An Interdisciplinary Introduction to Image Processing

AN INTERDISCIPLINARY INTRODUCTION TO IMAGE PROCESSING

Pixels, Numbers, and Programs

Steven L. Tanimoto

The MIT Press
Cambridge, Massachusetts
London, England

For information about special quantity discounts, please email special_sales@mitpress.edu

This book was set in Syntax and Times Roman by Westchester Book Group.
Printed and bound in the United States of America.

Library of Congress Cataloging-in-Publication Data

Tanimoto, S. (Steven)
An interdisciplinary introduction to image processing / Steven L. Tanimoto.
    p.   cm.
Includes bibliographical references and index.
ISBN 978-0-262-01716-9 (hardcover : alk. paper)
1. Image processing. I. Title.
TA1637.T37   2012
621.36'7—dc23
2011036233

10   9   8   7   6   5   4   3   2   1

Contents

Preface

To the Student

Traditionally, college subjects have been departmentalized. Computing is in one department, art is in the art school, mathematics is in its own department, and so on. Some subjects, such as international studies, at a typical university, span multiple departments. Other subjects, like writing, typically are taught by one department (e.g., English), even though writing applies to almost every subject; one writes about geography and about medicine; writing does more than tell stories or communicate poetry.

Image processing is a subject that relates to many different disciplines. Images are typically produced by photography. Yet photography itself can be artistic, commercial, medical, documentary, etc. When images are represented digitally, then mathematical methods apply to them. Images can be synthesized using computer graphics from models, virtual worlds, and so on. The techniques of image processing have often been associated with the fields of electrical engineering, applied mathematics, or statistics—electrical engineering because images can be considered signals and signal processing has been greatly developed by electrical engineers; applied mathematics because many methods of analyzing images require algorithms developed within the applied math field; statistics because the pixels of images can be considered to be samples from a population and these populations are subject to statistical distributions and relationships.

This book is about the basic principles of image processing and key concepts and techniques from mathematics, the psychology of perception, computer science, and to some extent, art, that connect directly to image processing. More specifically, the topics chosen for coverage include (1) the most important topics from an introductory image-processing course, such as image representation, sampling, enhancement, compression, and analysis; (2) the essentials of computer programming, using the increasingly popular Python language; (3) artistic applications of image processing, such as construction of stereogram and photomosaics; (4) key concepts from mathematics, such as symmetry groups, and (5) the psychology of perception, especially color perception and binocular stereo depth perception.

Once again, this book is intended to help you understand image processing from several perspectives: the creative, the theoretical (meaning mainly mathematical), and the programmatical (meaning telling computers how to do what you want them to do). We can only scratch the surface of the subject of image processing in a single course or a single book. However, I believe that this can be a good starting point if you are new to the subject and interested in working with images using technology.

Here is what you need. You should have completed high-school mathematics and understood that material. You don't need to have had calculus, and you don't need to have had either linear algebra or modern algebra. The few elements of these topics that are used here are covered in the text. You'll need a computer for the activities we describe. If you like working with large, high-resolution images, then you'll need a reasonably up-to-date computer. Otherwise, an older one should be fine. A few of the exercises ask you to find your own images and you might like to have the use of a digital camera in a few cases. However, most of the exercises do not require you to take your own photos; when images are needed, they are either provided at the book's website or you can find your own elsewhere on the web. This book and its associated software are intended to help you not only understand the key ideas but also to create neat images and effects. Have fun!

To the Teacher

Before giving descriptions of some of the possible courses that can be taught with the book, here are a few words about "subject area integration." This book addresses the interdisciplinary field of computer imaging. In order to avoid a heavy bias, it covers material from more than one subject area. Topics come from photography, art, mathematics, physics of light, psychology of perception, and computer science. In addition, image processing traditionally involves signal processing, which is considered part of the field of electrical engineering.

Thus the integration of diverse subject material reflects the interdisciplinary nature of imaging as a field. Imaging is not the only modern field requiring interdisciplinary treatment. Fields like modern musical composition, computational biology, and intellectual property law are other examples. Teaching an interdisciplinary course can be challenging, but its importance is increasing, and it's a way to keep college courses relevant for students preparing to work in the age of "digital everything."

In spite of this, one can teach image processing within a disciplinary framework. By emphasizing certain sections of the book, the flavor of the course can be varied considerably and made to fit within a program in, say, computer science, digital arts, mathematics, or possibly even perceptual psychology.

For a course on computer science, the following topics should be emphasized: number systems and their use in representing pixel values, red-green-blue (RGB) color representations, graphics formats, permutation groups, Python programming, and programming projects.

For a mathematics course, the following topics should be covered: formal properties of pixel arithmetic; combinatorics of RGB colors and palettes; coordinate transformations; invertibility of transformations; symmetry groups; permutation groups and modular arithmetic and their uses in image scrambling; convolution, filtering, and linear transformations of images; plotting of mathematical forms; discrete geometry; distance transforms; and morphological algebras.

For an introduction to image analysis, topics should include brightness, contrast, and color enhancement, thresholding, filtering, edge detection, Fourier transforms, graphics interchange format (GIF) and Joint Photographic Experts Group (JPEG) formats, contour following, connected components analysis, shape representation, morphological algebra, and pattern recognition.

For a course on imaging in graphic arts, the topics should include image representation, color systems, color enhancement, geometric transformation effects, morphing, stereograms, anamorphic images, photomosaics, computational photography, and image retrieval by contents.

A Few Words About Software

This book is intended to be used with software. A program called PixelMath2012 fully supports the book. It provides a special transparent view of digital images as both visual and mathematical objects that reinforces the connection between pixels and numbers. When the user zooms in on an image, the RGB values of pixels are superimposed on the colored-square rendering of the pixels.

In addition, PixelMath provides three different interfaces for controlling image transformations and synthesis: (1) the Pixel calculator, which supports part I of this book; (2) the Formula Page, which serves as an advanced extension of the calculator; and (3) the Python window, which supports part II of this book.

The software is portable. Most of it is written in Java, and all of it only requires a Java runtime environment. It can run in the browser (as an applet), or as a standalone application. The PixelMath2012.jar file is double-clickable in Windows, and so PixelMath can be started that way. There is a web version that supports educational research through an event-logging facility.

The Python language component of PixelMath2012 is, in fact, Jython, an open-source implementation of Python that runs in the Java virtual machine. Many Python programmers prefer Jython to native Python because it provides direct access to all standard Java libraries, including the Swing packages for building user interfaces. This means that a student who learns Python in this environment can go almost arbitrarily deeply into a rich programming environment. The Transcentration game presented in chapter 20 illustrates in detail how Python and Swing come together to afford a complete toolkit for developing interactive software involving images.

Although there have been a number of interesting image-processing tools on the market for a long time (such as Adobe PhotoShop), these tools have several limitations: first, they have tended to be expensive. Second, they have been designed primarily for artists and consequently their designers have gone to great pains to hide the mathematics and technologies that make them work. The PixelMath program used in this book takes a different approach. It's designed to reveal the digital image not only as a visual object but as a mathematical one, too. PixelMath helps reveal the power of mathematics by providing calculator and formula interfaces to the image. Users can draw on their own creativity to come up with entirely new image effects. Not only that, but more complicated sequences of operations can be automated by the user via programming with the built-in Python interpreter.

Acknowledgments

This book, the PixelMath software, and the many ideas, activities, and materials that go with them are an outgrowth of a project that began in 1991 entitled "Mathematics Experiences Through Image Processing." This project supported the development and testing of the Pixel Calculator (modeled after a pocket calculator and running under Windows 3.0), the Color Pixel Calculator, and the "METIP Programming Environment" (a combination of the Color Pixel Calculator and a Lisp programming system). Support by the National Science Foundation (NSF) under grant MDR-9155709 was instrumental in launching this effort. The author thanks the many students and colleagues who contributed in one way or another to that project, especially Prof. James King of the University of Washington's Mathematics Department in Seattle and teachers such as Gary Pounder at the Washington Middle School, Seattle. Some of the software developers include Dennis Lee, Jim Ahrens, Lauren Bricker, Alex Rothenberg, Evan McLain, Michael Van Hilst, Adam Carlson, Jeremy Baer. Contributors of materials or evaluations include Eric Artzt, Nicholas Benson, Donald Craig, Camberley Crick, Kirsten Hildrum, Susan Hubbard, Kenneth Perrine, Lori Postner, Robert Roos, and Daniel Teng. (I apologize to anyone inadvertently left out.)

The original version of PixelMath was written in 1999 by Jeremy Baer and included graphics by Chenoah Morgan, under support from an NSF Small Business Innovation Research award involving MathSoft, Inc.; Learner Empowerment, Inc.; and the University of Washington. Intellectual property rights to the PixelMath software were later transferred to the University of Washington. Since that time, PixelMath has been used in educational research and teaching at the university. National Science Foundation support of that research under grants EIA-0121345 and IIS-0537322 has contributed to the further development and maintenance of PixelMath.

As the one person who has been with the project the entire time, the maintenance and enhancement of PixelMath has been a job for the author over the past 12 years. However, I want to thank David Akers for the online "INFACT" extensions to PixelMath (for educational research). After having PixelMath versions with home-grown Common Lisp and then Scheme interpreters included, it was a revelation to find Jython, and thanks go to its development community for making it such a useful component. I'd like to acknowledge particular advisors of our projects who helped propel our efforts forward: E. Paul Goldenberg, Andee Rubin, Uri Wilensky, and our NSF program directors Andy Molnar, Nora Sabelli, Caroline Wardle, and Ken Whang, Thanks are also due to my research colleagues, Earl Hunt, Cynthia Atman, David Madigan, Jim Minstrell, Daryl Lawton, and especially the late William Winn, who all supported the teaching and research methodologies in which we used PixelMath.

I also thank my colleagues in the Department of Computer Science and Engineering who have supported this work even though it has gone against the mainstream of teaching Java and pushed beyond the boundaries of computer science. The following people supported the introduction of the course on which this book is based: Shawn Brixey, Brian Curless, Ken Etzkorn, Jenq-Neng Hwang, Hank Levy, Kevin Mihata, Mari Ostendorf, Richard Rice, Eve Riskin, Linda Shapiro, and Ming-Ting Sun. The strong interdisciplinary intellectual culture at the University of Washington has been a big help in making this kind of project practically feasible.

I would like to acknowledge the Helen R. Whiteley Center in Friday Harbor, Washington; the Center for Image Analysis in Uppsala, Sweden (and hosts Gunilla Borgefors and Ewert Bengtsson); and the University of Rome, Italy (and hosts Stefano Levialdi and Luigi Cinque) for allowing me to do some of my writing and programming on their hospitable premises. Thanks to Kevin Vixie, Tom Asaki, and the Park City, Utah Mathematics Institute for their support during the summer of 2010 when the institute's theme was image processing. Thanks also go to Tyler Robison for comments on the manuscript. I would like to thank the MIT Press staff for their care in the editing and production of this book, as well as the reviewers of the book proposal for their suggestions and comments.

I'd especially like to acknowledge my parents, Taffee and Mary-Mae Tanimoto, and my mentor, Theo Pavlidis, for inspiring me to not only undertake this project but finish it. Finally, a thank-you to my family and friends for supporting me in this seemingly endless project.

IMAGES AND FORMULAS

1 Introduction

1.1 Sources of Images

We are bombarded with images in our daily lives. They continue to come from television, magazines, newspapers, books, movies, and personal film and video cameras. However they now also come from digital scanners, digital cameras, Internet web sites, digital video cameras, and mobile phones (e.g., iPhones, Android, and the latest Windows phones). They can also be synthesized in computers using drawing and painting programs, and they can be synthesized directly from mathematical expressions. There are probably more pixels in the world now (on web sites, in people's personal computers, in their digital cameras, etc.) than there are printed characters in all of the libraries of the world. For example, the U.S. Library of Congress contains approximately 20 million volumes. if the average book contains about 250,000 characters, this means that there are about 5 trillion characters in that library. That's 5×10^{12}.

Suppose that the average digital photo contains 500,000 pixels. Certainly, some are much smaller and some much larger. Assume that the average home computer hard drive contains 100 images. (This is pretty conservative; there are many images cached by web browsers. And then there is video.) If we assume that there are 500 million such computers out there in the world, this comes out to about

$$5 \times 10^5 \times 1 \times 10^2 \times 5 \times 10^8 = 2.5 \times 10^{16} \text{ pixels}$$

Then there is video. Each video clip or movie is a sequence of images. A single feature-length movie, say 2 hours long, has approximately $120 \times 60 \times 30 = 216,000$ images in it, and at 500,000 pixels per image (fewer with old movies, more with high definition and 3D), that is about 100,000,000,000 pixels per movie. A hard drive with ten movies on it has on the order of 1 trillion pixels on it. (Image and movie files are usually compressed, so that you can usually fit more than the ten movies that you could squeeze onto a 1-terabyte hard drive if each pixel took 1 byte to store.) I won't try to estimate how many movies are found on the average home computer. We don't need that much detail.

The conclusion is this: Pixels are numerous! Pixels are the most ubiquitous data items in existence (other than bits or bytes themselves).[1] Furthermore, the volume of worldwide pixel data is growing as a result of more digital cameras, higher resolution, and richer formats.[2] One might say we're in a pixel tsunami.

1.2 What Is an Image?

This book is about image processing. Before we talk about processing, we should at least consider the question of what is meant by the term "image." The further we study image processing the less simple the answer may seem. Let's consider a representative collection of possible answers to the question of what an image is.

In everyday life, an image is a flat, physical representation of a scene, a picture, or a design. It can be a photographic print, a pattern of light emitted from a television screen or computer monitor, an oil painting, or a child's crayon drawing. In computing, an image may be a data structure containing a two-dimensional array of pixel values together with a set of attribute-value pairs (representing the "header" of an image file). In optics an image may be a convergence of rays on a plane or other surface in space, whether or not there is a physical surface present to reflect the rays. In psychology, an image may be a mental construct (e.g., "the mind's eye") generated deep in the brain. Dreaming is a visual experience, even though one's eyes are usually closed at the time. A person can also experience an afterimage— a perceived pattern of light that doesn't exist outside the eye, the result of prior stimulation with a related pattern. Visual illusions of many sorts are examples of mental images that exhibit striking differences from physical reality.

There are some other notable examples of perceived images that don't correspond directly to a physical two-dimensional stimulus. One is the depth image perceived by someone viewing a stereogram. The stereogram's two views of a scene are two-dimensional stimuli, but the depth map is not represented directly in either of them; it's represented by subtle differences in the positioning of corresponding points in these views.

A stranger example of a perceived image is the image one experiences when observing a piece of saccade art. Saccade art is rendered by one or more linear arrays of small, intense lights, such as light-emitting diodes (LEDs); the lights flash on and off under computer control in such a way that an observer, moving his or her eyes past the arrays, will have a pattern of light "painted" on the retina that shows a distinct and recognizable structure, such as the shape of an animal or some legible text. One of the best examples of a saccade

---

1. Assuming data are stored electronically, magnetically, or optically; this doesn't include the genetic material in DNA, which is even more plentiful.

2. Three-dimensional movies are gaining in popularity, roughly doubling the number of pixels per movie. The storage space required for just one minute of the movie *Avatar* is estimated at 17.28 gigabytes, and the movie runs for 166 minutes.

art display can be found at San Francisco's Exploratorium, where several linear arrays of lights have been set up on a high wall. Each array is vertically oriented and there are several feet between each of these strips. By illuminating first the leftmost array, then the next one to the right, and so on, the eye is directed to try to follow this apparent left-to-right motion. Once the eye is moving with roughly this speed and direction, much faster variations in the intensities of the lights cause the formation of retinal images that show butterflies, fish, text, etc. A simple online demonstration of saccade art can be found at http://pixels.cs.washington.edu/01-intro/SaccArt/.

The technology of virtual retinal displays (also known as retinal-scan display) offers an even more direct channel of visual communication from a computer to a human. It bypasses the use of any array of lights or pixels and uses a laser or a single high-brightness light-emitting diode to draw a raster-scan pattern of light onto the viewer's retina.

In all of these examples, there is a fundamental aspect to the image as a two-dimensional pattern of information that can be experienced in some way by a human observer. As we explore various image-processing techniques, we may lose sight of this general aspect of images. However, it is always there in the background.

A digital image is a particular kind of image. From a technical perspective, it's an image represented by numbers. However, there's a lot of leeway in that definition, and some people might not agree that numbers are a necessary part of the definition. Some might say that a digital image is a spatial arrangement of pixels. Then there's the question of what a pixel is and whether pixels themselves should be represented with numbers. We should note that file formats such as the JPEG image format use mathematical representations that are not particularly pixel oriented. It's theoretically possible to have digital images without pixels by using numbers to represent functions that in turn combine to represent the image. Nonetheless, pixels are a central concept in digital imaging.

1.3 What Is a Pixel?

When buying a digital camera, one of the first questions one asks is "How many pixels does it have?" This refers to the maximum number of individual colored dots a single photo can have when taken with the camera. The camera's sensor has to have a separate sensing cell (actually three cells—one each for red, green, and blue) for each pixel.

The usual answer to the question of what a pixel is goes something like this: A pixel is an atomic visible element of an image, a picture element or picture cell. A pixel represents a small area of an image. In most cameras, the area is square in shape. Before we give a definition that we'll use in the rest of the book, let's consider some special cases.

Consider a ceramic tile mosaic in which the tiles are arranged in a square grid. Each tile has a uniform color, although the colors of any two tiles might differ. The mosaic seems to be an image. Is each tile a pixel? A natural answer is "yes." However, that is not the whole story. In a real mosaic, the tiles are usually separated by thin zones of grout. The grout usually is neutral in color. However, the grout cannot help but have at least some effect on the observed image. Do zones of grout then count as pixels, too?

Some people would say that this mosaic is a digital image, even though we have not used numbers to represent it. The fact that it is made up of elements that we can call pixels (here actually just ceramic tiles) would be enough for them to call this a digital image. One could argue here that the image area has been divided up into a finite set of small components, and that structure is a key part of a digital image.

Or is it? Take a magnifying glass and look closely at the small dots on a cathode ray tube (CRT) as it displays an image. Are there distinct zones that can easily be called pixels? The answer is usually "no." The pixels of an image rendered by a CRT actually seem to be represented by fuzzy collections of small dots, and there are separate dots for each of the colors red, green, and blue. Where are the pixels?

A pixel is a more abstract entity than a colored region within an image. A pixel is a sample of the visual properties of an image that may be representative of a point or a region within the image.

Another example of a mosaiclike image is one of the graphic works of the artist Chuck Close. In figure 1.1 (plate 1) a baby's face is rendered using many small geometric shapes and blobs that we might call macro-pixels. Each macro-pixel carries color information for its region of the main image. However, it is also a little image in its own right. There is typically a distinct shape and perhaps other details in the macro-pixel. A generalization of this mosaic style is the photomosaic in which each macro-pixel is actually a little digital image whose details may be visible when inspected closely. An example of a photomosaic is shown in figure 1.2 (plate 2). While the generation of photomosaics usually involves computers, they can be made manually as collages with many small photos pasted onto a large board. There are many artistic decisions that can be made and some of these can be programmed into a computer, especially the criteria for choosing an image for each macro-pixel. This decision may include not only color but also dominant edge characteristics, color distribution within the image, and even the subject matter depicted. (A related kind of image is a mosaic made of tiles that have color variations within them, and that may have irregular shapes, such as fragments of glass, stone, or torn-up photographs.) We'll explore the fine art of photomosaic construction later in the book.

Finally, let's consider the saccade art at the Exploratorium once again. Where are the pixels of those images? They are in the controlling computer, they are on the observer's retina, and they are momentarily on the linear light strips, but they are never displayed on a separate two-dimensional medium. The areas represented by each pixel will be different for every observer because no two observers will scan their eyes across the light strips at exactly the same speed. So here, once again, we have a reason to treat the notion of a pixel as more abstract than the representation of a particular area.

Figure 1.1 (plate 1)
Chuck Close's "Emma," a woodcut completed in 2002, in which "pixels" are made up of colored lozenges and other shapes. Created in collaboration with Japanese woodblock artist Yasu Shibata, it is the woodblock with the world's most complex woodblock assemblage and printing process. Courtesy of Pace Editions, Inc. and the artist.

1.4   What Is a Function?

This book deals with images. It also deals with processing. Fundamental to the concept of processing is the concept of function. One meaning of function is "purpose," but the other, more important notion is the one used in mathematics: "determining relation." Imagine a function called double that can be used in the following way. "Double 5. What do you get?" The answer is 10. This function is a relation between numbers. It's a determining relation because given a number, say 5, the double is a unique number, in this case 10. Functions are essential to processing because they can be used to describe the relationship between the input and output data at each stage of processing.

A standard mathematical definition of a function is that it is a kind of mapping from one set of values to another (possibly the same set). The mapping must be single-valued—there must be only a single member of the second set corresponding to a given member of the first set. The first set is called the domain of the function and the second set is called the codomain (sometimes the second set is called the range of the function).

Figure 1.2 (plate 2)
A photomosaic image of a face composed of many small images of flowers using one of the methods described in this book.

Some functions relate pairs of numbers, like the doubling function just mentioned. Other functions relate pairs of numbers to other numbers: $z = f(x, y)$ or more specifically, $f(x, y) = 2x + y + 1$, for example. But functions don't have to work with numbers at all. They can relate pairs of symbols, such as $f(\text{dog}) = \text{cat}$. They can relate pairs of images, or they can relate complex data structures to others.

In traditional mathematics classes, one is typically presented with various functions and asked to solve for this or that, or to graph the functions. Can a function itself be the solution to a scientific problem? Can a function be a work of art? Yes and yes. As we'll see, an entire computer program can be considered to be a function. Also, an image (even the Mona Lisa) can be considered to be a function. Functions can also be used to represent artistic processes; for example, we can design a function that takes as input a photograph and that produces as output an image in the style of an Impressionist painter. In this book we will consider not only the design of functions for processing images but a little bit of the theory of functions themselves, particularly with regard to closed systems of functions called algebraic groups.

1.5 What Is a Program?

A computer program is usually defined as a sequence of instructions that tell a computer how to solve some problem or perform some activity. In this book we'll look closely at a particular set of conventions for programming: the Python programming language. However, there is also a more general sense of a program: a representation (of information) that causes a computer to behave in some particular way. Such a program might not be a sequence of instructions at all. It could be a set of rules, a set of answers to possible questions, a diagram, or even an image.

So now we have seen that images can be (macro)pixels, pixels can be images, images are functions, pixels and functions can be represented using numbers, programs are described by functions, and images can be programs. Programs can produce images, and with the right tools, can be visualized as images. So pixels, numbers, functions, and programs can all be considered to be different views of the same information, at least at a philosophical level. Yet, even at a practical level, these concepts are deeply intertwined.

1.6 Human Vision

In this section we consider how the human visual system works. There are several reasons that some understanding of human vision is important in a study of image processing. One is that an image is (usually) an artifact intended to be seen by humans and thus in order to know what is important in an image we need to understand how humans view it. Often we will judge images in terms of how they look to humans, and sometimes it is important to know about the human visual system in order to understand how certain judgments work (resolution, flicker, color, etc.) Another reason is that one kind of image is the representation in our brain of the scene in front of us, and we should understand how that can be, so that we'll know this meaning of the term "image." Finally, computer vision systems are often modeled after the human system, and when studying computer vision, it helps to know about the human system in order to understand analogies, strategies, terminology, and so on.

The rest of this section is organized as follows. First the human eye is discussed and its similarities and differences with modern cameras are mentioned. Then the part of the brain responsible for vision is discussed. Next, we consider illusions—manifestations of the limitations of human vision. Understanding illusions helps us to understand how human vision works. Finally, we summarize key issues for image processing as they relate to human vision.

1.6.1 The Human Eye

Human eyes, as the sensing organs for the human visual system, operate somewhat like a digital camera, but with many notable differences. Let's consider first the anatomy of the

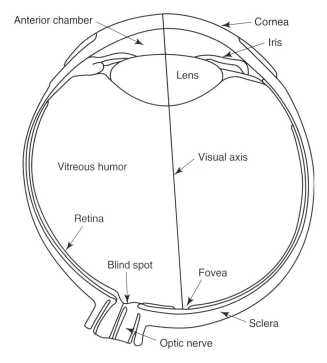

Figure 1.3
The human eye.

eye. Each eye is a roughly spherical organ located in an eye socket of the skull and controlled by muscles that effect eye movements. Figure 1.3 illustrates several important parts
of the eye. Following the path that a light ray takes as it enters the eye, it first passes through
the cornea and past an opening known as the pupil that is formed by a ring-shaped tissue
called the iris, then through the crystalline lens, and then through the transparent vitreous
humor that fills the eye cavity and then to the sensing layer of the retina. In the retina
there are many small, light-sensitive cells called rods and cones. The shape of the lens
is modified by muscles that control it to focus an image on the retina. The retina contains not only the rods and cones but also other neural cells that collect and process
the signals that come from the rods and cones. Figure 1.4 shows a cross section of the
retina.

An interesting difference between a digital camera and the eye has to do with spatial
resolution—the size of the smallest details that can be discerned by the imaging array.
In the case of a 4-megapixel digital camera, for example, the image area is divided into
(approximately) a 2000-by-2000 array of equal-sized pixels. But in the human eye, the sizes
of the the regions covered by rods and cones vary, depending on the area of the retina being
considered. There is a narrow, roughly circular patch of the retina right in the middle of the

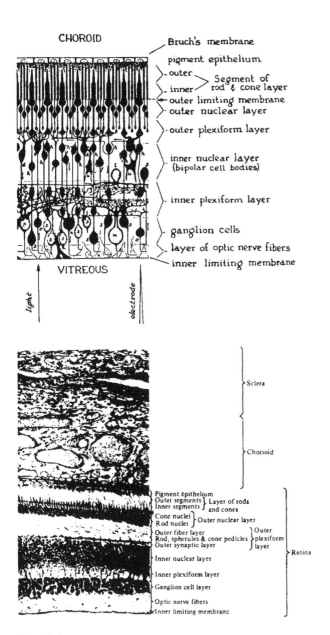

Figure 1.4
Cross-section of the retina.

field of view, called the fovea, and in the fovea tiny details of an image can be distinguished. Elsewhere in the retina, much less detail is captured. In the outer periphery of the visual field, the resolution is low. However, the part of the retina handling the periphery is very sensitive to motion. To see how different the fovea and periphery are, in terms of densities of rods and cones, look at figure 1.5.

The retina not only senses incoming light by the reactions of its rods and cones to the light, it also processes the information in certain ways. It can accentuate changes in the amount of light from one location to a neighboring one, and it can also accentuate changes of light intensity over time. We will discuss some of these kinds of processing in more detail in subsequent chapters.

Information about the image leaves the retina along a bundle of nerve fibers known as the optic nerve. The optic nerve leaves the retina at a location known as the "blind spot" and travels back in the head to the optic chiasm and the lateral geniculate body. These are shown in figure 1.6.

The blind spot is so named because at this particular location in the retina there are no rods or cones, and so the image on the retina cannot be sensed at this location. Most people are not aware that they have a blind spot in their vision because the brain fills in the missing information by integrating over multiple images. The eyes move rapidly during normal vision, so any particular part of a scene is captured many times and any missing information in one image is quickly filled in from the next.

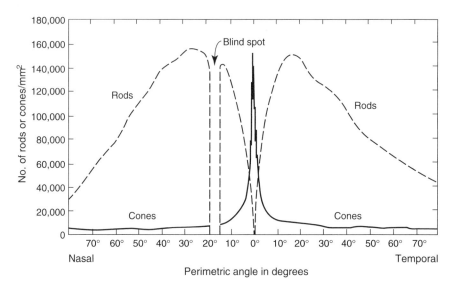

Figure 1.5
Density of rods and cones as a function of visual angle.

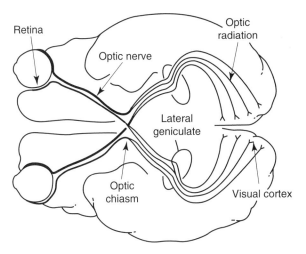

Figure 1.6
The visual pathway.

By carefully performing a simple experiment, it is possible for a person to experience his or her blind spot and even determine its size and shape. The experiment involves fixing one eye on a small black dot on a white sheet of paper and then moving the tip of a pencil toward the blind spot until the tip disappears. Then by carefully moving the pencil, one can trace the outline of the shape of the blind spot on the paper.

1.6.2 The Visual Cortex in the Brain

Information leaving the retina travels along the optic nerve to the optic chiasm, where the nerves from the left and right eyes meet, and each divides into two parts, with half proceeding to the left part of the brain and half to the right. The result is that information from both eyes proceeds to each side of the part of the brain known as the striate cortex.

The striate cortex, also known as area 17, is multilayered. Much of the low-level feature processing such as detection of light-dark differences at various angles occurs here. During the late 1960s, D. Hubel and T. Wiesel conducted experiments in which anesthetized cats were presented with various patterns: dark bars on light backgrounds in a certain position and rotated varying degrees. By implanting electrodes into specific cells of a cat's striate cortex, they found that there are cells that respond specifically to these stimuli. Changing the angle of the bar made one neuron stop firing and another one start, for example.

The striate cortex connects to other parts of the brain, and much research is currently focused on better understanding what happens to visual information after it is processed by the striate cortex.

Figure 1.7
The simultaneous-contrast illusion.

1.6.3 Illusions

This introduction to image processing features a section on visual illusions for several reasons. Illusions raise the question of how human vision works; how is it possible that we don't see the world the way it really is? Illusions can help us understand the limits of human vision. Finally, they help us understand the mechanisms of human vision and thus help us think about the design of artificial methods for image processing and vision.

Our first illusion is the simultaneous-contrast illusion (figure 1.7). Here we are presented with two gray disks. They are both the same color and are equally luminous. However, one is surrounded by a light-gray rectangle, and the other is surrounded by a dark-gray one. The one surrounded by the light rectangle seems to be darker than the other disk. From this illusion we can infer that the eye sees intensities in the context of nearby intensities. Although this illusion uses proximity in space, we can also do this using proximity in time.

Several additional illusions are shown in figure 1.8. While the first four of these involve perceived lengths, curvature, and noncolinearity, the sun illusion and subjective-contour illusion (e and f) prompt the viewer to perceive a contour that doesn't exist and to perceive the region inside the contour as brighter than the background.

A general type of illusion is the perception of some object or form within visual noise or a random arrangement of elements, such as in tea leaves, clouds, or a Rorschach ink blot. Such an illusion is called apophenia. An example of apophenia is the perception of the "Old Man of the Mountain" in a rock formation near Franconia Notch, New Hampshire. It was illustrated on a postage stamp (see figure 1.9). The formation is believed to have lasted thousands of years, but collapsed in 2003. Apophenia is an entirely expected product of the human visual system, which has evolved to perceive many possible threats and many possible hunting targets, even when they are largely hidden or camouflaged.

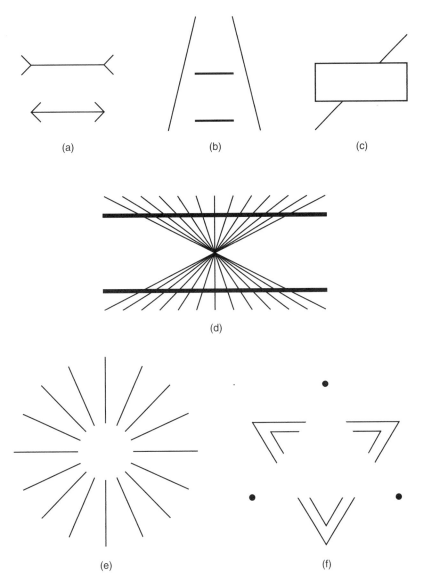

Figure 1.8
A variety of visual illusions: (a) Mueller-Lyer, (b) Ponzo, (c) Poggendorff, (d) Zoellner, (e) "sun," and (f) subjective contour.

Figure 1.9
A case of apophenia: the Old Man of the Mountain in New Hampshire.

In some cases, apophenia is simply a playful interpretation of an accidental or natural pattern. In other cases, people experiencing apophenia may attribute great significance to their perception, seeing it as a sign from a god or a threat from space aliens. This kind of apophenia is pareidolia—apophenia in which the perceiver attributes significance to the perception. Understanding pareidolia helps provide a psychological explanation for many reported sitings of unidentified flying objects, Jesus, Bigfoot, the Loch Ness monster, and so on.

Apophenia can occur in computer vision systems when the system matches a model of, say an automobile connecting rod, to a pattern of discoloration on an assembly-line conveyor belt. In extreme cases, machine vision systems can be considered to be hallucinating when their decision biases are adjusted so that the strength of evidence required to reach a recognition decision is zero. False positives are a problem for pattern recognition systems, whether human or artificial.

1.6.4 Relation to Image Processing

As we study image processing there are certain key concepts that we'll cover and that relate to human vision. These include resolution, light sensitivity, color, image stability, and other ideas.

Resolution is the capacity to represent spatial detail in an image. In the human eye, resolution is largely determined by the density of rods and cones in the fovea of the eye, although the brain can integrate multiple views to obtain somewhat higher-resolution information. The periphery of the retina senses information at a much lower resolution than does the fovea. In digital imaging, resolution is most strongly associated with the number of pixels in an image. For example, a 10-megapixel camera generally supports higher-resolution photography than does a 3-megapixel camera. The actual amount of detail in an image depends, not only on the number of pixels in the image, but also on the characteristics of the optical system that captured the image, as well as other forces that affect the image, such as light levels, fog, visual noise, motion, focus, and digital preprocessing.

Light sensitivity and color sensitivity relate to how much light and what wavelengths of light are necessary to stimulate a sensor to produce output. Human rods are more sensitive to light than cones, but they do not provide color distinctions. Closely associated with sensitivity is the concept of dynamic range, the extent to which we can make distinctions among slightly different low-intensity stimuli and slightly different high-intensity stimuli at the same time, i.e., in the same scene or image. The human retina has a remarkable dynamic range, but the eye must still adapt over a period of time when moving from bright environments to dark environments or vice versa.

Color is about the way humans perceive the distribution of light wavelengths in samples of light, especially those containing unequal amounts of the three additive primary colors (red, green, and blue). We will have more to say about this in another chapter.

Humans are sensitive and almost hypersensitive to contours. The subjective-contour illusion in figure 1.8f shows how strongly the human visual system tries to find contours in an image and can "see" them when they don't exist.

One kind of image stability is about the ability of the brain to integrate multiple "exposures" (between eye movements) to have a relatively constant mental image of a scene. We can compare this to the antijitter features of modern video cameras.

Humans see in a particular band of the electromagnetic radiation spectrum. Why? Does it have to be? No, some other animals see in other parts of the spectrum. For example, the honeybee has receptors for ultraviolet light as well as yellow-green and blue (but not red). People who are not color-blind perceive colors in a three-dimensional space spanned by the additive primaries red, green, and blue. The physics of color would permit much higher-dimensional color perception. Why are we limited to only three of them? A person has two eyes. Why not one, three, five, or more? There is a kind of arbitrariness of nature about the human visual system. Artificial systems can be created that have multiple cameras, cameras that respond to infrared or ultraviolet light, and that have lenses very different from the human lens. Some of these possibilities make sense in particular engineering applications. Chapter 19 on computational photography helps to broaden our perspective of how future cameras could work.

1.7 How Does a Digital Camera Work?

Digital cameras, like film cameras, use optical lenses to capture light and focus it into an image on an image plane. Instead of photographic film, a digital camera has a solid-state

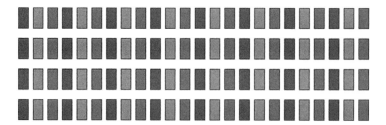

Figure 1.10 (plate 3)
How red, green, and blue photosites are arranged in the CCD array of a typical digital camera's sensor chip.

sensor in the image plane to record the image. Two types of solid-state sensors are commonly used today. More expensive cameras (such as those costing more than $200 in year 2011 dollars, have typically used charge-coupled device arrays (CCD arrays). Less expensive cameras have commonly used complementary metal-oxide semiconductor (CMOS) transducers. However, CMOS sensor technology has improved and today is competitive with CCD. The ways the sensors using the two technologies work are similar enough that the following discussion for the CCD case is representative of both.

Cameras with CCD arrays typically produce high-quality, low-noise images. In a CCD array, light falling onto each small zone of the image (known as a photosite) causes an accumulation of electric charge. The amount of charge depends upon the brightness of the light and the length of time during which the accumulation takes place. There are typically three photosites per pixel of the image: one for red, one for green, and one for blue (see figure 1.10—plate 3). The red photosites are covered with a filter layer that lets in red light and blocks blue and green. The green and blue photosites work in a similar manner. Right after the image is captured in the photosites, the charge accumulated at each photosite is electrically transferred to a small storage area next to the photosite. The storage area is protected from the light, so that any change in the charge there is minimized. From there, all the charges from the many storage areas can be shifted over to an analog-to-digital (A/D) conversion circuit, typically on the same semiconductor chip as the array of photosites. The A/D unit produces numerical representations of the charge magnitudes. These numbers are then transferred from the sensor chip to a bulk storage unit such as a CompactFlash memory card. Before the image data are written on the flash memory card, they may be digitally enhanced within the camera and then reduced in volume using a method such as JPEG compression.

1.8   What Can We Do with All These Pixels?

As mentioned earlier, pixels have been flooding the Internet at increasing rates. What can we do with all these pixels? Since we have a lot of them, we ought to know how to get value out of them. One way to obtain value is to extract information. Another is to make the pixels into beautiful objects (art). If we cannot obtain value or add value, we could of course delete images and recover disk space, memory space, etc. Or we could save the images but compress them to recover at least some of the space they take on disks.

How do we do these things that add value or save space? That's part of what this book is about. More than that, this is a book about empowering you to work with digital images using the rich languages of mathematics and computer programming, and about helping you understand at least some aspects of how the Internet and the objects in it really work.

Pixels are in some sense atomic units of visual information. They are analogous to digital audio waveform samples and to three-dimensional volume elements (voxels). Understanding how pixels are processed in computers provides a key to understanding the digital world more generally, and it's a big step toward fluency in information technology. Let's now begin to explore a world of visual information processing in a way that allows us to develop our artistic, technical, and mathematical faculties all at the same time.

1.9 References

Gregory, R. L. 1990. *Eye and Brain: The Psychology of Seeing*. Oxford, UK: Oxford University Press.

Luckiesh, M. 1922. *Visual Illusions: Their Causes, Characteristics and Applications*. New York: Van Nostrand. Available online at www.visualillusion.net.

Jeffries, S. 2010. The rise of the camera phone. *The Guardian*, Jan. 8, 2010. www.guardian.co.uk/technology/2010 /jan/08/-stuart-jeffries-camera-phones.

Metropolitan Museum. 2010. Chuck Close Prints: Process and Collaboration. Special Exhibitions. www.metmuseum.org/special/chuck_close/prints_more.htm.

Rath, J. 2009. The data-crunching powerhouse behind *Avatar*.www.datacenterknowledge.com/archives/2009/12 /22/the-data-crunching-powerhouse-behind-avatar/

Swanston, M. and Wade, N. 2001. *Visual Perception: An Introduction*. London, UK: Psychology Press.

Wikipedia. 2010. Digital Photography. en.wikipedia.org/wiki/Digital_photography.

1.10 Exercises

1. Choose the web site of some institution or corporation. Find a page there containing at least one image. (a) How many images are on that page? (b) Choose one of the images there and use your browser to download it and save it to your hard disk. Inspect the file and determine how many bytes are in the image file. (c) Determine how many pixels are in the image by loading the image into any popular image manipulation program, such as Microsoft Paint (which comes with Microsoft Windows), and examining the image attributes. (d) Compare the file's size with the number of bytes that would be required if 3 bytes per pixel were used. What is the compression ratio? (For example, 2:1 means two-to-one, or 1 byte compressed for every 2 bytes uncompressed.)

2. Assuming that a 3D movie is represented as a sequence of frame pairs and that each frame is a digital image having 1 million pixels, find the number of pixels in a feature-length 3D film (2 hours) running at 24 frames per second. Now assuming that each pixel has three color

components, each requiring 1 byte of memory to store, how many megabytes of memory are required to store the movie?

3. Find another example of a 3D movie file (not *Avatar*) and report its size. Estimate the size the movie file would be if it were not compressed at all. Take into consideration the number of pixels per frame, the frame rate, and the length of the movie. From these numbers, what is the compression ratio (number of bytes without compression divided by number of bytes in the compressed file)?

4. Most images that one can find on the Internet can be easily categorized as either photographs or synthetic graphics. Can you find an image that seems ambiguous? What is the Uniform Resource Indicator (URI) or Uniform Resource Locator (URL) of the image you found? What about it makes it difficult to classify?

5. Make up your own definition for the word "pixel." Does a pixel have to be square? Explain your answer. Does a pixel even have to have a shape? Why or why not?

6. Find an example of a mosaic image in which each tile is made of a material other than ceramic. Argue for and against each tile being considered as a pixel.

7. Is a movie presented using 16-mm or 35-mm film a kind of digital image? Why or why not?

8. At the website maintained by Michael Bach (www.michaelbach.de/ot/), choose one of the visual illusions related to motion. Prepare and deliver a 5-minute presentation about this illusion, explaining how to experience it, why it occurs, and any historical or related perceptual information that is associated with it.

9. Using a digital camera and your imagination, go out into the woods, to the beach, or into the kitchen and look for a natural pattern of branches, bark, leaves, stones, vegetable peel markings, or tea leaves that you can interpret as a face, figure, etc. (and which you don't have too much trouble convincing others to see that way). Capture at least two good pictures of the pattern, one showing it in its surrounding context and the other showing its details. Compare your example with one of the examples of pareidolia that you can find on the web; describe their (a) visual qualities and (b) possible spiritual, paranormal, or religious significance. Finally, explain why the human visual system (eye and brain) is ready to make or accept such interpretations as yours or others' in pareidolia cases.

2 Getting Started

In this chapter we begin to work with digital images in two ways: we discuss how they are represented in computers and we introduce a software program called PixelMath that makes it easy to do many things with images.

2.1 Representation of Digital Images

A digital image is normally represented in a computer as a two-dimensional array of numbers. For example, the image in figure 2.1 is represented as a 1600-column by 1200-row array of numbers in the range from 0 to 255. Figure 2.2a shows a small section that has been enlarged and (b) a smaller section (from the underside of the arch) that has been enlarged further. Figure 2.2c shows the numbers for this part of the image. This image is a *grayscale* image (allowing black, white, and shades of gray). A color image typically differs by having the numbers grouped into threes: each pixel has a separate number for each of the three additive primary colors red, green, and blue. Color and color representation are discussed in detail in chapter 4.

There are two fundamental aspects of digital image representation that we'll introduce in this chapter: sampling and quantization. Sampling refers to the selection of points or areas in the image that will be represented by particular numbers or collections of numbers. Quantization refers to the way in which the numbers correspond to particular light intensity levels (brightness, etc.) or color values. We'll cover sampling in the following section, and then we'll just introduce quantization in this chapter, with a more detailed treatment in chapter 3, which covers several aspects of the concept of brightness.

2.1.1 Sampling

Digital images are obtained in two fundamental ways: capture from the visual world and synthesis. There are some important ideas to understand about how images are captured. Of course, cameras or scanners are generally needed to capture images. The most important part of this capture is the way in which pixels are created from a scene or what let's call here the original image, the image prior to digitization. The allocation of pixels to locations

Figure 2.1
A grayscale (i.e., monochrome) image of Heidelberg, Germany. This image consists of 1200 rows each containing 1600 pixels. Each pixel is represented by a number in the range 0 to 255.

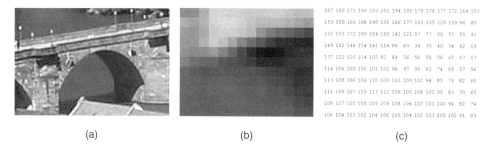

(a)   (b)   (c)

Figure 2.2
Closeup of one arch of the Stone Bridge in Heidelberg. (b) A detail of the arch. (c) The array of numbers for the detail.

or regions in the original image is called *sampling*. After an image is digitized, each pixel will represent a sample of the image from a particular place. Let's assume that each place is a point rather than a region.

Sampling to create a digital image refers to the number and choice of locations in the scene or picture that correspond to pixels. Usually the samples are arranged in a rectangular grid with even horizontal spacing and even vertical spacing. Both the spacing and the number of locations used are important. Also, the precise placement of the points can make a difference in some scenes.

Shopping for a camera, one is told about the megapixels of one model and then another. Supposedly the more pixels, the better. This is true to a certain extent. With more pixels, a scene can be sampled more densely than with fewer pixels, and that means that more fine details can be represented in the digital images. However, having more pixels can mean higher costs along several dimensions: (1) a more expensive camera, (2) more expensive memory cards, (3) longer times to transfer images, (4) more file space needed on web sites, (5) more main memory (random access memory, RAM) needed on the computer, (6) longer processing times for enhancement and analysis, and (7) longer upload and download times when sending the images over the Internet. Although data compression methods can be used to lower some of these costs in many cases, the basic rule is that more pixels usually means more details but greater costs. Therefore, finding the right number of pixels (in some approximate way) for an image is an important task. There are two approaches to finding the answer. One is subjective and requires viewing different representations of the same scene. The other is based on theory, the so-called Nyquist criterion.

2.1.2 The Nyquist Criterion

How many samples are enough to faithfully represent a signal? The signal might be an image, some audio, or the output of some scientific instrument like a seismograph. The answer depends on the size of the smallest details that must not be lost in the digitization. If the smallest details are dots of diameter d and they are separated by gaps no smaller than d, then we'll need our samples to be separated by a distance of no more than d. This is one form of the Nyquist criterion. The classic way of presenting the Nyquist criterion is using the terminology of oscillations: wave, frequency, cycle, phase, and amplitude.

We usually describe waves using mathematical functions. The two important basic wave functions are the square wave and the sine wave. The square-wave function is shown in figure 2.3. The x-axis on this graph of the square-wave function can represent either time (as one commonly does in studying audio signal processing) or horizontal position (as we often do in image processing; all the same arguments also apply in the vertical direction). At any particular horizontal location in the square-wave diagram, the y value is either -1 or 1. The y value changes every half cycle. The length of a cycle, following the mathematics tradition is usually, 2π or about 6.283. The sine-wave function is shown in figure 2.4. Just like the square-wave function, this one involves a repeating pattern, each repetition being

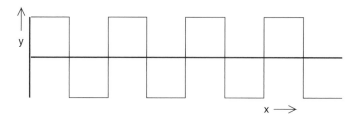

Figure 2.3
Square-wave function.

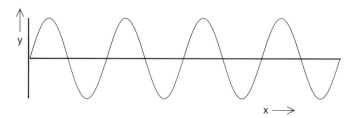

Figure 2.4
Sine-wave function.

called a cycle, with the length of the cycle being 2π. However, the sine function is smooth and curved. Both of these functions are important in image processing.

With any periodic (repeating-pattern) function like these, each occurrence of the basic pattern is a cycle. The length of a cycle is the *wavelength*, which doesn't always have to be 2π but can be any non-negative number. The *frequency* of the wave is the number of cycles per unit on the x-axis, such as 5 cycles per inch, 0.01 cycles per pixel, or 440 cycles per second (if the x-axis represents time). The concepts of wavelength and frequency are particularly important when we try to determine the minimum number of pixels required to accurately represent a scene.

The *phase* of a wave can be thought of as what part of the cycle a particular point is in, or how much the whole function has been shifted to the right in order to get a particular point lined up with the function at the beginning of a cycle. The phase is usually measured in angle units such as degrees (360 degrees to a cycle) or radians (2π radians to a cycle). The phase is measured this way even if the wavelength is not 2π.

In order to represent a wave function using samples, the number of samples will depend on how well we wish to represent the function. Although representing the shape of the function accurately could take many, many samples, in most analyses where we need to choose a sampling rate we focus on one aspect of the function: its frequency. (This is because other aspects, such as shape, can be accounted for by decomposing a function into other, usually simpler, functions and representing *their* frequency—and phase—information.) In

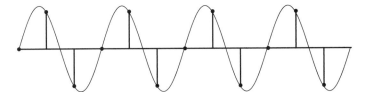

Figure 2.5
One possible sampling of the sine function with the minimum number of samples per cycle.

order to represent the frequency of the periodic function accurately, we need a minimum of two samples per cycle. Also, the phase of the sampling must be such that these two samples are not the same—one should have its wave at a high point and the other at a low point. Figure 2.5 is an example of sampling of a sine function. In this example the samples are slightly offset from the exact centers of the crests and troughs of the waves; this shows that the phase of the samples does not have to be perfect to represent the frequency correctly. The alternation of higher and lower sample values happens at the right rate. However, as we'll see shortly, the phase is important at this minimum sampling rate. Another series of examples is given in the context of images in the following discussion on representing a picket fence in a photo.

2.1.3 Picket Fence Examples

Consider the image shown in figure 2.6 (plate 4). There are various items in this image that might or might not be important to render faithfully. To take a simple example, consider the picket fence. Depending on how the samples are taken, the picture might end up with either the correct number of pickets discernable, or too few. In figure 2.7, a stylized picket fence is shown so that we can easily compare the effects of different sampling arrangements.

The Nyquist criterion for sampling is that we need more (at least a little more) than two samples per cycle of the highest-frequency oscillations (alternations of light and dark) that we wish to represent from the scene. In terms of frequency, this means that the frequency of the samples must be greater than twice the frequency of the highest-frequency oscillations to be captured. The frequency that is exactly twice the value of the highest-frequency oscillations to be captured is known as the *Nyquist rate*. The criterion says that we must sample at a frequency that is higher than the Nyquist rate.

If we were to sample at exactly the Nyquist rate, then we could end up with an inadequate representation, as shown in figure 2.8b. In this sampling, each sample point lies at an edge between a picket and the background. Each sample would see a little bit of the background and a little bit of the picket, and its value would be an average of the two. All the samples involving pickets are in this situation, and so all the pixels except the ones above the fence would be one color. This means that no alternation of light and dark would show up in the

Figure 2.6 (plate 4)
Photograph of a scene with a picket fence (taken at the garden at the historic English Camp on San Juan Island, Washington State).

Figure 2.7
A stylized picket fence for use in comparing sampling rates.

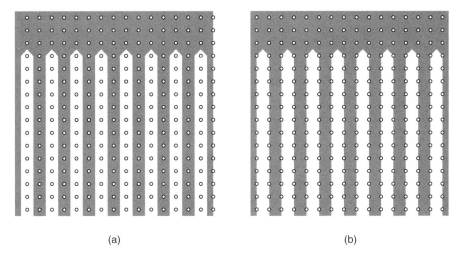

(a)   (b)

Figure 2.8
Sampling at the Nyquist rate with (a) good phase and (b) bad phase.

image. Even if the phase difference between the signal and the sampling is good enough to reveal the oscillation, the sampled signal does not reliably communicate either the amplitude or the phase of the oscillation. If the sampling rate is increased to a higher frequency than the Nyquist rate, the quality of the representation will increase. But, as we have already mentioned, having more pixels usually means greater cost.

A slightly different way of discussing resolution and sampling is when we start with a fixed sampling rate and ask "What is the highest frequency of oscillation in the image that can be faithfully represented?" If the sampling frequency is f_s, then only oscillations with frequencies less than $f_s/2$ can be correctly represented. The frequency $f_N = f_s/2$ is known as the *Nyquist frequency*. It represents an upper bound on what can be represented, whereas the Nyquist rate represents a lower bound on the sampling frequency that is needed. The two frequencies are related by

$$f_r < 2f_N$$

where f_r is the Nyquist rate. The relationships among these different frequencies are illustrated in figure 2.9.

At the core of what we have just discussed is the famous Shannon-Nyquist sampling theorem. Consider a continuous real-valued signal $f(x)$ that is bandlimited with frequencies in the range 0 to $f_r/2$. [In other words, $f(x)$ is a sum of sinusoidal waves of various amplitudes and phases but having frequencies only within the range of 0 to $f_r/2$.] Suppose $f(x)$ is sampled at a rate of f_s, where $f_s > f_r$. Then the samples $S(n)$ completely specify the function $f(x)$. In other words, the original function can, in theory, be reconstructed from the samples.

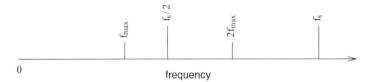

Figure 2.9
Graph illustrating the relative positions of frequency values related by the Nyquist criterion. The sampling frequency f_s should be strictly greater than the Nyquist rate $2f_{max}$. This condition is equivalent to saying that the Nyquist frequency $f_s/2$ should be strictly greater than the highest-frequency component occuring in the image, f_{max}.

This theorem is very important and it characterizes very well the main concern regarding image resolution. However, there are various practical limitations that make it, in general, impossible to exactly reconstruct the original function $f(x)$ from the samples. The theory assumes, first of all, that it is possible to have a bandlimited input signal; however, most natural images have discontinuities that involve an unlimited range of frequencies. Although filtering can reduce frequencies outside of a given band, filtering generally cannot fully eliminate the outside frequencies. Next, there is a difference between samples in theory and samples in practice. In theory, a sample is an infinitely precise number. In practice, samples need to be limited to a finite, and often small amount, of memory, such as a few bytes. So the samples in the computer are approximations of the real samples.

Finally, the process of reconstructing a function from samples involves a form of interpolation. This interpolation, done on a computer, can only approximate the theoretical process that would most accurately reconstruct the continuous analog function $f(x)$. Given these caveats, we understand that the Shannon-Nyquist theorem is valuable, but we should not expect to be able to fully reconstruct a detailed optically formed image from a computer representation of it.

When a signal is sampled at a rate lower than the Nyquist rate, then it is typical to have apparent oscillations at frequencies not present in the original signal. This phenomenon is called aliasing.

2.1.4 Moiré Patterns
A special aliasing-like effect occurs when an oscillating pattern with a slowly varying frequency or orientation is sampled with a sampling rate that is close to its frequency. The slight misalignments will give rise to a slowing changing pattern known as a moiré pattern. Moiré patterns can also be seen in physical situations, such as when one window screen is placed on top of another one (see figure 2.10). The holes in one screen serve as samples of the image created by the other. Moiré patterns are common when halftone images (typically produced by a color printing process) are digitally photographed or scanned.

Figure 2.10
Moiré pattern produced by two window screens overlapping with a slight rotational misalignment. The low-frequency wave pattern that emerges is analogous to beats in tuning musical instruments.

2.1.5 Quantization and Dynamic Range

We mentioned earlier that there are two key aspects to image representation. The first of these was sampling. The second is *quantization*. This is the business of assigning to each sample a number (or maybe three separate numbers, in the case of color images) to represent the amount of light at that sample's location. Quantization always involves some range of values. A typical range is the set of integers from 0 to 255. For a strictly black-and-white image, a range consisting of only 0 and 1 would be good enough. This range is the set of possible pixel values. (For a color image, there is typically a range for each of the red, green, and blue components.)

When a digital image is created there has to be a way of going from a particular light value in the scene or picture to a number in the image. Typically, 0 will be used to represent the darkest color expected in the scene and 255 the lightest expected. The spread of light intensities from darkest to lightest in the scene is its *dynamic range*. The term "dynamic range" comes from music, where it refers to the spread between the softest and loudest volume levels in a piece, performance, instrument, or recording. In image processing it refers to the spread of light-intensity values in a scene, image, display device, or representation.

The part of the dynamic range that is represented in a digital image depends on how the light values in the scene are sensed and then how they are converted to numbers. The sensing and quantization are done by the digital camera or scanner. However, once an image has been put into a computer, it can be requantized (also resampled), but not in a way that obtains new information that wasn't already captured in the image.

The PixelMath software that will shortly be described represents stored images using a range from 0 to 255 for each color component (red, green, and blue) of each pixel. The values are integers (no fractional parts). Zero represents the absence of light of the particular color, while 255 represents the maximum amount of light.

As an illustration of a quantization issue, consider figure 2.11. This shows an image of the English Camp, grayscale version, in four different quantization schemes, differing in the number of bits allocated to each pixel. (A bit is a unit of information, defined more precisely in section 3.5.) Having 8 bits per pixel gives a good rendering of the perceivable shades of gray from black to white. However, having only 1 bit per pixel means that each pixel is limited to one of two colors (e.g., black or white, or dark and light). Many details of the original image are lost, such as the texture of the distant trees and most of the flag. Also, there is an obtrusive false contour in the sky in the 2-bits per pixel version. We'll study quantization in more detail in the next chapter, which deals with brightness in an image.

Figure 2.11
Quantization of the grayscale English-Camp image at 8 bits per pixel (upper left), 4 bits per pixel (upper right), 2 bits per pixel (lower left) and 1 bit per pixel (lower right).

2.2 Starting PixelMath

PixelMath is an image-processing system tailored specifically for learning image processing and Python programming. PixelMath is used to work with digital images in various ways. It is possible to create new images in PixelMath. However, the most common way of starting some activity in PixelMath involves loading up a digital image that already exists in a file, such as a digital photo from a camera or something downloaded from the Internet. The image can be inspected, measured, edited, or used to produce other data. You can use PixelMath in either of two ways: as a standalone application on your PC or Macintosh, or at a PixelMath web site. This section tells your how to get started.

To start PixelMath on your Windows PC, double-click on the PixelMath icon. Depending upon how you have installed the software, this may be on the desktop, in the Programs folder of the C drive, or elsewhere. Another way to run PixelMath is directly from a CD that contains both the PixelMath program itself and the Java Runtime Environment (JRE). (PixelMath2012 needs Java 1.7 or later.)

To start PixelMath at a PixelMath web site, log in at the web site with your user name and password, and then select the PixelMath with Python link. If your browser is Java-enabled with Java 1.7 or later, then on the page that comes up you should see the PixelMath launch pad image, with four buttons below it.

The launch pad is shown in figure 2.12a (plate 5). Clicking on the first button, labeled Calculator, will bring up the PixelMath calculator, which is your first interface for using PixelMath. The calculator, with the cover closed, is shown in figure 2.12b. After the cover is open, the calculator appears as in figure 2.13 (plate 6). The Formula Page and Python buttons bring up interfaces for more advanced usage of PixelMath. The Help button brings up some text that gives an overview of using PixelMath.

2.3 Examining Your Image

2.3.1 Opening an Image File

Now let's load an image into PixelMath. Go to the File menu on the calculator window. Select "Open Image . . ." This will bring up a dialog window that you can use to select an image from somewhere on your computer. The dialog window will look like one of those shown in figure 2.14.

As mentioned before, there are two ways of using PixelMath: as an application on your computer or as an applet on the web. In application mode, you can navigate throughout your file system to find the image you want. PixelMath 2012 can read and write .jpg, .gif and .png files.

In applet mode, you can select (from the File menu) "Open Image from Server..." and you'll see a list of files that are on the server and that are currently available to your PixelMath applet. It will look something like that shown in figure 2.14b. It's also possible to upload an image file to the server from your PC in order to make it available to PixelMath.

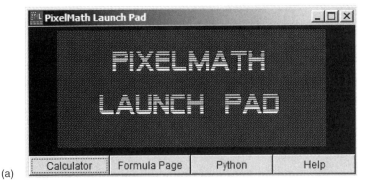

(a)

(b)

Figure 2.12 (plate 5)
PixelMath startup: (a) the launch pad and (b) the calculator with the cover still closed.

Once you have selected the image file and clicked on OK, the image will be read into the PixelMath program's memory area, a new window will be created, and the image will be displayed on the monitor. If there is any problem reading or downloading the image file, you may see an error message (possibly in the Java console of your browser). If you loaded the Mona Lisa image (mona-rgb.jpg), it should appear as in figure 2.15 (plate 7).

2.3.2 Zooming In and Out

Once your image is loaded, you are given a full view of it. The next thing to do is to zoom into the image. Simply click on the center of your image. It should zoom. If it does not, check to make sure that the zoom tool (depicted with the magnifying glass icon on the toolbar of the image window; see figure 2.16a) is selected and then try again.

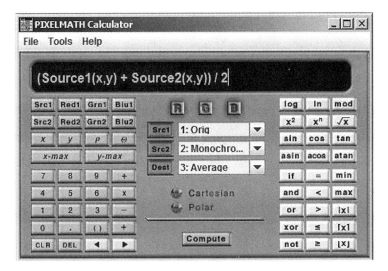

Figure 2.13 (plate 6)
The PixelMath calculator with cover open. It has a menu bar, a formula area, drop-down lists for selecting source images and destination, a Compute button, and additional buttons and controls.

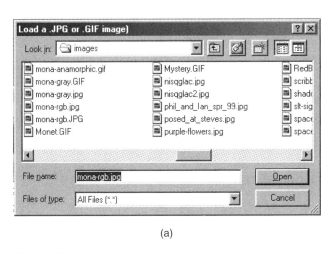

(a)

(b)

Figure 2.14
Selecting an image to load (a) in application mode and (b) in applet mode.

Figure 2.15 (plate 7)
An image window after loading is complete.

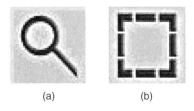

(a)   (b)

Figure 2.16
Tool icons: (a) the zoom tool's icon—a magnifying glass and (b) the selection tool's icon—a rectangle.

If you maximize the image window, you'll be able to see more of the image as you zoom into it.

2.3.3 RGB Values

Keep zooming in and you should soon be at a scale where the individual pixels will be visible. Each pixel is a small square region of the image. Its color is represented by three numbers: the red component, the green component, and the blue component. We'll refer to these three components of a pixel as the pixel's RGB values or its RGB triple. For example, the RGB triple $(0, 0, 0)$ represents the color having 0 units of red, 0 units of green, and 0 units of blue. This color is black.

As you keep zooming in, you should be able to see the RGB values of the pixels because PixelMath displays them right on top of their pixels. Figure 2.17 (plate 8) shows what these look like.

By the way, the largest value that can appear in an RGB triple is 255, and the RGB triple $(255, 255, 255)$ represents the color white.

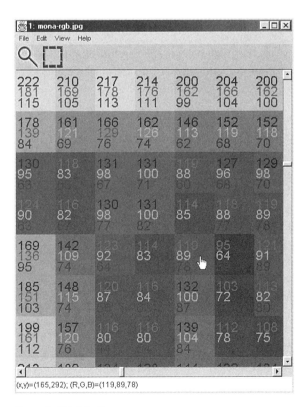

Figure 2.17 (plate 8)
A closeup of the Mona Lisa with RGB values of individual pixels showing.

To zoom out, simply hold the Shift key and click with the mouse on the image. As you zoom in or out, the location where you click is taken into account by the software. PixelMath usually centers the zoomed image around the pixel you last clicked on. However, when the image fits entirely within its window, the image is shown centered in the window regardless of where you last clicked on the image.

2.3.4 Scrolling

To move around in the image while it is zoomed in (i.e., it doesn't completely fit within the window), there are two ways to go. One is to zoom back out of the image, carefully choose the point on the image where you want to go, and click on that to zoom in around it. The other way to move around is to use the scrollbars. You can either pick up the scrollbar tab and slide it to the position you want, or you can use the fine-tuning scroll buttons at either end of each scrollbar.

2.3.5 Reporting Positions

You can tell where you are in an image in a precise way by looking at the coordinates of the pixel. Point to any pixel with the mouse cursor. That pixel's coordinates are reported at the bottom of the window. If you see, for example, (x, y) = (107, 38), this means that the pixel is in column 107 (counting from the left, with column 0 being the leftmost column of the image), and in row 38 (counting from the bottom, with row 0 being at the bottom of the image). These values are known as the *Cartesian coordinates* of the pixel.

2.4 Put a Twinkle in Your Eye

Now let's try changing some pixel values. First, load in a picture of a face. This could be a picture of yourself, suitably scanned or loaded from a digital camera. Or it could be the Mona Lisa image that comes with PixelMath.

Zoom into one of the two eyes in the face and don't stop until you can see the RGB numbers clearly. These numbers are probably fairly low (under 50), assuming you have located the iris of the eye, an area that is usually fairly dark.

Get the pixel selection tool, shown on the toolbar using an icon that has a rectangle on it (see figure 2.16b). Then use the tool to select a rectangular group of pixels in the middle of the person's eye. The rectangle should be small—perhaps 2 pixels by 2 pixels, or even just 1 pixel.

Next, find the PixelMath calculator window and enter the expression 255 into it. You can either type it into the black formula area or you can click on the calculator's number keys. After you have entered 255, click on the Compute button at the bottom center of the calculator.

You should see those formerly dark pixels turn white. If that worked all right, then you can go get the zoom tool once again and zoom out on the image (holding the Shift key and clicking on the image or clicking the right mouse button). After you have zoomed out about three or four times, look carefully at the image. Can you see a twinkle in the person's eye?

2.5 A Quick Overview of Features

If you have succeeded in putting a twinkle in the eye of someone, as described here, then you have exercised several key features of the PixelMath system: starting it up, opening an image, zooming, selecting pixels to be processed, and operating the calculator to enter new values into the selected pixels.

Some of the other features that you'll learn more about soon include the following: saving images to files, opening multiple images, selecting images for processing, arranging for the calculator to read pixels from one or two images and write pixel values to a third, using mathematical functions in formulas, controlling which of the three color components (red, green, blue) are written when a computation is performed, and programming sequences of operations so as to automate repetitive sequences of steps. The next step is to explore the use of PixelMath to control the color, brightness, and contrast of an image.

2.6 References

Gonzalez, R. C., and Woods, R. E. 2002. *Digital Image Processing*, 3rd ed., Reading, MA: Addison-Wesley.

Lyon, R. A brief history of "pixel." *Proc. IS&T/SPIE Symposium on Electronic Imaging*, 15–19 January, 2006, San Jose, CA. Reprinted online: www.foveon.com/files/ABriefHistoryofPixel2.pdf.

Shannon, C. 1949. Communication in the presence of noise. *Proc. Institute of Radio Engineers*, Vol. 37, No. 1, pp. 10–21.

Unser, M. 2000. Sampling 50 years after Shannon. *Proc. IEEE*, Vol. 88, No. 4, pp. 569–587.

2.7 Exercises

1. In film photography, an image is typically a pattern of pigment or opacity on a paper or film substrate. A digital image is generally a two-dimensional array of pixels. In either case, a good mathematical model for an image is a function whose domain is a set of coordinate pairs (x, y) and whose range is a set of possible pixel values, such as $\{v \in \Re \mid 0 \leq v \leq 1\}$ representing film opacity values, or the set of RGB triples $\{(r, g, b) \mid r, g, b \in \{0, 1, \ldots, 255\}\}$ used in the PixelMath system. Let $\mathbb{Z}_n = \{0, 1, \ldots, n-1\}$. For example, $\mathbb{Z}_4 = \{0, 1, 2, 3\}$. Give examples of small images (in particular 2-by-2 images where coordinates are either 0 or 1) with the set of pixel values indicated, having the following properties. (Give one image for each property. The first example is done for you.)

a. injective with range $\mathbb{Z}_7$ (An injection uses each range element at most once.) Answer:

6	2
3	5

b. surjective with range $\mathbb{Z}_3$ (A surjection uses each range element at least once.)

c. bijective with range $\mathbb{Z}_4$ (A bijection is both an injection and a surjection; it uses each range element exactly once.)

2. Suppose a scene contains a picket fence with thirteen pickets. Photographer Phrugal Phil wishes to take a digital picture of the fence with as few columns of pixels as possible while still allowing someone to correctly count the pickets in the image. How many columns of pixels will he need?

3. In the previous problem, what could go wrong if Phil uses the Nyquist rate as his sampling frequency but doesn't line up the samples quite right?

4. Suppose an image contains short oscillating patterns. One pattern repeats every 10 pixels. A second repeats every 8 pixels, and a third repeats every 6 pixels. Each pattern has a light-dark cycle with equal numbers of darker and lighter pixels. Phrugal Phil wants to resample the image with fewer pixels, but in such a way that the relationships among the frequencies of these oscillations are not lost. Can he just use one new pixel for every 10-by-10 block of old pixels? 8 by 8? 6 by 6? 5 by 5? 4 by 4? 3 by 3? Explain your answer.

5. For this exercise on sampling, obtain a copy, from your instructor or from the text's website, of the English-Camp.jpg image file. Open the PixelMath calculator. Then, from the File menu, choose "Open image…" and select this file. Find the number of rows and columns in this image by using the "Size Info" option in the image window's View menu.

a. What are the width and height (numbers of columns and rows)?

b. Consider the picket fence in the front of the garden. (Ignore the fences on the sides and back.) Use the mouse cursor to point to the lower left-hand corner of the picket fence. What are the x and y coordinates of this point?

c. Now click on this point to zoom in a little. Next find the point in the upper-right corner of the fence. You may need to scroll right to get there. You can also zoom back out by right-clicking on the image. What are its coordinates?

d. How many pixels wide is the fence?

e. How many pickets are there? Count carefully because you'll use your answer in a resampling experiment. (How many pickets are to the left of the gate, in the gate, and to the right of the gate? How many in total?)

f. If the pickets were perfectly aligned, how many samples would be required, at the theoretical minimum, to represent them in such a way that each picket could be distinguished from its neighbors?

g. Next create a downsampled version of this image. Using the File menu of the calculator (not the Image window), create a new image. Use your answer for the previous question for the width value. For the height use any positive integer in the range of 10 to 300, for example, 50. Leave the R,G,B values at their defaults.

Set the Destination choice on the calculator (lowest of three choices in the middle of the calculator) to the new window. It's "Untitled." Enter a formula such as the following[1] into the calculator's formula field: `Source1(x*2.5 + 171, y*2.5 + 273)`.

Now click on the calculator's Compute button to apply the formula. This formula tells PixelMath to fill each destination image pixel with a value computed by going into the Source1 image (your `English-Camp.jpg` original) at the coordinates given by

```
xsource = xdestination * 2.5 + 171
ysource = ydestination * 2.5 + 273
```

Thus the new image obtains its pixel values by starting at $x = 171$, $y = 273$ in the original and taking pixels every 2.5 pixels. PixelMath does automatic interpolation to compute values between pixel centers.

h. Adjust the resampling factor (here 2.5) to try to minimize the number of pixels you need to represent the picket fence with most of the pickets still distinguishable. What factor did you end up with? How many pickets were lost? If any pickets were lost, why?

6. Suppose a light sensor is to be used in a scanner and it has a dynamic range of 0 volts minimum to 5 volts maximum. Suppose that the designer of the scanner wants the pixels coming out of the scanner to be 0 for dark and 1 for light and nothing in between. What rule could the scanner hardware use to decide whether to output a 0 or a 1? What factors should the designer consider when setting up such a rule?

7. Start up PixelMath and load the Mona Lisa image (RGB color version). Place the mouse cursor on the middle of Mona's nose. What are the x and y coordinates of that position?

8. In the Mona Lisa image, find the pixel whose x coordinate is 50 and whose y coordinate is 75. What are the R, G, and B values for that pixel?

9. Identify the Mona Lisa's right eye. Report the x and y coordinates of the center of that eye. Select several pixels in her eye that represent the iris area (the part that is typically brown or blue in a person's eye). Change those pixels to a bright blue color. Do the same in the Mona Lisa's left eye. What R, G, and B values did you use to make the eyes blue?

1. Formulas for resampling are discussed in detail in chapter 5.

3   Brightness and Contrast

In this chapter you'll learn to control the brightness and contrast of an image. At the same time, your fluency will increase, both for PixelMath and image processing generally.

3.1   Brightness

3.1.1   The Phenomenon of Brightness

The intensity of light represented at a pixel is usually known as its brightness. This brightness is related to the amount of light energy received from the scene at that pixel's location in the original image. In a system in which colors are represented by RGB triples, black $(0, 0, 0)$ is the least bright color and white $(255, 255, 255)$ is the brightest color. We can consider the brightness of a pixel to be the average of its three RGB color values. In this way the brightness of black is 0, the brightness of white is 255, and the brightness of pure red $(255, 0, 0)$ is 85.

Sometimes the word "brightness" is used to refer to the perceived brightness, something that can depend upon the state of the eye. For example, if you have been in a dark room for an hour and then you walk out into clear sunshine, the world will seem brighter than it will 5 minutes later, after your eyes have had a chance to adjust to the change. When we use the word "brightness" in this book, we'll assume it refers to a property of the image itself, and not the state of the human eye.

3.1.2   A Scale of Gray Values

Let's consider the range of gray colors (the gray scale). Starting at RGB = $(0, 0, 0)$ we have black. You can see that in figure 3.1. At the other end of the scale is white $(255, 255, 255)$, and in the middle we have neutral gray $(127, 127, 127)$. We've taken the liberty of rounding $255/2$ down to 127. Between black and neutral gray is a range of dark grays, and between neutral gray and white are light grays.

The brightness of any gray is easy to obtain since it's the average of three equal values. In fact, it's the equality of the three RGB values that gives some kind of gray rather than some more general color like dark red, light orange, tan, etc.

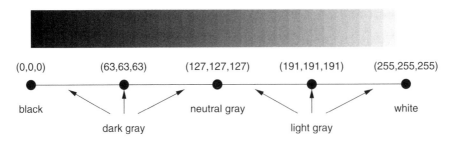

Figure 3.1
The gray scale. It goes from black, where RGB = (0, 0, 0), to white, where RGB = (255, 255, 255).

3.1.3 Brightening an Image

To brighten an image is to make it brighter than it already is. We might want to brighten an image because it seems too dark. Perhaps it was taken with a camera under dim lighting conditions. Or we may be trying to make an image fit better with some other images, which are all brighter.

Let's try brightening an image, just to see how it might be done. Start up a fresh session of PixelMath. Load an image into a PixelMath window. Now enter the following formula into the calculator:

```
Source1(x, y) + 100
```

and click Compute on the calculator. This should cause the RGB values of the pixels to be increased by 100. An example showing this adjustment on a black-and-white (grayscale) image is shown in figure 3.2. However, no value can go greater than 255, so some values may reach a maximum there.

This should have brightened the image. However, it tends to affect different colors differently, reducing the relative amounts of the brighter components while boosting the relative amounts of the darker colors. For example, if the starting color had been red (100, 0, 0), then the ending color would be a brighter but more pinkish red (200, 100, 100). This type of change in color in which the color becomes more of a blend of the three primaries is known as desaturation. Desaturation could have been avoided in this case by multiplying the RGB values by 2 rather than adding 100. That would have increased the red component to 200 while keeping the green and blue components at 0. You can try this by first selecting Undo from the Edit menu of the image window, and then entering the following formula and clicking Compute.

(a)   (b)

Figure 3.2
Brightening a grayscale image by adding 100 to each pixel component.

```
Source1(x, y) * 2
```

Generally, when we brighten an image we try not to upset the balance of colors in the image. This can sometimes make it a challenge to effectively brighten an image. Whereas multiplying the original red image by 2 will avoid the desaturation for that particular image, let's see what happens if the original color is not that particular red, but a brighter and slightly pinkish red (255, 100, 100). Multiplying these values by 2 results in (255, 200, 200) because the red value was already at its allowable maximum. This new color is brighter than the color before, but it's even more pinkish and unsaturated than before. So multiplication doesn't always avoid desaturation. Desaturation is one of the hazards of brightening, and often a difficult subjective judgment is required to decide whether the brightened version of an image is more useful than the original, even if the original was too dark.

3.2 Contrast

3.2.1 The Phenomenon of Contrast

Contrast describes the spread of values in an image within the range of possible brightness values. An image that is entirely made up of black pixels and white pixels has maximum contrast. High contrast can be effective when images of text or icons are involved and the text or icons must be easy to read under possibly low lighting conditions or from a great distance. However, this much contrast is usually considered bad in photographs of scenery and people since it usually means that many informative details of shading and color have been lost. Nonetheless, it is often helpful to be able to increase or decrease the contrast in an image, either to make distinctions clearer or to soften what would otherwise be a harsh appearance.

3.2.2 Stretching Contrast

Contrast can usually be increased by multiplying all the RGB values in an image by a number greater than 1, such as 2.0. As we saw earlier, this will also have the effect of brightening most images. In order to avoid saturation and too much brightening, it is common to first subtract some value from the RGB values and then perform the multiplication.

To see this in action, load a photographic image into a fresh PixelMath session and apply the following formula to it.

```
(Source1(x, y) - 100) * 2
```

For most images, one effect of applying this contrast stretch operation will be more black pixels as well as more very bright pixels. The effect of this operation on a grayscale image is shown in figure 3.3.

3.3 Histograms

A *histogram* is a bar graph that shows the number of occurrences of different kinds of items in a population. Figure 3.4 shows the number of times each letter of the alphabet occurs in Lincoln's *Gettysburg Address*. In this histogram one can see that the most frequently occurring letter is *e* and the letters *j*, *x*, and *z* don't occur at all; the letter *q* occurs only once. Just for reference, here is the text of the *Gettysburg Address*:

Four score and seven years ago our fathers brought forth on this continent, a new nation, conceived in Liberty, and dedicated to the proposition that all men are created equal.

Now we are engaged in a great civil war, testing whether that nation, or any nation so conceived and so dedicated, can long endure. We are met on a great battle-field of that war. We have come to dedicate a portion of that field, as a final resting place for those who here gave their lives that that nation might live. It is altogether fitting and proper that we should do this.

But, in a larger sense, we can not dedicate—we can not consecrate—we can not hallow—this ground. The brave men, living and dead, who struggled here, have consecrated it, far above our poor power to add or detract. The world will little note, nor long remember what we say here, but it can

(a) (b)

Figure 3.3
Enhancing contrast: (a) a grayscale image and (b) the contrast-enhanced result.

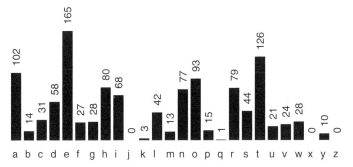

Figure 3.4
A histogram showing the number of occurrences of each letter of the alphabet in Abraham Lincoln's *Gettysburg Address*.

never forget what they did here. It is for us the living, rather, to be dedicated here to the unfinished work which they who fought here have thus far so nobly advanced. It is rather for us to be here dedicated to the great task remaining before us—that from these honored dead we take increased devotion to that cause for which they gave the last full measure of devotion—that we here highly resolve that these dead shall not have died in vain—that this nation, under God, shall have a new birth of freedom—and that government of the people, by the people, for the people, shall not perish from the earth.

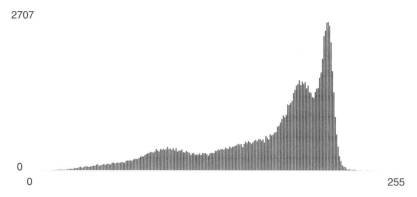

Figure 3.5
Histogram for a grayscale image of Lincoln.

A histogram is therefore a kind of statistical summary of a data set. In the case of text, the data consist of characters (or for some applications, words, phrases, or sentences).

3.3.1 Examining Image Histograms

A histogram for an image is a statistical summary of the set of pixels in the image. For a monochrome image, each pixel is represented by one number and the histogram is based on these numbers. In the case of a color image, we typically consider each color component separately, and so there is one histogram for the red values of the image, one for green, and one for red.

Let's consider the histogram shown in figure 3.5, which is based on the monochrome image of Abraham Lincoln shown in figure 3.3. The histogram shows, for example, that the most frequently occurring pixel value is 209, which occurs 2707 times. More importantly, the poor contrast of the original image is evident in the histogram because there are very few pixels near the left (black) end of the histogram, as well as few pixels near the right (white) end.

3.3.2 Histogram Equalization

An important use of histograms is in an image enhancement process known as histogram equalization. The idea behind histogram equalization is to try evenly distribute the pixel intensity values across the range of allowable intensity values. This can help enhance contrast in parts of the range where there are many pixels with similar (but slightly different) values. This means that all original pixels with a given value will be changed to have a new value. One constraint is that if two pixels happen to have the same value in the original image, then in the new image, although the values may have changed, their values will still be equal to each other. If the pixel values were evenly distributed within the range of 0 to

109326

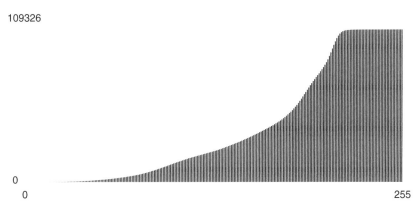

0

0   255

Figure 3.6
Cumulative histogram for the image of Lincoln.

255, then each bin of the histogram would have an equal value. It would have 1/256 of the total number of pixels. The histogram would be flat.

In order to explain the equalization process, we introduce the concept of a cumulative histogram. For a given histogram H, the cumulative histogram $C(H)$ is a bar graph where the kth bin gives the total number of items with value k or less. For an image, it's a count of the number of pixels with a value less than or equal to k. The cumulative histogram for the Lincoln image is shown in figure 3.6.

One method for equalizing a histogram uses a computer program that scans through the cumulative histogram of the image, at each position comparing it with the ideal cumulative histogram. At each position it will move the bin (specify a change of pixel value) left or right within the range in such a way as to make the new cumulative histogram closer to the ideal one at the new position for the bin. As the bins are moved, a table is filled out that tells what the new pixel value will be for each of the original pixel values. Then the image is processed by replacing each pixel value by its corresponding new value in the table.

After this has been done for the Lincoln image, we get the equalized Lincoln image shown in figure 3.7. The histogram after equalization is shown in figure 3.8. The cumulative histogram after equalization, shown in figure 3.9, is very close to the ideal one in its almost linear shape.

3.4 Thresholding

If we take contrast enhancement to the extreme, we change every shade of gray to either black or white. We decide in advance that a certain pixel value will be the threshold value—say 175. We apply the following rule: If a pixel's value is below the threshold value, then we make it black. Otherwise we make it white. This can be accomplished by the following formula, which happens to make use of the conditional construct: "if-then-else."

Figure 3.7
The Lincoln image after histogram equalization.

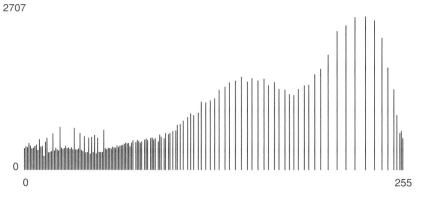

Figure 3.8
Equalized histogram for the image of Lincoln.

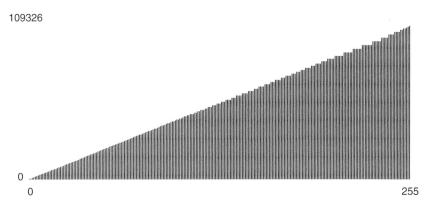

Figure 3.9
Cumulative equalized histogram for the image of Lincoln.

```
if Source1(x,y) < 175 then 0 else 255
```

Another way of accomplishing the same thing is to use the contrast-enhancing formula with a large gain value, in this case 255:

```
(Source1(x,y) - 174) * 255
```

Notice that we subtract 174 from each pixel value, not 175, since the pixel value 175 is supposed to end up changed to 255, not 0. The result of this operation, known as thresholding, can be seen in figure 3.10. Besides being a means to produce this graphical effect, thresholding is useful as a step in many other image-processing operations, such as creating stereograms, stencils, and computer vision.

3.5 Quantization

As we have just seen, thresholding produces a representation of an image that has only two kinds of pixels in it: black and white. Such an image has been quantized to 1 bit per pixel. A *bit* is a unit of information that represents a selection from a two-way choice. In thresholding an image, the choice is black or white. Quantization refers to making a choice, for each pixel of an image, as to what value (or values, in the case of color) will represent it.

(a)   (b)

Figure 3.10
The extreme case of increasing contrast, known as thresholding.

Let's consider another example of quantization. In this one, we'll use 2 bits per pixel. That means there will essentially be two two-way choices to make (or equivalently, one four-way choice). The first two-way choice will be "dark or light," and the second choice will be "darker or lighter." It is customary to use the numbers 0 and 1 to represent the selections in a two-way choice. Thus we can summarize the 2-bit quantization with the following rules.

• If the intensity of the pixel is in the range 0–63, select "dark" for the first choice and "darker" for the second. The two choices are thus represented by 00.

• If the intensity of the pixel is in the range 64–127, select "dark" and "lighter." The bit encoding is 01.

• If the intensity of the pixel is in the range 128–191, select "light" and "darker." The bit encoding is 10.

• If the intensity of the pixel is in the range 192–255, select "light" and "lighter." The bit encoding is 11.

Let's now assign decimal numbers to each 2-bit code. For 00 we'll use 0; for 01 we'll use 1; for 10 it's 2; and for 11 it's 3. The following PixelMath formula performs the quantization.

```
If Source1(x,y) < 64 Then 0
Else If Source1(x,y) < 128 Then 1
Else If Source1(x,y) < 192 Then 2
Else 3
```

For this set of four subranges (0–63, 64–127, 128–191, and 192–255), the following simpler formula achieves the same result.

```
Source1(x,y) / 64
```

A major advantage of performing quantization on images as we have just suggested is that the image can then be represented with fewer bits and requires less memory and less time to download. However, detailed information about shades of gray and color can be lost.

Note that the quantized image obtained with the formulas given here appears to be all black. This is because its values (in the range 0–3) are all close to 0. The image's brightness and contrast are limited with this range. The original brightness and contrast can be partially restored by multiplying the pixels' values by 64.

```
Source1(x,y) * 64
```

3.6 Bits and Bytes

As mentioned earlier, a bit represents a selection from a set of two possibilities. The term "bit" also refers to the unit of information that is embodied in the selection. A bit is customarily written using either 0 or 1. If the first item in the choice has been selected, the bit is written with 0; if the second item is selected, it's written with 1. Besides being a unit of information and representing a selection, a bit is a binary digit, a 0 or 1, which is used to represent the unit of information.

The *binary number system* is a way of representing the integers 0, 1, 2, . . . using only bits (0 and 1). Here is a table showing how the decimal numbers from 0 to 10 are represented in the binary system:

0	0
1	1
2	10
3	11
4	100
5	101
6	110
7	111
8	1000
9	1001
10	1010

The binary number system is also known as the *base*-2 number system. Each bit in a binary number represents the absence or presence of a power of 2 in the number. For example, the binary number 10011 contains 2^4, does not contain 2^3, does not contain 2^2, does contain 2^1, and does contain 2^0. Its value is therefore

$$2^4 + 2^1 + 2^0 = 16 + 2 + 1 = 19$$

When writing a binary number on a page that might also contain decimal system numbers, it is customary to use a subscript of 2 to indicate that it's in the binary system. Therefore we would write

$$10011_2 = 19$$

A group of 8 bits is often called a *byte*. (Note, however, that in the early days of computers, bytes sometimes referred to groups of more or fewer than 8 bits.) One byte can represent eight selections from two-way choices. Equivalently, it could represent one $2^8 = 256$ way choice.

In many image-processing software systems, each color component of a pixel (e.g., red, green, or blue) is represented by 1 byte. This means that there are 256 possible values for the component. Since a pixel in the RGB color system has three components, and each uses 1 byte, such an image is said to use 24-bit color. Theoretically, a pixel in a 24-bit color system can take on any of $2^{24} = 16,777,216$ different colors. In practice, computer monitors and color printers cannot produce such a broad range of colors effectively, so we don't really experience such a rich set. Nonetheless, there are some advantages to using 24-bit color, particularly when mathematical operations are applied to the pixels that amplify the slight differences among close colors.

3.7 The Memory Required by an Image

In order to store the red, green, and blue component values of all the pixels in a digital image having 512 rows and 512 columns, we need $512 \times 512 \times 3$ bytes, or about 750 kilobytes. Computer software such as PixelMath, however, uses more than this to store an image because its internal representation for images involves more than just the red, green, and blue values. As a rough estimate, about 2 to 4 megabytes of RAM might be used for one PixelMath image of this size, owing to the need for multiple internal representations of the image, such as those in the Undo buffer.

When saved to a file using the JPEG encoding method, an image can be compressed to take up less than what it would seem to require. This is achieved by reorganizing the pixel information and possibly giving up some of the fine details in the image. However, distortions known as artifacts can be introduced by the compression.

3.8 References

Floyd, R. W., and Steinberg, L. 1976. An adaptive algorithm for spatial grey scale. *Proc. Society of Information Display*, Vol. 17, pp. 75-77.

Wikipedia. 2010. Histogram Equalization. en.wikipedia.org/wiki/Histogram_equalization.

3.9 Exercises

1. Pixel values are limited to a fixed range in PixelMath. (a) If you enter 1000 into the calculator and attempt to store that value in the destination pixels, what value is actually stored? (b) If you attempt to store the value -1000 into the pixels, what value is actually stored?

2. Suppose you wish to take the photographic negative of an image using PixelMath. (a) A pixel that is black $(0, 0, 0)$ should be changed to what color and what values? (b) What formula should you use in the calculator to perform the negation?

3. In modular arithmetic, the results of each operation (addition, subtraction, multiplication) are taken modulo a number. For example,

$(13 \cdot 5) \bmod 7 = 65 \bmod 7 = 2$

If $x \bmod y = z$, that means that the remainder when x is divided by y is z. What is the result of $59 \cdot 3 \bmod 256$? What is the result of $193 \cdot 3 \bmod 256$?

Some computer image-processing systems force arithmetic results into a fixed range using truncation. Let A be a register that can hold any number in the range $\{0, 1, \ldots, 255\}$. Let's use expressions of the form $A \leftarrow expr$ to mean that A is assigned the value $\max[0, \min(255, expr)]$. Then, in the following sequence of steps, what is the value of A?

$A \leftarrow 17$

$A \leftarrow A \cdot A$

$A \leftarrow \sqrt{A}$

4. Suppose that a digital image is defined at the following set of coordinate pairs. [This notation defines a set of pairs of the form (x, y), where x is in a certain range of values and y is in a certain range of values.]

$\{(x, y) \mid x \in \mathbb{Z}, 0 \leq x \leq x_{\max}, y \in \mathbb{Z}, 0 \leq y \leq y_{\max}\}$

Here $\mathbb{Z}$ represents the integers, so the expression $x \in \mathbb{Z}$ says that x is an integer. The vertical bar ("|") can be read as "such that."

If $x_{\max} = 127$ and $y_{\max} = 63$, what is the area (in pixels) of that portion of the image where $x > x_{\max}/2$ and $y > 60$?

5. Suppose that you have a fairly bright image that you want to make about 10 percent darker. What formula should you use?

6. Express each of the following numbers (given in decimal) in the binary number system: (a) 7, (b) 16, (c) 31, (d) 100.

7. Give the decimal equivalent for each of the following numbers given in the binary system: (a) 1010, (b) 10001, (c) 11011, (d) 1111111.

8. Convert the numbers 41 and 22 to their binary representations. Show their sum in both decimal and binary representations.

9. Convert the number 1001001_2 to a decimal system representation.

10. The floor function returns the largest integer less than or equal to its argument. For example, floor(13.7)= 13, and floor(-5.1)= −6. These can also be written as $\lfloor 13.7 \rfloor = 13$ and $\lfloor -5.1 \rfloor = -6$. What is the value of $13.7 \cdot -5.1 - (\lfloor 13.7 \rfloor \cdot \lfloor -5.1 \rfloor)$?

11. The ceiling function is similar to the floor function except that it returns the smallest integer greater than or equal to its argument. For example, ceiling(13.7)= 14. This is also written as $\lceil 13.7 \rceil = 14$. What is the value of $\lfloor 13.7 \rfloor \cdot \lceil 13.7 \rceil$?

12. Suppose that a color image is 1600 pixels wide and 1200 pixels high. If it uses 8 bits to represent each of the red, green, and blue components of each pixel, how many bytes of memory does the image require?

13. Suppose we have a 1-megapixel image where each of its pixels is stored with 6 bits of red, 6 bits of green, and 4 bits of blue. How many bytes of memory are required for this image?

4 Controlling Color

In this chapter you'll learn to create palettes of colors, understand color transformations, and adjust the colors in images.

4.1 The Phenomenon of Color

We see light differences, not only in terms of brightness, but also in terms of color. Red and blue patches of an image could be equally bright, but we see them as different. We often associate color with temperature, with red being warm and blue being cool or cold. However, these associations don't really correspond very well to physical reality since red and blue light can both come from either hot or cold materials. The hottest part of a kitchen stove's gas flame is in the blue part. The red planet Mars is cold; it's red because of the iron content of that planet.

The phenomenon of light is known to be a part of a more general phenomenon of electromagnetic radiation—something that includes radio waves, infrared waves, X-rays, and cosmic rays, as well as visible light. Each type of radiation has a characteristic frequency range. Pure colors correspond to distinct points along a portion of the electromagnetic spectrum. Figure 4.1 (plate 9) shows the visible spectrum of colors. The wavelength of red light is the longest and that of violet is the shortest.

The human eye, except in color-blind or partially color-blind people, perceives color in a kind of three-dimensional color space. There are receptor cells in the retina that respond preferentially to each of three colors: red, green, and blue. The relative responses of the three types of color receptors to light stimulation of different wavelengths are represented by tristimulus functions that have peak responses at the wavelengths of their associated colors, and the responses taper off as the wavelength moves away from the special value. The tristimulus functions are approximated by the color-matching functions shown in figure 4.2 (plate 10).

Each color that we see can be expressed or at least approximated as some combination of the three primaries. Other systems of primaries than the red-green-blue one can be used to mix light and achieve rich sets of colors. However, the RGB system is preferred for most computer display systems.

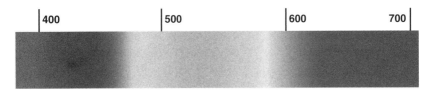

Figure 4.1 (plate 9)
Spectrum of visible light. Wavelength markings are in nanometers.

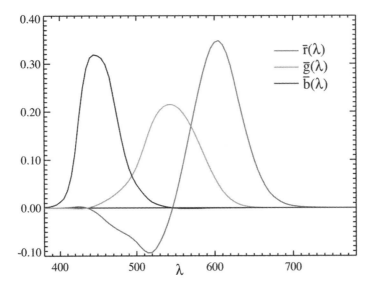

Figure 4.2 (plate 10)
Color-matching functions that show the relative amounts of red, green, and blue required to create a mixture that perceptually matches each spectral color. The curves also roughly indicate the sensitivity of each kind of cone to light across the spectrum. The horizontal axis shows wavelength in nanometers and the vertical axis shows relative magnitude. The curves have been normalized so that the areas under them are equal. These functions correspond to the 1931 CIE standard observer.

4.2   Controlling Color in PixelMath

In chapter 3 we considered monochrome images. Let us now consider both how PixelMath can use color information and how it can change colors in images. We'll start with changing colors (writing color information) and then accessing (reading) color information.

4.2.1   Enabling Color Changes

In order to create different colors using the PixelMath calculator, we need to be able to put numbers in the red components of pixels that are different from the numbers in green

Figure 4.3 (plate 11)
The enable-red, enable-green, and enable-blue toggles.

components and blue components, etc. To specify which components are to be modified, we use a special part of the calculator.

For each primary color, red, green, and blue, there is a pushbutton switch on the calculator to enable or disable changes to that component of the selected pixels. These are shown in figure 4.3 (plate 11). The "enable-red" button glows red when red is enabled and it's gray when red is disabled. The other colors (green and blue) work similarly. When PixelMath is started, all three components are enabled by default. Each one can be independently turned on or off. However, if they are all off, then no updates to any image are possible, and any computation using the calculator will not have an effect. We'll refer to these switches as the *enable-red toggle*, the *enable-green toggle*, and the *enable-blue toggle*.

Note that enabling a color is not the same as turning on a light of that color in the pixels. It just means that the values for that color component of the selected pixels can be changed. If, say, the enable-red toggle is off, then the red components of all pixels will be temporarily frozen at their current values no matter what formulas are applied with the calculator.

4.2.2 Creating a Block of Red

In order to practice the steps needed to control the color of some pixels, let's place a red square in the middle of some photograph. First, load up a photograph if one isn't open already. If you now have two image windows open, make sure that the calculator's Destination selection is set to the new image you just loaded so that its pixels can be modified rather than the pixels of the other image. Now, in order to create a nice block of red, we'll have to do three things: specify where the square will go, reduce the green and blue components of the selected pixels to zero, and finally, raise the red components of the selected pixels to the max, 255.

To select the pixels, zoom in or scroll if needed to find the pixels of interest. Then choose the selection tool from the toolbar and draw a box around the pixels to be modified. If you want to select only a single pixel, then just click on it.

Next, make sure that the enable-green and enable-blue toggles are on. It doesn't matter right now whether or not the enable-red toggle is on. Now enter 0 in the calculator and click Compute.

Finally, disable the green and blue components and make sure that red is enabled. Then enter 255 in the calculator and click Compute. You should see a bright red color in all the pixels you selected.

If you do not see red, then it may be for one of the following reasons: the Destination choice on the calculator does not match the window with your image, you didn't enable changing the pixel values, or you accidentally changed the selected set of pixels by clicking somewhere else on the image. Also, if you created a red square in a red area of an image, it might not be apparent.

4.2.3 Amplifying Only the Red Component of an Image

Suppose you want to make the red component of an image more intense, but you wish the green and blue components to remain the same. Then set the toggles so that red is enabled and green and blue are disabled. Make sure your image to be modified is listed as the Source1 as well as the Destination choice. If you have selected some particular pixels in that image, you might want to alter the selection to include all the pixels. Now enter and compute the formula

```
Source1(x,y) * 1.5
```

This should intensify the red. Here, you used the enable toggles to control what color component was affected by the computation.

4.3 Specific Colors and Palettes

The RGB system of color representation is widely used in computing and it's not only fun to express colors in it, but it can be useful to know it for tasks such as web-page design, computer graphics programming, and general work with digital images. In this section, we'll practice mixing colors both for the fun of it and in order to better understand the concept and processes of additive color mixing.

4.3.1 Creating Specific Colors

Let's begin our color mixing practice with a color whose RGB representation is consistent with our intuition: purple. In order to create purple, we'll need a lot of red and a lot of blue, but not much green, if any at all. Using the selection tool in the destination image, identify a group of pixels to be modified. Then enable all three colors using the toggles. Enter 0 into the calculator and click Compute. This will make the selected pixels black, giving you a clean slate on which to create purple. Now you do the rest!

Next, let's create yellow. If you did finger painting in kindergarten, you might have been told that yellow is a primary color and that you use it to make green. In the RGB system, yellow is not a primary and must be mixed from red and green. Can you come up with a nice yellow?

Cyan is considered a primary color in the printing industry, but we need to mix it from green and blue when working in the RGB system. The formula for cyan is RGB = (0, 255, 255).

In the RGB system, orange is like yellow because we must mix it from red and green. However, orange has relatively more red in it than yellow does, so if we start from yellow (255, 255, 0), we have to reduce the amount of green, since we cannot increase the amount of red. The precise shade of orange is going to depend heavily on how much green is retained, but here is one version of orange: (255, 127, 0). An even more reddish orange would use (255, 63, 0).

Pink is a color that involves us in a discussion of white. Pure white is obtained with a maximum of each of the primaries (255, 255, 255). However, we'll sometimes speak of "mixing in some white" to a color such as red by increasing the nonred components of the color. If we take red (255, 0, 0) and increase the green and blue components to something like 127, we get a kind of mixture of red and white, or pink (255, 127, 127). A lighter pink is obtained by mixing in more white, e.g., (255, 191, 191) or even (255, 223, 223).

We can do similar things with colors like purple, which are themselves mixtures. To add white to purple, we increase the green component from 0 to some higher value such as 127, resulting in lavender (255, 127, 255) or a lighter lavender (255, 191, 255).

Brown is a challenge. While it's a very common color in the natural world, coming up with a good-looking brown can take a bit of experimentation. Brown might be described as dark yellow, and you could make it by starting with yellow (255, 255, 0) and scaling it down to (127, 127, 0) or even (63, 63, 0). However, many nice-looking browns are in some sense mixtures of this dark yellow with dark gray (which itself is sort of dark white). To mix gray into a color is like mixing in white, but less of it, or we can achieve it by mixing in some white and scaling the whole color down to make it darker. In the case of brown, we could take dark yellow (127, 127, 0), add some white by raising the blue component, getting (127, 127, 95), and then scaling this down by a factor of 2, obtaining (63, 63, 47). Experiment a bit and you'll find it's not difficult to come up with some interesting earth tones.

4.3.2 Creating Color Gradients

Now that we've created several common colors one at a time, let's learn some ways to create many different colors at the same time. We can do this by generating images in which one color component (like red) gradually increases from left to right, while another (like green) gradually increases from bottom to top. Let's try this. Begin with a black image that's 256 pixels wide and 256 pixels high. You can create one by choosing New from the File menu and then specifying a width and height of 256 and red, green, and blue values of 0.

Now make sure that the new image is set as the Destination; then enable only red and compute

```
    x
```

This image is called a *gradient* image because it gradually increases from a low value (in this case 0) to a high value (in this case 255).

Now enable only green and compute

```
    y
```

There should be a nice blend of red, green, orange, yellow, etc., appearing in the destination image (see figure 4.4, plate 12).

You can repeat these steps using red and blue rather than red and green. Or you could use green and blue. However, this method only supports mixing two color components at

Figure 4.4 (plate 12)
Color gradients superimposed: red increases from left to right whereas green increases from bottom to top.

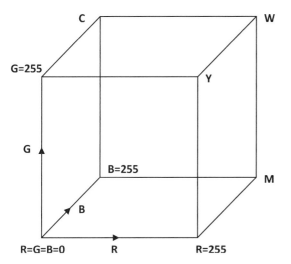

Figure 4.5
The RGB color space as a cube. Red (R) goes left to right, from 0 to 255. Green (G) goes up and blue (B) goes back in depth. Black is at the origin, where all three components are zero. Yellow (Y), magenta (M), cyan (C), and white (W) are also shown.

a time, with one equal to the x-coordinate value of each pixel and the other equal to the y-coordinate value.

The RGB color space is often conceived of as a cube. Figure 4.5 shows a cube where R increases along the horizontal dimension, G increases going up, and B increases going back in depth. If we had a z-coordinate value for each pixel, then we could combine all three components in a way that would create every possible combination of R, G, and B values. However, we are limited to only two coordinate dimensions in any one image, so how might we accomplish this or something like it?

One way would be to create several images, each with red and green blended as earlier, but each image having a different amount of blue. The first image might have no blue (blue = 0). If we had nine images, we could divide the range of possible blue values (0 to 255) into eight approximately equal subranges and choose, together with 0, the upper limits of each subrange. For example, we could use 0, 31, 63, 95, 127, 159, 191, 223, and 255. With this scheme, the blue value goes up by 32 (except from 0 to 31) from one image to the next, giving us a nice range of blue values. If we allowed 256 different images, we could have one image for every possible blue value. Then these 256 images could be combined into one image by laying them out in a 16-by-16 array of images, like tiles on a floor, and considering the arrangement of tiles to be one large image.

Another approach is to put all the colors in one image by taking small regions of the red-green image and mixing different amounts of blue into the pixels of each small region. To do this using 4-by-4 blocks of pixels as the subregions, take the red-green gradient image

Figure 4.6 (plate 13)
Palette of colors constructed by superimposing a pattern of locally varying blue with a horizontal gradient of red and a vertical gradient of green.

as the destination, enable only blue, and compute the following formula, which uses the mod operator.[1]

```
16 * (x mod 4) + 64 * (y mod 4)
```

The resulting image is a selection of colors, often known as a palette. This palette is shown in figure 4.6 (plate 13).

This method could be taken to the extreme (assuming you have enough memory in your computer) by starting with a much larger image (4096 by 4096) using 16-by-16 blocks of pixels and setting up the red, green, and blue components with the formulas as follows: for red, use

```
x / 16
```

1. As a reminder, the mod operator computes the remainder in division. For example, 21 mod 6 is equal to 3, and 39 mod 13 equals 0.

for green, use

```
y  /  16
```

for blue, use

```
(x mod 16)  +  16 * (y mod 16)
```

This image requires approximately 48 megabytes by itself. With the extra overhead of graphics support, it would require about 96 megabytes. Therefore, creating this image will not work or will not work well on a machine with less than about 256 megabytes of RAM in it. The one advantage of this image is that it contains each and every one of the 256^3 possible RGB colors in it. However, typical graphics cards in personal computers can render only a relatively small fraction of these colors on the screen at one time. Therefore there is not much practical value in creating this pan-color image.

4.3.3 A Spectrum

What if we wanted to show, not all possible colors, but a large, representative sample of the possible hues? Let us define a "whole" color as a maximally bright, fully saturated color of some particular hue. To be more specific, we will call an RGB color a *whole* color if one of its three color components is 0 and another is 255. The third can be any value in the 0–255 range. For example, RGB = (128, 0, 255) is a whole color (a violet color in this case).

How many different whole colors are possible in the PixelMath system? We can determine this by examining the number of choices available in creating a whole color. First we can choose which of the three components will be forced to be 0. There are three choices for that. Then we can choose which of the remaining two components will be fixed at 255. There are two choices left for that. So we have chosen among $3 \times 2 = 6$ possibilities so far. Then we have 256 choices for the value of the remaining component. This makes 1536 possible whole colors. However, some of these colors are double-counted because, for example, we can come up with (0, 0, 255) in two different ways, depending on whether red or green is selected as the color forced to be 0. The number of double-counted colors is 6. So there are 1530 distinct whole colors.

Let us create an image that shows all the whole colors. For convenience, we can make the image wide and not very tall, so that the color depends only on the x-coordinate. The idea will be to set the color component values of the pixels using ramp functions that increase or decrease as x increases. If the value of the function increases past 255, the value will automatically be truncated to 255 when it is stored in a pixel. Similarly, when a ramp descends below 0, the value stored in a pixel will be 0. A simple ramp function is $f(x) = x$. This function increases to the right. On the other hand, $f(x) = -x$ decreases to the right. Let us use functions that make one complete cycle of increasing and decreasing as we move across the image. A ramp up and then down again forms a triangular wave pattern. In order to obtain all the whole colors, the triangular waves for R, G, and B must be staggered or out of phase. Otherwise, we would get shades of gray rather than whole colors. We'll need an image that is 1536 pixels wide (ignoring the fact that six of the colors will be presented twice). The height of the image is immaterial, so let's use 64.

Three triangular waves out of phase can be obtained with the following three functions: (a) $f(x) = 511 - x$ if $x < 768$, $x - 1024$ otherwise; (b) $f(x) = x$ if $x < 512$, $1023 - x$ otherwise; and (c) $f(x) = x - 512$ if $x < 1024$, $1535 - x$ otherwise. In order to set these up to control red, green, and blue, we'll use the RGB operator[2] in the calculator. Here's our formula:

```
RGB(if x < 768 then 511 - x else x - 1024,
    if x < 512 then x else 1023 - x,
    if x < 1024 then x - 512 else 1535 - x)
```

The whole colors produced in this way are analogous to the colors one would visit traveling around a color wheel or traveling around the equator of a color globe that has white for a north pole, black for a south pole, grays along the north-south axis, saturated colors on the surface, and unsaturated colors in the interior.

4.4 Color Enhancements

Besides mixing colors to create specific colors or gradients, we often want to manipulate color in another way: to adjust the colors in photographic images. Let's consider some different kinds of adjustments, beginning with entirely removing the color in an image.

---

2. The RGB operator is described more fully in section 4.5.2.

4.4.1 Monochrome Conversions

Suppose we have a color image but wish to convert it to black and white. (This doesn't mean that black and white are the only tones we'll allow; shades of gray will be all right, too.) Removing the color in an image without changing the intensity of each pixel is what we're after. This is sometimes called *monochrome conversion*.

The key idea in monochrome conversion is to take a pixel's three color components and change them so that all three get values that are equal to each other, but to do this without much changing the sum of the values, which corresponds to the intensity. So a pretty straightforward way to make a monochrome version of a pixel is to take the average of the pixel's red, green, and blue components and replace all three components by this average. Here's a formula for this:

```
(Red1(x,y)+Green1(x,y)+Blue1(x,y))/3
```

This formula produces each destination pixel by looking at the Source1 pixel's red, green, and blue components and averaging them. Assuming you have all three color components enabled, then all three components of a destination pixel will receive that average value.

This monochrome image is an *unbiased* monochrome conversion because each of the red, green, and blue components had the same weight (namely one-third) in the average. A biased monochrome conversion gives unequal weight to the color components. For example, the formula

```
Red1(x,y)
```

gives full weight to red and nothing to green or blue. The result will still be a monochrome image, assuming all destination components are enabled. However, any variation in the source image's green or blue components that is independent of variation in the red component will not show up at all in the Destination. This biased monochrome conversion is a *red projection*. This kind of projection of an RGB image is an image derived from it by copying but that uses only one or two of the three RGB components.[3]

---

3. Technically, a projection can be more general: a reduction from three to one or two dimensions that could involve weighted averages rather than simply copying components.

4.4.2   Color Histograms

There are two aspects to the distribution of colors in an image that we might wish to consider from a statistical point of view. One is precisely what colors are in the image and how frequently each occurs. This is a topic taken up in chapter 14, when we explore the use of Python dictionaries to count colors. The other aspect is the frequencies of occurrence of each of the red, green, and blue values in an image.

Consider the Tree of Color photograph in figure 4.7 (plate 14). The color-component histograms are accessed in PixelMath by selecting the Histograms option from the image window's View menu. Separate histograms are shown for red, green, and blue. Figure 4.8 shows these for the Tree of Color photo. Although the image contains blue and bluish pixels (where the sky shows through and in some of the background foliage), blue is in the minority. The blue histogram shows a distinct spike at value 0. Although red also has a spike at 0, it is smaller. One might expect most of blue's zeros to come from the apparently black bark of the tree. However, a simple test can show that they come, not from the bark, but from almost everywhere else in the image; that is, everywhere except in the bark, in the sky, and in the background foliage. To see this, simply clone the image from the File menu of the

Figure 4.7 (plate 14)
The Tree of Color photograph. Courtesy of Bruce Hemingway.

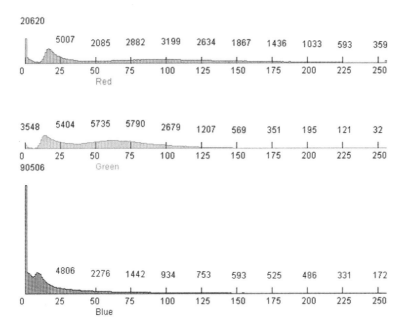

Figure 4.8
Red, green, and blue histograms for the Tree of Color.

image's window, set the calculator destination to this new image, Source1 to the original, and apply the formula

```
if blue1(x,y)=0 then 255 else 0
```

The result is shown in figure 4.9. The total number of pixels where blue=0 is surprisingly high. By clicking on the leftmost bin of the blue histogram, we get a popup box that reports not only the number of zeros (90506) but also the total number of pixels in the image (605790) and the percentage implied by these numbers (14.940 percent). By inspecting the color-component histograms and clicking on bins for specific counts and percentages, one may be prompted to ask where the pixels with a particular value or range of values are located in the image. Then, by applying formulas such as that given earlier, one may answer the question. The formulas can use more general criteria: for example, inequality tests rather than equality tests, and conditions on two or all three color components rather

Figure 4.9
The locations in the Tree of Color image where the blue component is zero. These are shown in white and all others in black.

than just one. This can also be a faster method for locating particular pixel values in the image than inspecting one pixel at a time.

4.4.3 Tinting

Rather than taking color out of a color image to create a monochrome image, we can do the reverse: take a monochrome image and tint it with some color. However, this doesn't make it a real color image. Rather, it's a monochrome image with a color effect.

Let's try tinting a monochrome image of the Mona Lisa. To begin, make a monochrome version of the Mona Lisa using the averaging technique described earlier. Then make the monochrome image of Mona Lisa be the Source1 image and make the original color image of the Mona Lisa be the Destination. We'll give a reddish tint to the Mona Lisa by enabling only the red component and computing the following formula that brightens the image a little.

```
Source1(x,y) * 1.3
```

Alternatively, one could enable only the green and blue components and then darken the image with

```
Source1(x,y) * 0.75
```

Starting again with the monochrome image and darkening only the blue component, we can get an effect similar to the sepia tone darkroom effect produced in old-fashioned photography studios.

4.4.4 Changing Color Saturation

The saturation of a color is the extent to which it is pure and not diluted with gray (or white).[4] For example, the color pink, with RGB = (255, 200, 200) is not saturated very much at all because we can express this as a sum of gray + red, with gray taking most of the intensity:

$(255, 200, 200) = (200, 200, 200) + (55, 0, 0)$

Here (200, 200, 200) is light gray (almost white) and the other part, the pure red (55, 0, 0), has a relatively low intensity.

On the other hand, the color violet (128, 0, 192) is completely saturated because to express this as a sum of gray plus something else is to end up with the gray part being all zeros (0, 0, 0). Saturated colors look pure. Unsaturated colors look like pastels (if they are bright) or like washed-out colors (if they are dark).

4.4.5 Reducing Saturation

One way to give a picture a more washed-out appearance is to desaturate it. Simply adding gray to it will usually reduce its saturation while at the same time lightening it. Another way of desaturating a color that tends not to brighten it as much is to consider the smallest of the three RGB components of the color and make it closer in value to the next smallest (middle) value. We'll compute each color component of the desaturated image separately, beginning with the red component.

---

4. This sense of the word "saturation" should not be confused with the sense meaning "getting to its highest value," for example, when a brightness enhancement leads many pixel values to become "saturated" because they have reached the limit of 255.

```
if ((Red1(x,y) < Green1(x,y)) and (Red1(x,y) < Blue1(x,y)))
then (Red1(x,y)+min(Green1(x,y),Blue1(x,y)))/2 else Red1(x,y)
```

This formula first checks whether the red component is the smallest of the three. If it is, then the average of red and the minimum of the green and blue is taken and used as the new red value. If not, the red value stays the same. We then do the same sort of thing for the green component (with green enabled) and the same sort of thing for blue. The result is a slightly brighter and less saturated image.

Another way of desaturating a pixel is to average each color component's value with the monochrome conversion value.

```
(3 * Source1(x,y) + Red1(x,y) + Green1(x,y) + Blue1(x,y))/6
```

4.4.6 Boosting Saturation
Saturation of a color can be increased by exaggerating the differences among the values of the color's components. A color that is almost gray, such as (126, 127, 128), could be turned into (125, 127, 129) or even (117, 127, 137).

To simplify the formula, let's first compute a monochrome version of an image and set up three windows so that the original is Source1, the monochrome version is Source2, and the Destination is the third image. Here's a formula that usually produces a more saturated version of the original:

```
Source2(x,y) - 1.5 * (Source2(x,y) - Source1(x,y))
```

Here the factor 1.5 controls the extent to which the saturation is boosted.

4.5 Specifying Color Components in Formulas

There are two questions that need to be answered when we are computing with colors in PixelMath. The first is from which component (red, green, or blue) in the source image are we taking values? The second question is into which component (red, green, or blue) in the destination image are we inserting values? Each of the following two sections addresses one of these questions.

4.5.1 Accessing Source Color Components

In the various formulas here, we've used two different ways of getting at the values of color components in pixels. One way is to specify Source1(x,y). Source1(x,y) is a kind of shorthand to obtain the component value in the Source1 image at (x, y) for the color currently being computed. The other is to use the specific component names, together with the number of the source image: Red1(x,y).

The expression Source1(x,y) may cause any or all of the three color components of the Source1 pixel to be accessed. When the red component of the destination pixel is being computed, then Source1 specifies the red component of the source1 image. Similarly, when the green component is being computed, Source1(x,y) retrieves the green value of the Source1 image, etc. If only red is currently enabled, then Source1(x,y) will only access the red value.

On the other hand, the expression Red1(x,y) always accesses the red component value in the Source1 image at location (x, y). The red component will be accessed no matter which of the three color components of the destination is being computed.

When we computed the unbiased monochrome conversion, we used the formula

```
(Red1(x,y)+Green1(x,y)+Blue1(x,y))/3
```

This value will be the same whether we enable red, green, blue, or any combination of them. However, if we used the following formula, it would compute an average of the three color components but simply add up three instances of one component at a time, divide by 3, and end up not changing the image at all.

```
(Source1(x,y)+Source1(x,y)+Source1(x,y))/3
```

This formula can be interpreted as equivalent to

```
(Red1(x,y)+Red1(x,y)+Red1(x,y))/3
```

when the red component is being computed and would be a similar sort of thing with green when green is being computed, etc.

4.5.2 Specifying Destination Color Components

As mentioned before, the current formula is evaluated, not only for each pixel in the destination image, but actually for each enabled color component in the destination. The enable-red, enable-green, and enable-blue toggles specify whether all three or some subset of the color components are to be computed for the destination image.

If we wanted to use different formulas for each of the three components, we could first enable only red and apply the first formula, then enable only green, and apply the second formula, and finally enable only blue and apply the third formula. This can be a little bit awkward. Fortunately, PixelMath provides a shortcut. By using the special function RGB, three different formulas can be entered all at once, and provided that all three color components are enabled, no further disabling and enabling is necessary.

As an example, suppose we wish to set the destination pixels to royal purple. First we make sure that all three color-enabling toggles are on. Then we enter and compute the following formula.

```
RGB(127,255,0)
```

The RGB function works as follows. Suppose the RGB expression being evaluated is RGB(expression1, expression2, expression3). Since this expression is computed for each of the red, green, and blue components of the destination pixel, it has the following effect. When computing the red destination value, RGB returns the value of expression1. When computing the green destination value, RGB returns the value of expression2, and when computing the blue destination value, it returns the value of expression3.

The RGB function can be used as part of a more complicated expression. For example, the following formula creates a gradient image in which the darkest pixel has color values (5, 5, 5) and which gets brighter going toward the right and up.

```
5 + RGB(x, y, x+y)
```

Since the function Source1 accesses the red component during the red computation pass, the green component during the green computation pass, etc., the following formula multiplies the red component of Source1 by 2, the green component by 3, and the blue component by 1.5.

```
Source1(x,y) * RGB(2, 3, 1.5)
```

It should be clear that the RGB function adds a powerful expressive capability to PixelMath formulas. A possible downside to using this method of doing different things to different colors is efficiency. If you are working on a very large image, and the expressions that you use as arguments[5] to RGB are large and complicated, it might take three times as long to perform the computation using RGB as it would using the direct method of enabling each color component in turn. If the efficiency problem affects you, you can take advantage of programming (see chapter 11) to streamline the process of using the direct method.

4.6 Hue, Saturation, and Value

The RGB method of representing colors, although widely used in computer systems, is not the one that most people are taught in art school. More common is the use of *hue*, *saturation*, and *value* (HSV). Hue refers to the dominant pure color, such as red, yellow, or orange. Saturation (as mentioned earlier) is the relative purity of the color, and value corresponds to brightness.

The representation of a color in terms of hue, saturation, and value is done with the HSV system. Figure 4.10 illustrates how this system can be visualized as a cylinder. PixelMath offers the user facilities for reading and writing colors in terms of the HSV system. First, it is possible to see the HSV values for any pixel by enabling the display of HSV values (see the View menu of the image window) and then looking on the status line. Second, to access the hue, saturation, and value of the Source1 image in a PixelMath formula, use the functions Hue1(x,y), Sat1(x,y), and Val1(x,y). Finally, to set a destination image pixel to a particular color expressed in the HSV system, you can use the pseudofunction HSV, which is similar in many ways to the RGB pseudofunction. For example, to set all the pixels of the destination to red, use the formula HSV(0.0, 1.0, 1.0).

4.6.1 Hue
The hue of a color corresponds to the dominant wavelength of light in the color. However, the numbers that represent hues in PixelMath (and other systems) range from 0.0 to 1.0.

---

5. An argument is a value passed to a function in order to help specify its behavior. For example, in the formula Source1 (x, y + 5), the first argument to Source1 is x and the second is y + 5.

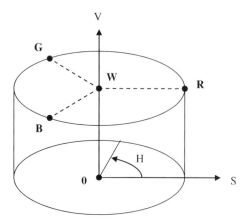

Figure 4.10
The HSV color system considered as the space within a cylinder. A point in the cylinder represents a color whose
hue corresponds to the angle around the central axis, whose saturation corresponds to the point's distance from the
axis, and whose value corresponds to the point's height. In the diagram, the locations of red, green, blue, white,
and black (0) are shown.

Figure 4.11 (plate 15)
A spectrum of colors created by varying the hue from 0.0 to 1.0 while the saturation and value are each maintained
at 1.0.

Hues form a circular range because 0.0 and 1.0 correspond to the same hue. The perceived
color spectrum starts at red and comes back to red. We can show a set of pure colors in
PixelMath by creating a 256-by-50 image and applying the formula

```
HSV(x/256, 1, 1)
```

which results in the image shown in figure 4.11 (plate 15).

An interesting color transformation involves shifting (rotating) all the hue values some
amount in the range of hue values. The following formula causes a hue rotation half of the
way around, thus causing each hue to be replaced by its complementary hue.

```
HSV(hue1(x,y)+if hue1(x,y)<1/2 then 1/2 else -1/2,
sat1(x,y), val1(x,y))
```

Rotation from blue to green, green to red, etc., can be effected by a hue rotation of one-third, as with the following formula:

```
HSV(hue1(x,y)+if hue1(x,y)<1/3 then 2/3 else -1/3,
sat1(x,y), val1(x,y))
```

The effects of various hue rotations on an image are shown in figures 4.12 and 4.13 (plate 16 and 17).

(a)   (b)

Figure 4.12 (plate 16)
Effect of hue rotation by one-half. The original (a) shows the true colors, while (b) shows the complementary hues obtained by going 180 degrees around the gray axis in the HSV color space.

(a)   (b)

Figure 4.13 (plate 17)
Effect of hue rotation by one-third and two-thirds. In (a) the effect of rotation by one-third (i.e., 120 degrees) is
shown and in (b) the amount of rotation is two-thirds (i.e., 240 degrees).

4.6.2   Saturation

The saturation of a color expresses its relative purity (as described in section 4.4.4). The
least-saturated colors are shades of gray. The most-saturated colors are those with as little
white in them as possible. In PixelMath, saturation values range from 0.0 (completely
unsaturated) to 1.0 (completely saturated).

The palette of colors shown in figure 4.14 (plate 18) is organized with hue going from 0.0
to 1.0 on the horizontal axis, while saturation goes from 0.0 to 1.0 going up on the vertical
axis. It was created using the formula

```
HSV(x/256, y/256, 1)
```

The purest (most-saturated) colors are at the top. The least-saturated colors, in this case all
tints—mixtures with white—are near the bottom.

Figure 4.14 (plate 18)
Palette of colors with a horizontal gradient of hue values and a vertical gradient of saturation values. The value
component of each color is 1.0 in this image.

Increasing the saturation of colors in an image tends to make the colors more brilliant, and
in the extreme case of taking saturation all the way to 1.0 can produce a garish appearance.
figure 4.15 (plate 19) shows the results of boosting the saturation of the image whose original
is in Figure 4.12a. Pixels that are white or almost white in the original change dramatically
as they are forced to take on a more saturated color. The formula for boosting the saturation
halfway to the maximum is this:

```
HSV(Hue1(x,y), (1+Sat1(x,y))/2, Val1(x,y))
```

4.6.3 Value
The third component in an HSV color representation is the value component. This expresses
the relative brightness of the color and it ranges from 0.0 to 1.0. If the value is 0.0, then the
color appears black, no matter what its hue and saturation may be. If the value is 1.0, then
the color is as bright as possible for a color with its particular hue and saturation. Note that
this is not white unless the saturation is 0.

The value component of the HSV color provides an easy way to control the brightness
of the color without changing the hue or saturation. Figure 4.16 (plate 20) is an example of
increasing the value of each color in the Mona Lisa image without changing either the hue

(a)   (b)

Figure 4.15 (plate 19)
Results of boosting the saturation of an image, (a) by averaging the original saturation with 1.0, and (b) by replacing
the original saturation by 1.0. The latter, representing maximum saturation, produces a somewhat garish effect.

or the saturation. The formula used for this enhancement is the following, which increases
the value of each pixel by averaging it with the maximum possible value, 1.0.

```
HSV(Hue1(x,y), Sat1(x,y), (1+Val1(x,y))/2)
```

4.6.4 Converting from RGB to HSV

To compute HSV values from RGB values, we can have PixelMath do the work. However,
it is instructive to consider the arithmetic involved in making the conversion. The following
method is equivalent to that used in PixelMath.

Let M be the maximum of R, G, and B, and let m be the minimum of R, G, and B.
Compute the value component as follows:

$$V = M/255$$

(a)   (b)

Figure 4.16 (plate 20)
(a) The Mona Lisa and (b) the result of boosting the value of each color in the HSV system.

Next compute saturation.

$$S = \begin{cases} (M - m)/M, & \text{if } M > 0; \\ 0, & \text{otherwise.} \end{cases}$$

Hue is more involved and there are four cases, depending on which component (R, G, or B) is largest or if they are all the same (in which case $S = 0$). Here is a formula for computing the hue component of the HSV representation given R, G, and B.

Let $C = (M - m)/6$. Then,

$$H = \begin{cases} 0, & \text{if } S = 0; \\ C(G - B) \bmod 1, & \text{if } R = M \\ C(B - R) + 1/3, & \text{if } G = M \\ C(R - G) + 2/3, & \text{if } B = M \end{cases}$$

In the case where $R = M$, we could have a negative value of $G - B$, leading to a value (before considering the "mod 1" part of the formula) such as $-1/6$. By taking the number mod 1, the negative value becomes positive, in this case $5/6$.

Sometimes having hue values in the range of 0 to 360 is desired, since hue is commonly interpreted as the angle around the gray axis from a red reference point. To obtain a number in this range, multiply the H value computed earlier by 360. (The method given here is equivalent to that presented by Alvy Ray Smith to the computer graphics community in 1978.)

4.6.5 The Munsell Color Model

A famous color system closely related to the hue-saturation-value system is the *Munsell* color model. This system is like the HSV system except that the ranges of numbers for hue, saturation, and value are adjusted so that equal changes in the numbers roughly correspond to equal perceptual changes. Munsell did experiments with human observers to determine the distribution of perceptibly different colors.

4.7 Indexed Color Formats, GIF and PNG

Two of the most popular image file formats are the Graphics Interchange Format (GIF) and Portable Network Graphics (PNG). Both of them support a representation scheme called indexed color. (The PNG specification supports other representations, too, such as straight RGB with 8 bits per component.) Indexed color representation is the scheme used in "paint by numbers" coloring books or the Venus Paradise™ colored-pencil system.

Whereas with straight RGB representation, each of red, green, and blue is represented directly by an integer telling how strong that component is, with indexed color representation, each color in the image, say, pink=(255,200,200), is given its own identification (ID) number, such as 17, valid in that image. There is a table that tells what the RGB values are for each ID number. The representation of the image consists of both the table (which is effectively a palette with its colors in a certain order), and a 2D array of values (the IDs of the colors at each pixel location).

With both the GIF and PNG formats, the palette can contain up to 256 colors. GIF images cannot have more than 256 colors in any one image. On the other hand, PNG images can have more colors, but then they are encoded directly as RGB triples, rather than with indexed representation. Both formats have additional options. For example, both support transparency; GIF supports animation by encapsulating several image frames within the file, and PNG supports other encoding schemes that are appropriate in situations where more (or fewer) bits per pixel are needed.

Because GIF images are limited to 256 colors, the encoding of an image having more than 256 distinct colors causes some distinctions among colors to be lost, and GIF is considered to be a "lossy" format. Because PNG encoders automatically choose direct RGB representation when there are more than 256 colors in an image to be encoded, PNG is a "lossless" format.

An interesting technical problem is how to choose the best 256 colors (or the best n for some given value of n) to represent a given image when that image contains more than 256 (or more than n) distinct colors. GIF encoders may use simple schemes that are fast but that may cause significant color distortion, or they may optimize various measures of fidelity. For example, an encoder may choose a palette that minimizes the squared error between the original image and the encoded image. Another approach is to cluster the colors of an image into 256 (or into n) groups; the K-means technique described in chapter 18 is one way to obtain such clusters. Simply counting the number of unique colors in an image efficiently is more interesting than it might seem; a technique for this is given in chapter 14.

Both GIF and PNG images are normally compressed. With indexed representation, the color table and the array of pixel color IDs are processed with methods such as Lempel-Ziv-Welch (LZW) or DEFLATE compression to reduce the number of bytes required for the file.

PixelMath supports reading and writing images in three formats: GIF, PNG, and JPEG. The JPEG format (also written JPG) is, in general, a lossy format that can achieve high compression ratios with relatively little loss in apparent visual quality for typical photographs taken of natural subjects, such as landscapes and portraits. JPEG does not use indexed color representations but performs a discrete cosine transform on 8-by-8 blocks of the image as a key step in the encoding process. We describe JPEG more fully in chapter 10.

4.8 References

Kang, H. B. 1997. *Color Technology for Electronic Imaging Devices*. Bellingham, WA: SPIE Press.

Meyer, G. W. 1986. Tutorial on color science. *The Visual Computer*, Vol. 2, No. 5, pp. 278–290.

Nassau, K. (ed.) 1998. *Color for Science, Art, and Technology*. Amsterdam: Elsevier Science.

Reinhard, E., Khan, E. A., Akyüz, A. O., and Johnson, G. M. 2008. *Color Imaging: Fundamentals and Applications*. Wellesley, MA: A. K. Peters.

Wikipedia. 2010. Munsell color system. en.wikipedia.org/wiki/Munsell_color_system.

4.9 Exercises

1. According to the spectrum in fig. 4.1, what color corresponds to 620 nanometers?

2. For the spectral color yellow (say at 575 nanometers), approximately what are the color-matching curve values? (Refer to figure 4.2.)

3. Identify the six double-counted colors in the spectrum described in section 4.3.3.

4. Give the RGB values for a whole color that is between cyan and blue.

5. Starting with a whole color that represents royal purple (less red than magenta), tint this color until it becomes lavender. How much white did you add? What is the resulting RGB triple?

6. Suppose a color palette is to be constructed in a 64-by-64 image. The palette should be representative of the whole color space. Give a PixelMath formula that will create this palette.

Hint 1: Use the RGB calculator construct. Hint 2: Notice that a 64-by-64 image has 2^{12} pixels. This means that each palette entry will be one choice out of 2^{12} possible. Treating R, G, and B equally means that there should be 2^4 choices for R, 2^4 choices for G, and

2^4 choices for B. Hint 3: Make R follow a (rough) horizontal gradient, make G follow a (rough) vertical gradient, and make B follow a scanning pattern inside each 4-by-4 tile.

7. Come up with a formula that creates an 8-by-8 palette of pastel colors. Assume this means colors of the form (R, G, B) where these R, G, and B values are always in the range of 192 to 255. All the colors should be different. Ideally, the palette will treat R, G, and B equally in terms of representation in the palette.

8. Imagine the RGB color space as a cube, with 256 distinct values on each axis: R, G, and B. Now consider the black-to-white axis; it's an interior diagonal of this cube going from (0, 0, 0) to (255, 255, 255). Now imagine a plane perpendicular to that axis, bisecting it at (127.5, 127.5, 127.5). That plane creates a hexagonally shaped cross-section of the cube that represents a palette of equal-brightness colors. Design a PixelMath formula that will create this particular palette.

9. Load a photographic image or art image of your choice. Amplify only its blue component by 20 percent. What steps did you take?

10. Make a desaturated version of the Mona Lisa image. What steps did you take?

11. Use the method described in this chapter to boost the color saturation of a photographic image. How would you describe the change in appearance of your image (better? worse? more lively? garish? unnatural?)?

12. Find both the RGB and the HSV representations of the following colors:

a. hot pink (Hot pink is somewhat more saturated than normal pale pink.)

b. beige

c. olive green

d. dark brown

e. bright orange

f. turquoise

g. chartreuse

13. For the RGB color represented as (0, 150, 200), find the HSV representation using the formulas in the text. Then use PixelMath to check your work.

14. For the average HSV color represented as (0.5, 0.5, 0.5), find the RGB representation. Is this in any sense an average color from the RGB point of view? What is arguably the average RGB color and what is its HSV representation?

5 Geometric Transformations

5.1 Overview

This chapter describes how the image-processing engine within PixelMath actually works. The direction in which it processes pixels (in the destination window, reaching into the source window) is very important. Another matter is how the x and y values of the pixel currently being computed can be used in formulas. A key concept is the distinction between the "push" method of image processing and the "pull" method. In order to see why we often want to use two windows rather than one for performing an image transformation, we'll first show some one-window transformations and what might go wrong.

5.2 Scaling with One Window

In order to shrink an image of size 158×200 by a factor of 2 in each direction, we want to reduce the dimensions to 79×100 and appropriately sample every other pixel in every other row of the original. We can accomplish this by setting Source1 and Destination to the window containing the image of interest and then computing the formula

```
Source1(x * 2, y * 2)
```

Try this. Why do we specify the operation $*$ (multiplication) and not $/$ (division)? Because our formula is used by the PixelMath image-processing engine to determine what value(s) to put at location (x, y). This formula says that the values to be put at (x, y) should come from $(2x, 2y)$. This moves the data toward the origin (lower left), thus shrinking the image. This is illustrated in figures 5.1 and 5.2.

Now let's try scaling an image up rather than down. We'll aim to make it twice as wide and twice as high, rather than smaller as we did last time. The formula

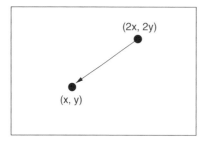

Figure 5.1
Reducing an image by a factor of 2, which involves taking pixel values from $(2x, 2y)$ and moving them to (x, y). This is done for each pixel position (x, y).

(a)   (b)

Figure 5.2
Reduction by a factor of 2, showing (a) image before reduction and (b) after reduction, but occupying a buffer of the original size.

```
Source1(x / 2, y / 2)
```

would seem appropriate, assuming that to figure out the pixel at (x, y) we should obtain the values of the pixel at $(x/2, y/2)$. This is illustrated in figure 5.3. Try this.

Surprise! This doesn't work. What does the image look like? Is it one big rectangle, all the same color? Why that particular color? (The color depends on your image.) For the Snow Lake image of figure 5.2a, we get the one-color image shown in figure 5.4a. What we want is shown in figure 5.4b.

In order to understand this strange behavior, you need to realize that the image-processing engine tries to compute the new pixel values in a particular order. (This order is shown in figure 5.5.) It starts at the origin and scans along to the right. So the first pixel it computes

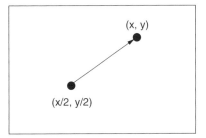

Figure 5.3
Desired movement of pixels for expanding an image by a factor of 2. This would seem to invert the shrinking operation (figure 5.1). However, there is a glitch (see text).

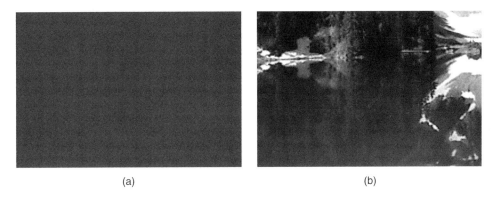

        (a)   (b)

Figure 5.4
Results of applying the expansion formula (a) using one window and (b) using two windows.

will be at $(0, 0)$. It takes $0/2$ and $0/2$ getting 0 and 0, and it accesses the Source1 pixel at $(0, 0)$ and puts it right back in the same place—the same image and the same location. There's no change. This is good.

Now for the second pixel. It's going to be put at $(1, 0)$, so $1/2$ and $0/2$ are computed. When accessing pixels in Source1 or any other image buffer, fractional coordinate values are rounded down, and so it is the value at $(0, 0)$ that is placed in $(1, 0)$. This is good because when the image is doubled in width, each pixel needs to be repeated once in the horizontal direction. (And since we are doubling both the width and the height, each pixel and its copy will need to be repeated once in the vertical direction, also.)

Next, let's figure out the third pixel. It will be placed at $(2, 0)$. We compute $2/2$ and $0/2$, getting 1 and 0, and so we grab the values at $(1, 0)$. The only problem is that this is where we just put a copy of the pixel at $(0, 0)$, and so the original value at $(1, 0)$ isn't there now. Instead, we get another copy of the pixel at $(0, 0)$ to put in $(2, 0)$. As we continue with pixels at $(3, 0)$, $(4, 0)$, etc., we keep getting copies of the pixel at $(0, 0)$ because the

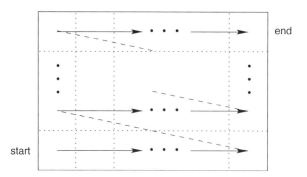

Figure 5.5
Standard scanning order used by PixelMath to compute the pixel values of a destination image.

values we really want have already been overwritten. After the entire row has been filled up with copies of the $(0, 0)$ pixel, we begin with the first pixel of the second row: $(0, 1)$. This produces a copy of the pixel at $(0, 0)$, too, since $(0/2, 1/2)$ is rounded to $(0, 0)$. As it turns out, this row and every row receive nothing but copies of the pixel at $(0, 0)$, and we end up with a big, boring rectangle of whatever color happened to be in the $(0, 0)$ pixel of the image. This process is illustrated in figure 5.6.

Because of the problem of overwriting pixel values that may yet be needed to compute the rest of the destination image, it is often necessary to place the computed pixels in a separate buffer (and in a separate window), where they do not interfere with the data in the source. Hence, we'll frequently set up *two-window transformations*.

To fix the bug in our expansion-by-2 operation, all we need to do is to allocate a suitable new window and set the Destination to be this window. To avoid losing three-quarters of the image, the new window's image should be set up with twice as many rows and twice as many columns as the original.

5.3 Push versus Pull

Now let's investigate the difference between using the source pixels and using the destination pixels to control the computation process. Suppose someone gives you the grid full of numbers shown in figure 5.7 and says, "Make a copy of these numbers, but with 1 added to each of them." She also gives you an empty grid on the right, in which to place the new values.

You might scan through the grid on the left, going from one number to the next, but stopping at each long enough to add 1 to it and write the answer in the corresponding box on the right. This is the "push" method. You scan the array that already contains data.

Alternatively, you could scan the empty grid, stopping at each box long enough to find the corresponding number on the left, add 1, and write down the answer. This is the "pull"

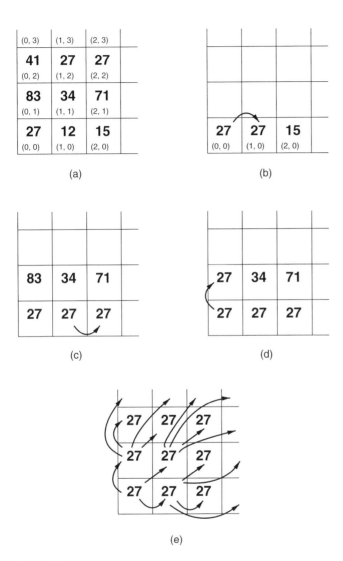

Figure 5.6
Actual movement of pixel values in a straightforward attempt at expanding an image.

method. You scan the destination array. Are the push and pull methods the same? Well, they seem to produce the same results in this example.

Now let's consider another example. Suppose you've been given the same grid of data and asked to stretch out the data, moving each value to a position twice as far from the origin as it already is. Let's begin. The 5 at the lower left corner is at $(0, 0)$ and so it can stay where it is. But the other values move. For example, the 4 in position $(1, 0)$ moves to $(2, 0)$. Actually, most of the values move too far to stay in the grid, and the result is the

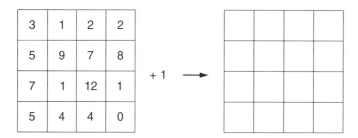

Figure 5.7
Two grids, one full of numbers, the other to be filled by adding 1 to the value in each corresponding cell.

–	–	–	–
7	–	1	–
–	–	–	–
5	–	4	–

Figure 5.8
The result of expanding the grid on the left of figure 5.7 using the push method.

array shown in figure 5.8. This "image" has data at only four of its sixteen boxes. How did this happen? We used the push method, scanning the source array and doing something with each value—moving it and writing it down in the right-hand grid, if it's still in the grid.

Now let's perform the stretching operation with the pull method. We scan the destination grid, considering each empty box. The box at $(0, 0)$ gets its corresponding value from the source grid. The box at $(0, 1)$ should get its data from $(0/2, 1/2)$, which we round to $(0, 0)$; so it gets a copy of the data from $(0, 0)$. Next, let's take $(0, 2)$ in the destination. It takes its value from source box $(0/2, 2/2)$, which is $(0, 1)$. This is a 4 in the example. As you can see, every box in the destination gets filled in with something this way, although there are a lot of repeated values in this case.

The pull method is almost always preferred over the push method-in image processing systems because it doesn't leave gaps in the destination. However, it is possible to try to pull in the values of nonexistent pixels. For example, if the operation is to move all the pixels to the right by one space, the push method leaves a gap in the first column of the destination image whereas the pull method tries to fill that column with values from $(-1, 0)$, $(-1, 1)$, etc. PixelMath handles this situation by generating the value 127 for any color component of any nonexistent pixel. Note that the value 127 is deemed to be neutral, since (127, 127, 127) is the RGB triple for neutral gray.

One consequence of using the pull method for image transformation is that the formulas for geometric transformations for a particular task such as enlarging an image will look a little bit like what you would expect to have for the inverse of that transformations. Thus

```
Source1(x/2, y/2)
```

is used for *expanding* the image whereas

```
Source1(x*2, y*2)
```

is used for reducing it. (These transformations should be used with two windows; the setting-up process is described in the next section.)

As with scaling, the pull method makes us think in terms of inverse operations for transformations that move an image around relative to their windows. The formula

```
Source1(x+5, y)
```

is for moving the image 5 pixels to the left even though x values increase as one goes to the right, and

```
Source1(x-5, y)
```

is for moving it 5 pixels to the right.

One more point to make is that the variables x and y used in PixelMath formulas refer to coordinates of the destination pixel whose values are being computed and not necessarily to the location in the source array from which values are being picked up. It will often be important to remember that the pull method is being used in image processing and to think about scanning the destination array when performing image transformations.

5.4 Setting Up for Two-Window Operations

To make these transformations work, you should have two image windows open. You can do this by opening the image of your choice from the File menu of the PixelMath calculator and repeating the procedure to obtain the second window. The second copy can be distinguished from the first by its window number on the title bar of the window. After opening the second window, use the mouse to pick up the window by the title bar and move it over to the right, so that you can see the first window. Before applying a formula, go to the middle of the calculator and select the first window for Source1 and the second window for the Destination.

Now that you know what is needed for a two-window operation, here's a shortcut. The calculator's File menu has an option "Open Two...". If you choose this command, you'll only have to select the input image file once and two windows will be created. In addition, the windows will be nicely arranged on the screen with the calculator, and the Source1 and Destination choices will be made automatically.

5.5 Widths and Heights

The width and height of an image are often useful in transformation formulas. For example, to specify the last pixel in the bottom row of the Source1 image, use the coordinates (xmax1, 0). To reflect the image horizontally (in a vertical axis), use the formula

```
Source1(xmax1 - x, y)
```

In general, the bottom row has y coordinate 0. The leftmost column has x coordinate 0. In Source1, the top row has y coordinate ymax1, which is equivalent to w1−1. The rightmost column of Source1 has x coordinate xmax1, which is equivalent to w1−1. The names of the dimensions in Source2 are similar except that they end with 2 instead of 1. The names for the destination window coordinates don't have any 1 or 2 at the end. Figure 5.9 shows how the various dimensions of the Source1, Source2, and destination image buffers are named. These names are the same whether you are performing a one-window, two-window, or three-window transformation. For a one-window transformation, both sources must be the same as the Destination, and so you can use the destination's width, say, to refer to the width of Source1 or Source2. In a two-window transformation, at least two of the three image buffers

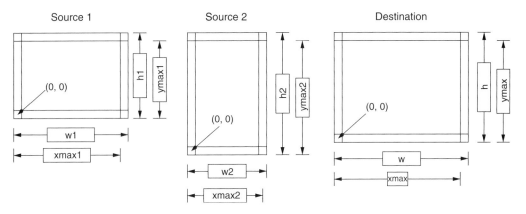

Figure 5.9
Names of the widths, heights, and maximum *x* and *y* coordinates for the sources and destination image buffers.

will be the same. In general, if two of your image buffers have the same size, then it doesn't matter which of their width symbols (w1, w2, or w) you use; they'll all have the same value.

The following three-window transformation adds the corresponding pixels of Source1 and Source2 and places the sums in the Destination, except that the Source1 pixels are used upside-down and the Source2 pixels are taken flipped left to right.

```
Source1(x,ymax1-y)+Source2(xmax2-x,y)
```

If all three images have the same size, then the following formula works.

```
Source1(x,ymax-y)+Source2(xmax-x,y)
```

Now let's transition from the mechanics of PixelMath to studying particular transformations and a theory of image transformations.

5.6 Reflections

In this and the following sections you'll learn how some transformations on images, such as horizontal and vertical reflections (or for square images, rotations by multiples of 90 degrees), form coherent groups and have nice properties like invertibility. If a scrambling transformation is a member of a group, it's possible to unscramble the image with its inverse.

Flipping an image upside down is an operation known slightly more formally as a reflection around a horizontal axis. We can apply such a reflection with the following formula, assuming that the source and destination are separate windows.

```
Source1(x, ymax - y)
```

Here `ymax` is a symbol that refers to the y coordinate of the pixels in the top row of the destination image. In a 256×256 image, `ymax` would be 255. Figure 5.10 shows an image before and after this transformation is applied.

The comparable reflection around a vertical axis is given by

```
Source1(xmax - x, y)
```

(a)   (b)

Figure 5.10
An image (a) before and (b) after reflection in the horizontal line that bisects the image.

Each of these transformations is a *self-inverse*. Applying one of these to an image and again to the result will bring back the original. Since it's possible to transform the result of the reflections back to the original, these transformations are called *invertible*.

One of the simplest transformations to specify is a reflection around the diagonal axis whose equation is $y = x$. This formula does it:

```
Source1(y, x)
```

Provided the source and destination images are square-shaped (with equal width and height), this is an invertible transformation. It will also work for unequal width and height provided that the width of the destination image is equal to the height of the source and that the height of the destination is equal to the width of the source.

5.7 90-Degree Rotations

To put an image on its side by turning it [rather than flipping it as we just did with the `Source1(y,x)` formula], we need a transformation that moves the pixel at one corner of the image to the next corner (see figure 5.11). In the destination image, the pixel at B should be taken from A. In general, the pixel at (x, y) should be taken from $(y, \text{xmax} - x)$; so the formula should be the following:

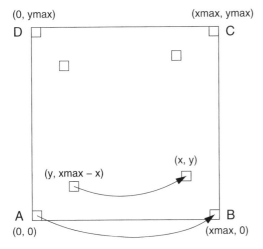

Figure 5.11
Illustration of some corresponding pixels in a 90-degree rotation.

```
Source1(y, xmax - x)
```

For a 180-degree rotation, we can use

```
Source1(xmax - x, ymax - y)
```

and for a 270-degree rotation, the formula should be

```
Source1(ymax - y, x)
```

These three rotations, together with one more (a rotation by zero degrees, which is an *identity* transformation) form a collection with notable properties (called group properties) that we'll discuss shortly.

5.8 Two Transformations in Succession

How do we apply two transformations in succession? Let's use three windows: an original (Window 1), a first result (Window 2), and a second result (Window 3). To perform the first transformation, we make Window 1 the Source1 in the choice on the calculator, and we make Window 2 the destination. (We don't care about how the choice for Source2 is set up, because we don't use it.) We enter our first formula, say a 90-degree rotation: `Source1(y, xmax - x)`, and then we click Compute, obtaining the first result.

Next we make Window 2 be Source1 and Window 3 the destination, and enter the next formula, say a 180-degree rotation: `Source1( xmax - x, ymax - y)`, and click Compute. The second result, in Window 3, shows what happens when a 90-degree rotation counterclockwise is followed by a 180-degree rotation counterclockwise.

Using this setup for two transformations in succession, we can verify that a rotation by 90 degrees counterclockwise followed by a rotation of 270 degrees counterclockwise produces an image identical to the original (provided that the width and height were equal). This indicates that rotation by 270 degrees counterclockwise is an "inverse" of rotation by 90 degrees counterclockwise. One transformation (let's call it T_1) has another transformation (call it T_2) as its inverse provided that applying T_1 and then applying T_2 to the result brings back the original image.

5.9 Modular Arithmetic on Coordinates

When we divide whole numbers like 17 and 5 and want a whole number result, we get a quotient and a remainder. Here, 17 divided by 5 is 3, with a remainder 2. If only the remainder is of interest, then it's customary to use the mod operator and to write 17 mod 5 = 2. The mod operator is useful for keeping numbers within a given range of values. Thus 47 + 13 = 60, but 47 + 13 mod 7 = 4. No matter what integers x and y may be, the result of $x + y$ mod 7 is in the range 0 to 6.

The symbol xmax on the calculator refers to the largest x coordinate value of any pixel in the current destination image. In an image with width 256 and height 256, xmax is 255, since the first column of pixels has x-coordinate 0 and so the last column has x-coordinate 255. Now let's consider a two-window transformation that shifts the image 100 pixels to the left. This is

```
Source1(x + 100, y)
```

You can see the result of applying this in figure 5.12. The pixels in the first 100 columns of the original image have been shifted out and do not appear at all in the result. At the same time, gray values have been shifted into the right side of the image by accessing "pixels" with x-coordinates greater than 255. For example, as the destination pixel at location (175, 3) is computed with the formula Source1(x + 100, y) the Source1 image is accessed at (275, 3), which lies to the right of the last column of pixels, and by the PixelMath convention, the color outside the image is gray.

A simple way to prevent access to locations outside the image is to restrict the x-coordinate value to remain within the range from 0 to xmax. One way to do this is to make as many copies of the rightmost column of pixels as needed to fill the gap. This is accomplished with the formula

```
Source1(min(x+100, xmax), y)
```

(a)   (b)

Figure 5.12
Shifting pixels to the left by 100: (a) original and (b) result.

A more common way to do this is to take the computed x-coordinate value modulo w. Use the following formula instead of the previous one.

```
Source1((x + 100) mod w, y)
```

You can see the results of this in figure 5.13a. The pixels in the rightmost 100 columns of the image are no longer gray, but are the ones previously lost from the left side of the image. The destination pixel at (175, 3), in particular, is taken from the Source1 image at x position 175 + 100 mod 256, which is 275 mod 256 or 19. The y position, of course, is 3. This x position of 19 is the twentieth column of the source image and not some place to the right of the image as before. This transformation that shifts an image using the mod operation to keep coordinates in range is sometimes called shift with wraparound or horizontal rotation.

An image transformation of the shift-with-wraparound type is an invertible operation. For example, the formula Source1((x + 156) mod w, y) is the inverse for the operation shown in figure 5.13a. Because xmax is equal to 1 less than the width of the destination image, the sum xmax+1 represents the width. This is the number of columns of pixels in the image. This can also be specified with the symbol w. Similarly, ymax+1 gives the height of the

(a)   (b)

Figure 5.13
Shifting pixels to the left by 100, (a) bringing those pixels shifted out back in on the right side (this is horizontal rotation) and (b) padding the gap with copies of the rightmost column.

destination image, which is the number of rows of pixels; the symbol h is equivalent to ymax+1.

If the Source1 and destination images have different dimensions, then the Source1 dimensions should be specified using w1 and h1. Note that just as w =xmax+1, we have w1=xmax1+1. So, to reference the width, height, maximum x, or maximum y value of the Source1 image, append a 1 to the same symbol used for the destination. Alternatively, you can append a 2 so as to reference the information from the Source2 image, as per figure 5.9.

5.10   Resampling

A digital image taken by a digital camera can be considered as a collection of color samples taken from a scene. A single 1.3 megapixel image contains about 1.3 million samples. Such an image carries a lot of detailed information.

If we "take a picture of a picture" and these pictures are both digital, then we are collecting samples of samples. This is called *resampling*. In a typical resampling situation, there is a (somewhat natural) mismatch of the sampling pattern of the new image and the samples of the first image. For example, the new image might have 103 columns and 97 rows, whereas the first image might have had 256 columns and 128 rows. If the new image covers the same image area as the first, then each new column covers 256/103 first-image columns and each new row covers 128/97 first-image rows. The following formula describes this resampling transformation.

```
Source1(x * 256/103, y * 128/97)
```

There is a distortion in the aspect ratio (ratio of height over width), not only of the image as a whole, but also of the region covered by each pixel. There is also a loss of information because there are fewer samples in the new image than in the first.

In the formula, the resampling is controlled by two numbers called resampling ratios. The resampling ratio for x is 128/97. This ratio is greater than 1, and so this specifies *undersampling* horizontally. The resampling ratio for y is 256/103, which is also greater than 1. Therefore, there is vertical undersampling here as well. If the resampling ratio is less than 1 in the horizontal direction, then it specifies *oversampling*, and this usually has the effect of enlarging some portion of the image horizontally.

5.10.1 Using Coordinate Wraparound

Resampling can be used to enlarge or reduce an image. With a minor modification, it can also be used to turn one image into a collection of smaller ones that look like the larger one. Under certain circumstances, resampling can be information-preserving, i.e., invertible.

We saw earlier how modular arithmetic could be used to turn an information-losing image shift operation into an invertible horizontal rotation. Let's now consider applying modular arithmetic on the coordinates of pixels to create invertible resampling transformations.

First we need to make sure that the destination image has the same size as the source image, so that there is a place for every pixel to go. Then we must make sure that no two source pixels get mapped into the same destination pixel because if they did, one of them would be overwritten and its information lost.

One way to guarantee that image columns will be mapped one-to-one from the source to the destination is to set up the source image and resampling ratio so that they are relatively prime. That means that there should be no positive integer other than 1 that divides both of them evenly. For example, 100 and 9 are relatively prime, but 102 and 9 are not, since they have the common factor 3.

So let us assume we have an image in Source1 that has a width 100. We'll assume that the destination image has the same size. So xmax is 99. We'll perform a resampling by taking every ninth column, but wrapping around whenever the x-coordinate exceeds xmax. Here's the formula:

(a)

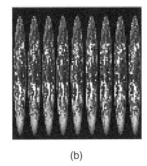

(b)

Figure 5.14
(a) An image that's 100 pixels wide and (b) a new version resampled horizontally with ratio 9 and coordinate wraparound.

```
Source1((9 * x) mod 100, y)
```

The effect of this transformation is illustrated in figure 5.14. This image of Earth has a width 100. The previous transformation can be undone by applying its inverse, given by

```
Source1(x * 89 mod 100, y)
```

In the next chapter we'll see more uses of relatively prime pairs of numbers to scramble images in such a way that they can still be unscrambled.

5.10.2 An Array of Miniatures

Whether or not the transformation is invertible, the technique of resampling with a ratio greater than 1 and using coordinate wraparound can be used to create a new image that appears to be a mosaic of many miniature versions of the original image. For example, for a 3×3 array of miniatures, use the formula

```
Source1((3 * x) mod w1, (3 * y) mod h1)
```

(a)   (b)

Figure 5.15
(a) An original and (b) the array of miniatures created using undersampling with wraparound.

The effect of this is illustrated in figure 5.15. If we wanted to have five copies horizontally, instead of three, then we would change the resampling ratio for x to be 5 instead of 3.

5.11 Composition of Transformations

We've now seen a number of examples of following one transformation with another. For example, rotating an image by 90 degrees counterclockwise and then reflecting it in a horizontal axis has a net effect on the image in figure 5.12a that is different from the result of either transformation alone. We can think of the combination of the two transformations as a single new transformation. Applying the new transformation has the effect of rotating by 90 degrees and then flipping around a horizontal axis.

The act of combining two transformations to obtain the single new transformation that corresponds to the sequence of the two transformations is called *composition*. If T_1 represents a rotation by 90 degrees counterclockwise and T_2 represents the reflection in the horizontal axis, then $T_1 \circ T_2$ represents the composition of T_1 with T_2, which is considered a single transformation having the net effect of the sequence of T_2 followed by T_1. (The symbol $\circ$ is the composition operator. Just as $+$ is used to add two numbers to get a new one, $\circ$ is used to compose two transformations to get a new one.)

It's interesting to note that we can describe the composition of two transformations without having to choose a particular image to apply the transformations to. By composing transformations independent of any particular images, we can create image transformations and work at an abstract level. The image transformations can then be applied to any image (provided that the transformations and images are compatible in size, etc.).

When we actually perform a transformation on a particular image, it is called the *application* of the transformation to the image. The result of applying a transformation to an image is a new image (unless the transformation is an identity transformation).

5.11.1 Associativity of Composition

There's an important property of the composition operation that we can illustrate using a setup that involves three transformations that are to be composed. Consider the the following sequence of image horizontal rotations (where we use the abbreviation HR to mean "horizontal rotation"):

T_1: `HR left 50`

T_2: `HR left 20`

T_3: `HR right 40`

This sequence can be written $T_3 \circ T_2 \circ T_1$. Note the reversed order. If we combine T_2 and T_1, we have `HR left 70`. Let's call this T_4. If we combine T_3 and T_2, then we have `HR right 20`. Let's call this T_5. Using parentheses to order the composition, we have

$$T_3 \circ T_2 \circ T_1 = (T_3 \circ T_2) \circ T_1 = T_5 \circ T_1$$

$$T_3 \circ T_2 \circ T_1 = T_3 \circ (T_2 \circ T_1) = T_3 \circ T_4$$

The important fact is that we can group the transformations in either of two ways and end up with an overall transformation that is the same:

$$(T_3 \circ T_2) \circ T_1 = T_3 \circ (T_2 \circ T_1)$$

When this regrouping yields the same net transformation either way, we say that the composition of transformations is *associative*. It turns out that the composition of transformations is always associative, no matter what the transformations are!

5.12 Invertibility and the Identity

5.12.1 The Identity

The formula `Source1(x,y)`, used by itself, has the effect of putting a copy of the Source1 image in the destination window. This is technically a transformation like any other except that since the new image is the same as the original, the transformation is called the *identity* transformation, or simply the identity.

5.12.2 Inverses

If two transformations, when composed, result in the identity transformation, then they are inverses. More specifically, if $T_2 \circ T_1 = I$, then T_2 is a left inverse of T_1, and T_1 is a right inverse of T_2. If not otherwise specified, by "inverse" we'll mean a left inverse.

Some transformations have inverses and some do not. Consider the transformation that rotates an image by 180 degrees. This transformation is a self-inverse. On the other hand, the shrinking transformation given by `Source1(x*2,y*2)` gives up three-fourth of the typical image's information and has no inverse, although `Source1(x/2,y/2)` might give the appearance of being an inverse. This might be considered to be a partial inverse because it restores the general appearance of the image; however, it cannot restore the details that have been thrown away by the shrinking transformation.

5.12.3 The Importance of Invertibility

In certain applications, invertibility is especially important. For example, when encrypting an image to make its contents secret, a transformation can be used to scramble all the pixels. If that transformation is not invertible, it will not be possible to recover the original image from the encrypted version.

Invertibility is a property of many transformations that form groups of related transformations. It's often important to know whether or not a transformation is invertible. With images, an invertible transformation is one that preserves all the information in the image in some recoverable form. A transformation that loses any of the image information cannot be a truly invertible transformation, although it might be partially invertible.

Any invertible transformation must have an inverse. It is common to use a kind of exponential notation to denote an inverse. The inverse of a transformation T is written T^{-1}. Note the similarity of the inverse of a transformation to the reciprocal of a number:

$$T^{-1} \circ T = I$$

$$x^{-1} \cdot x = 1$$

5.12.4 More Examples of Invertible Transformations

Here are some examples of invertible transformations: any horizontal rotation, any vertical rotation, any combination of a horizontal rotation followed by a vertical rotation, reflection in a vertical axis, reflection in a horizontal axis,[1] any combination of one of these reflections and the horizontal and vertical rotations.

Regular rotations of an image, such as around the center of the image and by an angle of 45 degrees, are not fully invertible because information is lost in two ways. First of all, if the destination image has the same width and height as the source, as we generally assume, then the pixels near the corners of the source image get rotated outside the bounds of the image and are lost. They are cut off. Not only that, but even those pixels that are not cut off become distorted by the resampling process. Some of the source pixels are copied twice, while others are missed entirely, simply because the sampling grids don't line up very well when one of them has been rotated.

An example of a regular rotation that *is* invertible is rotation by 180 degrees around the center of the image. This transformation is its own inverse. The one other rotation

---

1. The axis must bisect the image. Otherwise some pixel data will be lost by the transformation.

that definitely has an inverse (no matter what image is being rotated) is rotation by 0 degrees—just another name for the identity transformation. The identity is another invertible transformation whose inverse is itself.

There are invertible transformations on images that have nothing to do with moving the pixels around. For example, the photonegative transformation given by the following formula is a self-inverse.

```
255 - Source1(x,y)
```

This is an example of permuting the range of pixel values: black trades places with white; pure red trades places with cyan; only neutral gray stays pretty much the same, with $(127, 127, 127)$ trading places with $(128, 128, 128)$—a perceptually indistinguishable difference.

Another example of permuting values in pixel range is adding one to every component, modulo 256. This transformation causes every shade of gray to become imperceptibly brighter, except for white, which is dramatically changed to black. The formula for this is

```
(Source1(x,y)+1) mod 256
```

The inverse of this is simply the following:

```
(Source1(x,y)+255) mod 256
```

The transformations that permute colors rather than brightnesses are conceptually similar. A transformation that causes each pixel's red and green components to be swapped is a self-inverse. Computing this transformation with PixelMath requires three passes. In the first, we enable blue only and perform an identity operation, Source1(x,y). In the second, we enable only red and apply the formula Green1(x,y), and in the third, we enable only green and apply the formula Red1(x,y). The effect is more easily achieved with the formula

```
RGB( Green1(x,y), Red1(x,y), Blue1(x,y) )
```

5.13 Closure

Suppose that we take a small number of transformations and consider them as a collection. Let's use reflection in the horizontal axis as one transformation, and let's take one more: the photonegative transformation. Let's denote this $T_{\text{upsideDown}}$ and T_{photoNeg}. If we compose them, we get a new transformation that we can call "upside-down photonegative" and write $T_{\text{upsideDownPhotoNeg}}$. Since we used composition to obtain it, we can express it as

$$T_{\text{upsideDownPhotoNeg}} = T_{\text{upsideDown}} \circ T_{\text{photoNeg}}$$

Let's add this new transformation to our set. We now have three transformations. What if we compose this new transformation with one of the original two? We might get a fourth transformation. Let's try combining it with $T_{\text{upsideDown}}$ and define

$$T_{\text{upsideDownPhotoNegUpsideDown}} = T_{\text{upsideDownPhotoNeg}} \circ T_{\text{upsideDown}}$$

It turns out that applying this new transformation to an image has the same effect as doing only the photonegative. The upside-down operation has been effectively undone by doing it twice. That means

$$T_{\text{upsideDownPhotoNegUpsideDown}} = T_{\text{photoNeg}}$$

and we really did not get a new transformation by doing that last composition.

On the other hand, there is one more distinct transformation we can achieve by composing a pair of transformations from our current set of three. If we compose any one of the three with itself, we'll get a fourth transformation that is different from the other three, and it will be the identity transformation.

Then no matter what pairs from the set we compose, we don't get any new transformation. This set of four transformations is the *closure* of the original set of two transformations. And if we have some set of transformations such that composing any two (including one with itself) does not produce a new transformation, then the set is said to be *closed* with respect to composition.

Given any starting set of transformations, we can in principle proceed to generate the closure of that set by trying successive pairs of transformations to obtain new transformations and adding any new ones to the set. This worked out nicely in the earlier example; we started with two transformations and ended up with four in the closure. However, it might not always be so easy. For the pixel range-shifting transformation that we mentioned earlier—the one computed with (Source1(x,y)+1) mod 256, composing this with itself over and over again can be done 255 times before we finally regenerate a transformation that we already had, for a net total of 256 transformations in the closure. And then if we started not only with this one but also the red-green swap transformation, we would get a closure with 512 transformations in it.

The closure of a set of transformations is an important concept. It's a way of describing all the possible results you can get by combining just a few transformations over and over. It's also useful in helping us define a group of transformations that share properties and have inverses.

5.14 Groups

A collection of transformations that has certain properties can form something called a group. The word "group" has a special, technical meaning in mathematics. It refers to a set of elements and a binary operation such that the following properties are satisfied: there is an identity element in the set; the binary operation is associative; the set is closed under the operation; and every element in the set has an inverse that's also in the set.

The set of four image transformations we defined earlier, namely,

$$\{I, T_{\text{upsideDown}}, T_{\text{photoNeg}}, T_{\text{upsideDownPhotoNeg}}\}$$

together with the composition operation $\circ$ form a group. This is because first, the set contains I, the identity; second, composition is associative; third, the set is closed under composition; and fourth each element has an inverse (because in this case each of the four happens to be a self-inverse).

The notion of a group is a general one. The elements of the set do not have to be transformations. They could be be integers. For example, the set $\{0, 1, 2\}$ together with the following operation form a group. The operation $\oplus$ is defined as

$$x \oplus y = x + y \bmod 3$$

The element 0 serves as the identity element because no matter what x is, $x \oplus 0 = x + 0 \bmod 3 = x$. The operation $\oplus$ is associative because we can see that $x \oplus (y \oplus z) = x + (y + z \bmod 3) \bmod 3 = x + (y + z) \bmod 3 = (x + y) + z \bmod 3 = (x + y \bmod 3) + z \bmod 3 = (x \oplus y) \oplus z$. The set is closed under $\oplus$ because no matter how many times or which values from the set we take, whenever we compute $x \oplus y$, we get a result that is already in the set $\{0, 1, 2\}$. Each element has an inverse because 0 is a self-inverse, 1 has inverse 2, and 2 has inverse 1. That is $1 \oplus 2 = 0$ and $2 \oplus 1 = 0$. So this set of three integers with this operation $\oplus$ is definitely a group.

Knowing about the theory of groups can often be helpful in image processing. For example, groups called permutation groups can be used to scramble and unscramble the pixels of an image. Using a few simple transformations such as having the even and odd rows of an image trade places or switching the left-hand side of the image with the right-hand side, it is possible to come up with quite complicated transformations by combining the simple ones. Group theory provides tools for planning and analyzing such combinations of transformations.

The branch of mathematics that includes the theory of groups is commonly known as modern algebra or abstract algebra. It's quite different from high-school algebra in which one solves linear equations, etc., to find the values of variables.

5.14.1 The 90-Degree Rotation Group

Let's assume for the moment that we are working with square images. Then it is possible to rotate an image by 90 degrees without losing any pixels. Let's use T_{90cc} to represent the transformation that rotates the image 90 degrees counterclockwise. Composing this with itself gives us a 180-degree rotation. Composing it with this again gives us a 270-degree rotation. Once more, and we have a 360-degree rotation, which is the identity transformation. The single transformation T_{90cc} thus generates the full collection of four transformations that, together with the composition operation, forms the 90-degree rotation group. It's easy to see that this set is closed and that each of the rotations has an inverse in the group.

5.14.2 Group Operation Tables

When the number of transformations in a group is not too large, it may be convenient to describe all the combinations of transformations in a table. A *group operation table* has a row and a column for each transformation and it gives, in row i and column j, an entry representing the result of combining (through composition) the transformations T_i and T_j.

For the 90-degree rotation group, the group operation table is as follows:

$\circ$	T_0	T_{90cc}	T_{180}	T_{270cc}
T_0	T_0	T_{90cc}	T_{180}	T_{270cc}
T_{90cc}	T_{90cc}	T_{180}	T_{270cc}	T_0
T_{180}	T_{180}	T_{270cc}	T_0	T_{90cc}
T_{270cc}	T_{270cc}	T_0	T_{90cc}	T_{180}

The circle in the upper-left corner denotes the binary operation used to combine elements, which in this case is composition of image transformations. The table tells us, for example, that a 180-degree rotation, composed with a 270-degree rotation counterclockwise, is equivalent to a 90-degree rotation counterclockwise. That is, the entry in the row for T_{180} and the column for $T_{270\text{cc}}$ is $T_{90\text{cc}}$.

5.14.3 Displaying Groups Using Large Images

It can be fun and instructive to take a group, such as the one generated by $T_{\text{upsideDown}}$ and T_{photoNeg}, and apply all its transformations to your favorite image. One way to do this is to open up a window for each transformation, putting a copy of the original image in each one. Since one of the transformations is the identity, one of these copies will be left as it is. The others will be replaced by computing new versions of the image.

Another way of displaying the same information is to create one large image, tiled with the different versions of the original. Let's illustrate this using the upside-down and photonegative group. We'll open one window for the original image alone and one large window for all four transformed versions (including the original). The large window must be twice as wide and twice as high as the original. Let's assume the windows have been set up and that the original image is in the small window. The original image is selected in the calculator as Source1 and the large window is selected as Destination.

In order to compute all the transformed versions of the image at once, we need one formula that somehow includes all the other formulas in it. Here it is:

```
if x < w1 then if y < h1 then Source1(x,y)
else Source1(x,ymax - y) else
if y < h1 then 255 - Source1(x - w1, y) else
255 - Source1(x - w1,ymax - y)
```

This formula compares the x-coordinate of the current pixel to w1, and if it is smaller, does one of two possible things, depending on the y-coordinate. If not, it does one of two possible other things, also depending on the y-coordinate. There are thus four possible expressions to compute, and these correspond to the four different transformations in the group. Note that w1 is the width of the Source1 image, and not the large destination. On the other hand, xmax and ymax refer to the destination image. The result of applying the formula to a portion of the Tree of Color image by Bruce Hemingway (figure 4.7) is shown in figure 5.16.

5.15 Summary

Formulas are used by PixelMath's image-processing engine to compute a new image for the currently selected destination window. The formula is applied up to three times at each pixel location of the destination image. If all of red, green, and blue are enabled on the

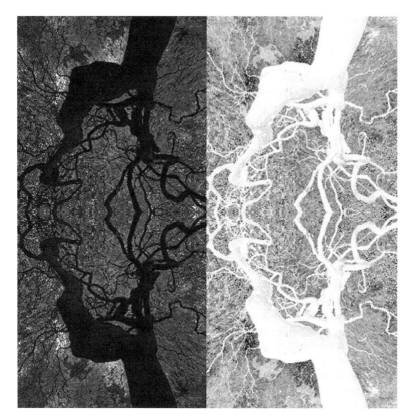

Figure 5.16
A single image showing the results of applying all the transformations in the upside-down and photonegative group.

calculator, then the formula is applied three times at each location. The pixel locations are processed in a standard scanning order, starting at $(x, y) = (0, 0)$, and then $(1, 0)$, $(2, 0)$, up to (xmax, 0), then $(0, 1)$, $(1, 1)$, etc., all the way to the upper-right corner: (xmax, ymax). For special purposes such as transforming or measuring the shape of an object, this order can be modified using one of the Python functions described later in this book.

No matter how many windows are involved in a transformation, the coordinates x and y in the formula always refer to the position within the destination image where pixel values are being computed. When the destination image's red, green, and blue values at position $x = 13$, $y = 36$ are being computed, then the values of x and y used in the formula are 13 and 36. The use of x and y to refer to destination-image positions and not necessarily source-image positions is a property of the pull method of computing image transformations.

5.16 References

Miller, W. 1972. *Symmetry Groups and Their Applications*. New York: Academic Press. Available online at www .ima.umn.edu/ miller/symmetrygroups.html.

Wikipedia. Permutation Group. en.wikipedia.org/wiki/Permutation_group.

5.17 Exercises

1. When a pixel value is to be retrieved from a source image but the specified coordinates lie between coordinates where source pixels are stored, interpolation is often used to blend the values of nearby pixels. Suppose we want the source pixel value at $(4.5, 7.0)$. Assume the source image is monochrome at its pixel value at $(4, 7)$ is 23 and its value at $(5, 7)$ is 37. What should be the value of the interpolated pixel?

2. Suppose, in the same image as the previous problem, we wish to have the value of the image at the coordinate pair $(4.25, 6.8)$. Suppose that in addition to the values at $(4, 7)$ and $(5, 7)$ already given, the value at $(4, 6)$ is 15, and the value at $(5, 6)$ is 21. What should be the value of the interpolated pixel? Use linear interpolation in both directions. (Show your work.)

3. Which of the following transformations will produce a drastic distortion of the image if used in one-window rather than two-window mode? (a) `Source1(x,y)`, (b) `Source1(x+1,y)`, (c) `Source1(x-1,y)`, (d) `1+Source1(x,y)`, (e) `Source1(x+1,y-1)`. Why?

4. Suppose that we are scaling an image up so that the destination is three times as wide and two times as high as the `Source1`. What is the correct formula to use?

5. Suppose that you need a formula that will take any-sized Source1 image and completely fill any given destination image with a stretched and/or compressed version of the Source1 image. What formula should you use? (Note: The horizontal and vertical scale factors are potentially different here.)

6. A formula such as `Source1(x*2, y*2)` shrinks an image into the lower-left corner of its window. (a) Give a formula that will shrink the image by the same scale factor but maintain its center in the same place. (b) If the scale factor is not 2 but an arbitrary value k, how would you determine the formula that maintains the center while shrinking the image?

7. Using an image of the Leaning Tower of Pisa, design a transformation that will "fix" the tower by rotating it so that it is no longer leaning. Use a rectangle of interest (set using the rectangle tool for the destination window) to restrict the rotation to the pixels of the tower and some of the surrounding sky.

8. Give formulas for each of the following operations: (a) shifting an image up 10 pixels (without any wraparound), (b) shifting an image up 10 pixels (with wraparound), (c) reflecting an image in the axis $x = 100$, (d) simultaneously rotating an image by 90 degrees and taking its photonegative.

9. Colors can be manipulated by transformations in ways that change the image but preserve all the information in the image. (a) Give an example of an invertible transformation that drastically changes the color of each and every pixel in an image but does not move pixels around in the image. Note that the photonegative transformation will not drastically change the color of a gray pixel. (b) Generalize your answer to the previous problem to obtain a mathematical group of transformations that (with the exception of the identity transformation) change the colors of the pixels of an image. Show that your transformations satisfy the requirements for a group. (c) Create a tiled image that shows all the transformations in your group applied to some image, such as a reduced version of the Mona Lisa. (This will be difficult if there are many transformations in the group, but not so difficult for a group of size 4 or so.)

10. Suppose we have an image of width w1 and height h1, where w1 = m*k and h1 = n*k. Thus the image can be divided into k-by-k tiles, arranged in an m-by-n array. Any symmetry operation on a tile, such as reflection or rotation, can be made into a transformation of the entire image by applying it to all the tiles at once. (a) Make up a group of transformations for such images, based on this approach. Your group should contain at least four transformations in it. Prove that it meets all the requirements for being a group by showing that each property required for a group holds. (b) Create a PixelMath formula page that illustrates all the transformations in this group on an image of your choice.

11. A simple color transformation that is invertible is taking the photonegative. Instead of this, consider the following kind of pixel "inversion". Each color component is represented in the computer as a byte of information (8 bits). A byte can be broken down into two 4-bit parts called nibbles. The inversion consists of interchanging the two nibbles of each byte of the image. (a) Show that this operation is invertible and that with the identity transformation it forms a group. (b) Come up with a formula that performs the inversion and apply it to an image. Verify experimentally that the inversion of the inversion of an image is the original.

12. Give the group operation table for the group whose transformations are illustrated in figure 5.16.

13. Give the 8-by-8 group operation table for the group generated by the 90-degree rotation transformation and the upside-down reflection transformation.

14. Suppose we have two different groups, but they both have the same number of transformations in them. We say they are *isomorphic* if the group operation table of one group can be rearranged into that of the other using only the following steps: (1) renaming the transformations in the first group with names from the second, (2) permuting the rows of the table (for example, interchanging two rows, any number of times), and (3) permuting the columns. (a) Give an example of an image transformation group that is isomorphic to the 90-degree rotation group but that does not involve moving pixels and instead modifies the colors of pixels. Show that it is isomorphic by explaining the one-to-one correspondence between rotations and the transformations in your new group. (b) Come up with a scheme

for producing many more groups of image transformations that are isomorphic to these two (yours and the 90-degree rotation group). Describe your scheme. How many groups can someone make using the scheme?

15. An invertible image rotation is a kind of pixel permutation in which all the pixels move somewhere else in the image. Another kind of pixel permutation is like a volleyball rotation in which the players shift to the right and the rightmost player in a row moves to the leftmost position of the next row. (a) Does this permutation generate a group? Why or why not? (b) How many elements will result when closure is reached? (c) Suppose the image can be divided into k-by-k tiles and the rotation is applied independently within each tile. How many elements will result in that case? (d) Write a PixelMath formula that performs the operation using the whole image. (e) Write a PixelMath formula that performs the operation within each tile. Assume $k = 8$ for this formula.

6 Geometric Distortions

In this chapter you'll learn to make a mild mess of an image, in a controlled way, of course! We'll learn techniques that can be used to create bathroom window effects, warps, and invertible encryptions of an image. In this last activity, we'll see how one image can serve as a code for encrypting and decrypting another.

6.1 Perturbing Coordinates

A typical geometric distortion is produced, not by changing the colors of pixels, but by moving pixels around in the image, stretching, shrinking, warping, curving, or just cutting and pasting. We don't need to disable any of the color components when performing geometric transformations.

6.1.1 Skews

We have already seen how to scale an image, translate it in any direction, or rotate it around an axis. Now let's see some transformations that do nastier things to the shapes and figures in an image. We begin with a skew because it is so simple.

Try setting up two windows of the same size for Source1 and Destination, loading in the image of your choice, and then compute the formula

```
Source1(x, y - x)
```

If this is too drastic, scale down the skewing part of the formula as in

```
Source1(x, y - 0.2 * x)
```

A similar effect can be achieved by distorting the x coordinate rather than the y coordinate.

```
Source1(x - 0.2 * y, y)
```

If we apply the skewing perturbation to both coordinates, we can get tighter compression of the image.

```
Source1(x - 0.5 * y, y - 0.5 * x)
```

However, if we let the two components get the same formula (or opposite formulas), the image shrinks down to a somewhat boring line:

```
Source1(x - y, y - x)
```

To make life more interesting, let's consider some perturbations that are not quite so straight.

6.1.2 Wavy Versions Using sin

The function $\sin x$ is one of the trigonometric functions like $\cos x$ that describes a pure and smooth oscillation such as you might observe looking at a bicycle pedal going up and down from a viewpoint right behind the rear tire. When PixelMath is given the function $\sin x$ to compute, it considers the value of x to be given, not in degrees, but in radians. Although we usually think of $\sin x$ as a function of the measure of an angle, we can think of it as a function taking some number as its input. This function returns a value in the range -1 to $+1$. If we want to show this function in an image, we should adjust the range of values of the sine function so that it better matches the 0 to 255 range of possible pixel values. Let's now plot a sine function into an image. To do this, enter the following formula and click Compute.

```
127 * (sin(x) + 1)
```

The result should be a pattern of vertical stripes, and if you zoom into the image, you'll see that the stripes repeat every 6 pixels or so. The sine function repeats a cycle every 2π radians, and in this PixelMath example, this is about every 2π pixels in the x direction.

To lengthen the cycle period, we slow down the oscillation by scaling the argument x down to something like $x/5$. You can observe the result of the formula

```
127 * (sin(x / 5) + 1)
```

Now let's apply such a wave in the form of a coordinate-perturbing modulation to a photograph. What we'll do is copy an image from the Source1 buffer to the destination buffer, but along the way we'll adjust the coordinates from where the pixel values are taken so that instead of coming from the identical (x, y) position where they're to be written, they will come from $(x + f(x), y)$ where $f(x)$ is our perturbing function based on the sine function. Here it is:

```
Source1(x + 10 * sin(x / 5), y)
```

The scale factor 10 means that the perturbances to x will be in the range $[-10, 10]$, which is large enough to produce notable waviness, but not so large as to completely obliterate the face of the Mona Lisa. The Mona Lisa and her wavy version created with this formula are shown in figure 6.1.

6.1.3 Modulating Both x and y

What we just did to the x coordinate can, of course, be done to the y coordinate. To make the image a little more interesting, let's do something to x and y at the same time. Here's the application of a sine modulation to both coordinates, but with different frequencies:

```
Source1(x + 10 * sin(x / 5), y + 10 * sin(y / 8))
```

(a)   (b)

Figure 6.1
The Mona Lisa (a) before and (b) after perturbing x-coordinates with a sine function.

If you are applying a distortion like this to an image of a face, you might need to adjust the phase of the oscillations to line up nicely with facial features like the eyes. You adjust the phase by adding a constant to the angle, i.e., to the argument of the sine function. Here's an example where we add 2 radians to the phase in the horizontal oscillation:

```
Source1(x + 10 * sin(2 + x / 5), y + 10 * sin(y / 8))
```

What we've learned is that the sine function can be used to produce controlled waves, which can in turn be used to distort an image for a special effect. If you see an image that has such a wave distortion, you can imagine how it might have been produced.

6.2   Modulator Images

What if instead of using a function like sin to perturb the coordinates of an image, we use the values in another image for that purpose? This will give us a way to control distortions that is conceptually different and in some ways more powerful.

First let's simulate the sin x perturbation by filling an image with values from the function sin x. As we did previously in this chapter, we scale the values into the range 0 to 255 rather than -1 to 1 because we're filling a PixelMath image buffer. But other than that, there is nothing fancy going on here. So here is an image similar to those we saw previously:

```
127 * (sin(x/5) + 1)
```

Now let's modulate another image using this one. We load in a scanned photograph and make that image Source1. We load another copy of that and make it the Destination. Next we set the sine function image to be Source2. Finally, we apply a formula that uses the sine image to modulate the photo:

```
Source1(x + 0.1 * (Source2(x, y) - 127), y)
```

This is taking the value in Source2 at (x, y), moving it into the range -13 to $+13$ and adding it to the x value of the coordinates of the location from which the Source1 pixel is copied.

6.2.1 Relative Displacement Using a Monochrome Image

Using the sine function image to modulate a photograph is just one example of using one image to control the distortion of another. Any image can be used as a control image here, but the effects can seem strange and harsh if the modulator image is not continuous and has values that change by a large amount from one pixel to the next. In addition, we are only modulating one of the two coordinate values in the transformation, namely x, while y is unaffected.

We can of course add something to y and modulate it, too. This allows us to perturb either x or y or both together in the same way (they both get the same perturbation). Next let us see how to perturb both x and y independently at the same time.

6.2.2 Using Color Components to Perturb x and y Independently

A color image can be thought of as three separate images: one for red, one for green, and one for blue. By using two of those, we can arrange for one color image to control modulations for each of x and y in a photograph. Here is how we could do that. Let's arrange for the red component to modulate the x component of the mapping and for the green component to modulate y.

Let's again simulate one of our previous distortions so that we can see the difference in how the methods work. First let's create a modulator image. We open a new image with dimensions equal to those of the photo to be distorted. Next, we make this new image the Destination. We define the contents of the modulator using two separate formulas. Let's enable red and disable green and blue, and then let's compute

```
127 * (sin(x / 5) + 1)
```

Next, we disable red and enable green, and then compute

```
127 * (sin(y / 8) + 1)
```

At this point, we go ahead and re-enable all the color components so that when we apply the main mapping all three color components will be copied and distorted.

Next, we open the photo in a source window and another copy of it in a new destination window. We make sure that Source1 is the photo and Destination is a copy of the photo or a blank image of the same dimensions. Then we set Source2 to be the modulator image.

The formula that will map the photo to its distorted version will use the red component of the modulator image to adjust the x values and the green component to adjust the y values. Therefore it accesses the values of Red2(x,y) and Green2(x,y), which are the red and green component values for the pixel at (x, y) in the Source2 image. Here is the formula:

```
Source1(x + 0.1 * (Red2(x,y)-127), y + 0.1 * (Green2(x,y)-127))
```

This should result in an image with an appearance similar to that produced earlier, but now it has been done using a modulator image rather than using the sine function directly. The point of this is to show that one can use an image to specify a distortion rather than simply using a function within the mapping formula.

It's possible to use any image as the modulator. Try opening some random image, possibly a photo, and using it as a modulator. This means making it the Source2 image and then applying the above formula once again.

Note that this method used the modulator image's red and green components. The blue component was not used. What can we do with the blue component? It is possible to use the blue component to gain extra bits with which to represent displacements, but this is a little complicated and we'll not discuss it further here. It's mainly of interest when absolute coordinate mapping is involved (as described in the next section) and the images to be mapped are larger than 256×256 pixels.

6.2.3 Absolute Coordinates: An Identity Transformation

In the examples we just considered, the source photograph was distorted using a formula of the form Source1$(x + f(x, y), y + g(x, y))$, where f and g are represented by the red and green components of the modulator image. Now, rather than adding these values to x and y, let us use them directly as the coordinates going into Source1. In this way, we'll be using the modulator image to provide the absolute coordinates of the source pixel to be copied. The following example illustrates this. First, we construct a modulator image that is just a pair of gradients, the red component representing a horizontal one and the green component representing a vertical one. If the gradients increase from left to right, we might have an image that represents an identity transformation. Let's illustrate this and then change it.

Create a new image of size 256×256 and make it the Destination. Enable the red component, disable green and blue, and enter the simple formula

```
x
```

Then disable red, enable green and enter

```
y
```

Zoom in on a pixel of this image, and you should see that the red value matches the x coordinate value shown on the status line, whereas the green value matches the y coordinate value.

Use this identity image to transform a photograph by setting Source1 to your photograph, Destination to another image buffer of the same dimensions as the photograph, and Source2 to the modulator image. Make sure all three color components are enabled and then enter the following formula:

```
Source1(Red2(x,y), Green2(x,y))
```

We'll call this last formula the modulator image-mapping formula (or MIM formula).

If the width and height of your source photograph did not exceed 256, the transformation should have been equivalent to a copy operation. There should not have been any distortion involved. However, if either the width or height exceeded 256, then you could expect to see something peculiar at the right, top, or both right and top of the destination image. This effect can be explained by checking what's going on as, say, the x coordinate exceeds 255.

Suppose we are computing the value for a destination pixel at (500, 39). The x coordinate, 500, is much larger than the x coordinate of the rightmost pixel in the modulator image (which is at $x = 255$). Therefore the value retrieved by the PixelMath image engine is the default value for any position outside the image, i.e., 127. The Source1 pixel value at position (127, 39) is what is written into the destination position (500, 39), which appears as a rather arbitrary value. This value will be the same at (501, 39), (502, 39), and in fact all pixels in the same row beyond the position 255. The effect produced is a series of stripes, horizontal at the right side of the image and/or vertical above. The stripes that can arise in these situations are known as *artifacts*, and their cause can be described as an *8-bit addressing restriction* owing to the use of color components as coordinate values. (Two alternative ways of avoiding the artifacts are (1) to use 12-bit addressing by dividing the 24 bits of the red, green, and blue components equally between the x coordinate and the y coordinate; or (2) performing scaling on the inputs and outputs of the Red2 and Green2 access functions.)

6.2.4 Absolute Coordinates: 180-Degree Rotation

The point of showing the identity transformation here is to show (1) what the identity modulator image looks like and (2) the hazard of using images with a width or height greater than 256 with the current method. (If needed, this hazard can be overcome, albeit with some added complexity in the process.)

Let's now change the modulator image slightly, so that we can see a slightly more interesting transformation done with this method. Let's create the red and green modulator components as earlier, except that we'll use the following two formulas:

```
xmax-x
```

```
ymax-y
```

Then, applying this transformation using the MIM formula (with the same source and destination settings as with the earlier identity example), we should get a 180-degree rotated version of the photograph.

As with the relative coordinate modulators, any PixelMath image can, in principle, be used as an absolute coordinates modulator image. However, most images, when used as modulators, will mess up the photograph pretty badly. Therefore we'll typically use artificial images with nice mathematical properties as our modulators. In the next section we'll look at more drastic yet invertible distortions generated by more radical permutations of the Source1 pixels.

6.2.5 Permutations Using Modular Arithmetic

Let's suppose we are transforming a 256×256 photograph using the MIM method. By moving each pixel to a distant location in the image and separating adjacent pixels with a lot of space, we can make the resulting image unintelligible without discarding any of the pixels or changing any of their colors. One way to come up with such a permutation is to use a scaling factor that is much larger than a factor of 2 or 3, but which is relatively prime to the dimensions of the image (256), and wrap all large values back into the image region of the plane by taking the values modulo 256.

Here are a pair of formulas that give us the red and green components of the modulator image for such a permutation:

```
(x * 73) mod 256
```

```
(y * 73) mod 256
```

This modulator image is shown in figure 6.2a. Let's apply this modulator to our 256×256 photo using the MIM formula. The results can be seen in figure 6.3.

To prove that this transformation is invertible, let's just show that the following formulas give us a modulator image that inverts the first transformation.

```
(x * 249) mod 256
```

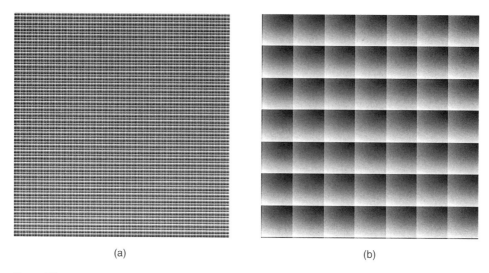

(a)   (b)

Figure 6.2
Modulator images (a) for permuting the pixels of an image and (b) for inverting the permutation.

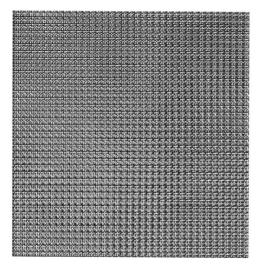

Figure 6.3
The Mona Lisa image after permuting the pixels. All information of the original is retained but is unintelligible.

```
(y * 249) mod 256
```

This image is shown in figure 6.2b.

In creating this pair of modulator images for scrambling and unscrambling an image, it was not necessary that the same factor (e.g., 73) be used in the x permutation and the y permutation; we could have used different factors. For example, we could scramble the image with the modulator

```
(x * 171) mod 256
```

```
(y * 27) mod 256
```

and unscramble it with the inverse modulator

```
(x * 3) mod 256
```

```
(y * 19) mod 256
```

6.3 Invertibility Once Again

One of the lessons we can learn about invertibility is the following: Just because a transformed image becomes completely jumbled does not mean that we have lost any information or performed a noninvertible operation. And even if a transformation does not seem to jumble an image at all, it might lose information and be noninvertible.

6.3.1 Partial Invertibility

Some image transformations perform a distortion that can be partly reversed. For example, rotating an image by half a right angle (this is 45 degrees or $\pi/4$ radians) and then rotating

Figure 6.4
The Mona Lisa image after rotation by 45 degrees counterclockwise around the lower-left corner and then rotation
back. This is an example of partial invertibility because some pixel values have been lost.

it back results in an image like that in figure 6.4. Here the center of rotation is the Cartesian
coordinate system origin, $(0, 0)$. The image looks fine, except that some of the pixels are
now missing. The first rotation is one example of a partially invertible transformation. To be
completely invertible, *all* the pixels would have to be restorable to their original values by
an inverse transformation. By the way, the rotations by 45 degrees (first counter-clockwise,
then clockwise) are accomplished with the formulas

```
Source1((x * 0.707)+(y * 0.707), (x * -0.707)+(y * 0.707))
```

and

```
Source1((x * 0.707)+(y * -0.707), (x * 0.707)+(y * 0.707))
```

In the next section, using polar coordinates, we'll see a simpler way to rotate an image.

6.4 Polar Coordinates

In previous chapters we have been using (x, y) coordinate pairs to describe the location of a pixel. There are other ways to specify the location of a pixel, and the most important of these is with polar coordinates. Also, using polar coordinates, we can define transformations to obtain a variety of interesting effects.

6.5 Angles and Radii

Consider figure 6.5, which shows two points. The "pole" is the point in the center of the image. The point Q is another point, one whose location we wish to describe. In the polar coordinate method, we describe the location of Q by describing how to get there from the pole using an angle value and a distance value.

It's common to use the Greek letters ρ (rho) and θ (theta) to stand for the distance value and the angle value. We reach the point $Q = (\rho, \theta)$ by moving a distance ρ out from the pole (moving to the right), reaching a point we can call Q' (read Q prime). Then we rotate a line that begins on the horizontal axis (with Q' on it) counterclockwise, pivoting it at the pole. We carry the point Q' along for the ride. We stop rotating it when it has turned an angle equal to θ. The new position of Q' is Q.

The angle θ could be given in degrees, but traditionally (at least in mathematics, science, and engineering) it is given in radians, where 1 radian $= 180/\pi$ degrees. We can approximate this with 1 radian ≈ 57.3 degrees. In PixelMath, the distance ρ is given in pixel widths. One pixel width is the width of 1 (square-shaped) pixel.

6.6 Visualizing the Polar Coordinates

PixelMath has a switch on the calculator to put it into polar mode (as opposed to Cartesian mode). Once in polar mode, it displays the polar coordinates of the pixel under the mouse cursor.

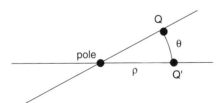

Figure 6.5
Polar coordinates: the point Q is described by the pair (ρ, θ), where ρ represents its distance from the pole and θ represents the angle (in radians) that the line from the pole to Q makes with the horizontal axis.

Another way to see polar coordinate information is to use a simple formula to make an image based on the coordinates and then examine the image. First, let's examine the values of ρ for each pixel of an image. Create a new image of size 512 by 512. Set R, G, and B all enabled and enter and compute

```
rho
```

You should see a circular blur with black in the middle and white at the edges. This shows how the ρ values increase as the distance from the pole increases. This is shown in figure 6.6a.

Now let's try something similar with θ. Enter and compute

```
theta
```

Surprise! The result is all black. Are all the values 0? Look closely at different regions in the image. PixelMath angles for polar coordinates are given in the range $-\pi$ to $+\pi$. Since

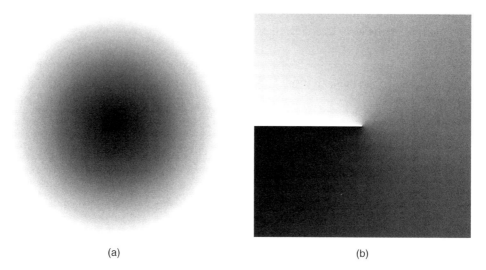

(a)   (b)

Figure 6.6
Images in which the intensity of each pixel is based on its polar coordinates: (a) rho and (b) theta—actually (theta + 3.14159) * 255 / 6.2832.

negative numbers are changed to 0 as they are written into the destination image, the entire bottom half of the image consists of 0 values. In the upper half, the values vary from 0 to 3. The intensities of all these pixels are low and they appear black.

In order to see a pattern, let's amplify these values and get them into the full range of allowable pixel values: 0 to 255. Enter and compute

```
(theta + 3.14159) * 255 / 6.2832
```

Now you should see a pattern in which black changes to white as the angle increases from the horizontal axis going counterclockwise. (It's shown here in figure 6.6b.) You can combine these two images for showing the ρ and θ patterns into a single color image by storing the ρ pattern in the red component of the destination and the θ pattern in the green component.

6.7 Transformations with Polar Coordinates

Set up an image for a two-window transformation. Rotations around the center of the image are particularly simple using polar coordinates. Try

```
Source1(rho, theta - 0.7854)
```

Compare this with the transformation

```
Source1(rho, theta + 0.7854)
```

The pull method (see chapter 5) has its effect in polar coordinates too!

It's also easy to scale an image up or down with polar coordinates, and since PixelMath sets the pole in the middle of the image, the scaled image remains centered. Try these scaling transformations:

```
Source1(rho / 2, theta)
```

```
Source1(rho * 2, theta)
```

Strange things happen if we scale the angle, however:

```
Source1(rho, theta / 2)
```

```
Source1(rho, theta * 2)
```

or if we add to or subtract from ρ:

```
Source1(rho + 50, theta)
```

```
Source1(rho - 50, theta)
```

6.8 Fisheye Transformations

A fisheye lens has two observable effects: one is to take in a wide field of view and the other is to enlarge objects in the center of the image relative to those on the periphery. By performing a transformation that adjusts the ρ values of the accessed source pixels so that they are relatively reduced near the pole and relatively larger near the maximum value of ρ, we can create the distorting effect of a fisheye lens. A way to do this is by squaring

Figure 6.7
The fisheye transformation applied to the Mona Lisa.

ρ and then bringing the value back into range by dividing it by the largest possible value of ρ in the destination image:

```
Source1(rho * rho / rhomax, theta)
```

This is shown in figure 6.7.

The effect can be intensified by taking the third power of ρ and bringing those values back into range by dividing them by the square of the maximum ρ value.

```
Source1(rho * rho * rho / (rhomax * rhomax), theta)
```

Doing something similar to the θ coordinate produces a strange warp.

```
Source1(rho, theta * theta / 6.2832)
```

Figure 6.8
A ripples-on-a-pond effect.

6.9 Ripples on a Pond

Whereas the fisheye transformation works by adjusting the ρ parameter to Source1 to grow slowly and then more quickly as the destination ρ parameter grows, we can obtain another effect by making it alternately grow more slowly and more quickly. The effect is a waviness along the ρ dimension that results in a rippling effect (see figure 6.8).

```
Source1(rho + 8 * sin(rho / 2), theta)
```

Try adjusting the amplitude (the factor 8 in this example) and the frequency (controlled by the divisor 2 in this example) to obtain the effect that you find most pleasing.

6.10 Polar Pixellation Effects

Some notable effects can be created by undersampling with polar coordinates. This means that only a fraction of the Source1 pixels will actually be used in the destination, and to fill the gaps that would otherwise be there, copies will be made of the selected few pixels. Here's a way of doing it where we use all the θ values but only 1 out of 10 of the ρ values to access some pixels.

Figure 6.9
A polar pixellation of the Mona Lisa.

```
Source1(rho - (rho mod 10), theta)
```

Let ρ_d represent the ρ coordinate of the current destination pixel and let ρ_s be the ρ coordinate of the corresponding Source1 pixel: the one that is to be copied into the destination. Then the above formula uses $\rho_s = 0$ for the first 10 values of ρ_d, $\rho_s = 10$ for the second 10 values of ρ_d, $\rho_s = 20$ for the next 10 values of ρ_d, etc. The effect of this is to make the image into a collection of noticeable rings or *annuli*.

Suppose we wish to reduce the resolution in the angular coordinate rather than in the radial one. Doing something like this with angles is tricky since the mod function is not usually defined for noninteger arguments. We can accomplish it by first scaling up the θ value from the range $-\pi$ to $+\pi$ to the range -10π to 10π, then truncating these (converting these to integers by eliminating the fractional parts), and then scaling them back into the original range.

```
Source1(rho, floor(theta * 10) / 10)
```

We can combine the effects using the following formula. The resulting image can be called a polar pixellation of the original.

```
Source1(rho - (rho mod 10), floor(theta * 10) / 10)
```

The result of this on the Mona Lisa can be seen in figure 6.9.

The uniform regions that we obtain in this image might remind you of a diagram showing blocks of storage space on a hard disk. By requantizing the angular divisions in the image, we define sectors on the image. The scaling factor 10 used here is arbitrary. A smaller factor will lead to larger sectors whereas a larger factor will cause smaller sectors because the effects of truncation to integers will be less after the rescaling is done.

6.11   About Anamorphic Images

In this and the following sections we consider specials kind of distorted images called anamorphic images. You'll learn to create distorted images that are meant to be viewed in special ways. One kind is a sort of squashed or stretched image that needs to be viewed on a slant. Another kind is an image that needs to be viewed reflected in a cylindrical mirror. This sort of image is called a cylinder anamorphosis.

Like stereograms, which we will consider in a later chapter, anamorphic images can be thought of as patterns that carry hidden images within them. However, rather than using the special way of seeing with two eyes that stereo requires, the anamorphic image requires an optical viewing technique that does not depend on using two eyes. Consequently, it may be easier to see the hidden image of an anamorphic image than it is to see the depth dimension in a stereogram.

6.12   Definition and Motivation

Anamorphic images are images that look strange because of a geometric distortion until they are viewed in a special way that inverts the distortion. For example, looking at an image reflected in a cylindrical mirror can reveal what is distorted in a cylinder anamorphic image.

Anamorphic images have been used for parlor entertainment since the 1500s, and a number of outstanding examples of carefully painted distorted images can be found. For example, the nautical image shown in figure 6.10 attributed to James Steere is believed to be from the late 1700s (see Leeman, 1975).

Figure 6.10
Cylinder anamorphic image. To view the hidden image, place a cylindrical mirror in the center of the anamorphic image and examine the reflection.

Anamorphic images are not only a source of fun, they can be used to illustrate important aspects of digital image transformations such as invertibility and interpolation. In the following sections of this chapter we'll learn several techniques for creating anamorphic images.

6.13 Obtaining a Cylindrical Mirror

In order to view a cylinder anamorphosis such as that in figure 6.10, you need to place a cylindrical mirror in the center of it and look at the the image's reflection. There are several ways to obtain a cylindrical mirror. One that sometimes works is to shop at a plumbing supply store to find a section of chrome-plated bathroom washbasin drain pipe that is smooth, round, and reflective. However, not all drain pipes are shiny and smooth enough, and it might be better to make your mirror yourself.

To make your own mirror, you need a cylinder (possibly a piece of drain pipe that is quite round but that doesn't reflect well enough to be the mirror itself. A 6-inch section of a sturdy cardboard mailing tube will also do. The core of a roll of paper towels or an empty juice can may also work. The diameter is not critical, but from 1.5 inches to 3 inches will work best with typical anamorphic images that are easy to create.

Next, you need a rectangular piece of reflective Mylar sheet that is big enough to wrap once around the cylinder. Such mylar is typically available at art supply stores. When you buy the Mylar, be sure that there are no wrinkles in the piece you are buying. You might wish to buy enough to make more than one mirror; think of this as insurance against accidentally wrinkling your Mylar. You might also get a friend so excited about anamorphic images that he or she also wants to have a mirror.

Carefully cut the Mylar sheet to fit the cylinder and wrap the cylinder with the Mylar, fastening it along the seam with double-faced tape. (Single-faced tape can be used, with a slightly less appealing result.) It's possible to create a mirror this way that appears to be made of silvered glass or polished stainless steel.

6.14 Slant Anamorphosis

Let's begin our look into anamorphic images with a simple example, by Leonardo da Vinci, of *slant anamorphosis*. Then we'll look at some other examples of this type of distortion and see how to create our own.

6.14.1 Examples of Slant Anamorphosis

Figure 6.11 shows a drawing by Leonardo da Vinci of a distorted form. Upon viewing this image at a sharp angle, one sees the forms of an eye and a face. This is an example of slant anamorphosis. Leonardo's example is considered to be the earliest example of an anamorphic image.

A later example of a slant anamorphosis occurs in the famous painting by Holbein called *The Ambassadors* (figure 6.12). In this case, the anamorphosis is confined to a small portion of the image. However, this portion is sufficiently different from the rest of the painting that the viewer's attention is called to it quite well.

A more elaborate visual effect is shown in figure 6.13, in which a slant anamorphosis is camouflaged within another scene. When one image or message is carried secretly within another, we call this *steganography*.

As one more example of slant anamorphosis, we consider the combined effects of including an anamorphic image within another image while also camouflaging it to make its presence a secret. The fallen tree depicted in figure 6.14 contains a likeness of a well-known U.S. president when viewed obliquely.

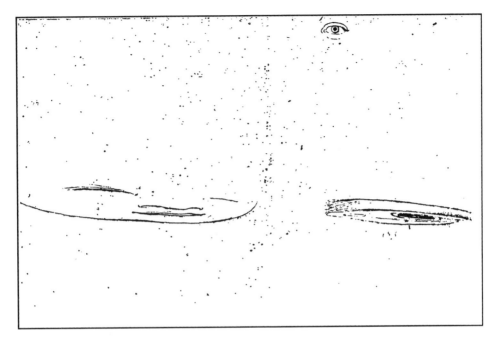

Figure 6.11
Slant anamorphosis by Leonardo da Vinci. To invert the distortion, view the image at a sharp angle from the left or right.

These examples show that as simple an idea as squashing or stretching an image can be used to novel effect. In the next section we consider some simple means of creating slant anamorphoses.

6.14.2 Construction of Slant Anamorphoses

Constructing a slant anamorphosis essentially means stretching an image horizontally. The first step in doing this is to choose an image to start with. Let's use the picture in figure 5.12. The next step is to decide how much to stretch it; let's use a factor of 4 so that the effect is quite noticeable and so the image will not be too easily recognized when viewed straight on.

Using PixelMath, we must set up two windows, one for the original image and one for the destination image. The latter image needs to be dimensioned with a width four times that of the original. Once all that has been done, we need to select on the calculator the Source1 image to be the original and the wider one to be the Destination. Then we can apply the formula

Figure 6.12
The Ambassadors, painted by Hans Holbein. The picture contains a slant anamorphosis within it.

```
Source1(x / 4, y)
```

to perform the stretching. This transformation essentially repeats each column of the original image four times in the destination. The results of performing this transformation are shown in figure 6.15. This version works to some extent, but makes the unrealistic assumption that the viewer is infinitely far away from the picture. Hence there is still some distortion even when the image is viewed on a slant from any finite distance.

A more satisfactory slant anamorphosis is obtained by making two additional distortions to the image. First, we compress the image vertically according to how close it is to the viewpoint. Second, we sample the source image more densely when far away from the viewpoint. Let's assume that the destination image is twice as wide and half as high as the source. For a viewpoint on the right of the image, we can use this formula:

Figure 6.13
One image hidden within another using slant anamorphosis. The otherwise rural scenes reveal the portraits of four important figures upon viewed from the side. This work is by Erhard Schoen.

Figure 6.14
A scene that contains an embedded camouflaged slant anamorphosis within one part of it. To discover the secret, view the tree from an angle. This is by Sam Loyd.

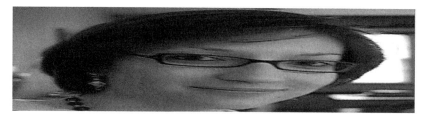

Figure 6.15
The image from figure 5.2 transformed into a slant anamorphosis by simple stretching.

Figure 6.16
A better slant anamorphosis, incorporating foreshortening.

```
Source1(x*x/(w*2), 2*((y - (h/2))*w/(w*1.2-x) + (h/2)))
```

The vertical compression is done as follows: First, the y value of the destination is translated down by $h/2$ so that we can scale it with respect to the central horizontal axis. Then we scale it by the ratio w/(w * 1.2−x). Then we add the $h/2$ back on to invert the vertical translation. Finally, we multiply by 2 to account for the destination image being half as high as the source. The key step here is multiplying by the scaling ratio; as x increases, the ratio's denominator $w * 1.2 - x$ decreases, thus increasing the ratio. As the ratio increases, the height of the transformed image seems to decrease because of the pull method of computation. The second part of the distortion is the changing density of samples in the horizontal direction. The expression x*x/(w*2) grows slowly near $x = 0$, thus reusing the points on the left side of the source image more frequently than points on the right. The *2 in the denominator accommodates the overall stretch in width from source to destination by a factor of 2. The resulting slant anamorphosis is shown in figure 6.16.

It's a significant artistic challenge to create a camouflaged slant anamorphosis of the sort shown in figure 6.13 or 6.14. A strategy for doing it is to begin with a computed slant anamorphosis, perhaps in black and white rather than color, and then to open the image in a program such as Photoshop or PaintShop Photo Pro and make lots of small modifications

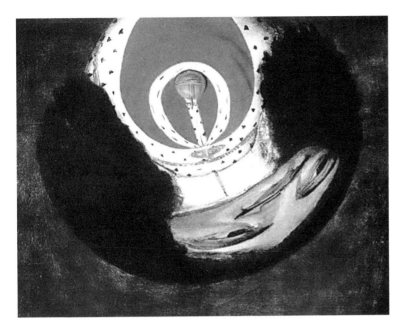

Figure 6.17
A cylinder anamorphosis of King Charles II of England.

to the image that render various figures and features in the details without upsetting the more global distribution of light and dark that represent the hidden image.

6.15   Cylinder Anamorphosis

A cylinder anamorphosis is a distorted image that looks normal when viewed reflected in a cylindrical mirror. Their production goes back at least to the 1600s and they remained popular into the nineteenth century. A number of examples have been collected in the book *Hidden Images* (Leeman, 1975), and three are shown here. In figure 6.17 the portrait of King Charles II of England has been distorted so that although we might recognize it as a face, we cannot recognize who it is.

Figure 6.18 shows an erotic example; the anamorphosis served the practical purpose of hiding the naughty image from view under normal conditions.

6.15.1   Manual Drawing of Cylinder Anamorphoses

In order to gain an appreciation for the experience that some artists had centuries ago, it's instructive to set up a cylindrical mirror on a table, with a piece of white paper under it, and to draw some forms on the paper so that they come out in the reflection as a square, a

Figure 6.18
The scene in this anamorphosis may have been hidden to avoid censorship.

triangle, a circle, etc. Then try to draw a pair of faces so that one looks like a man's face
and the other a woman's.

An easy way to get started is to use a piece of paper containing polar-coordinate guidelines,
such as those shown in figure 6.19. This image was produced using the following formula
in polar-coordinate mode.

```
if (rho > 30 and (abs(24*(theta-0.1)/pi
- ceil(24*(theta-0.1)/pi)) < 0.1))
or (ceil(rho/10) - rho/10 < 0.1) then 0 else 255
```

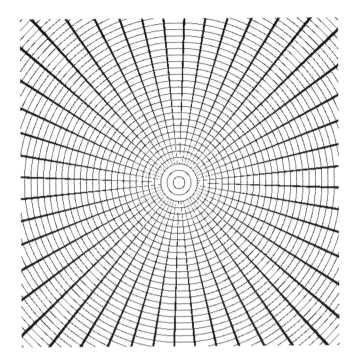

Figure 6.19
Polar-coordinate guidelines that can be helpful in drawing cylinder anamorphoses. These guidelines were plotted using a polar-coordinates PixelMath formula.

A nice challenge is to use the guidelines to write the message "Happy Birthday!" so that it looks correct in the cylindrical mirror.

6.15.2 The Full-360 Method

Let's now consider the business of producing anamorphic images by computer. A straightforward approach is to consider a one-to-one correspondence between the cells in a rectangular array and the cells in a polar array like that in figure 6.19. Let's assume that the polar array is to go completely around the center. Then we will need a mapping that takes a normal image and wraps it around the center in the polar array so that the bottom of the original image is near the center (the pole), and so that the left and right sides of the original end up butted together in the polar version. This mapping is illustrated graphically in figure 6.20.

This method can be implemented with the following formula:

```
Source1(((w1/(2*pi)) * Angle(x-w/2,y-h/2)+1.5*pi) mod w1,
(h/(h-100)) * (sqrt(sqr(x-(w/2)) + sqr(y - (h/2)))) -50)
```

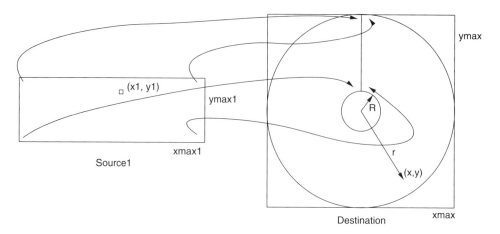

Figure 6.20
The correspondence between original image pixel positions and locations in an anamorphic version using the full-360 method.

This formula determines first what angle (in the range of 0 to 2π) the pixel to be drawn is at in the destination image. `Angle` is a built-in function that is based upon the arc tangent of the slope of the line that connects the pole with (x, y). In order to place the "seam" of the anamorphic image at the top rather than the right, we rotate the image 90 degrees counterclockwise (actually 270 degrees or $3\pi/2 \approx 4.712$ radians clockwise). The angle is then scaled (by `w1`/2π) and wrapped (using `mod w1`) into the range of 0 to `xmax1`, which is the largest x-coordinate value in the Source1 image. The resulting value is used as the x-coordinate of the source pixel. To get the y-coordinate, first we compute the distance (shown as r in figure 6.20) from the center of the destination to the pixel to be drawn. Then we subtract from this the radius of the cylindrical mirror (given as R in figure 6.20, which in this example is assumed to be 50 pixels.

An example of an anamorphic image constructed this way is shown in figure 6.21. The source image is a section of Caravaggio's painting *The Calling of Saint Matthew*. Although cylinder anamorphoses were created for entertainment in past centuries, recently special cameras have been developed to produce them for such purposes as videoconferencing and panoramic photography (see chapter 19).

6.15.3 Precomputed Mapping Method
Although the method discussed here works well in practice, the images that result have a certain distortion that remains even in the reflected image. There is an alternative approach, which is to use a mapping based on optical ray tracing.

Consider the diagram in figure 6.22. From a particular viewpoint E, in order to make it appear that a particular color is at location (u, v) in the reflection image, it is necessary to

(a)

(b)

Figure 6.21
Example of an anamorphic image constructed using the full-360 method: (a) original and (b) cylinder anamorphosis.

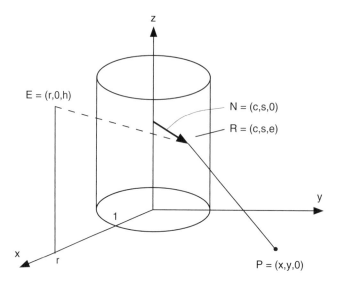

Figure 6.22
Optical ray-tracing diagram showing the cylindrical mirror, viewpoint, virtual image point, and point on the anamorphic image. Here E is the viewpoint. It lies in the x-z plane at a distance r from the x axis, and its height is h. A ray from E meets the cylinder at a point of reflection R, and reflects to the x-y plane hitting it at point (x, y, 0). Point R has coordinates (c, s, e), where c is the cosine of an angle θ and s is its sine. The normal vector (perpendicular to the cylinder) at R is represented by N.

color the corresponding anamorphic image pixel at (x, y) with that color. The ray from the viewpoint to the cylinder hits the cylinder at an angle that depends upon how far to the side of the cylinder's central axis it hits the cylinder. The angle of reflection is equal to the angle of incidence at the point of reflection. Where the ray hits the anamorphic image then depends upon that angle, the point of reflection R, the height e of the point of reflection, and the downward angle. All these dependencies make for a somewhat messy set of fourth-order polynomial equations (which don't have a closed-form solution). However, it is possible to send rays out from the viewpoint that pass through successive (u, v) positions and determine where on the anamorphic image plane each ray leads. The resulting mapping can be interpolated in such a way that each pixel position in the anamorphic image is assigned an appropriate value from the original image.

If the anamorphic mapping obtained this way is represented as a modulation image, such an image reveals in a visual way some of the structure of the mapping. This can be seen in figure 6.23. Such a modulator image cannot be successfully saved in GIF format, owing to its need for more than 256 distinct pixel values, and lossy JPEG would lead to inaccuracies of the mapping. Consequently, (lossless) PNG format is the best method for saving the image.

An attractive feature of the modulator image approach is that the ray tracing can be done once and for all to obtain the modulator image. Then the modulator image can be used to create any number of anamorphic images (figure 6.24).

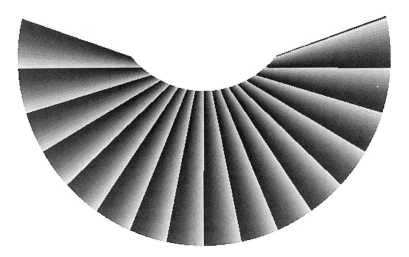

Figure 6.23
A cylinder anamorphic mapping represented as a modulator image.

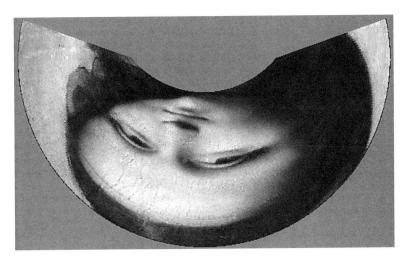

Figure 6.24
A cylinder anamorphosis of the Mona Lisa produced using a modulator image, in turn created by ray tracing.

More details on the geometry and algebra used to compute such a modulation image can be found in Tanimoto et al. (2000). An exercise the reader may wish to try is applying this mapping to an original image to obtain an anamorphic image.

6.16 Connections

Anamorphic images clearly have connections to art, mathematics, and computing. Let's look at some of these connections.

6.16.1 Modern-Day Art

Producing anamorphic images continues as an art form today. The graphic artist Kelly Houle has created cylinder anamorphoses, analogous to the slant anamorphosis of Schoen, in which a likeness of Lewis Carroll is hidden in a busy collage of Carrollabilia. (See her web site at http://www.kellyhoule.com.)

6.16.2 The Trompe-l'Oeil Effect

Slant anamorphosis is sometimes used to create an illusion of a three-dimensional structure on a flat surface, typically a wall, canvas, or pavement. This technique, called trompe-l'oeil (French for "fool the eye"), has been widely applied in the interiors of Renaissance and Baroque buildings. A fine example of trompe-l'oeil is the false cupola of the church of St. Ignatius in Rome. When the viewer enters the church and looks up and ahead at the ceiling, there appears to be a large dome over the far end of the room. The low lighting enhances the effect, and only upon walking forward and thus destroying the special geometric relationship of the viewpoint to the painting, is the illusion dispelled.

6.16.3 Ray Tracing in Computer Graphics

Anamorphic art depends upon geometric distortions of images brought about by mirrors or slanted surfaces. The detailed workings of light and surfaces are often studied by examining the paths of optical rays as they reflect. Even more elaborate distortions are possible if the rays are allowed to pass through transparent materials such as glass, plastic, or water. Then refraction plays an important role. Computer-image synthesis or computer graphics has typically used such techniques.

6.17 Tuning Parameters

When an artistic effect is desired, an experimental approach is often needed. This consists of an idea, the choice of an original image, an initial formula, and then a sequence of trial-and-error steps culminating in the achievement of the artistic goal. Let's consider an example motivated by the theme of global warming and cooling. These terms are ubiquitous in the news. Climate change is an important concern, and yet it is often difficult for many people to visualize these ideas.

To illustrate global warming, we'll start with an image of a subject that contains snow and ice, and we'll transform it into an image that appears to contain water, the result of melting the snow and ice. The starting image will be a picture of a glacier, in this case the Nisqually Glacier at Mt. Rainier National Park in Washington state. In order to give the effect of melting, we'll transform the image in two ways: (1) reflecting the upper part of the image so that there appears to be a lake at the bottom and (2) adding ripples to the lake to make it seem more liquid and realistic.

The formula for reflecting the upper part of the image is straightforward:

```
S1(x, if y<h/2 then ymax-y else y)
```

However, putting the ripples on the lake is more complicated because we have some questions to answer. What should be the frequency of the ripples? What should be their amplitude? Should these parameters be fixed or change in the image? If they should vary, then how? A good strategy in answering questions like these is to answer one question at a time, try some experiments, make some decisions, and move on to the next question. After answering these questions and performing several experiments, the following formula was found to meet the artistic objectives without becoming overly complicated.

```
S1(x, if y>h/2 then y else h-y+5*sin(y/(0.05*(h/2-y)))))
```

The result is shown in figure 6.25 (plate 21).

In the case of global cooling, we'll try to create a transformation that has the opposite effect: taking something considered to be normal and making it look frozen. In this case, we'll start with an image of the Earth, since that is something "global." The transformation should make the image look icy. This can be accomplished by warping the image in such a way that it seems to be refracting light in the same way that a blob of glass or ice would. We can achieve this by reusing the technique presented at the beginning of the chapter for the wavy Mona Lisa effect. However, now we'll apply it in both the horizontal and vertical directions. With some experimentation in adjusting the amplitudes and frequencies of the oscillations, we arrive at the following formula and the effect shown in figure 6.26 (plate 22).

Figure 6.25 (plate 21)
Simulated effect of global warming on the Nisqually Glacier at Mt. Rainier National Park.

Figure 6.26 (plate 22)
Simulated effect of global cooling on the Earth.

```
S1(x + 5*sin(x/5), y + 5*sin(y/5))
```

Neither the global warming nor the global cooling transformation is based on scientific simulation. They're both artistic. However, artists' illustrations of ideas can often help to clarify discussions of complex issues.

6.18 References

Leeman, F. 1975. *Hidden Images: Games of Perception, Anamorphic Art, and Illusion from the Renaissance to the Present*. New York: Harry N. Abrams.

McLoughlin Brothers (circa 1900). *The Magic Mirror or Wonderful Transformations*. Republished in 1979 as *The Magic Mirror: An Antique Optical Toy*. New York: Dover.

Tanimoto, S., King, J., and Rice, R. 2000. Learning Mathematics through image processing: Constructing cylindrical anamorphoses. *Proceedings of MSET 2000: International Conference on Mathematics/Science Education and Technology*, held at San Diego, CA Chesapeake VA: AACE, pp. 381–386.

6.19 Exercises

1. Devise an alternative to the MIM formula that will handle photographs with widths and/or heights greater than 256 without the striping artifacts. Hint: Provide a means to scale the inputs and outputs of the Red2 and Green2 functions.

2. Come up with another permutation modulator that's based upon a prime number other than 73 or the others demonstrated. Can you discover the inverse modulator? Apply the inverse to be sure you retain the original.

3. What happens when a 256×256 image is transformed using a modulator that is based on a number that is not relatively prime to 256? Is the transformation invertible?

4. A "perfect shuffle" of a deck of cards is achieved by splitting the deck in half and then alternately taking a card from the bottom of each pile and putting it on a new pile. In general, the perfect shuffle is a way to permute any finite sequence. The sequence

$$x_0, x_1, \ldots, x_{n-2}, x_{n-1}$$

becomes (for even values of n) the sequence

$$x_0, x_{n/2}, x_1, x_{n/2+1}, \ldots, x_{n/2-1}, x_{n-1}$$

For example, the list

$$[0, 1, 2, 3, 4, 5, 6, 7]$$

becomes

[0, 4, 1, 5, 2, 6, 3, 7]

a. Show the result of applying the perfect shuffle twice to the sequence [0, 1, 2, 3, 4, 5, 6, 7].

b. How many times does one have to repeat the perfect shuffle operation on a length-8 sequence to get back the original?

c. Suppose the rows of a 256×256 image constitute sequences to be shuffled. How many times must the perfect shuffle be applied to each row before the image comes back to the original?

d. Consider the group (see chapter 5) generated by two transformations: perfect shuffling of the rows of this image and perfect shuffling of the columns of this image. How many transformations are in this group?

e. Create a PixelMath formula for each of these two perfect shuffle transformations.

5. The ripple distortion that was applied to the Mona Lisa in figure 6.1 can be applied to affect both the horizontal and vertical directions. Try the following formula on an image of your choice. As we saw in figure 6.26 if applied to the Earth's image, one makes the Earth look like it's made out of blocks of ice. (Perhaps this is an antidote to global warming!)

```
Source1(x+5*(1+sin(x/5)),y+5*(1+sin(y/5)))
```

6. Find the equivalent angle in radians: (a) 180 degrees, (b) 90 degrees, (c) 360 degrees, (d) 45 degrees.

7. Use a polar coordinate formula to rotate the Mona Lisa image 180 degrees.

8. What happens when we apply the formula Source1(rho, theta*2) in polar mode? Why?

9. Make up a polar mode formula that creates an image that looks like the sun: bright yellow in a central circle and blue outside, but with the blue starting out bright and getting darker as the distance from the sun increases.

10. Try creating a slant anamorphic image (similar to Leonardo's example in figure 6.11 by sketching on a sheet of paper. To keep your viewpoint constant as you draw, tape to a table a folded piece of cardboard with a quarter-inch viewing hole in it so that the hole is about 1 inch above the table top. You might try to draw a cat, ghost, skeleton, or other Halloween-related figure.

11. As suggested in the text, create your own cylindrical mirror by wrapping a sheet of reflective Mylar-coated plastic around a can, a piece of pipe, or a cardboard tube. Use double-faced tape to secure the Mylar to the cylinder along the seam. Use care to avoid creasing the Mylar. Then place the cylindrical mirror in the middle of a blank sheet of paper and draw your own anamorphic image of (a) your initials, (b) a cat, (c) a human face.

12. Use the full-360 method to create your own cylindrical anamorphic image from a landscape or other scene. For best results, use an image that is quite a bit wider than it is tall.

7 Synthesizing Images

In this chapter we explore how to create new images without using a source image. In principle, any image can be constructed with a suitable PixelMath formula, but it might be a ridiculously long formula. Here we'll focus on a number of techniques that relate directly to basic mathematical forms.

The topic of synthesis is important in image processing for several reasons. First, many special effects use synthetic images with geometric forms. Some of these are stereograms, framing, stenciling, and cinematographic transitions. Another reason is that in image analysis and computer vision, an image may be described or interpreted automatically in terms of geometric primitives or artificial basis images. One of the issues we'll confront here is the fact that the realm of images and pixels is not quite the same as the pure world of mathematics; a pixel is not the same thing as a point, and a digital line or curve is different from a line or curve in geometry.

7.1 Rendering Points

Perhaps the most basic geometric object is the point. We think of it as a dimensionless, infinitesimally small entity that has no attributes other than a location—a place in some space, perhaps described by a pair (for the 2D case) of coordinates, perhaps with the form (x, y). We might use metaphors such as "pinpoint" to describe how small it is.

If we have a large image (that is, one with many, many pixels), one pixel may seem small enough in that image to play the role of a point. Yes, a pixel has a pair of coordinates associated with it, and thus it bears an important resemblance to a point. However, a pixel is typically understood to represent more than a single point. It is "responsible" for representing all the many scene or geometric points in its little square area of coverage. If there are even two points in that area with significant contributions of value (i.e., light or colors) to an image, then it is probably important that the pixel covering them include the contributions from them both and represent the color mixture.

Another problem we may have is that the coordinates of an arbitrary point, such as (5.8, 11.33), probably do not match perfectly with the coordinates of an image pixel, such as

(6, 11). Consequently we may end up with one of the following problems in a rendering: (1) failure to show the point at all, (2) positional inaccuracy, or (3) inappropriate color. We'll typically err on the side of some positional inaccuracy, assuming that it is better to convey an approximation of the correct information than to convey nothing at all.

To illustrate these issues, the following two formulas take a similar approach to rendering, but one works and the other doesn't.

```
if x=6 and y=11 then 255 else 0
```

```
if x=5.8 and y=11.33 then 255 else 0
```

The latter can be made to force its coordinates to nearby integer values with the `floor` function:

```
if x=floor(5.8) and y=floor(11.33) then 255 else 0
```

and this at least shows something. An approach that requires more effort but that seems to do a better job of accurately representing the point has each neighboring pixel light up in proportion to how close it is to the point.

```
256 * max(0,1-abs(x-5.8))*max(0,1-abs(y-11.33))
```

This formula first computes the horizontal distance between the center of the pixel (at x) and the point (at 5.8), and it subtracts this from 1. This number tells what fraction of the point's light should be rendered by the combination of this pixel and the closest one above or below it. If the distance was more than one pixel, then the pixel is out of the neighborhood of the point, and its share of the light (as well as that of any pixel above or below it) is zero, not something negative. It does something similar in the vertical direction to determine what fraction of the light should be rendered by this pixel and the closest one left or right. By multiplying these two fractions, it determines what fraction should be put into this particular pixel at (x, y). The result is a little blurrier than if the full 255 were put into a single pixel, but the result is arguably a more positionally accurate representation of the true location of the original point.

In this example, the division of light between the pixels with $x = 5$ and $x = 6$ is 20 percent and 80 percent. The division vertically is that the two pixels at $y = 11$ get 67 percent of the light and the two pixels at $y = 12$ get 33 percent of the light. The pixel at $(5, 11)$ gets about 13 percent of the light or a value of 34. The pixel at $(6, 11)$ gets about 55 percent of the light or a value of 137. The pixels at $(5, 12)$ and $(6, 12)$ get values of 16 and 67, respectively.

16	67
34	137

This sort of problem is avoided if the points to be displayed all have integer coordinates or if they can be faithfully transformed into a new set of points (perhaps by scaling, shifting, etc.), all of which have integer coordinates.

7.2 Drawing Lines

After the point, perhaps the most important geometric object is the line.

7.2.1 Traditional Linear Functions

The most familiar line formula is probably the linear equation $y = mx + b$, where m represents the slope of the line and b represents the height of the line where $x = 0$. Depending on the particular slope value, m, we may sometimes be able to translate this equation in a straightforward way into a PixelMath formula. Let's take the case $m = 1$. Then the equation is $y = x$. The pixels that lie on this line can be easily identified and colored black with the following formula.

```
if y=x then 0 else 220
```

The result is the expected diagonal line from the origin in the lower left going up and to the right, shown in figure 7.1. (We are using value 220 to produce a light gray background for these displays, to make them stand out from the page.)

Figure 7.1
The line $y = x$ rendered with `If y=x then 0 else 220`.

Figure 7.2
Result of applying `if y=3*x then 0 else 220`.

Now let's consider a different slope, say $m = 3$. The corresponding formula in this approach is the following, and its resulting image is shown in figure 7.2.

```
if y=3*x then 0 else 220
```

However, this image does not show a continuous line. It shows a dotted line. There is a black pixel in every third row. Furthermore, if we put in an intercept such as 0.1, there are no black pixels.

```
if y=3*x+0.1 then 0 else 220
```

Clearly if we multiply x, which must be an integer, by 3, we get another integer. But when we add 0.1 to that, it cannot be any integer. Since y is always an integer, the equation is never true for any pixel, and so every pixel ends up white. To be able to plot lines with general slopes and intercepts, we'll need a more robust method. For that, we'll take advantage of the notion of a half-plane.

7.2.2 Working with Half-Planes

A line in a two-dimensional plane divides the plane into two parts. Each of these parts is called a *half-plane*. A *closed half-plane* contains the dividing line, and an *open half-plane* contains all the points on one side, up to, but not including points on the line.

A *digital half-plane* consists of all the pixels (normally in some given image) whose centers are on one side of a given line. As with "real" half-planes, we can make a distinction between open and closed digital half-planes.

An image of an open half-plane for the line $y = 3x$ is produced with the formula

```
if y<3*x then 0 else 220
```

The pixels under the line are all black, as shown in figure 7.3a. By taking two overlapping half-planes constructed with closely spaced parallel lines, and on complementary sides of their lines, we can produce a rendering for the median line that passes between these two lines. Such a representation is shown in figure 7.3b.

```
if y>3*(x-1) and y<3*(x+1) then 0 else 220
```

7.2.3 Polar Formulation of a Line

One problem with using the standard line equation $y = mx + b$ for drawing lines is that vertical lines cannot be handled directly. Not only that, it is a little complicated to keep the thickness of lines uniform because the lines have different slopes.

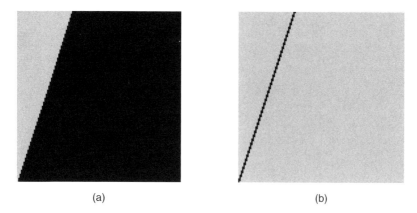

(a)   (b)

Figure 7.3
(a) Construction of a half-plane and (b) a rendering of a line as the intersection of two half-planes.

There is another representation of lines that is based on angles and the trigonometric functions sine and cosine, and this formulation makes it easy to handle vertical lines and to keep the thickness of lines uniform at different angles. This form of equation is $x \cos \omega + y \sin \omega = d$. Here ω represents the angle that a perpendicular to our line makes with the x-axis and d represents the distance of our line from the origin. (The origin is the lower-left corner of the image.) Here is a formula that gives us a line at 112.5 degrees ($5\pi/8$ radians) at a distance of 75 from the origin:

```
if floor(x*cos(pi/8)*y*sin(pi/8))=75 then 0 else 220
```

Note that the angle $\pi/8$ in the formula differs by $\pi/2$ from the angle of the line ($5\pi/8$), since the line is defined in terms of the angle of its perpendicular. We use the floor function here to adjust the value of the expression down to an integer, so that it has a chance to match the integer value 75 and produce a black pixel. Also note that this formula works in PixelMath's Cartesian mode or polar mode equally well. It doesn't actually rely on the polar-mode features of using rho, theta, or polar-mode access of source image pixels.

The half-plane method for drawing lines can be adapted for this polar line formulation. The following formula produces a line this way. Here the thickness has been set to 10.

```
if x*cos(pi/8)+y*sin(pi/8)>70 and
x*cos(pi/8)+y*sin(pi/8)<80
then 0 else 220
```

Besides being useful in drawing lines at any angle, this polar formulation of a line is important in an image analysis technique known as the Hough transform, described in a later chapter.

7.3 Nonlinear Functions of the Form $y = f(x)$

If we wish to plot a quadratic function such as $y = x^2 + 5$, then, as with lines, we need to make sure that suitable pixels will be chosen to represent the function visually, and that the pixels don't all miss the function by a hair. The use of inequalities or converting function values to integers by rounding are helpful techniques. This lets us have margins within which pixels can respond to the function. When using margins, we must decide whether to base the margins on variations along the vertical direction or the horizontal direction. We obtain variations along the vertical direction by adding to or subtracting from the value of the function. We obtain variations along the horizontal direction by using expressions such as $(x - 2)$ and $(x + 2)$ in place of x. Here is an example of plotting $y = x^2 + 5$ in a 128-by-128 image using margins of plus or minus one half based around x:

```
if y>sqr(x-0.5)+5 and y<sqr(x+0.5)+5 then 0 else 220
```

The plot based on this formula is shown in figure 7.4a. Enlarging the margins from 0.5 to 2 might be done to thicken the curve. The result is shown in figure 7.4b. However, there is an unintended defect that arises. At $x = 0$, the value of x with the negative margin is at $x = -2$, which when squared by the function gives the value 4. This value is equal to that produced at the positive margin where $x = 2$, and no y values in the column where $x = 0$ can be both greater than 4 and less than 4 at the same time. The result is that there aren't any black pixels at $x = 0$, which is bad for a plot of a function that should at least have the pixel at $(0, 5)$ colored black. This shows that one has to be careful about applying these methods involving margins; some functions will play tricks.

A plot based on vertical margins is created by the following formula and is shown in figure 7.5a.

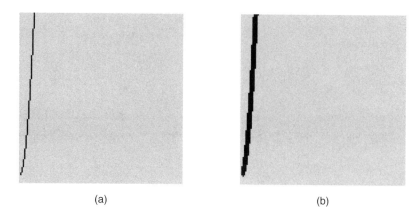

(a)   (b)

Figure 7.4
Plots of the function $y = x^2 + 5$ using (a) margins of ± 0.5 based on x and (b) margins of ± 2 based on x.

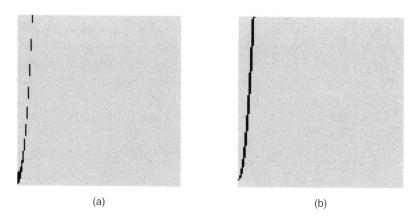

(a)   (b)

Figure 7.5
More plots of the function $y = x^2 + 5$. Here we use (a) margins of ± 5 based on y and (b) a combination of horizontal and vertical margins.

```
if y>sqr(x)+5-5 and y<sqr(x)+5+5 then 0 else 220
```

The problem with using any vertical margins for a quadratic is that no fixed margin is guaranteed to work to produce a connected set of pixels to represent the curve. With the margins of ± 5 used here, part of the curve near the origin looks okay, but it gets disconnected as soon as x gets to 7.

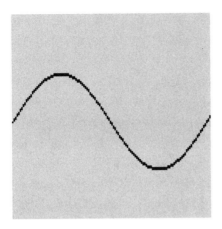

Figure 7.6
A plot of the function $y = 30\sin(x/20) + 60$.

One more thing we can try is using both kinds of margins. In this approach, we take the union of the sets of pixels colored black by each method independently. The following formula implements this for horizontal and vertical margins of ± 1.

```
if y>sqr(x-1)+5 and y<sqr(x+1)+5 or
y>sqr(x)+5-1 and y<sqr(x)+5+1
then 0 else 220
```

The result is shown in figure 7.5b.

Functions whose slopes are known to be bounded pose fewer problems. For example, using vertical margins of ± 1 does a reasonably good job of giving us a representation of the function $y = 30\sin(x/20) + 60$.

```
if y>30*sin(x/20)+60-1 and y<30*sin(x/20)+60+1 then 0 else 220
```

This plot can be seen in figure 7.6.

Figure 7.7
An antialiased representation of the line $y = 3x$.

7.3.1 Antialiasing of Lines and Curves

The various plots presented in figures 7.1–7.6 were done using 128-by-128 images, and they look "blocky." This appearance is an artifact of using such a low resolution that the eye can easily see that the pixels are square. The resulting image seems to contain spatial frequency components that were not in the original—here not intended to be part of an observer's perception. This is a form of frequency aliasing, which was introduced in chapter 2. There are two approaches to countering this (normally) undesirable effect. One is to increase the resolution, usually reducing the pixel size at the same time, so that the effects will appear smaller and less obtrusive. The other approach is to change some of the pixel values along abrupt brightness or color boundaries, to blur them slightly. This technique is known as *antialiasing*.

When drawing lines and curves as we have been doing so far in this chapter, one way to obtain antialiasing is to change the structure of formulas in such a way that we compute the distance of each pixel from the desired line or curve. Then we use the distance to determine the color (or brightness). The following formula does this for the line $y = 3x$, using the vertical distance. To obtain a reasonable brightness value, we multiply by 64.

```
abs(y - 3x)*64
```

Finally, to make the background consistent with that in the other illustrations, we cap the value at 220 using the min function. The result is shown in figure 7.7.

```
min(abs(y - 3x)*64,220)
```

The polar line formulation given earlier can also be used with antialiasing. A formula for it is this:

```
min(64*abs(x*cos(pi/8)+y*sin(pi/8)-75),220)
```

7.4 Other Planar Figures

Besides functions of the form $y = f(x)$, we often want to plot curves such as circles and ellipses. These are also described by equations; however, the form doesn't have y isolated on the left side of the equals sign. These more complicated functions are not really more complicated for PixelMath. For example, the following formula shows the pixels that lie (perfectly) on the circle centered at (64,64) having a radius 25.

```
if sqr(x)+sqr(y)=sqr(25) then 0 else 220
```

For an antialiased circle, we can use this:

```
min(abs(sqr(x-64)+sqr(y-64)-sqr(25)),220)
```

The results for these formulas are shown in figure 7.8

One application of the circles formula is in making a color-mixing image. The following formula produces a Venn diagram (figure 7.9—plate 23) that shows additive color mixing of red, green, and blue in the RGB system.

```
if sqr(x-w/2-RGB(0,w/5,-w/5))+sqr(y-h/2-rgb(-h/5,h/8,h/8))
 < sqr(w/4) then 255 else 0
```

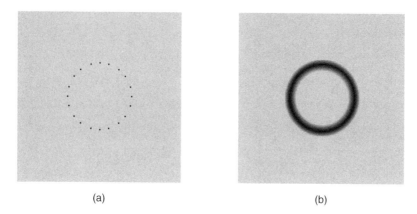

(a)   (b)

Figure 7.8
(a) A circles with pixels whose centers lie exactly on the circle and (b) an antialiased circle based on distance from the circle.

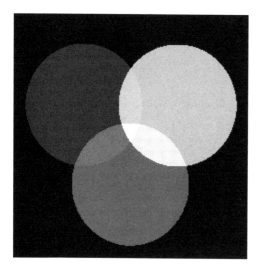

Figure 7.9 (plate 23)
A Venn diagram showing additive RGB color mixing produced using the circle formula.

This formula looks like it might draw only one circle, but it draws it differently for each of the red, green, and blue components of the image because of the way the RGB operator is used. It's used to adjust the horizontal and vertical center coordinates of the circle differently for each color. In the case of red, it shifts the circle down, relative to the others, by $h/5$, which is one-fifth the height of the image. Yet the green and blue circles are shifted up by $h/8$. The additive mixing is a by-product of the normal combination of R, G, and B values in each pixel.

Closely related to the circle is the ellipse. One formula for ellipses is $x^2/a + y^2/b = 1$. Let's apply this to create an "elliptical frame" image.

```
if sqr((2*x-w)/w)+sqr((2*y-h)/h) < 1 then 255 else 0
```

Here, we have set the center of the ellipse at the center of the image, and we have used w and h for its major and minor axes. (If $w \geq h$, then w is the major axis. Otherwise h is the major axis.) By using pixels of a source image instead of white, we get the image in an elliptical frame.

```
if sqr((2*x-w)/w)+sqr((2*y-h)/h) < 1 then s1(x,y) else 0
```

The result of applying this to the image of the Nisqually glacier on Mount Rainier is shown in figure 7.10.

7.5 Functions of Form $z = f(x,y)$

Let's now consider ways to synthesize images in which pixels all over the image are set to various values. A function that assigns a value to each point in a plane has the form $z = f(x, y)$.

7.5.1 Functions of the Plane

We have already seen some examples of such functions. First of all, every PixelMath formula does something like define a value (or three separate R, G, and B values) to each (x, y) location in the image. However, here our emphasis will be on more traditional mathematical functions, such as $z = x^2 + y^2$.

When we discussed gradient images in chapters 3 and 4, we worked with the simple formula

```
x
```

Figure 7.10
Result of framing Mount Rainier in an ellipse.

and this corresponds to $z = x$. If we think of z as a depth value, then we can think of the image as representing a 3D surface. The function $z = x$ represents a tilted (inclined) plane. Similarly, $z = y$ represents a tilted plane, but rotated 90 degrees. The function $z = x + y$ represents another tilted plane, one rotated around the z-axis by 45 degrees and pulled in $1/\sqrt{2}$ of the way to the origin.

An important type of function in image analysis is a product of two waves: $z = \alpha_x \sin(f_x x + \phi_x) * \alpha_y \sin(f_y y + \phi_y)$. Here α_x is the horizontal wave amplitude, f_x is the horizontal wave frequency, and ϕ_x is the horizontal wave phase, etc. Such a function can be plotted with a formula such as this, which has specific values for each parameter:

```
7*(1.1+sin(0.1*x + 2))*8*(1.1+sin(0.16*y + 1))
```

Interesting textural effects can be obtained by setting different frequency values for each of R, G, and B in each of the horizontal and vertical directions.

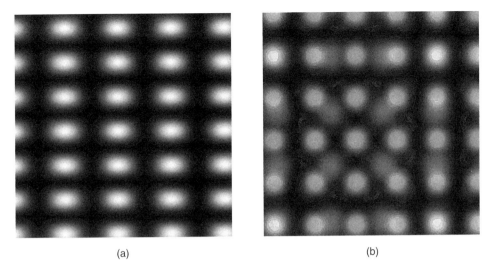

(a)   (b)

Figure 7.11 (plate 24)
Products of sinusoidal functions: (a) monochrome and (b) with different horizontal and vertical frequencies in each of R, G, and B.

```
7*(1.1+sin(RGB(0.1,0.13,0.16)*x))*
8*(1.1+sin(rgb(0.1,0.13,0.16)*y))
```

These images are shown in figure 7.11 (plate 24).

7.5.2 A Strange Image

A somewhat popular synthesized image results from taking a well-known mathematical function, the paraboloid $z = x^2 + y^2$, and "wrapping" its values modulo 256. Trying to account for the repeated patterns is an exercise in number theory. Let's call this image the *ringing paraboloid* (figure 7.12).

```
(sqr(x-w/2)+sqr(y-h/2)) mod 256
```

Another strange image results from exclusive-or'ing the corresponding bits from the x and y coordinates of each pixel. Since it is so highly dependent on the binary digital representation of coordinates, and since the image seems to have little value other than as a

Figure 7.12
The beautifully strange "ringing paraboloid" produced with `(sqr(x-w/2)+sqr(y-h/2)) mod 256`.

visual novelty, let's call it the "digital doodle" (figure 7.13). Our formula to produce it takes advantage of PixelMath's bitwise exclusive-or operator `bxor`.

```
x bxor y
```

7.6 Mountain Ranges and Distance Transforms

An important family of techniques both for image synthesis and image analysis is the computation of distance transforms. Here's a mathematical definition of the term. Let S be a set of points in a space (such as a 2D plane). The *distance transform $D(S)$* is a function that assigns to every point p in the space a non-negative real number d_p, so that d_p is the distance from p to the closest element of S.

Here are some consequences of this definition. If S is empty, then d_p is infinite for all p. If S consists of a single point s_0, then d_p is simply the distance from s_0 to p. If p is a point in the x-y plane, and we take $z = d_p$ to be the height of a surface, then the surface has the shape of a cone. The cone's vertex is at s. If S consists of a finite number of points, at least two, then d_p can be obtained as the minimum of the values of the various cones corresponding to elements of S at p. If p is an element of S, then d_p is zero.

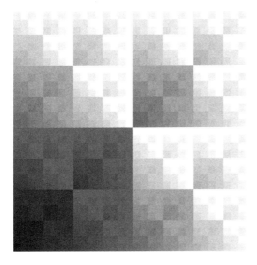

Figure 7.13
The digital doodle formed by exclusive-or'ing together the corresponding bits from each pixel's x and y coordinates.

Here is a formula that generates a digital representation of the distance transform of a single point, in this case the point in the center of an image:

```
sqrt(sqr(x-w/2)+sqr(y-h/2))
```

The resulting monochrome image is shown in figure 7.14. It's interesting to note that using PixelMath's polar mode, the same image is produced by the much simpler formula

```
rho
```

but this only works for the distance transform of this particular point, the pole of the polar system.

If we take the complement of this image, using the formula 255-s1(x,y), then the value is maximized at the vertex of the cone and we have a sort of mountain surface. If we do something similar for a collection of points rather than a single point, we get a sort of

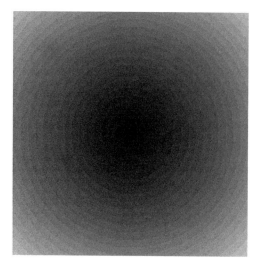

Figure 7.14
The distance transform of a point in the middle of the image.

Figure 7.15
Side view of a cylindrical trough.

mountain range. If we did it for a set of points on a circle, we would get a craterlike surface, and for any filled-in region of points, we would get a sort of mesa or plateau at whose edges downward slopes lead away.

One use for synthesized images with surfaces like these is in creating depth maps for stereograms. However, we might also wish to have surfaces that not only slant down but curve down.

7.7 Making Curved Surfaces

In addition to cones, it would be useful to have cylinders and spheres, particularly for use in making stereograms. Let's consider now how to produce a surface that rounds away as it goes up or down. The logical way to approach this is to take the formula for a circle and rotate it out of the image plane and into, say, the x-z plane. Now the equation is $x^2 + z^2 = r^2$. Here z is the depth of a point and r is the radius of the circle. If we compute these z values all over the image where it is possible, we should get a view of a cylinder. This is because at every y position we'll be looking at a similar side view of the circle. To compute z, we use a formula in which we have solved for z and put in a value of 250 for r. We'll also subtract $w/2$ from x in this formula, so that the cylinder appears in the center of the image. This will work well with an image having a width of at least 500, say 512.

```
sqrt(sqr(250)-sqr(x-w/2))
```

Note that we only see one side of the cylinder (figure 7.15. Since the greatest depths are in the middle, it seems that we are actually looking at a concave cylindrical trough. If we wanted the reverse, we could have subtracted each pixel value from 255.

Now let's make a spherical surface. For this we use the same idea as for the cylinder: we assume that the planar circle has been rotated up so that we see only a side view of it. However, instead of considering every y value the same way and using x as the distance from the center, which gave us the cylinder, we'll use a distance based on both x and y. Our equation is $x^2 + y^2 + z^2 = r^2$. Solving for z, we have, $z = \sqrt{(r^2 - x^2 - y^2)}$. A formula based on this equation is the following. Once again, we translate to the center of the image, so the ball will be in the middle.

```
sqrt(sqr(250)-sqr(x-w/2)-sqr(y-h/2))
```

We show this in a 512-by-512 image in figure 7.16.

7.8 Exercises

1. Digital half-planes and traditional mathematical (continuous) half-planes have similarities and differences.

a. Are all the points of a digital half-plane always within the corresponding continuous half-plane?

b. Are there any points of the continuous half-plane that are not part of the corresponding digital half-plane? Why or why not?

Figure 7.16
A spherical depression.

2. Create a formula that draws the line $y = x/5$ with black pixels.

3. Create a formula that draws the line $y = 5x$ with black pixels. Do whatever is necessary to make sure it is not a dotted line.

4. Use a single formula to plot two lines at the same time, one with a slope of 2 and the other with a slope of $-1/2$. Make both lines pass through the center of the image.

5. Use a slanted line to create an image from two source images so that the pixels on one side of the line come from source 1 and those on the other side of the line come from source 2.

6. Use a sinusoidal curve such as that used in figure 7.6 in the manner of the previous exercise to separate the pixels of two source images.

7. Use a single PixelMath formula to create an image in which two intersecting diagonal lines divide the image into four regions, two of which are filled with parts of two different photographs and the other two of which are filled with bright colors (or patterns of colors, if you wish to get fancy).

8. Create an image in a manner similar to that of the previous exercise, but instead of using straight lines to divide up the image, use a pair of intersecting sinusoidal curves (possibly with different frequencies, amplitudes, and phases).

9. Create a PixelMath formula to plot a centered red ellipse 128 pixels high and 384 pixels wide, on a black background, inside a 512-by-256 image, so that the ellipse has a thickness of approximately 10 pixels.

10. Change the formula that creates a spherical surface so that it creates an ellipsoidal surface.

11. Further modify your solution to the prevous exercise to produce an egg-shaped surface.

8 Stereograms

8.1 Introduction to Stereo

Stereo vision allows two-eyed creatures (and two-camera robots) to sense the distance of objects away from them. Perceiving the distance of objects is usually called depth perception. Stereo vision relies on the fact that two views of an object taken from viewpoints slightly separated but along parallel directions will have the object appear in slightly different image locations. The farther away the object, the more similar the views look. The closer the object is, the more pronounced the differences in the images.

Stereo is obviously important in allowing humans and other animals to see depth. However, stereo is also important in image processing. The mathematics and technology of stereo are important in two main categories of applications: (1) the creation of three-dimensional viewing experiences for humans and (2) depth perception by robots and computer-vision systems. Category 1 includes producing stereo photographs and other stereo imagery; three-dimensional television and movies; and immersive, virtual-reality experiences such as games, simulations, and virtual meeting places. Category 2 includes automatic construction of 3D computer models from images and video, as well as robot navigation.

In this chapter we consider first some historical examples of stereo photography. Then we study the mathematical basis of stereo vision. Finally, we explore the use of PixelMath for constructing autostereograms.

8.2 Traditional Stereo Pairs

At the end of the 1800s and in the early 1900s, photography was still relatively new. A particularly popular form of parlor entertainment was looking at stereo photographs using a special viewer. The stereo pictures were taken by professional photographers and published in sets of "slides" (cardboard-mounted pairs of photographs about 3 inches high and 6 inches wide). These stereograms were put into a viewer that made it easier to fuse the stereo images by using lenses that allowed the eyes to focus at a great distance even though the images were actually only about 12 inches from the user's face.

Figure 8.1
Stereo pair of photographs on a card. Taken by Carleton Watkins in the 1860s, this view shows Yosemite Falls
with horseback riders in the foreground.

It's not necessary, however, to use a viewer if you can relax your eyes and decouple
your focusing (flattening or unflattening your lenses to sharpen or blur the image) and your
verging (pointing your eyes inward or pointing them along parallel rays to align or misalign
the two eyes' separate views).

In figure 8.1 we see a pair of images photographed from left-eye and right-eye viewpoints. When viewed properly, this stereo pair gives a three-dimensional illusion. The
men and horses are distinctly closer to the viewer than the trees, and the cliffs are far
back.

8.2.1   How Two-View Stereograms Work

A two-view stereogram works by presenting, to each eye, a view of a scene that is geo-
metrically consistent with the actual views that might be projected to the eyes if the viewer
were actually looking at a real 3D scene.

The perception of depth by stereo vision is based on the fact that points in a scene at
different depths will have corresponding points on the two images that have different horizontal separation distances. If the two points in a corresponding pair are in the same
position in each image, the point appears to be at an infinite distance from the viewer. But
if there is a large displacement (or disparity) between the points, then the perceived point
appears to lie close in depth to the viewer. This can be readily experienced if you hold
a finger near your nose and then view it alternately with the left eye and the right eye.
The left eye sees the finger as over to its right whereas the right eye sees the finger as to
the left.

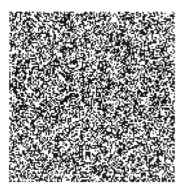 

Figure 8.2
Random-dot stereogram, in the style of Bela Julesz.

A good example of a simple two-view stereogram is a *random dot stereogram* as first created by Bela Julesz. Such a stereogram consists of two images of random black-and-white pixels. The two images are identical except that in one of them a square region has been moved to the right (or left) by a few pixels, with the cut being filled in on the left (or right), and on the right (or left) side, some old pixels are covered up by the ones that have moved over them. Such an example can be seen in figure 8.2 in which the pixels within a square region of the right image have been shifted 5 pixels to the right. If the stereogram is viewed with the left eye seeing the left image and the right eye seeing the right image, the central square region will appear to be behind the rest of the image. If it is viewed with the cross-eyed method, then the central region will appear to be in front of the background. The random-dot stereogram is an example of a kind of stereogram in which a hidden depth map (in figure 8.2 having the recessed square) seems to have nothing to do with the texture or image used to represent it (in figure 8.2 the random pattern). This is in contrast to the stereo-pair photographs such as those in figure 8.1, in which the depth map and the flat picture represent the same scene.

8.2.2   Creating Two-View Stereograms
In order to generate a synthetic two-view stereogram that represents a hidden depth map, what is needed is essentially a kind of 3D scene. Rather than deal with the full complexity of 3D objects, we can make a simple assumption: that each eye can see each point on the surface. This implies that the scene consists of a horizontally continuous (but not necessarily smooth) surface. This is because if there were any discontinuity in depth going from left to right, then that would be a sort of cliff, and one eye or the other would not be able to see some surface points in the depths of the cliff.

With this assumption, we can represent the scene using two image arrays: one for the depth of each surface point and one for the color of each surface point. We could generate a depth map this way using a paraboloid function, such as

```
(sqr(x - 128) + sqr(y - 128))/100
```

Then we could color the image in a somewhat arbitrary way, such as with a series of vertical stripes, as with the formula

```
if (x / 10) mod 2 = 1 then 255 else 0
```

Let's assume that the depth and color information have been given, and that the depth image is in Source1 and the color image is in Source2. We can generate a two-view stereogram either in two windows or in one window. The two-window method is easier to understand, and the two windows can be easily moved on the screen to accommodate people with eyes that are closer together or farther apart. The one-window method has the advantage that the two views are already aligned and ready to be printed as a single printout.

To compute the left view of the scene, we should use a formula such as

```
Source2(x + (20 / (Source1(x,y) + 1)), y)
```

and for the right-eye view, we simply negate the sign after the x.

```
Source2(x - (20 / (Source1(x,y) + 1)), y)
```

8.3 Autostereograms

Another type of stereogram is a single, large graphical pattern that may look like a jumble of texture, but that seems to have repeated patterns in it. Such images are sometimes called

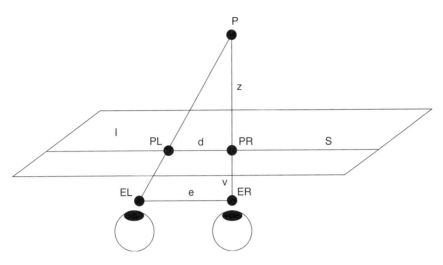

Figure 8.3
Stereogram geometry. The viewer's eyes are a distance v from the image plane. When the viewer fixes her left eye on point PL and her right eye on point PR and considers them to be the same point (because of coloration and stereo fusion), she perceives a surface point P at depth z behind the image plane.

single-view stereograms or Magic Eye pictures. Let's call them *autostereograms* to avoid infringing on any trademarks.

An autostereogram carries a hidden depth image or depth map. To see the depth map, the observer must carefully view the autostereogram in a way that allows the left and right eyes to settle on adjacent copies of the repeated pattern and to see them as one. It takes most people some practice before they are able to see depth maps in these stereograms. Someone with one bad eye might not be able to see the depth maps no matter how much they try. However, some people give up before they can see the depth maps because they don't know how to go about looking for the depth map. (We'll discuss how to view an autostereogram shortly.)

8.3.1   How Autostereograms Work
Figure 8.3 shows the geometric arrangement of eyes and image for single-view stereograms. To produce the stereo effect, the stereogram should provide pairs of corresponding points, such as PL and PR, and color each member of the pair with the same color so that the viewer can imagine them to be left-eye and right-eye views of the same point P. In order to make P seem to be z units in back of the image plane, the disparity d must be calculated proportionately. The proportion is based on the fact that triangles P-EL-ER and P-PL-PR are similar. This means that $d/z = e/(v+z)$. Thus $d = ez/(v+z)$.

8.3.2 How to View an Autostereogram

It's important to view the stereogram directly in front of you, with no tilting of the image in any direction. You need to be viewing the image along a line of sight that is almost exactly perpendicular to the image. And both your head and the stereogram need to be level so that there is no relative twisting or turning of the image in front of you. You must let your eyes relax so that you are aiming them at a point behind (through) the image. If you don't do this, you will never see the depth map. Once you succeed in looking "through" the image in this way, the next step is to "fuse" the separate perceived images from each of the two eyes. You do this by learning to control your "vergence," relaxing and slightly unrelaxing your eyes so that you make the images move left or right toward or away from each other. When you can control this apparent movement of the images seen by the left and right eyes, make the images line up, and at that point you will probably see the depth image. However, it's possible that you will make two nonadjacent copies of the pattern line up, in which case you will see a 3D pattern, but not the intended one; it will probably then be a sort of broken-up version of the proper depth map. In this case, relax your eyes again and try to fuse two adjacent copies (copies of the pattern that are actually right next to each other rather than separated by another copy or copies).

8.4 Making an Autostereogram: Basic Ideas

The basic procedure for creating an autostereogram involves three steps:

1. Create a depth map that will be hidden in the stereogram. A depth map is normally represented as a monochrome (grayscale) image in which the value 0 represents the closest possible depth value and 255 represents the most distant possible depth value.

2. Create a "carrier image" that will represent the textural element(s) to be repeated in order to hide the depth map.

3. Create a modulated and tiled pattern (the autostereogram itself) based upon the depth map and the carrier image.

8.4.1 Making a Depth Map

Your depth map should be the same dimensions as the final autostereogram. A good size is 512 pixels wide by 256 pixels high. Using Pixelmath, you can create a nice smooth surface with a formula such as

```
(sqr(x - 256) + sqr(y - 128)) / 100
```

8.4.2 Setting Up a Carrier Image

The carrier image should have lots of sharp edges or busy textures in it. Without these, the eyes will have a difficult time fusing the copies and seeing the depth map. However, the carrier image should not have periodicity in the horizontal direction; such periodicity is likely to interfere with the perception of the hidden depth map.

The carrier image does not need to be wider than about 256 pixels unless you are going to produce a very high-resolution stereogram. If you are going to view your autostereogram on the computer monitor, a width of 200 is probably sufficient. Basically, the width of the carrier image should match the distance between your eyes, measured in pixel widths. To use an existing image as a carrier image, go to the File menu, select Open, then choose an image. Alternatively, you can create your own carrier image.

A good way to create abstract carrier images is to take a photograph and manipulate the low-order bits of the pixels. Let's take a 256-by-256 color version of the Mona Lisa as our source for this. The following formula uses two "octaves" in an approximation of Perlin noise (described in chapter 9).

```
128*((S1(x,y) mod 4)+S1(x/8,y/8) mod 2)
```

Here `S1(x,y)` represents one of the two octaves and `S1(x/8,y/8)` represents the other; the latter gives us 1/64th of the original, blown up to fill the original space. The two together give us high-frequency and low-frequency components in our texture. Taking values modulo 2 and then multiplying by 128 gives us either 0 or 128 for each color component at the low frequency. Taking values modulo 4 allows maximum brightness in two out of the four cases, leading to frequent occurrences of bright, saturated colors and white. There are innumerable other ways to obtain carrier images for stereograms, but this approach often does well in terms of creating textures that facilitate fusing (perceiving) the final stereogram.

8.4.3 Determining Horizontal Displacements

Suppose that we wish to render a pixel in the autostereogram so that the perceived depth at that location is z. This means that the perceived 3D surface should appear z pixel widths in back of the image plane (the screen).

Then we must determine d, the horizontal displacement, which corresponds to z. We can use the following formula:

$$d = e * (z/(z+v))$$
$$= e * (1/(1 + (v/z)))$$

where d = horizontal displacement between current pixel and its corresponding one, e = interocular distance, z = desired depth of the surface point behind the image plane, and v = viewing distance (from eyes to screen).

8.4.4 Computing the Autostereogram

The computation of the stereogram works as follows. The Pixelmath image-processing engine begins computing the pixels in the destination buffer at the lower-left corner of the image [starting with the pixel at coordinates (0, 0); pixels in this vicinity are simply copied from the Source2 buffer, the carrier image. As pixels further to the right are computed, the left-to-right processing gets to a point where the pixels are simply copied from somewhere to the left. This somewhere is d pixels to the left. We call d the *displacement*. It varies from place to place and it depends on the value of the depth map [which is in the Source1(x,y) location]. The pixel to the left is a recently computed pixel. It is not in either Source1 or Source2, but in the destination buffer. So we get its value with an expression of the form dest(x - d, y), where d is actually given by another formula that computes the displacement.

The following sketch of a formula specifies the method that computes the autostereogram.

$$\text{dest}(x, y) = \begin{cases} \text{Source2}(x, y \bmod h2), & \text{if } x < d(x, y) \\ \text{dest}(x - d(x, y), y), & \text{otherwise} \end{cases}$$

The displacement values $d(x, y)$ can either be precomputed from the depth map before rendering the autostereogram or computed within the rendering formula. The PixelMath subexpression for $d(x, y)$ is 250*(1/(1+800/(100+Source1(x,y)))). This formula is an implementation of the formula for d given earlier. It uses 250 for e, with 800 for v, and 100+Source1(x,y) for z. (Adding 100 to the depth from the depth map not only prevents division by zero, it also tends to protect against ugliness in the stereogram, which can happen if d values approach 0.)

If we compute the d values within the rendering formula, the overall formula for Pixel-Math is the following:

```
if x<250*(1/(1+800/(100+source1(x, y))))
then source2(x,y mod h2)
else dest(x-250*(1/(1+800/(100+source1(x, y)))),y)
```

8.4.5 Putting the Steps Together

Let's now perform the steps we have described and create an autostereogram. The most convenient PixelMath interface for this construction is the Formula Page interface. In Window 1, we create our depth map. Let's expand a little on this step and make the size 600 by 300. The following formula creates a version of the paraboloid depth map that has a reasonably gradual change in depth, yet one that is still dramatic. It centers the shape slightly to the right of the center of the image in order to compensate in advance for a product of the left-to-right scanning process used in rendering the stereogram.

```
(sqr(x-9*w/16)+sqr(y-h/2))/200
```

Next we load the Mona Lisa image in Window 2 and create a carrier image in Window 3, using the formula already presented. We are using only the low-order bits of the Mona Lisa image for texture; she will not be recognizable anywhere in the stereogram. (Alternatively, we *could* use the Mona Lisa image itself as the carrier, and with some adjustments for scaling and positioning, she *would* be quite recognizable in the final stereogram.)

Before we render the stereogram, there is a small detail to attend to. PixelMath normally uses bilinear interpolation when it retrieves a pixel from an image and the coordinates are not integers. In typical image resampling tasks, this tends to make the result look better. However, it's not good for stereograms. The autostereogram rendering formula calls for accessing pixels in the destination image (i.e., stereogram pixels already computed) a distance d to the left of the current pixel, where d is computed from the depth, which can vary a great deal. Values of d will seldom be integers, and that means interpolation would happen a great deal if we did not turn it off. Interpolation would ruin a stereogram because it causes the sharp boundaries within the carrier image to become blurred as the pattern is copied, and it changes the colors of the right-side pixel of each left-right pair, causing the colors to not match perfectly any more. PixelMath2012 has a Python function for turning interpolation on or off. To use it, (1) open the Python window and evaluate any expression, which causes a Python interpreter instance to be activated; and (2) either enter `pmSetInterpolateSourcePixels(False)` in the input line at the bottom of the Python window and follow it by a carriage return, or in the Formula Page formula bar's formula area, enter `!pmSetInterpolateSourcePixels(False)` and then click on "Go!" for that formula bar. If you do not get an error message, the call was successful.

Finally, we render the stereogram in an image array having the same dimensions as the depth map: 600 pixels wide by 300 high. The rendering formula given earlier does the job.

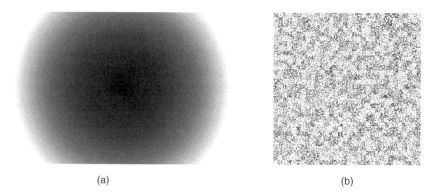

(a)   (b)

Figure 8.4
Setup for creating an autostereogram: (a) a depth map, and (b) a carrier image.

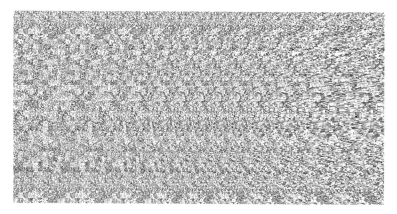

Figure 8.5 (plate 25)
Autostereogram resulting from the setup in figure 8.4.

The results of each step are shown in figures 8.4 and 8.5 (plate 25). The result needs to be viewed at a good magnification. If you maximize the window containing the stereogram and zoom in so that it fills your screen, you'll probably have an easier time fusing it than if it is small.

8.5   Challenges

Here are some things to think about when designing your stereogram. First, there is a relationship between a depth image and a suitable carrier image. If there is fine detail in the depth map to any extent, then the carrier image will also have to have a lot of detail.

And yet there should also be gross structure in the carrier image or it will be difficult for the viewer to lock onto the proper view.

8.5.1   Creating Depth Maps

There are lots of possible ways to create depth maps. You can simply create an image and use it as a depth map. This means you can draw one with a pen and then scan it. However, you can more easily create smooth surfaces that come forward and recede if you use PixelMath to create the depth image. A depth map should be represented by a monochrome image. Otherwise, different R, G, and B values at a pixel would make the depth ambiguous.

Besides creating one surface, it is possible to create depth maps that seem to contain multiple surfaces, with transparency in the closer ones. One approach is to make one surface have small holes in it that reveal another surface behind it. Another approach is to simulate transparency with a kind of close juxtaposition of different depth values in the image.

Another way to create a depth image is to scan a 3D object with a laser scanner, or use a stereo vision system to synthesize a depth map from two digital camera images. Such systems are gradually becoming more readily available.

8.5.2   Challenges Aligning Carrier and Depth Features

Another artistic challenge is to select carrier images that not only have a fine enough texture to render a depth map effectively, but also that use visual patterns or textures that themselves carry part of the artistic message of the stereogram. A carrier image can be abstract or it can be a photograph, possibly with some texture added to make it work better as a carrier.

If one is rendering a depth map of a face, it is possible to use a corresponding face image as the carrier and align one period of the carrier with the face in the depth map, thus painting the face in a natural way. Other periods of the carrier in the stereogram will probably not align with faces unless the depth map itself has a repeated pattern of faces. Coming up with depth maps and carrier images that can be aligned in this fashion is an art.

8.6   Further Discussion

In this chapter we've discussed two-image, side-by-side stereo pairs, and we've explored the construction of autostereograms in depth. There are a number of other ways of presenting stereo images, and it's interesting to compare them and to consider the future of stereo viewing.

In addition to viewers for stereo pairs on cards (such as that shown in figure 8.1, image pairs have commonly been provided by the Viewmaster company on cardboard disk frames holding seven pairs of transparencies. Using a special viewer that holds the disk, one can advance to the next stereo pair by depressing a lever.

Another means of presenting 3D images is using a lenticular grid; some souvenir postcards have a layer of lenticular clear plastic over the image so that the plastic bends the light to each eye in such a way that each eye sees a different image. Although precision is needed to interleave two or more images and register them with the lenticular plastic, the principles underlying the determination of views are essentially the same as for other stereo image display methods.

The *anaglyph* is a type of stereo image that has its two views printed in complementary colors, most commonly red and cyan. For a good example of an early anaglyph, see the online collection of stereo photos by Carleton Watkins at http://3dparks.wr.usgs.gov/yose /html/1s01355.html. To view the anaglyph, one uses colored glasses that have a red filter in front of one eye and a cyan filter in front of the other. A drawback of this method, if applied directly, is that one loses the normal use of color in rendering a scene. However, variations on the technique have been developed in which a color image and an anaglyph of the same scene are combined. When viewed without colored glasses, the image looks slightly fuzzy and with a little bit of red or cyan ghosting around the edges of objects, but otherwise normal. Then, when colored glasses are used, colors other than the specific red and cyan colors used in the anaglyph are attenuated and the viewer sees the depth and some of the natural color. The natural colors do not interfere with the depth perception because not only are they somewhat attenuated, they have been rendered without the sharp edges needed to convey depth by stereo.

A 3D movie such as James Cameron's *Avatar* is displayed in theaters using circularly polarized light. Each frame is polarized in one or the other of two ways. Polarized glasses for this kind of movie have filters for each eye that either block or transmit the two kinds of circularly polarized light. In this way, the left image always gets only to the left eye of the viewer and the right image gets to the right eye.

8.7 References

Julesz, B. 1971. *Foundations of Cyclopean Perception*. Chicago: University of Chicago Press.

National Gallery of Art. 2010. *Carleton Watkins: The Art of Perception*. Available online at http://www.nga.gov /exhibitions/watkinsbro.htm.

Priester, G., and Levine, G. 2004. *Eye Tricks: You Won't Believe Your Eyes*. London: Arcturus Publishing.

Wikipedia. 2010. Circularly Polarized Light. http://en.wikipedia.org/wiki/Circular_polarization.

8.8 Exercises

1. Binocular stereo is just one of several mechanisms that humans and other animals have for perceiving depth. Try closing one eye and walking around, going up to objects and touching them. To what extent are you able to judge distances to objects? How do you account for your ability to perceive depth even though one eye is closed?

2. Refer to the diagram in figure 8.3. Suppose that we wish to create an image in which some perceived point P is z pixel widths behind the screen, the eyes are v pixel widths from the screen, and their centers are e pixel widths apart. If e is 200, v is 500, and z is 800, then what should be the distance d between the two similarly colored pixels used to represent P?

3. When creating an autostereogram, one can either begin with a depth image provided by special software (e.g., a geometric modeling program) or create one from scratch. Make up your own formula that creates a "bump" in the middle of a new depth-map image. Try to make your bump rounded, for example, hemispherical.

4. Using PixelMath, create your own random-dot stereogram similar to that in figure 8.2, but make the "hole" round instead of square. Explain where your random dots came from and the formulas you used.

5. Create a new depth map that consists of a sum of three circular 2D Gaussian surfaces, each having a different center $(\bar{x}, \bar{y})$, amplitude A, and standard deviation σ. A circular 2D Gaussian surface is defined by

$$G_{\bar{x},\bar{y},\sigma}(x, y) = Ae^{-((x-\bar{x})^2 + (y-\bar{y})^2)/\sigma^2}$$

After you have your depth image, use the same or a similar carrier image as that used with the paraboloid stereogram example in section 8.4.2 to create your own autostereogram of the new depth map. An example formula for creating a single circular 2D Gaussian surface is the following:

```
200*pow(e,-(sqr(x-64)+sqr(y-64))/400)
```

This formula specifies an amplitude of 200, a center located at (64, 64), and a standard deviation of 20. The square of the standard deviation, known as the variance, in this case is 400.

6. Create a new carrier image by using the method in section 8.4.2, but with a photograph that you choose, other than the Mona Lisa. Is there enough texture and contrast in your carrier image to serve the purpose well?

7. Create a stereogram in which the Mona Lisa figures in both the carrier image and the depth image.

a. Create a two-level depth image based on the Mona Lisa. One way to do this is the following. Using an image-oriented drawing program such as Microsoft Paint, first make a monochrome version of the Mona Lisa and then manually trace the outline of her head and

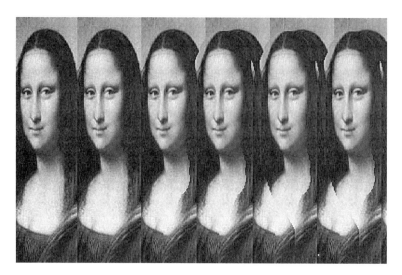

Figure 8.6
Stereogram to be constructed in exercise 7.

body using the paintbrush tool and the color white. This defines two regions: the figure and the background. Color the figure white and the background black.

b. Using PixelMath's Formula Page interface, work out formulas to render the stereogram using the Mona Lisa as the carrier and using the special depth map. Your final stereogram should look something like that shown in figure 8.6.

8. Create your own stereogram using your own depth map and a carrier image of your own choosing or construction. Redo your stereogram a few times to make the effect as easy to see and as striking as you can.

9 Images Within Images

This chapter describes four different forms of images within images: (1) steganography, in which one image is intentionally concealed within another; (2) watermarking, in which a watermark image is embedded unobtrusively but robustly within an image; (3) photomosaics, in which many small images combine to form one large, emergent image; and (4) fractals, in which forms, often identical or statistically similar, can be seen at multiple scales.

9.1 What Is Steganography?

"Steganography" means "covered writing" and is based on two Greek words (*steganos* and *graphē*). Covered writing, or hidden writing, refers to messages that are written so that most people who see the media on which the messages are written do not notice that the hidden message exists.

An early example of steganography was employed in ancient times to transmit a short message to someone in another town. The head of a messenger was shaved; the message was tattooed on his head; his hair was allowed to grow back; he traveled to the next town, passing the guards; upon reaching the recipient of the message, he shaved his head again, and the message was revealed. Another kind of steganography involves writing with invisible ink. Milk, vinegar, and urine can each be used as an invisible ink that darkens when heated.

Some forms of steganography are like codes. For example, the following text carries a secret message within it.

Good old Tom. Incomparable talent.

Taking the first letter of each word spells out the message "Got it." Unlike a code, however, each letter of the message is not so much changed as hidden by being distributed within the "carrier" text.

Here is an example of a message hidden with a technique involving extra spaces:

```
Terminate each line with a carriage  return in
order  to register with the  base of the form.
```

Taking only those words preceded by a pair of spaces, we get "return to base."

Another steganographic method is the use of microdots. During World War II, German messengers sent letters in which the periods sometimes contained detailed images in miniature. Unless someone knew what to look for, these letters looked like ordinary correspondence.

9.2 Discovering Information by Stretching Contrast

A basic method of hiding a message in an image is essentially by writing very faintly onto an image. This means making slight changes in the values of certain pixels. If the background color of the image in the area where the writing is located does not change too much, it may be possible to read the message by amplifying the differences in pixel values. This can often be done by simply multiplying all the pixel values with some constant such as 5. This might not work, however, if the resulting values "saturate" (that is, if they reach the maximum value of 255).

You can try out this method of revealing hidden messages by loading a copy of the image having the file name `mystery.gif`. This is a monochrome image of Mt. Rainier taken from the University of Washington campus. In the trees directly below the mountain is a dark area. If this entire dark area is selected and all the values are multiplied by 5, the message should be quite clear.

Upon close inspection of this image, you can see that the pixels that represent the message generally have slightly brighter values than those of the surrounding pixels, prior to the multiplication step. Enhancing brightness and contrast by multiplying the pixel values by a small constant is one of the simplest and often effective kinds of enhancement.

There is another message hidden in the snow of Mt. Rainier. Can you find it? As a hint, note that it uses a "key value" that is an odd number, and none of the other pixels in the vicinity have odd values. If you determine what the key value is for the message in the snow, the next problem is to enhance the contrast so that you can easily read the message. Let's say the key value is represented by the symbol k. You can stretch the contrast around the value k by first subtracting $k - 1$ from all the pixels in the vicinity and then multiplying the result by 128. This will have the effect of changing all message pixels into pixels having a value $128 \cdot (k - (k - 1))$ which is the same as $128 \cdot 1$ or just 128. A pixel with RGB $= (128, 128, 128)$ has the color neutral gray. Any nonmessage pixel in the area will have a value either less than k or greater than k. If it has a value less than k, then subtracting $k - 1$ from it will give zero because PixelMath converts negative values to 0 before storing them in pixels. Multiplying the zero by 128 gives zero again. The pixel ends up with RGB $= (0, 0, 0)$, which is black. If the pixel has a value greater than k, say $k + a$ for $a \geq 1$, then $128 \cdot (k + a - (k - 1))$ equals $128 \cdot (a + 1)$. Since a is at least 1, we know that $a + 1$ is at least 2. That means $128 \cdot (a + 1)$ is at least 256. But any pixel given a value of 256 saturates at 255. Such a pixel gets RGB = (255, 255, 255), which is white. So the message shows up as gray pixels on a background of black pixels and white pixels.

There is yet another secret message hiding in the pond of the fountain near the bottom of the image. You can use the contrast stretching technique just described to find out what is underwater near the end of the fishing pole.

9.3 Hiding Messages Using Key Values

Let's explore some ways to write messages on images in such a way that the messages are difficult or impossible to see under normal viewing conditions.

The method that was used to prepare the hidden messages in the snow and in the pond of the `mystery.gif` image was the following: (1) subtract 1 from each odd pixel value to make it even; (2) find a region of fairly uniform brightness in which to hide a message; (3) select a key value which which to write the image; it should be close to the values in the image where the message will be put, and it should be an odd value, rather than even; (4) write the message into the selected area by setting each message pixel equal to the key value.

This method has a significant disadvantage. Many images do not have large regions of uniform color. Rather, they tend to have slight gradients that are due to lighting variations. Thus it is difficult to really hide the message well because it will tend to stand out a little bit from the background in some places.

Another method is to let the message pixels have different values, depending on the brightness or color of the original image, so that the message can blend in with the background as the background changes. In this case, rather than using a single key value to distinguish the message pixels from the others, multiple key values are needed, or some other criterion is needed. One way to do this is to make all odd values key values. Here is how we hide a message with this method.

9.3.1 The Method of Least Significant Bits

This method consists of using the least significant bit of each pixel value to encode the message. First, we prepare a separate image with the message, using white letters on a black background. This image should be the same size as the one in which the message will be hidden. Next, we divide each pixel value by 255 in the message image. This will make all the message pixels have the value 1 whereas the others will have the value 0. The image will look black since both 0 and 1 are very small values when considered within the 0–255 range.

Next, we prepare the background image by making all the pixels have even values, just as for the previous method. By dividing each pixel value by 2 and then doing another transformation that multiplies each of the resulting values by 2, the final pixels will all have even values. Better yet, we apply the following formula to make the pixels all even in a single step:

```
   2 * Floor(Source1(x,y)/2)
```

Here, the floor function computes the largest integer that is less than or equal to its argument. For example, Floor(2.5) = 2 and Floor(7) = 7.

Now we add the (darkened) message image to the (even-pixel) background image. This can be done by making the background image be Source1, making the message image be Source2, and putting the result in a Destination that has the same dimensions. The sum image now contains the hidden message.

In order to extract the hidden message from this image, we use the following formula.

```
   If (Source1(x,y) mod 2 = 1) then 255 else 0
```

The method of least significant bits is straightforward and it can be quite effective in many situations. However, it has two disadvantages. First, lots of people know about it, so they might try decoding it with something like the formula given here, and then they will discover your secret. Second, when you save your image containing the hidden message and use compression, such as JPEG compression, the message may be corrupted so much that it will be unrecognizable when the decoding is later performed.

The first disadvantage can be partially overcome by using the method in conjunction with a scrambling technique. By scrambling the pixels of the message before they are put into the background image, someone who tries to decode the message will see only a scramble of pixels and possibly conclude that they are on the wrong track. We'll discuss scrambling methods a bit later.

The second disadvantage is more difficult to overcome. First, when you save your image, you need to make sure that the pixel values are not corrupted. Choosing the GIF of PNG format rather than JPEG is a good start. However, the GIF format can only write out the pixel values correctly if there are no more than 256 distinct colors in your image. If you are using a monochrome image, then it will have no more than 256 values, and so the GIF method should save all the values correctly. If you are using a color background image, you can preprocess the image to reduce the number of distinct colors to no more than 128. Then, when you add the message image, you will have no more than 256 colors.

9.3.2 Limiting the Number of Colors in an Image
Here is one way to reduce the number of colors in an image to 128 or fewer. The idea will be to turn off some of the less significant bits of each pixel component, so that we end up with

only 7 bits in each pixel that can have nonzero values. This will usually cause a significant distortion in the colors, since 17 of the 24 bits in each pixel will become nonfunctional. First, we decide how to allot the 7 bits to the three color components. We'll give 3 bits to Red, 2 to Green, and 2 to Blue. Red seems to be perceptually more significant than Green or Blue, and that is why we give it the extra bit.

For this operation, the Source1 and Destination can be set to the same image. First, enable only red and apply the formula

```
32 * Floor(Red1(x,y)/32)
```

This divides the red component of each pixel by 32, throws away the fractional part, and multiplies what's left by 32. The effect is to convert the red value to the largest multiple of 32 that is smaller than or equal to the old red value.

Next, enable only green and apply the formula

```
64 * Floor(Green1(x,y)/64)
```

Finally, enable only blue and apply the formula

```
64 * Floor(Blue1(x,y)/64)
```

After all these steps have been performed, your image will have no more than 128 distinct colors in it. It might have a lot fewer colors in it. If so, this method might not be the best one for you. You might explore a way to turn off a different set of 17 bits in each pixel, for example.

9.3.3 Directly Manipulating Bits

There are some facilities in PixelMath for dealing directly with the bits of an image's pixels. In order to use these, it's important to remember that each pixel component (such as the red component) is represented as 1 byte, and 1 byte is 8 bits. Each bit corresponds to a power of 2: 1, 2, 4, 8, 16, 32, 64, or 128.

The PixelMath operators for manipulating bits are "bitwise" versions of the logical operators AND, OR, and XOR. The bitwise versions are named BAND, BOR, and BXOR. Whereas AND, OR, and XOR operate on Boolean values (values that are true or false), the bitwise versions operate on numbers. They treat each number as a sequence of bits, and they perform the logical operation on each pair of corresponding bits. For example, let's consider the expression 5 BOR 9. The 5 is represented in binary as 101, and the 9 is represented as 1001. To make both binary numbers the same length, we pad the shorter one with leading zeros. So we have $5 = 0101_2$ and $9 = 1001_2$. Scanning each binary number from the left, we take 0 OR 1 and get 1; then 1 OR 0 gives 1; then 0 OR 0 gives 0; and finally 1 OR 1 gives 1. The resulting binary number is therefore 1101_2, which is equal to 13.

Suppose we wanted to force the most significant bit of each color component of every pixel to be 0, and we didn't want to change any of the other bits in the image. We could do that by doing a bitwise AND operation (with BAND) between each component and the number whose binary representation is 01111111. This number is equal to 127. The following formula does it.

```
Source1(x,y) BAND 127
```

9.4 Hiding Messages Using Bitwise Exclusive-OR

Note that by using the bitwise exclusive-OR operation we can hide a message in the least significant bits of pixels without having to first make all the background pixels even. All we need to do is prepare our message image as a binary image (message pixels have a value 1 and all others have a value 0), and then, with the original image as Source1 and the message image as Source2, create a new Destination and apply the formula

```
Source1(x,y) BXOR Source2(x,y)
```

Revealing the message will be easy, provided that the original background image is still available. Simply make Source1 be the image with the hidden message, make Source2 be the original background image, and apply the formula

```
(Source1(x,y) BXOR Source2(x,y)) * 255
```

The message image does not actually have to be a binary image. It can be any image at all. However, the "hidden" version may not actually be well hidden if the values of the message image pixels are much bigger than 4 or 5. Also, multiplication by 255 will not be appropriate for other than binary images.

9.5 Hiding and Finding Messages Using Masks

In this method of hiding messages, certain pixels of the background image will be used for the message. These pixels can be sparsely distributed, and they can be arranged either in a regular way or in a seemingly random way.

To reveal a message that is hidden in this manner, we multiply the image with a mask image. This essentially selects the key pixels, lifting them out of the background so that they are easily visible. If desired, these pixels can then be brought together by shrinking the image or by making each of these pixels "dilate" into a more visible blob.

9.5.1 Hiding with a Mask

Let's assume the message has been written using white on black in a 64-by-64 image. We'll hide it in an image of size 256-by-256. First, we spread out the pixels of the message to create a 256-by-256 version of it. To do this, create a new 256-by-256 image, make it the Destination, and make the message image be Source1. Then apply the formula

```
if (x mod 4 + y mod 4 = 0) then Source1(x/4,y/4) else 0
```

What this does is to place a message pixel at each place where x and y are both multiples of 4 in the destination image. All other pixels are black.

Now let's combine the message with the background image. We do this by replacing only those background pixels that have x and y coordinates that are multiples of 4 by the message pixels. Assume the background image is Source1, the (blown-up) message image is Source2, and the Destination is a new 256-by-256 image. Then the following formula will perform the combination.

```
if (x mod 4 + y mod 4 = 0) then Source1(x,y) else Source2(x,y)
```

9.5.2 Revealing with a Mask
To reveal the image, we apply the formula

```
if ((x mod 4)+(y mod 4) = 0) then Source1(x,y) else 0
```

This turns off all the nonmessage pixels. To make the message easier to read, we can shrink this image to retrieve the original message by making this image the Source1 and setting up a new 64-by-64 image in the Destination. Then we apply the formula

```
Source1(4*x, 4*y)
```

This last formula could have been applied directly to the image in which the message is hidden. It would obtain the message without the separate masking step. However, if the mask pattern were not such a regular one, then we would need to apply the masking separately, and instead of shrinking with this last formula, we would need to do something else to enhance the message.

9.5.3 Creating a Random Mask
Imagine taking out a sheet of white paper and sprinkling ground pepper around on it. The grains of pepper would form a random pattern of points on the page. A random pattern like that would make a nice mask for hiding a message.

There are several ways to create such a mask using the computer. One is to generate random numbers using a special computer program and then have the program select black or white on the basis of those numbers.

Another way is to take some natural process that has a random character (e.g., tossing dice, sprinkling pepper) and record that in an image. Taking a digital photo of a sheet of paper with pepper grains on it would fit right in, but you can probably get a decently random mask without going to this much trouble.

Take almost any digital photo of an outdoor scene. The photo should not be over- or underexposed. Load that into PixelMath. The least significant bit of each pixel component is likely to be fairly random, owing to the minute fluctuations of light in the photo. If we were to consider all pixels whose red component is an odd number to be mask pixels, we would get a random mask, but it would probably be too dense with pixels. It would be better to have about one out of each 16 pixels, on the average, in the mask. To do this, we could take pixels so that four of its low-order (i.e., not very significant) bits have prescribed values, such as 0, 0, 0, and 0, or perhaps better, 0, 1, 0, and 1. Such a mask can be computed from the source image using a transformation like the following, which uses two bits from the red component and one each from the green and blue components:

```
If ((Red1(x,y) mod 4 = 2) and (Green1(x,y) mod 2 = 0) and
(Blue1(x,y) mod 2 = 1)) then 255 else 0
```

Assuming that these low-order bits are randomly distributed with a mean 0.5, then about one in 16 of the pixels should be set to white in the mask.

9.5.4 Encoding with a Random Mask
Let's assume that we have a 32-by-32 message to encode in a 256-by-256 image using a random mask. Assume the message is in Source1, the random mask is in Source2, and the background image is in Destination. Then the following formula will use the mask to insert copies of most of the message pixels into the background image.

```
If (Source2(x,y)=255) then Source1(x/8,y/8) else Dest(x,y)
```

9.5.5 Decoding with a Random Mask
To reveal the message from this encoding, make the image containing the message be Source1 and make the mask be Source2. In Destination, set up a new image of the same size as the mask and apply the formula

```
If (Source2(x,y)=0) then 0 else Source1(x,y)
```

The message pixels have now been selected. To thicken them, apply the following transformation without changing any of the source or destination settings.

```
Dest(x,y)+Dest(x+1,y)+Dest(x,y+1)+Dest(x+1,y+1)
```

This formula can then be applied again to dilate the message pixels even more.

9.6 Scrambling and Unscrambling

Although the method of hiding a message in the least significant bits of an image is well known and therefore not ideal for keeping secrets, it can be combined with other transformations so that it's not so obvious. For example, the pixels of the message can be rearranged with a permutation of the pixels, so that even if the least significant bits are visualized, they will not seem to form a coherent message.

One way to scramble the pixels of an image is to apply modular arithmetic to their coordinates as explained in chapter 5. Another way to scramble the pixels is to use a suitable modulator image of the sort described in chapter 6. The modulator image should represent a permutation transformation. Let's consider how to come up with a suitable modulator image.

9.6.1 Creating Random Permutations

The simplest permutation is the identity permutation. It doesn't change the ordering of the pixels in an image at all. A modulator image representing this permutation is actually a good starting point for us because we'll be able to make a more interesting permutation by altering this modulator image. In order to perform permutations of 256-by-256 images, we'll use modulator images that encode the (x, y) coordinates of source pixels using the Red byte (for x) and the Green byte (for y) at each pixel.

To construct an identity permutation modulator image, create a new 256-by-256 image, make it the Destination, and then do the following: enable only Red, and apply the formula

```
x
```

and then enable only Green and apply the formula

```
y
```

You now have a modulator image for the identity transformation.

To make a more interesting permutation matrix out of this one, we can apply any combinations of permutations to the pixels of this image. Although we could easily do things like modular arithmetic on pixels to scramble things, the resulting permutations will still be somewhat regular. It would be nice if we could create more random permutations.

Here is a way to use any scanned image to create a permutation. Different scanned images will tend to produce different permutations. We will assume that the scanned image, like the permutation matrix and other images in this section, is 256 by 256.

The idea here will be to use bits from the pixels of the scanned image to determine whether or not each of two corresponding pixels in the modulator image swaps with a partner. Suppose that the identity modulator image is Source1, that the scanned image is Source2, and a blank 256-by-256 image is in Destination. Then the following formula applies the first step of the method.

```
if (Red2(x band (255-1),y) mod 2 = 1) then
if x mod 2 = 0 then Source1(x + 1, y) else Source1(x - 1, y)
else Source1(x, y)
```

After this transformation has been applied, some of the permutation matrix elements have changed places with a neighbor. We need to perform more steps with longer distance swaps in order to get general permutations. Here is the next step:

```
if (Red2(x band (255-2),y) mod 4 > 1) then
if x mod 4 < 2 then Source1(x + 2, y) else Source1(x - 2,y)
else Source1(x, y)
```

In the third step, some pixels change places with partners that are 4 pixels to the left or right.

```
if (Red2(x band (255-4),y) mod 8 > 3) then
if x mod 8 < 4 then Source1(x + 4, y) else Source1(x - 4,y)
else Source1(x, y)
```

There should be five more transformations. In each one, the distance between partners is double that of the previous step. Also, we keep checking the next bit of the red component of each pixel to decide whether or not to swap. There is no particular reason to use the red component of the scanned image. The green or blue can be expected to do just as well. Note also that it is important to make each resulting image the Source1 image for the next step, and to set the Destination either to a new image or to the old Source1 image in order to reuse it. In the eighth and final step of the horizontal swaps, some pixels swap with partners that are 2^7 pixels away. After all eight steps, a given pixel could end up anywhere else in the same row, depending on the values of various bits in the red components of scanned image pixels. Now, to make the permutation really general, we need to perform eight more similar steps, but with movement in the vertical direction and using the green component of the scanned image for the decisions.

After all sixteen of these steps have been performed, we have a new modulator image that represents a permutation of pixels that is dependent on the values of the scanned image. Now if the scanned image's red and green components were 0 everywhere, then none of the pixels in the modulator image would ever have swapped, and the resulting permutation image would still be the identity. But with a more natural scanned image, the resulting permutation can be expected to seem random.

The permutation represented by this image can be used to scramble the pixels of an image in a random yet invertible way. To perform the unscrambling, an inverse permutation is required. A modulator image representing the inverse permutation can be created by applying the same transformations used to make the forward permutation, but in the reverse order.

While using the modulator image to permute the pixels of a message all at once, the pixels could also be scrambled by applying the same sequence of steps as that used to create the permutation modulator. Although this might be more painstaking, if performed on more than one image, than doing the full sequence on only the modulator image and then reusing it, there is a possible benefit to running the full sequence on each image: you can see what the partially scrambled image looks like after each step. The image would first get slightly scrambled, then more scrambled, etc. It might be even more fun to unscramble an image gradually, so that the image seems to "develop" before your eyes.

Figure 9.1 illustrates one step of this kind of pixel permutation. A 256-by-256 image of the Mona Lisa is processed with the formulas below. The key image used to determine the permutation has been taken here to be the same as the source image, but it could be any

(a)   (b)

Figure 9.1
One step of (a) horizontal permutation and one step of (b) vertical permutation using an exchange distance of 128 and the seventh bit of each (a) red component and (b) green component.

image. The first formula uses the red pixel values of the key image to decide whether or not to make a horizontal pixel exchange with another pixel 128 units apart.

```
if (Red2(x band 127,y) band 128 > 0) then Source1(x bxor 128,y)
else Source1(x,y)
```

Here the original Mona image is Source1 and the key image (which happens to be the same Mona in this case) is Source2. The expression x band 127 has the effect of turning off bit 7 of the x value. This will cause any pixel in the right side of the image (having $x > 127$) to swap or not on the basis of the key image pixel in the corresponding position on the left side of the image. Let's call this pixel the decision pixel. It takes two pixels to make a swap, and they both need to decide to swap together, and so they both make their decision on the basis of the same decision pixel. The decision pixel is in the same position as the left-hand pixel of the swapping pair. One particular bit of a decision pixel is used: the red component's bit 7 (counting from 0, with bit 0 being least significant). Bit 7 is represented by the number 128 (which is 2^7). The bitwise AND operation "band" serves here to extract bit 7 from the red component of the decision pixel. That completes the explanation of the condition after the "if" in the formula. Then there are two Source1 expressions. The first one specifies the value to use in case of a swap. The second one is an identity, leaving the pixel unchanged. The swap works by figuring out the x-coordinate of the other pixel and taking its value. To obtain the other pixel's x coordinate, we simply change bit 7 of the current x coordinate. That either adds or subtracts 128, depending upon whether the pixel is the left or the right pixel of the swapping pair. Changing bit 7 is accomplished using the bitwise exclusive-OR operation with the value 128, which is 10000000 in base 2.

Now here's the second formula:

```
if (Green2(x,y band 127) band 128 > 0) then Source1(x,y bxor 128) else
Source1(x,y)
```

This formula uses a bit of each green component to make a similar decision, but for a vertical swap.

In later chapters we'll introduce programming that can be used to automate the sequence of steps we have just described. Then it will be easy to come up with new permutation images or to apply the gradual scrambling and unscrambling of images. In particular, chapter 13 contains an example program that performs a scrambling operation similar to that described here.

9.7 Watermarks

In papermaking, a watermark is a pattern intentionally created in the paper during manufacturing. The pattern is typically created by arranging for some parts of the paper to be thinner than others, typically by placing extra wires in the screen used to hold the pulp while the paper is setting. High-quality bond paper sometimes carries a watermark showing its brand name. Some U.S. currency, such as new $20 bills, has watermarks that can be seen when the bills are held up to the light. A watermark often helps to identify a piece of paper or a document as authentic. A $20 bill with a watermark image of Andrew Jackson seems less likely to be counterfeit than one without it.

A watermark is difficult to insert without the proper facilities. For example, it cannot be photocopied onto a piece of blank paper. You would need access to a paper factory to get paper with your own watermark. Similarly, a watermark is difficult to remove. Removing or changing a watermark without destroying the paper that carries it would require somehow thinning the paper without breaking it. Doing this in a way that produces some other watermarklike pattern would be a huge challenge.

For digital images, there is a similar notion of a watermark. It is a pattern that is either invisible or almost invisible under ordinary viewing conditions, and it helps identify the image in some way. It is intended to be difficult to remove, to help prevent piracy of intellectual property.

A digital watermark has much in common with the hidden messages we have been discussing in this chapter. There are some differences, however. A watermark is not necessarily supposed to be a secret message, although it should be unobtrusive and not interfere with the image it's in. A watermark should be difficult to remove. That typically means that it is embedded in its host image in a redundant fashion. It may be embedded in the same image in a variety of ways, so that if a pirate succeeds in removing some of the embeddings, the watermark may still be embedded in other ways.

A message that is hidden in the least significant bits of an image can be considered to be a kind of watermark. The message is normally difficult or impossible to see, but with a little enhancement becomes visible. However, it's quite easy to remove a watermark of this sort. Simply rounding all pixel values to the nearest even number would do it.

A better watermarking method would be one that embeds the message in more than one way. For example, it could use both the least-significant bits method and the masking method described earlier. It could even use more than one masking method at the same time, and some of the embedded copies of the message could be scrambled to make it harder for pirates to discover those embeddings. Although pirates might succeed in removing some of the embeddings, the true owner of the image could demonstrate in a court of law that the image is his or hers by revealing the watermark in one or more of the embeddings that remain intact.

One approach to creating robust watermarks is to use so-called spread spectrum techniques. In this approach, the image is first analyzed to determine the relative strengths of its oscillating patterns of various frequencies.[1] Then the watermark information is embedded by making adjustments to these strengths. The watermarked image is synthesized from the adjusted strengths. One aspect of such a scheme is that the watermark information becomes spread out among all the pixels of the image and so it becomes harder to remove.

9.8 Photomosaics

9.8.1 Overview

A *photomosaic* is an image made up of other images sometimes called tile images arranged next to each other. Depending on the kind of photomosaic we are talking about, the overall image may be based on a separate photograph (the subject image) or may be an abstract pattern. Alternatively, it may be a panoramic scene that smoothly integrates the tiles of which it is composed. Unlike stenciling, multiple exposures and composite images based on

---

1. Two methods of frequency-based analysis are described in the next chapter: the discrete cosine transform and the discrete Fourier transform.

superposition, photomosaics are formed using *juxtaposition*, the placement of images next to each other rather than on top of each other.

We have already discussed one type of image close to the photomosaic in an earlier chapter: large tiled images that we used to illustrate groups of image transformations. Now we will consider photomosaics in which there is an explicit subject image—an image that an observer of the photomosaic will see emerge when the tiles are viewed from a great-enough distance. When we need to distinguish this type of photomosaic from others, we will call it a macropixel photomosaic.

9.8.2 Macropixels

In a typical macropixel photomosaic, each tile plays the role of a single pixel in rendering the subject image. Later we will consider a variation on macropixel photomosaics in which each tile represents multiple subject-image pixels.

In chapter 1 we considered the question, "What is a pixel?" In a macropixel photomosaic, we adopt an answer that says "A pixel is anything that plays the role of representing a single positioned sample in a digital image." A *macropixel* is an image in its own right that also serves as a pixel in representing the subject image. An example of a photomosaic with hand-designed macropixels is the work "Emma" by artist Chuck Close, shown in figure 1.1.

A fundamental question in the design of photomosaics is whether the internal geometric structure of macropixels will be a significant factor for their use in representing the subject image. We will come back to this issue as we discuss multiple-tile-image photomosaics. Before we do that, we discuss a simpler type of photomosaic.

9.8.3 Single-Tile-Image Photomosaics

Let's consider two different ways to create macropixel photomosaics. The first method uses only one image as the basis for creating the tiles for the photomosaic. The other method uses a collection of tile images. In order to obtain the variations in color, brightness, etc., needed to render the subject image, the single-tile-image method creates modulated versions of the given tile image. On the other hand, the multiple-tile-image method takes advantage of the differences among the given images. The single-tile-image method is simpler, both in terms of implementation and in terms of achieving an aesthetically consistent result.

Here we give an outline of the steps needed to create a photomosaic using the single-tile-image method.

1. Select the subject image.

2. Select the tile image.

3. Reduce the size of the subject image through such methods as cropping and resampling (possibly with low-pass filtering). Let's say the subject image is now of size $w1$ by $h1$.

4. Reduce the size of the tile image. Optionally, give it a square aspect. Let's say the size of this image is now $w2$ by $h2$ (and perhaps $w2 = h2$).

5. Create a blank image of size `w1*w2` by `h1*h2` and make it the destination for the photomosaic synthesis operation.

6. Make the resized subject image be Source1 and the resized tile image be Source2.

7. Apply a formula such as that below, and then adjust the two values that together control brightness and contrast in the photomosaic in order to achieve the best-looking result.

The following formula creates multiple copies of the tile image, adjusting their colors to make the entire tile's average color better match the corresponding pixels of the subject image.

```
S1(x/w2, y/h2) * (s2(x mod w2, y mod h2)-32)/96
```

Here the parameter 32 adjusts the brightness and the 96 adjusts both the contrast and brightness. For more contrast, reduce 96 to a smaller value, such as 64 and to compensate for the increased brightness, raise the 32 to approximately 50.

The formula in this method accomplishes two things. First, it places enough copies of the tile image in the photomosaic to fill up the space there. Second, it amplifies or reduces each color component of the pixels in each copy of the tile image in accordance with the value of a pixel in the subject image.

Reasonable sizes for the images used in this process might be these: `w1 = h1 = 64`. `w2 = h2 = 16`. For the photomosaic itself: `w = h = 1024`. With these values and the Mona Lisa used as both subject and tile, a single-tile photomosaic is created as shown in figure 9.2 (plate 26). The replicas of the tiles can be seen better in the detail of the face shown in figure 9.3 (plate 27).

9.8.4 Multiple-Tile-Image Photomosaics

By using many different tile images, a macropixel photomosaic can be created that has much visual interest and complexity. Creating an aesthetically consistent result becomes a greater challenge, for several reasons: The tiles themselves must have sufficient visual variation that they can effectively play their roles as pixels for the subject image. The tiles should "go well together" in the sense that their own subject matter has a relationship to the subject image. The method for selecting tiles to represent particular parts of the subject image should be capable of obeying aesthetic constraints such as avoiding immediate repetitions of the same tile, but not unless there are enough viable alternative tiles.

In the following paragraphs we'll describe two approaches to constructing multiple-tile-image photomosaics. The first approach follows the macropixel methodology of one tile

Figure 9.2 (plate 26)
Photomosaic constructed with the single-tile method, with the Mona Lisa image used both for the subject and the tile.

per subject-image pixel. The second approach assumes a somewhat larger subject image and uses one tile per equal-sized subimage of the subject image (e.g., one 32 by 32 tile per 32 by 32 subimage of the subject image).

9.8.5 Macropixel Approach

In this method, each of the possible tiles is summarized; its average R value, average G value, and average B value are computed and entered in a table. This is done in advance of computing the photomosaic. The table can be reused for different photomosaics provided only the subject image is changed and the tile image set is not changed.

Then, for each pixel of the subject image, the tile image whose average R, G, and B values most closely match it is selected to represent that pixel. The matching is based on the Euclidean RGB color distance as follows:

$$d(s, t) = \sqrt{(r_s - r_t)^2 + (g_s - g_t)^2 + (b_s - b_t)^2}$$

Here s represents the subject pixel, t represents the tile, (r_s, g_s, b_s) are the color values of the subject pixel, and (r_t, g_t, b_t) are the average color values of the tile. The tile with the minimal distance to the subject pixel is the best-matching tile.

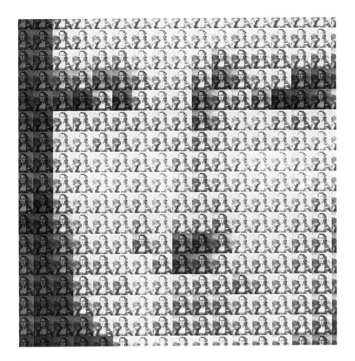

Figure 9.3 (plate 27)
Detail of figure 9.2 in which we see the face made up of many small Mona Lisa images whose colors have been adjusted.

9.8.6 Subimage Approach

In the subimage approach, each tile represents, not just a single subject image pixel, but a region having the same number of pixels as the tile itself. As with the macropixel approach, each tile is evaluated by computing a distance, and the tile with the lowest distance value is the best-matching tile. However, now the distance is computed in a way that takes all the pairwise pixel differences into account. In particular, the distance between the tile and the subimage of the subject image is the average of the Euclidean RGB color distances for all the corresponding pairs of pixels.

This method of selecting tiles has one significant advantage over the macropixel approach: it tends to find tiles that represent not only the dominant color in the region but that also more accurately match the spatial distribution of colors within the region. This tends to result in a photomosaic that better conveys the details in the subject image. The computer implementation of this method depends on the use of programming in Python, and so it is discussed later, in chapter 20.

9.9 Panorama Stitching

A different kind of photomosaic is a panorama image constructed from multiple views of a scene taken from the same viewpoint but in different directions. There are typically several objectives in creating a panorama photomosaic: (1) coverage, (2) geometric continuity, and (3) continuity of color. Coverage refers not only to the amount of the scene that is represented in the panorama but also to the shape of the coverage region, and whether it has gaps. Coverage can be described by imagining the photographer to be at the center of a sphere; the sphere represents the potential field of view for the panorama. Each photo taken from the viewpoint corresponds to a roughly rectangular patch on the sphere. A typical panorama corresponds to a band that follows the horizon and that stretches some number of degrees around the sphere horizontally. It might even go all the way around (360 degrees). It might also go up and down in places. In principle, the entire sphere could be covered, although this is seldom done, not only because of the bother to take so many photos, but because the ground under the photographer is seldom of much interest.

Obtaining thorough coverage of a scene is a matter of numbers: take enough images and you get the coverage. There might be some photographic challenges along the way: maintaining the same viewpoint for all the shots, perhaps with the aid of a good tripod, or making sure that no gaps are left between shots.

When the shots overlap in their fields of view, it is possible for an algorithm to align and blend them into a photomosaic. Recent algorithms are effective at doing this provided there are suitable visual features that appear in the overlap areas to aid in the alignment.

Geometric continuity and continuity of color are desirable properties that can sometimes be attained by automatic means. One of the most successful methods to date is one known as Autostitch developed by Matt Brown and David Lowe at the University of British Columbia. It begins by computing in each image a collection of scale-invariant feature transform (SIFT) features, where particular points in the image are identified and described in terms of notable changes in color ocurring at those places. Then the images are aligned in ways that maximize the consistency of the aligned SIFT features. The images may be warped slightly to achieve this alignment. Finally, the images are "blended" at the seams, to avoid sudden changes in color that are due to differences in photographic exposure, etc.

9.10 Fractals

A *fractal* is a mathematical object that has self-similarity across multiple scales. There several different kinds of fractals, depending on the nature of the self-similarity. Fractal curves are one family of fractals and they come in two varieties: regular and irregular. A regular fractal curve has a structure that is reliably repeated at a succession (typically an

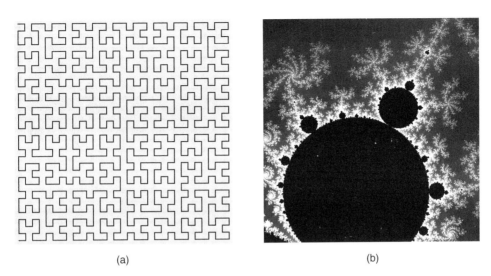

(a)   (b)

Figure 9.4 (plate 28)
(a) Approximation of the Hilbert curve fractal to five levels and (b) a portion of the Mandelbrot set.

infinite succession) of scales. An example of such a curve is the Hilbert curve. A level-5 approximation of the Hilbert curve is shown in figure 9.4a (plate 28). An irregular fractal curve is one that is either generated by a random process or that simply has random statistical properties so that the statistics are similar across scales. The trace of a point undergoing Brownian motion (a random walk) is an example of an irregular fractal curve. Some irregular fractals are generated by completely nonrandom processes. An example of this is the Mandelbrot set, a portion of which is shown in figure 9.4b.

Fractal images may also be regular or irregular. A regular fractal is one that has been created by a process that combines scaled copies of a prototype pattern so that the result contains all the copies (typically averaged together with a possibly weighted average). An irregular fractal image is one that represents a combination of images from a succession of scales that are not necessarily constructed from the same prototype but which nonetheless have statistical self-similarity.

9.10.1 Regular Fractal Images
Let's explore the use of PixelMath to create fractal images of these last two types. (In later chapters we'll use Python programs to revisit the topic of fractals.) Let's start with a regular fractal image based on a prototype consisting of a simple geometric shape: a circular disk.

A formula page for constructing a 256-by-256 example of this kind of fractal contains fifteen formula bars. The first creates the circular disk (the prototype). The disk is created by this formula:

```
if sqr(x-w/2)+sqr(y-h/2) < 1600 then 0 else 255
```

The next seven create seven "octaves" from the prototype. The prototype serves as the first octave. Each octave after the prototype is obtained from the preceding one by resampling it, modulo w1 or h1 with a factor of 2. This formula, used seven times with a different Source1 and Destination each time, is this:

```
s1(x*2 mod w1, y*2 mod h1)
```

There are seven more formula bars, and they are used to add up the eight octave images, two at a time. The first two are added as follows, with 256 subtracted to keep the values in the range from 0 to 255.

```
(s1(x,y)+s2(x,y))-256
```

The same formula is used with different sources and destinations to combine, not only the first and second, but the third and fourth, fifth and sixth, and seventh and eighth octaves. Then the first two of these combinations are combined with the formula

```
(s1(x,y)+s2(x,y))/2
```

as are the latter two of these combinations. Division by 2 makes good use of the 0-to-255 pixel range here because there are overlaps of dark with dark and light with light areas in this combination. Finally, the two sums of sums are combined to obtain the overall fractal, using this last formula once again. Several steps in the process are illustrated in figure 9.5: the prototype, third octave image, sum of the first four octaves, and the final fractal image. Although fractals such as this can serve decorative purposes, with minor variations the same method becomes a useful tool for synthesizing natural-looking textures.

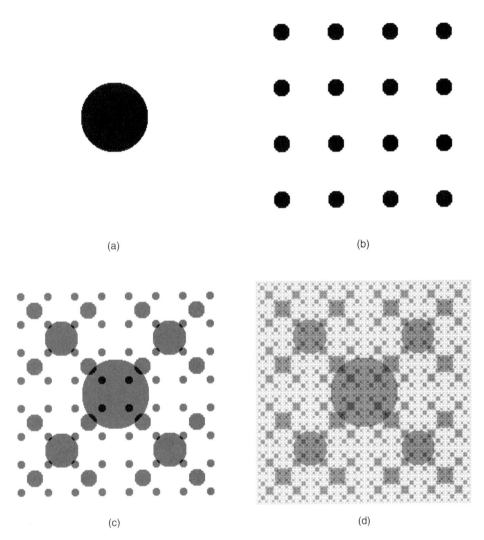

(a)   (b)

(c)   (d)

Figure 9.5
Steps in the creation of a regular fractal image: (a) prototype, (b) third octave, (c) adjusted sum of the first four octaves, and (d) final fractal.

9.10.2 Semiregular Fractal Images

In order to make a natural-looking texture, it helps to start with something that looks random. A good source of random-looking data is often the low-order bits of a photograph. Provided the photograph was not over- or underexposed (leading to saturation of pixel values or insufficient light to break above zero in the pixels), the value of the least significant bit of any particular pixel is about as likely to be 0 as to be 1. The decision of whether or not to accept the data obtained this way from a photograph can usually be made by looking at the data. (Alternatively, one could do a statistical analysis.) Here is the formula that not only extracts the low-order bit of one color component of an image (here red, but it should not matter which), but also scales it up so that we have an image of pixels that are either black or white.

```
255*(red1(x,y)mod 2)
```

To make a texture that seems natural, we'll usually want to make its structure seem random at multiple scales. Whereas in the case of the circular disk fractal we started with a simple pattern and then made higher and higher spatial-frequency versions of it (with finer and finer detail), we will now take the opposite approach; we'll start with the finest degree of detail and work toward coarser and coarser textural components.

Our goal is still to create a kind of fractal image; it should have a similar statistical structure at multiple scales. We'll accomplish this in much the same way we did with the circular disk fractal; that is, we'll make scaled copies of our starting material. Since we are starting with the most detailed level, each step to create a new octave will reduce the frequency by a factor of 2 instead of doubling the frequency as before. Reducing the frequency is sometimes called decimation. Because the source and destination images have the same dimensions, we are effectively blowing up the lower-left quadrant of our image and ignoring the other three quadrants in the construction of each new octave of texture.

```
s1(x/2, y/2)
```

The resampling specified by this formula involves some (many) pixels that are between source pixel centers, and the PixelMath engine performs bilinear interpolation on the values of nearby pixels to obtain their values. This contributes to a certain degree of smoothness in the resulting texture.

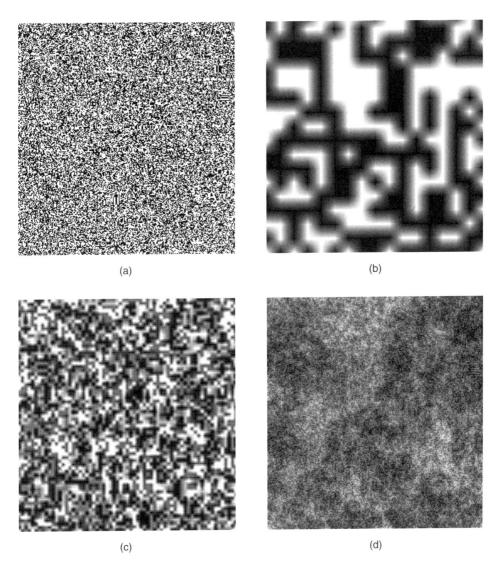

(a)   (b)

(c)   (d)

Figure 9.6
Steps in the construction of a semiregular fractal image: (a) apparently random binary texture, (b) fifth octave, (c) average of octaves 3 and 4, (d) final fractal.

After constructing seven new octaves, in addition to the original random pattern, we are ready to combine them into a single image. Although they could easily be weighted differently, we'll take each octave with an equal weight, thereby doing straight averaging. Taking the images in pairs in the same manner as for the circular disk fractal, we use this formula seven times:

```
0.5*s1(x,y)+0.5*s2(x,y)
```

Several steps of this process are illustrated in figure 9.6.

This method of creating a random-looking texture is a particular variation of Kenneth Perlin's technique, known widely as a *Perlin noise* construction (see Perlin, 1986). Given the starting data, it deterministically (nonrandomly) creates a random-looking texture. With minor variations in the process, the same starting data can be used to create many different textures. To obtain more textures with a similar appearance from the same data, it would suffice to generate octaves taking a variety of patches (not precisely the first quadrant). To get differences in textural granularity, the weights used to average the octaves can be adjusted. This method is considered to be a *procedural* graphics method because the graphical material (the texture) can be synthesized when it is needed, rather than designed in advance. Such techniques are important in multimedia games when new textures are needed as parts of new game levels. The textures should always be the same when players are in the same places, but new textures may be needed for all the new places a player can get to.

9.11 References

Baron, R. 2006. Digital Mona Lisas: A survey of the use of the Mona Lisa as a metaphor for digitizing images, including related efforts. www.studiolo.org/Mona/MONA43.htm.

Brown, M., and Lowe, D. 2007. Automatic panoramic image stitching using invariant features. *International Journal of Computer Vision* Vol. 74, No. 1, pp. 59-73.

Ebert, D., Musgrave, F. K., Peachey, D., Perlin, K., and Worley, S. 2002. *Texturing and Modeling, Third Edition: A Procedural Approach*. San Mateo, CA: Morgan Kaufmann.

Eglash, R. 1999. *African Fractals: Modern Computing and Indigenous Design*. New Brunswick, NJ: Rutgers University Press.

Finkelstein, A. 1995. Web Gothic. (photomosaic). Mossy Bits, Autumn. Seattle WA: University of Washington Dept. of Computer Science and Engineering. cs.uw.edu/publications/mossybits/autumn95/page.gothic.html.

Finkelstein, A., and Range, M. 1998. Image Mosaics. Technical Report: TR-574-98, Computer Science Department, Princeton University. www.cs.princeton.edu/gfx/proj/mosaic.

Mandelbrot, B. 1982. *The Fractal Geometry of Nature*. New York: W. H. Freeman.

Peitgen, O., and Hichter, P. H. 1986. *The Beauty of Fractals*. Heidelberg, Germany: Springer.

Perlin, K. 1985. An image synthesizer. *ACM Computer Graphics*, Vol. 19, No. 3, pp. 287–296.

Silvers, R., and Hawley, M. 1997. *Photomosaics*. New York: Henry Holt.

Silvers, R. 2000. Digital composition of a mosaic image. U.S. patent 6137498.

9.12   Exercises

1. Make up steganography examples of your own using the following techniques: (a) the first letter of each word belongs to the message and (b) each word preceded by two spaces is part of the message.

2. Hide your own initials in the Mona Lisa image using the key-values technique. First, decide where in the image you will hide your initials. Next, decide which of the three color components you will modify. After that, choose the key value you will use. Then, prepare the Mona Lisa image so that it does not use the key value in that color component by using a formula of the form, If Red1(x,y)=79 then 80 else Red1(x,y). Next, make a black image of the same size as the Mona Lisa and draw your initials in there with white letters. Finally, combine the initials with the Mona Lisa, making up a formula that tests the value in the initials' image and either puts in the key value or the Mona Lisa's current value, depending on whether the pixel is part of the initials. Finally, try decoding your image to extract the initials again by making up a suitable formula that compares the pixel value in your image with the key value.

3. Create a 256-by-256 version of an image of your choice by stretching and/or compressing the original with an appropriate formula. Then apply the first five steps of a random-permutation creation process using the new image. The result should be a permutation matrix of size 256 by 256. Then apply the permutation to the Mona Lisa image. Some of the pixels may move by up to 31 pixels, depending upon the configuration of bits in the scanned image.

4. Select a subject image and a separate tile image. Then make a single-tile-image photo-mosaic using the method described in this chapter.

5. The single-tile-image photomosaic method can be modified to use two or even more tiles by embedding an IF-THEN-ELSE construct within the formula so that one tile is used in dark areas and another in light areas, for example. Explore this technique and create a photomosaic to illustrate it.

6. The conditional-expression technique of the previous exercise can be applied to other problems. Consider the task of taking a group operation table such as that shown in chapter 5, and portraying it, not as a table of text, but as an array of transformed images, somewhat like the large tiled image of the Tree of Color (figure 5.16), but having more copies of possibly smaller versions of each image. Demonstrate this idea for the 90-degree rotation

group and an image of your choice. Your image should have four rows and four columns of subimages, and they should correspond one-to-one with the entries in the table.

7. Create a regular fractal image using, as a starting prototype, a square rather than the circular disk used in the example in the text.

8. Create a fractal image using the same method as for the circular disk-based fractal, but starting with an arbitrary photograph as the prototype rather than a geometric form such as the circular disk.

9. Create a semiregular fractal image using the Perlin-noise method in the text, except that by putting relatively low weights on the high-frequency (fine-grained) textural components and higher weights on the low-frequency components, obtain a cloudlike texture. Furthermore, adjust the colors to fall within a range of light blue to white, so that a semblance of white clouds on a blue sky background can be achieved.

10 Filtering

10.1 Introduction

Perhaps the most important form of image enhancement after brightness, contrast, and color adjustment is filtering. Filtering involves adjusting pixel values as a function of their neighbors' values as well as their own.

The most common form of filtering is to reduce the amount of "noise" in an image. Noise is a form of image distortion most commonly occurring as spurious variations in pixel values that result from somewhat inadequate photographic processes or interference, degradation, or heavy enhancement for brightness and contrast. We'll describe noise in more detail later.

Filtering of images is useful not only for improving their appearance but also as part of image analysis processes, in which filtering can be a step of feature extraction in order to describe the contents of the image. Another application of filtering is to produce special effects such as embossing and producing outline images. Filtering is also a basic concept behind the linear transforms that play important roles in image compression and image communication, described later in this chapter.

10.2 Filtering Out Noise

Let's begin our study of filtering by seeing how it can be applied to reducing the amount of noise in a raw (unfiltered) image. Our first example image shows a grayscale image of part of a television test card for adjusting the parameters of a television system. Figure 10.1a shows this image with Gaussian noise added to it. Then parts b, c, and d show the results of filtering it with three different methods.

The essential idea in filtering out noise in images is that we have a model for the process that generates the noise and we apply a filter that is suited for removing such noise. The most common model for noise is Gaussian additive noise, meaning that each pixel in the image has a value p that is the sum of the "true" signal value s and the noise n.

$$p = s + n$$

The noise n is random and at each pixel it is independent of the noise at any other pixel. The random numbers are normally distributed, with mean μ and standard deviation σ. Typically $\mu = 0$. The value of σ corresponds to the intensity of the noise, with higher values corresponding to heavy noise. The term "signal-to-noise ratio" (snr) is used to refer to the relative strength of the true pixel values to the strength of the noise. The term is also used in electrical engineering, audio engineering, and communications, and has somewhat different mathematical definitions in different contexts. In image processing with pixel values in a non-negative range from 0 to p_{max}, one definition is

$$\text{snr} = \mu_s / \sigma_n$$

This considers the signal-to-noise ratio as the average true pixel value (which can be taken as the average value of p, since the noise is assumed to have zero mean) divided by the standard deviation of the noise.

The job of filtering is to determine, for each pixel position, a new value to replace p that is likely to be closer to s. In order to do this successfully at all, we make an assumption that the s values of nearby positions in the image are close to each other. That is, we assume a degree of continuity of s values from one pixel to the next. This assumption is not valid at a sharp edge or in the midst of fine texture, and filtering under this assumption will not necessarily replace p by a value closer to s.

The continuity assumption leads us to assume not only that two adjacent pixels should have s values that are close but that all the points in a small neighborhood of the image should have s values that are close to each other. Under this assumption, it is reasonable to estimate s by taking an average of all the p values in the neighborhood. The points where the noise is positive will tend to be balanced by the points where the noise is negative, and the balance is likely to improve as the neighborhood size is increased. However, there is a tradeoff, since increasing the size of the neighborhood represents an assumption of greater continuity in the true image. This means that we can reduce the amount of noise in uniform-color regions of the image by increasing the neighborhood size, but at the cost of blurring any sharp edges in the image.

The filtering in figure 10.1b is done with a box filter. The box filter replaces each pixel by an average value for pixels in its neighborhood. The neighborhood is normally square (or at least rectangular) in shape. In this example it is 3 by 3. All the pixels in the neighborhood contribute equally to the average. (Other filters use weights that can be different for each pixel in the neighborhood.) The pattern of weights for neighbors in this average is known as the filter's *kernel*. The 3-by-3 box filter's kernel is the following. (Not shown is the final division by 9, which turns the sum into an average.)

1	1	1
1	1	1
1	1	1

The filter can be applied in PixelMath by using the following formula.

```
(1/9)*(S1(x-1,y-1)+S1(x,y-1)+S1(x+1,y-1)+S1(x-1,y)+S1(x,y)+
S1(x+1,y)+S1(x-1,y+1)+S1(x,y+1)+S1(x+1,y+1))
```

The box filter succeeds in reducing the high-frequency noise in this image; however, it tends to smear the results, losing sharpness in the edges between black and white areas.

In figure 10.1c, the filtering uses an approximation to a Gaussian function (bell-shaped), so that the farther away a pixel is from the center of a neighborhood, the less it contributes to the weighted average. This filter smears the image less while still reducing the amount of noise. The particular Gaussian filter used here is a 3-by-3 approximation to a Gaussian having standard deviation 1. Its kernel is the following (not shown is the final division by 3.013, which turns the sum into a weighted average).

0.135	0.368	0.135
0.368	1.000	0.368
0.135	0.368	0.135

The corresponding PixelMath formula for this filter is this:[1]

```
(0.135*S1(x-1,y-1)+0.368*S1(x,y-1)+0.135*S1(x+1,y-1)+
0.368*S1(x-1,y)+S1(x,y)+0.368*S1(x+1,y)+
0.135*S1(x-1,y+1)+0.368*S1(x,y+1)+0.135*S1(x+1,y+1))/3.01285
```

---

1. Formulas such as these can be constructed automatically with the help of Python programs such as MakeConvolutionFormula.py, described in chapter 13.

10.3 Median Filtering

An alternative approach to eliminating salt-and-pepper noise from an image uses a statistical approach. Within each neighborhood, the median pixel value can be found and used to replace the pixel at the center of the neighborhood. This way, if there are any outlier pixels with extremely high or low values, they will usually be replaced by nonoutliers and thus the salt (high outliers) and pepper (low outliers) are removed.

Figure 10.1d shows a median-filtered version of the noisy test-card image. As can be seen, the sharp edges are better preserved in the median-filtered version than in the box-filtered version, and one can see some subtle improvements over the Gaussian-filtered version.

Median filtering with a very small neighborhood (e.g., 1 by 3) can be accomplished with a PixelMath formula. However, with larger neighborhoods this is awkward. The following formula obtains the median of a 1-by-3 neighborhood by subtracting the minimum and maximum from the sum of all three pixel values.

```
S1(x-1,y)+S1(x,y)+S1(x+1,y)
-min(S1(x+1,y),min(S1(x,y),S1(x+1,y)))
-max(S1(x+1,y),min(S1(x,y),S1(x+1,y)))
```

When we use Python programming, we'll see how to implement median filtering for larger neighborhoods.

Median filtering is a form of nonlinear filtering. As such, its characteristics are different. An important property of median filtering, in comparison with box filtering and Gaussian filtering, is that it does not introduce new pixel values into the image, and yet it still helps maintain sharp edges while eliminating noise in the form of outliers. No new pixel values also means that if the original image has integer-valued pixels, then median filtering does not create fractional-valued ones, whereas linear filtering usually does so. The results for median filtering seem similar to the Gaussian filtering result; however, we can see that the white areas are cleaned up better by the median filtering.

10.4 High-Pass Filtering and Sharpening

Whereas low-pass filtering is typically used to eliminate high-frequency noise from an image, high-pass filtering is a way to emphasize or isolate small details in the image. High-pass filtering tends to accentuate noise. However, there are applications in which this is acceptable, either because there is little noise, or because enhancing the details takes a higher priority than suppressing noise.

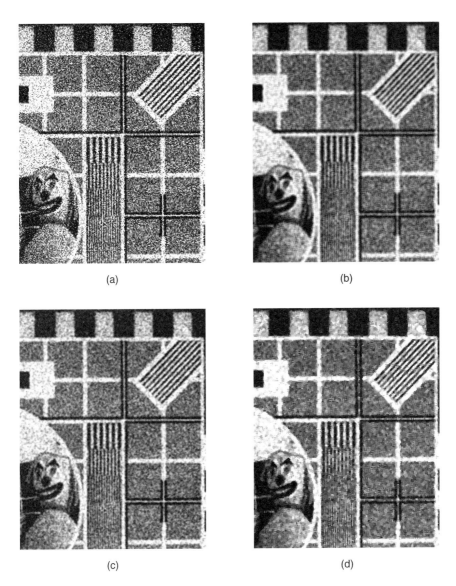

(a)　　　　　　　　　　　　　　(b)

(c)　　　　　　　　　　　　　　(d)

Figure 10.1
A comparison of filtering methods: (a) noisy original, (b) result of 3-by-3 box filter, (c) result of 3-by-3 Gaussian filtering, and (d) result of 3-by-3 median filtering.

A simple high-pass filter involves performing the same kind of weighted averaging oper-ation as for low-pass filtering except that the kernel will have a mix of positive and negative coefficients in it, leading to a canceling out, from one neighbor to the next, of the constant or slowing changing parts of the image values, and an amplification of rapidly changing values. Here is a 3-by-3 kernel that achieves this.

−1	−1	−1
−1	8	−1
−1	−1	−1

Although translating this filter transformation into a PixelMath formula is simple in prin-ciple, the images that result would not be displayed well. For example, we could expect roughly half of the computed pixel values to be negative, and PixelMath would convert them to zero before storing them in an image buffer. Thus, viewing the result of high-pass filtering requires some judicious scaling and shifting the range of pixel values to match the range of the display software (i.e., PixelMath image frames) and hardware (e.g., your computer's LCD screen).

The following formula computes the high-pass output, scales it up to enhance contrast, and then adds 127.5 to put the expected mean output value (zero) at the middle of the PixelMath range (from 0 to 255).

```
(4*S1(x,y)-S1(x-1,y)-S1(x,y-1)-S1(x+1,y)-S1(x,y+1))*10+127.5
```

The result of applying this transformation to the test-card image is shown in figure 10.2b.

10.4.1 Laplacian Filtering

A more commonly used method of high-pass filtering is Laplacian filtering. Laplacian kernels, like Gaussians, can be constructed for any size of kernel, but 3-by-3 kernels are most common. As with Gaussian filtering, the influence of neighboring pixels drops off with their distances from the center pixel. When using integers to represent the Laplacian coefficients, the following kernel nicely approximates the two-dimensional Laplacian.

0	−1	0
−1	4	−1
0	−1	0

The image that results from applying the Laplacian can serve as the mask image for unsharp masking, which is the technique we describe next. As we'll see in chapter 17, Laplacian filtering also plays a role in some image edge-detection methods.

The following formula computes the Laplacian output, and like the high-pass filtering formula given earlier, scales it up to enhance contrast and then adds 127.5 to put the expected mean Laplacian value (zero) at the middle of the PixelMath range (from 0 to 255).

```
(4*S1(x,y)-S1(x-1,y)-S1(x,y-1)-S1(x+1,y)-S1(x,y+1))*10+127.5
```

The result of applying this transformation to the test-card image is shown in figure 10.2c.

10.4.2 Unsharp Masking

Another approach to high-pass filtering is known as *unsharp masking*. The goal here is to enhance the fine detail in an image rather than eliminating the lower-frequency content. For unsharp masking, we first compute the difference between the original and a low-pass filtered version of it. This difference, known as the mask, contains the high-frequency content of the image. The mask is then combined with the original, in proportions that can be adjusted, to give a boost to the high-frequency content in the image. This is also known as *high-boost* filtering.

Figure 10.2d shows an example of unsharp masking applied to the test-card image. The effect of unsharp masking can be obtained using a single filter kernel such as the following, which consists of the Laplacian plus an impulse that adds back in a multiple of the original.

```
(6*S1(x,y)-S1(x-1,y)-S1(x,y-1)-S1(x+1,y)-S1(x,y+1))/2
```

This has the effect of heightening the contrast at edges in the image without altering the average brightness in regions of uniform brightness. For example, there is more contrast around the lips of the doll, in figure 10.2d than in the other versions.

10.5 Convolution

It's time that we put a name on the general family of image transformations that we have been computing. In each of the cases in which we have used a kernel to define a filter, we have essentially taken one image (the original to be processed), let's call it *A*, and another

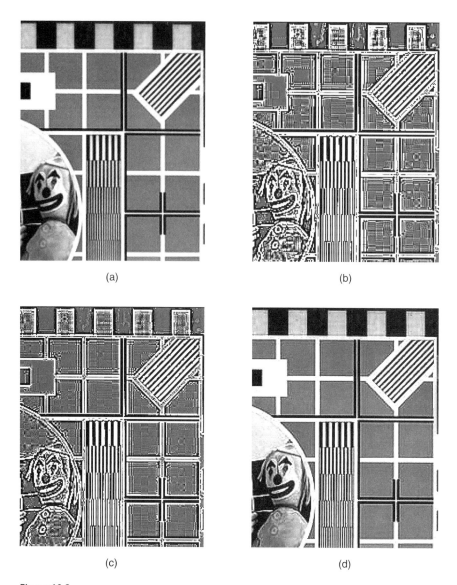

(a)   (b)

(c)   (d)

Figure 10.2
High-pass filtering methods: (a) original, (b) result of using the basic filter, (c) result of 3-by-3 Laplacian filtering, and (d) result of unsharp masking based on the Laplacian.

(in these cases a very small) image (the kernel), let's call it B, and combined them to obtain a filtered result, which we can call C. A key part of this operation is effectively lining up B over and over again at each pixel location of A so that every neighborhood of A that is the size of B gets treated. Taking two images A and B, and lining them up at every position (and then taking the sum of the products of corresponding pixels as the output pixel value) is called the *cross-correlation* of images A and B.

Let $\neg B$ represent the result of rotating B by 180 degrees around its center. Then the cross-correlation of A with $\neg B$ is known as the *convolution* of A with B. (Image convolution is a particular form of a more general mathematical concept of the convolution of two functions, a topic normally introduced after integral calculus.)

As we have seen, the second image, B, is typically small. However, this does not have to be the case. In fact, if $A = B$, then the cross-correlation output would be an image whose values indicate the extent to which A is similar to itself at each of the possible alignments between the two copies. The convolution of A with itself represents, at each position, the extent to which A is similar to $\neg A$.

So far, all the kernels we have considered have been rotationally symmetric. That is, they satisfy $B = \neg B$. Therefore, for these rotationally symmetric kernels, there is no difference between the cross-correlation and the convolution of A with B.

It is easy to confuse cross-correlation with convolution. In the case of rotationally symmetric kernels, they have the same effect. Otherwise there is a difference, but that difference can be eliminated by rotating the kernel 180 degrees. It is therefore common for people doing image processing to use the term "convolution" even when, strictly speaking, they should say "cross-correlation."

Both cross-correlation and convolution are simple ideas, but there are a few details that have to be addressed when they are computed. In particular, what happens near the borders of A (or both A and B, in general)? Some of the alignments of the center pixel of B with a pixel of A cause part of B to go outside the bounds of A. How then should the sum of products be defined and computed? There are several answers, and the best one depends on the circumstances.

One answer is to assume that A is simply the nonzero region of a larger image, so that product terms involving pixels external to A are zero. This is simple, but it sometimes has the undesirable effect of adding a dark border to the resulting image C. The next choice is to treat the exterior locations as if they had the neutral value in the middle of the range of pixel values. (In PixelMath the neutral value is 127.5, or 127 if we stick to integers.) However, this again is insensitive to local context in the image. A more sophisticated policy is to take, as the value of a pixel outside of A the value of the closest pixel inside A. The extra logic involved in doing this directly could slow the convolution operation substantially. Therefore it is often the case that A is first changed into a slightly larger A' where the values of A are used to pad the surrounding framelike region, and then the convolution is performed using A' with B. The output C is based only on alignments of B that fit completely within A'.

Although producing the padded image A' takes a little extra time and memory, the resulting output C tends to be better in some applications, and no extra time is needed within the main convolution loop to test for and handle boundary cases.

Convolution of one image by a (small) kernel is such a common image-processing operation that many pieces of specialized hardware have been designed and built to do it quickly.

10.6 Systems of Filters

Now that we have seen examples of both low-pass and high-pass filtering, we can consider a broader array of filters: everything from extremely low pass to extremely high pass. A sequence of audio filters from low frequency to high frequency constitutes a filter bank. Any particular audio tone can be analyzed by finding out how much sound energy gets through each filter in the bank. The result is a spectral analysis of the tone.

In image processing, a similar approach—a two-dimensional (and spatial rather than temporal) kind of spectral analysis is often used to analyze or process an image. It can be used for many purposes: image noise filtering, high-frequency boosting, data compression, pattern recognition, and image classification.

In most cases, a spectral analysis of an image is performed, not by running an image through a sequence of filters, but by producing all the filter outputs together through a special process called computing a linear transform. We cover two of the most important of these methods: (1) the discrete cosine transform (DCT), which, among other things, is a key step in JPEG image compression, and (2) the discrete fourier transform (DFT), which is the computer version of a classic and powerful mathematical concept, the Fourier transform.

Books that cover these techniques normally assume that the reader has previously studied both linear algebra and calculus. These are subjects taught in separate college mathematics courses. This book, on the other hand, does not make that assumption. Consequently, we first present the discrete cosine transform from a qualitative point of view and then give a definition of it that involves weighted averages of images, but no other linear algebra and no calculus. Then, in order to present the discrete Fourier transform, those aspects of linear algebra needed for using it are given here. These transforms embody important ideas in image processing and they can be understood on multiple levels. Some of these levels are accessible without calculus. Spectral analysis of images is not only an extremely useful set of tools, it is also a powerful way of thinking that is very much a part of the language and culture of image processing.

10.7 The Discrete Cosine Transform

The discrete cosine transform is a way to turn an image into another image. However, the new image looks nothing like the original and yet it contains the same information. It contains it in terms of how much of each of various frequencies are present in the original. (This is also true for the discrete Fourier transform, but the discrete cosine transform is simpler in notable ways.)

Before we attempt to define the discrete cosine transform, let us consider how a familiar image (the Mona Lisa) can be broken down into a sum of simpler images. To keep the discussion concrete and simple, we'll assume a low-resolution version of the Mona Lisa (16 by 16), and monochrome.

Let's first consider an extremely simple set of images. This set is called the 16-by-16 canonical basis set. Each image has 16 rows and 16 columns, and each pixel has a value 0 except for one of them, which has a value 1. There are 256 of these images, with one for each pixel position. We can denote by $B_{x,y}$ the basis image having a 1 at position (x, y). This set is shown in figure 10.3a. Any other 16-by-16 monochrome image I can be expressed as a weighted sum of these 256 images. The weight for a basis-set image $B_{x,y}$ is the value of I at (x, y). Adding up all these weighted basis images gives I. The image I itself is the collection of weights for the canonical basis.

The discrete cosine transform representation of I is also a weighted sum of basis images, but it uses a different basis set. Each basis image is a pattern created by multiplying a cosine function based on x by another cosine function, one based on y. For the 16-by-16 case, there are again 256 basis images shown in figure 10.3b.

Let's look at a small, monochrome version of the Mona Lisa image (figure 10.4a) and at its discrete cosine transform (figure 10.4b). This version of the Mona Lisa is 16 by 16, and so has the same number of pixels as there are basis images in figure 10.3a or b. As the theory will explain (in the next section), there is a unique way to represent this Mona Lisa image as a weighted sum of a set of basis images. In the case of the basis in figure 10.3b, that collection of weights constitutes the discrete cosine transform of the image.

The weights in the DCT representation of the Mona Lisa can be organized in the same 2D array as the basis image in figure 10.3b. Some of the weights are negative, meaning that a (possibly fractional) multiple of the image is essentially subtracted rather than added. To illustrate the array of weights as an image, their absolute value has been taken and then multiplied by a scaling factor, enhancing the brightness and contrast so that some of the structure of the DCT array is visible. The result is shown in figure 10.4b. Figure 10.4c shows the weighted sum of the first fifty-three basis images, giving a filtered version of the Mona Lisa in which the higher-frequency terms (in the vertical direction) are missing. Figure 10.4d shows the fifty-third basis image, the last used in the partial reconstruction. (This basis image can also be seen in figure 10.3b, where it is in the fourth row from the bottom and sixth column from the left.)

There is an important observation that we can make about figure 10.4. Most of the bright pixels are in the lower-left corner of the array. This means that the weights that are strongly positive or strongly negative correspond to wave patterns with low frequencies (see figure 10.3b). At the same time, the weights in the other parts of the array tend to be close

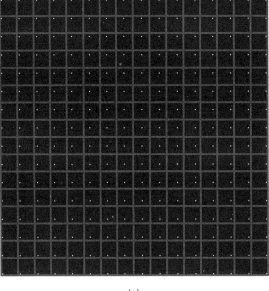

(a)

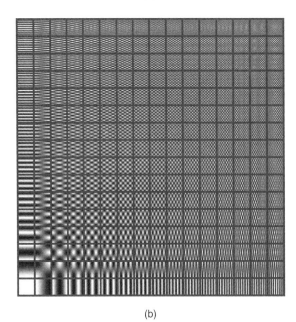

(b)

Figure 10.3
The images of (a) the canonical 16-by-16 basis set and (b) the images in the basis set for the 16-by-16 version of the discrete cosine transform.

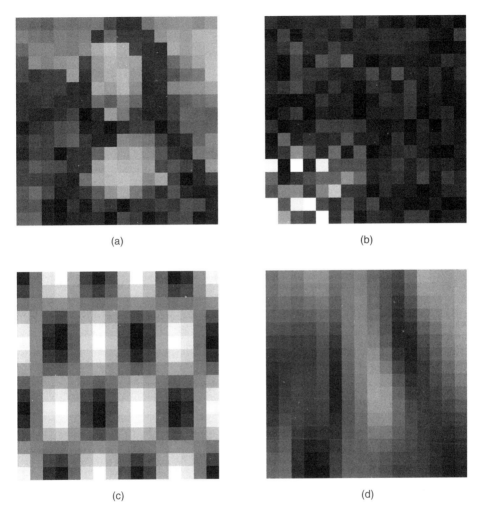

Figure 10.4
(a) Monochrome 16-by-16 version of the Mona Lisa, (b) its DCT shown as an image, (c) the fifty-third basis image, and (d) partial reconstruction with the first 53 out of 256 terms.

to zero. This observation is the key to JPEG image compression. By simply dropping the weights from the upper-right part of the DCT array or by using fewer bits to represent their values, it is possible to compress the representation of the image without doing too much damage to its appearance. Most of the technical details of JPEG encoding are concerned with how best to take advantage of the observation.

The theory of linear transforms, which we'll consider in the next section, tells us something important. Transforms such as the DCT are invertible. It is possible, in theory, to completely recover the original image from its DCT. The invertibility of the DCT, however, is not perfect in a computer implementation because the fixed limits of numerical precision mean that there will be some roundoff or truncation errors that lead to small changes (usually imperceptible) in the image.

The JPEG compression method works, essentially, by taking the DCTs of each 8-by-8 section of an image, approximating the DCTs by dropping some of the weights, and encoding others with small numbers of bits. A JPEG decoder does the reverse, inverting the DCTs and then putting all the 8-by-8 blocks together into a (usually good) approximation of the original image. There are more details in actual JPEG encoding and decoding, but the use of the DCT is at the heart of the method. It's a very effective method and the most popular in the world of digital photography, supported by almost all digital cameras these days.

Before leaving this section, we give the definition of the most common version of the discrete cosine transform. This is for the one-dimensional case where we have a list of input values, $[f_0, f_1, \ldots, f_{N-1}]$. The output is a list with the same number of values: $[g_0, g_1, \ldots, g_{N-1}]$. The first output value, g_0, is amplified twice as much as the others to achieve a property called orthogonality that is discussed in the next section.

$$g_u = C(u) \sum_{k=0}^{N-1} f_k \left[\frac{(2k+1)u\pi}{2N} \right]$$

where

$$c(u) = \begin{cases} \sqrt{\frac{2}{N}}, & \text{if } u = 0; \\ \sqrt{\frac{1}{N}}, & \text{otherwise.} \end{cases}$$

Since each output value is a weighted sum of all the input values, every input value has an effect on every output value. Both the discrete cosine transform and discrete Fourier transform (described later) have this property.

In the next section we'll consider the theory of linear transforms. We'll begin with some mathematical background on *vectors*, which are sequences (i.e., lists) of numbers. This material is typically covered by courses in linear algebra; however, we only need a small part of the content of such a course for our discussion of the DCT and the discrete fourier transform.

10.8 Vectors and Vector Spaces

As indicated, a vector is a sequence of numbers. An n-dimensional vector is a sequence of n numbers. For example, $[2.2, 5.7, -101.6, 0.0]$ is a four-dimensional vector of real numbers and $[0, 4, 2]$ is a three-dimensional vector of integers. A vector can be used for many things. In physics, three-dimensional vectors are often used to represent velocities, forces, displacements, or accelerations. In geometry, vectors can be used to represent points in space, lines, and other objects. In pattern recognition, vectors are used to represent measurements of the properties of a pattern, such as area, perimeter, density, and average curvature. Vectors are used in economics, materials analysis, biology—practically all the fields of science and engineering.

Several mathematical operations on vectors are particularly important: vector addition, multiplication of a vector by a scalar, and dot product. Let's look at these briefly. Let $X = [x_0, x_1, \ldots, x_{n-1}]$ and $Y = [y_0, y_1, \ldots, y_{n-1}]$ be two n-dimensional vectors, and let a be a scalar (a single number, such as 2.5).

The vector sum $X + Y$ is defined as $[x_0 + y_0, x_1 + y_1, \ldots, x_{n-1} + y_{n-1}]$. This is simply adding corresponding elements.

The product aX is defined as $[ax_0, ax_1, \ldots, ax_{n-1}]$, and the product Xa is defined as $[x_0a, x_1a, \ldots, x_{n-1}a]$. Clearly $aX = Xa$. Thus, multiplication of a vector by a scalar means getting a new vector by multiplying each element of the vector by the scalar.

The dot product $X \bullet Y$ is defined as $x_0y_0 + x_1y_1 + \cdots + x_{n-1}y_{n-1}$. This means first doing multiplications of corresponding elements and then adding all these products up to get the overall value.

The n-dimensional vector space V over the real numbers consists of these components: (1) all n-dimensional vectors whose elements are real numbers; (2) the vector addition operation, defined here; (3) the scalar multiplication operation, defined earlier; and (4) the dot product operation, defined here.

10.9 Bases for Vector Spaces

A fundamental idea for vector spaces is the idea that any given vector can be expressed as a weighted sum of some other vectors. If these other vectors are special basis vectors, as they often are, we might write this as follows:

$$V = a_0 B_0 + a_1 B_1 + \cdots + a_{n-1} B_{n-1}$$

Here, each term $a_i B_i$ is the result of multiplication of a vector B_i by a scalar a_i. These scalars a_i are called the weights and the vectors B_i are the basis vectors.

If V (with its operations) is an n-dimensional vector space, then the set $\mathcal{B} = \{B_0, B_1, \ldots, B_{n-1}\}$ is a *basis* for V provided that (1) its vectors span V and (2) they are linearly independent. A set of vectors V_1 spans another set V_2, provided every vector in V_2 can be expressed as some weighted sum of vectors in V_1. A set of vectors V_1 is linearly independent provided none of the vectors in the set can be expressed as a weighted sum of the others.

Thus a basis for an n-dimensional vector space V is a set of vectors in V that can serve for representing all the other vectors in V with no redundancy. There will always be exactly n vectors in any basis for an n-dimensional vector space. If there were any fewer, some vectors in the space would have no representation in the basis. If there were any more, there would be redundancy, and each vector in the space would have multiple representations in the basis.

There is a special, standard basis for every vector space. It's sometimes called the *canonical* basis and sometimes just the *standard* basis. Each element of the canonical basis consists of all zeros, except in one position, where there is a one. Here's the canonical basis for a three-dimensional vector space.

[1, 0, 0]

[0, 1, 0]

[0, 0, 1]

The normal expression of a vector, e.g., $v = [5, 2, -7]$ can be thought of as the weighted sum $5B_0 + 2B_1 - 6B_2$.

Bases have more interesting applications when we use other bases than the canonical one. Consider the basis $\mathcal{B}'$:

[1, 1, 1]

[0, 1, 1]

[0, 0, 1]

Our vector $v = [5, 2, -7]$ can be expressed in this basis as $5B_0' - 3B_1' - 9B_2'$.

By reexpressing v in a new basis, we can get the effect of rotating the vector v in space. For example, the basis $\mathcal{B}''$ defined below has the effect of rotating a 3D vector in space by angle θ in the x-y plane.

[$\cos\theta$, $\sin\theta$, 0]

[$-\sin\theta$, $\cos\theta$, 0]

[0, 0, 1]

We'll see later that computing the Fourier transform is essentially expressing a vector in a new basis.

Before we start considering special bases, let's take note of two properties that bases may have. One property is orthogonality. A basis $\mathcal{B}$ is said to be *orthogonal* provided that the dot product of one vector in the basis with any other vector in the basis is zero. In other words, all the vectors in an orthogonal basis are pairwise orthogonal. In the case of a 2D

Image 1:   Image 2:   Image 3:   Image 4:

7   5   2   3   9   8   14   10

3   4   4   1   7   5   6   8

Figure 10.5
Four 2-by-2 images, to be considered as vectors.

or 3D vector space, where it makes sense to talk about angles between vectors, all pairs of pairs of vectors in an orthogonal basis form right angles (90 degrees).

The other property is the normalized or normal property, by which we mean that each vector in the basis has a length 1. The length of a vector v is defined as $\sqrt{v \bullet v}$. This means that a normalized vector has 1 as its dot product with itself. If a basis is an *orthonormal* basis, then it is an orthogonal basis in which every basis vector has a length 1.

10.10   Image Vector Spaces

Although an n-dimensional vector is a sequence of n numbers that seems in its shape to be one-dimensional, a digital image, which has a two-dimensional shape, can also be considered to be a vector. For example, an image with 256 rows and 256 columns of pixels can be thought of as a single 65536-dimensional vector. This high dimensionality may seem strange, but it is not a problem for computers to handle.

Once we accept the idea that an image can be treated as a vector, we immediately have at our disposal all the techniques that go along with vector spaces: vector addition, multiplication of a vector by a scalar, dot products, bases, changes of bases, etc. These are all important in image processing.

Let's briefly look at some simple examples of treating images as vectors (see figure 10.5). Here we have Image$_1$+ Image$_2$ = Image$_3$. Also, Image$_4$ = 2 Image$_1$. The dot product Image$_1 \bullet$ Image$_2$ = 45.

Although a set of images can be thought of as a set of vectors, a vector space containing these vectors may contain some vectors that might not be valid images. If the pixels of an image are limited to the range 0 to 255, for example, the values obtained by adding corresponding pixels of images might go above 255. Similarly, the additive inverse of an image would have to have pixel values less than zero, which is fine for a mathematical vector but problematic for a PixelMath image. We'll get around this problem in two ways. Sometimes we'll just apply the vector space operations and accept the results we get with Pixel Arithmetic. Sometimes we'll define a wider class of images than standard PixelMath images, and we'll let pixel values have arbitrary floating-point values: negative as well as positive, fractional as well as integral, very large as well as narrowly bounded. PixelMath actually supports a type of image like this; the complex color image structure will be described later in this chapter.

10.11 Bases of Complex Exponentials

In this section we review the concept of complex numbers. Then we take a look at how exponential functions of complex numbers can be used to represent oscillating patterns. Finally, we'll put together sets of these functions to form a basis that will allow us to re-represent a signal in terms of its component oscillating patterns.

10.11.1 Complex Numbers

A quadratic equation such as $x^2 - 3x + 2 = 0$ has two roots: $x = 1$ and $x = 2$. On the other hand, another quadratic equation, $x^2 + 1 = 0$, has no real roots since we can't have any real x such that $x^2 = -1$. Motivated in part by the desire to have roots to all algebraic equations, a new kind of number was invented in the 1500s by Gerolamo Cardano and Rafael Bombelli. Originally called fictitious numbers, they later came to be called *complex* numbers. Complex numbers not only provide solutions to algebraic equations that would not have them otherwise but are particularly useful in physics and electrical engineering.

The first step in building the complex numbers is to posit the existence of a special imaginary number i whose defining property is $i^2 = -1$. Thus it is defined to be the square root of negative one. A complex number c is any number that can be expressed as the sum $a + bi$, where a and b are real numbers. Thus c has two parts: a is the real part and bi is the imaginary part.

The arithmetic operations of addition, multiplication, subtraction, and division can all be performed on complex numbers by applying the usual rules of addition and multiplication, together with the fact that $i^2 = -1$. For example, for $c_1 = a_1 + b_1 i$ and $c_2 = a_2 + b_2 i$, $c_1 + c_2 = (a_1 + a_2) + (b_1 + b_2)i$. In the case of multiplication, it's a little more interesting: $c_1 c_2 = (a_1 a_2) + (a_1 b_2 i) + (a_2 b_1 i) + (b_1 b_2)i^2$. This simplifies to $a_1 a_2 - b_1 b_2 + (a_1 b_2 + a_2 b_1)i$.

Any complex number $a + bi$ can be visualized as a point (a, b) in a two-dimensional plane where the real part a is treated as a horizontal coordinate, and the coefficient b of the imaginary part is used as a vertical coordinate. This 2D space is called the *complex plane*. We can also consider a complex number to be analogous to a two-dimensional vector $[a, b]$. Then the addition of complex numbers corresponds to vector addition.

10.11.2 Complex Exponentials

In 1748, Leonard Euler determined that there is a close relationship between exponential functions and trigonometric functions when the arguments and values are complex numbers. By working with a power series, he discovered the following identity now known as Euler's formula:

$$e^{i\theta} = \cos\theta + i\sin\theta$$

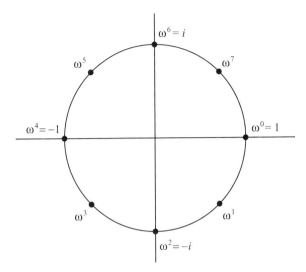

Figure 10.6
A unit circle in the complex plane showing the n-th roots of unity for the case $n = 8$. The principal root used to generate the others is $\omega = e^{-2\pi/n}$.

This states that raising e to an imaginary power corresponds to taking the sine and cosine of an angle.

As a consequence of Euler's formula, it is clear that $e^{i\theta}$ is a periodic function that repeats itself every 2π. Whenever $\theta = 0$ or $\theta = 2\pi$, etc., $e^{i\theta} = 1$. Then, because of the additive laws for exponents (i.e., $e^a e^b = e^{a+b}$), we have $(e^{i\theta})^n = e^{ni\theta}$. That means that $e^{2\pi/n}$ is an n-th root of 1. Call this quantity u. The powers of this root, $u^0, u^1, u^2, u^3, \ldots, u^{n-1}$, are all n-th roots of unity and they are distinct. The same roots can be produced in another order by starting with $e^{-2\pi/n}$ and taking its powers. This ordering is important in the definition of the discrete Fourier transform, which we'll discuss later.

There is a nice graphical representation for the n-th roots of unity in the complex plane (see figure 10.6). All these roots lie on the unit circle centered at the origin. The first root, 1 itself, lies one unit to the right of the origin. The next root, $\omega = e^{-2\pi/n}$, is on the circle at $1/n$ of the way around from 1, going clockwise. This root is known as a *principal n-th root of unity* because its powers give the others roots. (It is not the only principal n-th root of unity; as we mentioned earlier, $u = e^{2\pi/n}$ also generates the others, and there may be more principal n-th roots of unity, depending on the value of n. In general ω^k is a principal n-th root of unity if k and n are relatively prime.) All the n-th roots of unity are found evenly spaced around the circle, every $1/n$ of the way around.

Clearly the real and imaginary parts of these roots represent samples of oscillating patterns. The real parts represent a cosine function of θ and the imaginary parts represent a sine function.

10.11.3 Vector Spaces with Complex Numbers

Just as we defined vector spaces for real numbers, we can do it for complex numbers. The n-dimensional vector space over the complex numbers consists of all possible vectors of length n having complex numbers as elements, together with the operations of vector addition, scalar multiplication, and dot product. The scalars are now complex numbers, too.

10.11.4 Bases

Using the n complex roots of unity, we can generate some interesting vectors. Starting with the first root, 1 itself, and multiplying this by itself $n-1$ times, we get the n-dimensional vector $[1, 1, \ldots, 1]$. The next root is ω, our chosen principal n-th root of unity. Taking its first n powers, we get the vector $[1, \omega, \omega^2, \ldots, \omega^{n-1}]$. The next root is ω^2. Its first n powers give us $[1, \omega^2, \omega^4, \ldots, \omega^{2n-2}]$. Continuing in this manner, we end up with n vectors, all based on powers of ω. This set of vectors forms an orthogonal basis. It's the basis for the length-n discrete Fourier transform.

10.12 Fourier Transforms

A Fourier transform is a way of taking one function and getting another function that represents the same information but in a different way, giving explicit values for the different frequency components in the original function.

There are two basic categories of Fourier transforms: those for continuous functions (which are defined using integrals) and those for sequences of numbers (which are the discrete Fourier transforms and which are defined using summations). We will restrict our attention to the discrete class since we are working with digital images that consist of finite collections of samples (pixels).

The Fourier transform is normally defined in terms of one-dimensional sequences rather than two-dimensional images. It is a straightforward matter to extend it to images by using separate phases of transformation for the rows and for the columns of an image. However, to keep the discussion simple, we start with the one-dimensional case.

Let v be a vector. Its discrete Fourier transform is a new vector: the vector of weights obtained by expressing v as a weighted sum of the discrete Fourier basis vectors. (Actually the weights may all be a factor of n larger, by convention.)

The discrete Fourier transform can be computed using matrix-vector multiplication. By expressing the basis as an n-by-n matrix, we can use the following scheme.

$$
\begin{bmatrix} F_0 \\ F_1 \\ \vdots \\ F_{n-1} \end{bmatrix} = \begin{bmatrix} 1 & 1 & \cdots & 1 \\ 1 & \omega & \cdots & \omega^{n-1} \\ \vdots & & & \\ 1 & \omega^{n-1} & \cdots & \omega^{n^2-2n+1} \end{bmatrix} \begin{bmatrix} v_0 \\ v_1 \\ \vdots \\ v_{n-1} \end{bmatrix}
$$

This corresponds to the formula commonly used to define the discrete Fourier transform:

$$F_k = \sum_{j=0}^{n-1} e^{-2\pi jki/n} v_j$$

When n is large, this method of computing the Fourier transform is inefficient. An improvement results from precomputing all the powers of ω, but that still leaves n^2 complex multiplications and $n^2 - n$ complex additions. There is a clever algorithm called the fast Fourier transform (FFT) that computes the same results with many fewer multiplications and additions—on the order of $n \log_2 n$ multiplications and additions. PixelMath uses that algorithm in its Fourier transform method because the FFT is hundreds of times faster than the direct method for typical images of 1 megapixel or more. A simple version of the FFT is described in more detail in chapter 15.

10.12.1 Complex Color Images in PixelMath

The basic representation for an image in PixelMath is an RGB representation with one integer for each of R, G, and B, with values in the range 0 to 255. This representation is not adequate for representing Fourier transforms of images for three reasons: (1) Fourier transforms require the use of complex numbers; (2) the range 0 to 255 is insufficient because values may need to be negative and sometimes of large magnitude; and (3) the accuracy is too limited—fractional values are needed. Any one of these limitations alone makes it impossible to perform reasonable FFT-inverseFFT cycles that return a reasonable facsimile of the original.

Therefore, PixelMath provides a way to represent a color image using floating-point representations of the real and imaginary parts of complex numbers. In order to use this representation, one either selects the option from an image window's "Rep." menu, or uses the Python function `pmSetComplex(wn)`. It is also possible to specify such an image in the Formula Page interface by appending the letter "c" after the size specification.

A complex color image has six floating-point numbers for each pixel. These can be seen in an image window's status line when the mouse is positioned over a pixel. For example, an orange pixel could have the following complex representation:

```
(Rc,Gc,Bc) = (250.00 + 0.00 i, 190 + 0.00 i, 0.00 + 0.00 i)
```

Here the complex number representing the red component is $250.00 + 0.00i$, etc. When a complex color image is created, the real part of each color component is given the regular R, G, or B value and the imaginary part is given 0. When the complex color image changes, the displayed R, G, and B values are automatically computed from the Rc, Gc, and Bc values by taking the modulus of the corresponding complex number. The modulus of the complex number $a + bi$ is defined to be $\sqrt{a^2 + b^2}$.

10.13   Two-Dimensional Fourier Transforms

Normally, the Fourier transform is applied to a one-dimensional signal, such as an audio clip, resulting in a one-dimensional transform. For example, a sequence of 512 audio values would be transformed into 512 spectral values. When processing images with a frequency-analysis approach, we want to detect the frequency components of the image in both the horizontal and the vertical directions. This is done by applying a two-dimensional version of the discrete Fourier transform. In practice, this is done very simply. First, the discrete Fourier transform is applied to each row of the original image. This produces an intermediate image of row transforms. Then the image of row transforms is processed by applying the discrete Fourier transform to each column. That results in a third image, which is the two-dimensional Fourier transform of the original image.

The result of performing the discrete Fourier transform on first the rows of the original and then the columns of that result is the two-dimensional discrete Fourier transform (2D DFT). Taking the modulus of each R, G, and B value (and then clipping those values to be integers in the range from 0 to 255) gives us a viewable PixelMath image, and that is what we see in the following examples when a 2D DFT is shown. An image of this kind is known as a Fourier spectrum, and if we take the squares of these modulus values as the pixels, then the image is known as the *power spectrum* of the original image. Sometimes the power spectrum is called the spectral density.

10.14   Filtering with the Fourier Transform

A general method for filtering an image A involves the following steps. First, the 2D discrete Fourier transform F of the image is computed. Then F is modified, either by manual editing or by applying a mask or other automatic technique. The result is a modified Fourier transform F'. This modified transform is then mapped back into the space domain by applying the 2D inverse Fourier transform to it. The filtered image A' is the result. Typical modifications to F are to zero out the frequency components for frequencies above a threshold. This results in low-pass filtering. Alternatively, the lowest frequencies can have their coefficients zeroed out, resulting in a high-pass filtered version of A.

Figures 10.7 and 10.8 (plate 29) illustrate this method of filtering applied to the Mona Lisa image. A PixelMath formula page was used to generate the transforms and filtered versions shown here. The formulas used are the following (each preceded by its window number):

```
1: @Mona256.png
2: complex(s1(x,y),0)
3: #fft
4: s1((x+w/2) mod w, (y+h/2)mod h)
5: if {abs(x-w/2)>8} or {abs(y-h/2)>8} then 0 else S1(x,y)
```

(a)

(b)

(c)

(d)

Figure 10.7
Low-pass filtering with the Mona Lisa image: (a) original, (b) 2D discrete Fourier transform, (c) edited transform, and (d) inverse of the edited transform.

```
6: s1((x+w/2) mod w, (y+h/2)mod h)
7: #ifft
8: if {abs(x-w/2)>20} or {abs(y-h/2)>20} then 10*S1(x,y) else 0
9: s1((x+w/2) mod w, (y+h/2)mod h)
10: #ifft
```

In window 1, the original image is kept. A copy of it is made in window 2, but it is converted into a complex color image (in which each R, G, and B value is a double-precision complex number with its own real and imaginary parts). The imaginary parts of each component in window 2 are zero. The two-dimensional discrete Fourier transform is computed by the special formula #fft (which works only in the Formula Page interface, not the calculator). The resulting transform image is still a complex color image, and now its imaginary components are no longer zero. The origin of the frequency-space image is still in the lower-left corner of the image. However, traditionally, the origin is placed in the center of the image. Consequently, the formula in line 4 translates the origin to the center. The image produced by this formula is the transform image that we see in Figure 10.7b. In line 5, the low-frequency components of the 2D Fourier transform are retained while the high-frequency components are set to zero. This edited transform has all parts set to 0 (black) except those within a square region of low-frequency values (Figure 10.7c). Line 6 is the same as line 4 because the translation of the origin that we are using is a self-inverse transformation. We apply it here to prepare the edited Fourier transform image for inverse Fourier transformation. Line 7 computes the inverse 2D discrete Fourier transform, resulting in the low-pass filtered version of Mona that we see in figure 10.7d. For the high-pass filtering case, we edit the transform in a complementary way, removing the low-frequency components (which are in a square around the origin). This edited transform and its inverse (the high-pass filtered version of Mona) are shown in figure 10.8a and b.

The use of the 2D discrete Fourier transform for filtering images is a standard method, and it's often considered as one of the first techniques to try when designing a new image enhancement method or texture analysis technique. Because the editing is performed in the transform (the frequency domain), filtering with the Fourier transform is often called a spectral method.

10.15   References

Castleman, K. R. 1996. *Digital Image Processing*. Englewood Cliffs, NJ: Prentice-Hall.

Cooley, J. W., and Tukey, J. W. 1965. An algorithm for the machine calculation of complex Fourier series. *Mathematics of Computation*, Vol. 19, pp. 297–301.

Gonzalez, R. C., and Woods, R. E. 2002 *Digital Image Processing*, 3rd ed., Reading, MA: Addison-Wesley.

Shapiro, L., and Stockman, G. 2001. *Computer Vision*. Upper Saddle River, NJ: Prentice-Hall.

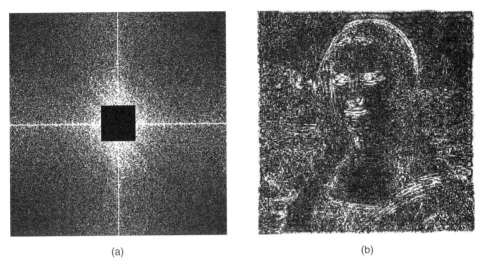

(a)   (b)

Figure 10.8 (plate 29)
High-pass filtering with the Mona Lisa image: (a) edited transform and (b) inverse of the edited transform.

10.16 Exercises

1. Compute by hand the result of applying the 1-by-2 box filter with kernel [0.5, 0.5] to the following 2-by-5 image.

```
0    8    0   16    2
0   10   10   10    0
```

2. Compute by hand the result of applying the 2-by-2 box filter below to the image next to it.

0.25	0.25
0.25	0.25

0	0	0	0	0
0	0	0	0	0
0	0	64	0	0
0	0	0	0	0
0	0	0	0	0

3. Design a 7-by-7 mask (convolution kernel) to detect arrowheads pointing up.

4. Show the result of median filtering (using a 1-by-3 horizontally arranged neighborhood) of the image shown:

7	1	5	7	8
2	3	2	4	2
1	2	3	2	9
2	8	7	3	8
3	9	5	4	7

5. Create a PixelMath formula that will perform median filtering with a 1-by-3 neighborhood.

6. Compute the dot product of the two vectors $[2, 9, 8]$ and $[-5, 3, -1]$.

7. Compute the dot product of the following two images

```
V0:           V1:
 1  0          4  2

 2  1          6  3
```

8. Consider the basis:

```
B0:         B1:         B2:         B3:
 1  1        -1  1        1  1        1 -1

 1  1        -1  1       -1 -1       -1  1
```

Express V1 (from the previous problem) as a linear combination of B0, B1, B2, and B3.

9. Determine the value of $e^{-2k\pi i/n}$ for $n = 4$ and $k = 3$ and $i = \sqrt{-1}$.

10. Use the following Python program to compute the DFT of the following (real) vector.

```
1    f = [1,    2,    0,   -2,   3,    0,   -4,   -2]
2
3    ''' DFT.py
4        Direct computation of the Discrete Fourier Transform.
5        This short program computes Fourier transforms using the
6        simple, but slow method.  It's fine for small experiments
7        and learning about the Fourier transform.
8
9        The input to the DFT function should be a list of numbers.
10       The numbers can be integers, floating point numbers, or
11       complex numbers.  The length of the list can be any whole
12       number greater than 1.
13       (This is unlike most Fast Fourier Transform programs,
```

```
14        which require that the lengths be powers of 2.)
15
16    '''
17
18    from cmath import exp, sqrt, pi
19    i = sqrt(-1)
20
21    def DFT(f):
22      N = len(f)
23      F = N*[0]
24      for k in range(N):
25        F[k] = 0.0
26        for j in range(N):
27            F[k] += f[j]*exp(-2*pi*i*j*k / N)
28      return F
```

11. Using PixelMath and the Formula Page on computing Fourier transforms, starting with the Tree of Color image, introduce a low-frequency modulation in the vertical direction by adding a large impulse (a high value like 1000 in a single pixel) to the Fourier transform of the image and then applying the inverse transform. Note that the image should be resized to 256 by 256 before taking the transform. Save and show the resulting image.

12. Compute the (discrete) Fourier transform of the ramp vector [$1 + 0\,i, 2 + 0\,i, 3 + 0\,i, 4 + 0\,i$].

II   IMAGES AND PROGRAMS

11   Introducing Python

In this chapter you'll learn to create a file containing a sequence of PixelMath commands so that you can automatically run the sequence without having to go through each step manually. This is particularly helpful when you want to run the sequence a number of times.

11.1   Why Use Programming in PixelMath?

The PixelMath software can be operated in two ways. One is by directly clicking on buttons, pulling down menus, selecting tools, and clicking on the image, etc. The other is by running little programs or typing commands in a programming language. The previous chapters have all assumed that the user is directly manipulating the software. Now, we'll begin to explore the second way to operate the software.

The language used for programming in the PixelMath software is called PixelMath Python. It's a version of Python, which is a well-known programming language developed during the early 1990s. Python is used today in software systems such as Plone (a web content management system), Alice (an introductory programming environment for animation), and experimental software for artificial intelligence. It's also used in scientific computing, scripting inside applications such as GIMP (an open-source image manipulation program) and website scripting. PixelMath Python provides two kinds of capabilities: functions for operating PixelMath and general computing capabilities.

The general computing capabilities of PixelMath Python include using symbols to represent numbers, character strings, other symbols, and lists. They also include ways to perform arithmetic and other mathematical operations. Then there are control constructs for causing operations to be repeated in loops, executed conditionally, or based on calling subprograms in various ways.

The facilities for controlling PixelMath in PixelMath Python correspond to nearly all the things a user can do by direct manipulation, such as opening image windows, arranging them on the screen, zooming in and out, selecting sources and destinations, enabling R, G, and B color component modification, and computing image transformations.

Having all these capabilities in a programming system makes it possible to automate the process of setting up windows for a particular demonstration or experiment. It also allows the user to set up somewhat complicated experiments without the tedium of manually laying everything out each time the setup is wanted. For example, using a small program, you can set up a screen with twenty windows, tiling the screen area in a 4-by-5 array. In the remainder of this book we will not usually refer to our programming language as PixelMath Python, but simply Python, because it will usually be clear from the context whether the features we discuss are general Python features or are specific to PixelMath.

11.2   Introducing the Programming Interface

To find out a little bit about how to use Python to control PixelMath, let's begin an interactive programming session. From the PixelMath launch pad, click on Python. This will cause the programming portion of PixelMath to be set up. This may take a few seconds on an older computer, but should be fast on any newer machine. When it's ready, you should see a large new window with three text areas: a shallow one at the bottom (where you can type things in), a middle-sized one in the middle, where session history is shown (where you can see a history of what you have typed in and what the Python interpreter has responded with), and a larger one above that where the currently open buffer or file is shown.

The lower two panes constitute what we call the Python listener; we'll just call them the listener. You can see the listener in figure 11.1 (plate 30).   The listener contains a history pane and an input pane. The user types Python expressions into the input pane at the bottom of the listener. In figure 11.1 the user has just typed into the input pane an expression but has not yet typed the enter key.

The pane above the input pane is the history pane. Here, a record is shown of what has been entered into the input pane and what each response by the system was. In figure 11.1 the first expression entered by the user was 5 + 7, and the response from Python was 12. The expression the user is about to enter is pmNewImage(0, "Blue Box", 100, 50, 0, 0, 255). The system will respond to this in two ways. First it will make a new window and put a new image in it with blue pixels. This won't show in the listener because it is a separate window. Then it will return the number of the new window that it created. This number, 1, will appear as the response in the history pane. The user can see this number and use it in subsequent commands or function calls, such as pmSetSource1(1). You can select and copy from the history pane, but you cannot delete or replace text there.

11.2.1   Entering Commands in the Listener
To start out, type the following into the listener (bottom of the window) followed by the Enter key.

```
pmNewImage(0, "Blue Box", 100, 50, 0, 0, 255)
```

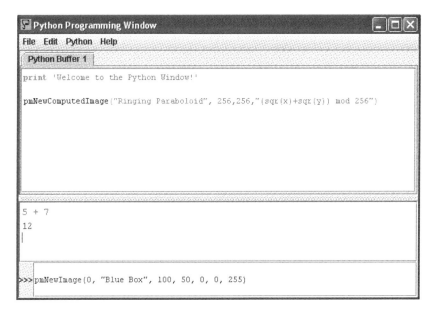

Figure 11.1 (plate 30)
The PixelMath Python window showing the buffer pane (just below the menu bar) and listener panes (lower half). The buffer pane shows what file (program) the user is currently editing or testing, in this case a two-line program beginning with a print statement. The history pane (here containing the two lines 5 + 7 and 12) contains a transcript of what the user has entered and what the responses from Python were. The input pane, at the bottom, holds the last line of the expression the user is currently typing in. In this case it is a call to the function pmNewImage.

In typing this, it's important to spell the function name "pmNewImage" correctly; the various items following it are separated by commas. By the way, this function should cause a new image to be created on the screen having a title "Blue Box," a width of 100 pixels, a height of 50 pixels, and all its pixels a bright blue color: RGB = (0, 0, 255).

In the listener history you should see what you typed, followed by a response. In this case the response is an integer that represents the window number of the new image window. This number should be used in subsequent commands involving this window. For example, if this was window number 1, then you could type the following to adjust its position.

```
pmPositionWindow(1, 200, 300, 0, 0)
```

This causes window number 1 to have its upper-left corner placed at screen-coordinates position (200, 300). The two zeros indicate that the width and height of the window should not be changed. If the width and height parameters are nonzero, then they would be used to resize the window. The screen coordinate system is assumed to have its origin in the upper-left corner of the screen, so that x increases to the right and y increases going downward on the screen. This is different from the (mathematical) convention used within PixelMath images, but it is consistent with what most graphics systems do.

Notice that most of the commands are typed using a combination of lower-case and uppercase letters. It is a standard requirement of Python systems to type names just as they appear. Python is case-sensitive.

11.3 Editing Sequences of Commands

The various Python functions for controlling PixelMath are given in section 11.6 near the end of this chapter. By selecting from these and arranging your selections in a file, you can set up a little program that we call a script that can be used to automatically do a bunch of things in PixelMath. Here is an example of a script:

```
1    pmNewImage(0, "My Design", 250, 200, 255, 0, 0)
2    pmSetDestination(1)
3    pmSetFormula("((x * x) + (y * y)) mod 256")
4    pmCompute()
```

Running this script does the work that otherwise might involve manually making a new window, setting the destination choice on the calculator, typing a formula, and clicking on the Compute button.

11.3.1 Python Buffers
You can set up any number of buffers with space for editing Python programs by using the Python programming window's File menu item "New." This creates not only the new buffer but also a tab that you can use to select it from all the other buffers. Another way to create a new buffer is to load a file that already exists on the local hard disk or a PixelMath server that you are connected to. To load a file, use the File menu's "Load . . ." command. Computer program text in Python (or in any other programming language) is often called *code*. Consequently, a Python buffer is a code buffer, and what one typically does with it is write and edit code.

Note that the text in a Python buffer is shown in several colors. These colors are used for highlighting syntax. The editing program associated with the buffers does a partial analysis of the text in the buffer, considering it as a possible Python program. When it recognizes certain words or phrases as having potential significance in the program, it colors them according to a simple classification. It uses brown for built-in Python commands like `print` and `def`. It uses green for literal text strings that are given within quotation marks. It uses red for comments, black for user-defined variables and functions, purple for operators, gray for numbers, and cyan for parentheses. Syntax highlighting is particularly helpful for identifying incorrectly quoted strings and various other typographical errors.

You can evaluate the commands in a Python buffer by selecting from the Python menu the Evaluate Buffer command. Evaluation means that the commands are performed. The results of any print commands are put in the history pane. If you only wish to evaluate part of the contents of a Python buffer, use the mouse to make a selection and then use the command "Eval. Selection in Buffer." When evaluating from the buffer, printing is handled differently than when typing into the input pane. When you type into the input pane, the evaluated commands themselves are copied into the history pane. But when you evaluate from a buffer, the commands are not copied to the history pane. Also, evaluation in the buffer does not automatically lead to a printed value in the history pane. For example, if you type into a buffer the expression $2 + 5$ and then select it and evaluate the selection, you will not see any result in the history pane. On the other hand, if you type `print 2+5` and then select and evaluate that, you'll see the value 7 printed in the history pane. In this way, the programmer has the option of having values printed, but by not doing so automatically, the program execution can run more quickly and can do so without cluttering the screen with extra printing.

If your Python program opens up too many windows or results in a clutter, you can select "Reset Calculator and Close Windows" from the calculator's File menu, or you can select "Close all Image Windows" from the Python window's File menu, and this will restart everything except for your Python buffer window. You can then modify your program and try it again.

11.3.2 Using an External Editor

Using a text editor (such as WordPad under Microsoft Windows, or Emacs), your Python program could be edited and saved in a file, even if you are running PixelMath from a website and don't have permission to load to or save from the applet directly from or to your hard disk. You will need to be able to cut and paste either to/from the listener or to/from a Python buffer window.

If you have permission to read files directly from the hard disk or if the program is on the applet's server, you can load your Python program without using a Python buffer. Let's suppose that the program is saved in a file named MyScript.py and this file is either on your hard disk (if you are using PixelMath in application mode) or on the server (if you are using PixelMath on the web). The file is assumed to be in the same directory as your images. Then you can execute the script by using the Load menu command (on the File menu) of the Python window.

11.4 How to Deal with Errors in the Commands

Much of the time when one is developing a program, there are errors in it. These may cause any of a number of things to happen: an error message might be printed in the listener or in a special window called the Java console; the desired command may be performed, but in an unexpected manner; the PixelMath software might get stuck in a state where it does not seem to respond to anything; or possibly nothing at all may happen. The most usual error condition is the first of these, when some error message is printed out.

11.4.1 Typical Diagnostics from PixelMath Python

A typical error results from misspelling something. Then you will get something like "SyntaxError: invalid syntax" or "nameError." A "nameError" message happens when a name is not the correct name of a function or variable that the system knows about. For example, either of the following two expressions would cause such an error:

```
1   pNewImage(0, "My image", 100, 50, 0, 0, 0)
2   print xyz
```

The first expression fails because "pNewImage" should have been "pmNewImage". The second fails because the name xyz has not been defined as a function or given a value as a variable.

Another typical error is to use a function with too few or too many arguments. The function pmSetFormula takes one argument. If we tried to use it as follows, we would get a "TypeError: pmSetFormula(): expected 1 args; got 0" error, because 0 arguments are given.

```
pmSetFormula()
```

If you type in an expression that has too few right-hand parentheses, then the interpreter will usually wait until you type in enough right-hand parentheses to balance all the left-hand parentheses in the expression. So if you type something in and nothing happens, Python might just be waiting for you to type another right-hand parenthesis.

11.4.2   The Java Console

PixelMath itself is written in the Java language. If you are running PixelMath in application mode, then you will be able to see certain diagnostic messages as they are printed in a console window. If you are using PixelMath on the web with a browser, then you normally can use a browser menu item to open up a window called the Java console. This console will show certain error messages, and you might be able to get a clue about what's going wrong with your Python script by taking a look at the Java console.

The Python interpreter in PixelMath is a software component called *Jython*; it's Python for the Java Virtual Machine (JVM). The JVM is part of the Java Runtime Environment or JRE.

11.4.3   Saving Your Work

If you are developing a Python script more than a page or so in length, then it would be a good idea to use an external text editor and keep your script in a file on your hard disk. It is a good idea to save the latest version of this file each time you go to test the script. Get in the habit of saving your work in a text file before errors happen. It would be a shame to lose any of your work because your script caused a "fatal error" in PixelMath and you had not saved the latest version of your script.

11.4.4   Restarting

You may need to restart PixelMath for a variety of possible reasons: you feel that your setup is too cluttered and you want to start over, or you have run into some kind of error that prevents you from proceeding, or you want to run a script that assumes that PixelMath is in its starting state.

You may be able to restart using the calculator's File menu option "Reset Calculator and remove images." If this fails, you'll need to do one of two things, depending on whether you are using PixelMath with a web server or as a standalone application. So you'll either be reloading the applet or restarting the application. To reload the applet in Mozilla Firefox, simply reload the web page by clicking on the browser's Reload button while holding down the shift key. Note that this will abort the current PixelMath session, closing all of its windows and discarding any work you may have done, so don't restart PixelMath without considering this. To restart the PixelMath application, kill the current session either by quitting or by typing Control-C in the Windows Command (DOS) window (if applicable). Then repeat whatever command you used to start PixelMath before.

11.5   A Longer Example

The following is an example Python script. It opens three image windows, lays them out on the screen, zooms in on each one, and puts a different pattern in each.

```
1    # Open 3 windows
2    window1 = pmNewImage(0, "First image",  200, 100, 0, 0, 0)
3    window2 = pmNewImage(0, "Second image", 200, 100, 0, 0, 0)
4    window3 = pmNewImage(0, "Third image",  200, 100, 0, 0, 0)
5
6    # Lay them out on the screen
7    pmPositionWindow(window1, 100, 50, 0, 0)
8    pmPositionWindow(window2, 100, 300, 0, 0)
9    pmPositionWindow(window3, 100, 550, 0, 0)
10
11   # Zoom into each one
12   pmZoom(window1, 64, 128)
13   pmZoom(window1, 64, 128)
14   pmZoom(window2, 64, 128)
15   pmZoom(window2, 64, 128)
16   pmZoom(window3, 64, 128)
17   pmZoom(window3, 64, 128)
18
19   # Put a different pattern in each
20   pmSetFormula("x * 32 mod 256")
21   pmSetDestination(window1)
22   pmCompute()
23   pmSetFormula("y * 32 mod 256")
24   pmSetDestination(window2)
25   pmCompute()
26   pmSetFormula("(x+y) * 32 mod 256")
27   pmSetDestination(window3)
28   pmCompute()
```

This script is mostly a sequence of PixelMath commands with some comments (lines starting with "#") and blank lines. There are also three assignments where a variable such as window1 is set equal to a value returned by pmNewImage. All these constructions will be described later.

11.6 PixelMath Commands

The PixelMath Python functions that interface with the image-processing environment we call PixelMath commands. Their names begin with "pm" and the rest of the name is somewhat descriptive. Most of these simply cause things to happen in PixelMath. However, some of them obtain information and return it; for example pmGetPixel is used to obtain the RGB information for a particular pixel of an image so that it can be used in a program, and using this function does not change the image in any way.

Some of the PixelMath commands are described below. A few more, such as those for manipulating dialog boxes, are introduced in chapter 16. Appendix c contains descriptions of all of them, along with many of those for standard Python functions. In each description that follows, there is a prototype expression in italic type. For example, *pmSetFormula(formula)* is a prototype that provides the name of the command, "pmSetFormula" and some more information about how the function is called. In most cases, the command name is followed by a number of names, such as "windowNum". These names are called parameter names and they represent argument values that need to be provided when the command is executed.

pmNewImage(windowNum, title, width, height, r, g, b)   This is used to put an image on the screen. If `windowNum` is 0, this creates a new window and a new image having the specified width, height, and color. If `windowNum` is the number of an image window on the screen already, the new image is put in that window. Example: `pmNewImage(0, "My image", 400, 300, 0, 0, 128)` creates a new window with a 400-by-300 array of pixels, each of which is initialized to dark blue (0 red, 0 green, and 128 units of blue). This function returns an integer that is the window number for the newly created image window or for the existing image window.

pmOpenImage(windowNum, filename)   If `windowNum` is 0, this creates a new window and downloads the specified image from the server or loads one from the local file system. Then it returns an integer representing the window number for the new window. If `windowNum` is the number of an image window already on the screen, the downloaded image is put into that window rather than a new one.

pmSetSource1(windowNum)   Sets the choice box for Source1 to the chosen window.

pmSetSource2(windowNum)   Sets the choice box for Source2 to the chosen window.

pmSetDestination(windowNum)   Sets the choice box for the destination to the chosen window.

pmSelectRGB(r, g, b)   Enables or disables each color component for updates. Each argument here should be true or false for selected or deselected. Example: To select only red and blue, use `pmSelectRGB(True, False, True)`.

pmSetRectangle(windowNum, x, y, width, height)   Places the selection rectangle so that one corner is at (x, y) and so that it will have the given width and height.

pmSetFormula(formula)   Puts a string into the formula box on the PixelMath calculator. This string should be in a form that is ready for the calculator, just like those that get entered by hand. Example: to negate the source image, use `pmSetFormula("255 - Source1(x,y)")`

pmCompute()   Simulates clicking on the Compute button on the calculator.

pmPositionWindow(windowNum, x, y, width, height)   Repositions and resizes the specified Image Frame window. If `windowNum` is given as 0, it repositions the calculator itself. If either the width or height value is 0, then only repositioning is performed. The *x* and *y* values specify where the lower-left corner of the window should be placed, in terms of the screen's coordinates. The screen coordinate system has its origin, with coordinates (0, 0), in the lower-left corner of the screen.

pmSetTitle(windowNum, title)   Changes the title in the specified window. (Note that the window number is always automatically shown as part of an image window's title.) The `title` is a Python string.

pmGetPixel(windowNum, x, y)   Reads a pixel from the specified window, performing array bounds checking.

pmSetPixel(windowNum, x, y, r, g, b)   Stores a pixel in the specified window, performing array bounds checking. Also puts each of R, G, and B into the range 0–255 if any of them are negative or greater than 255.

pmRefresh(windowNum)   Updates the display. This should be called after one or more calls to either `pmSetPixel` or `pmSetPixelQuickly`, so that the new pixel value and color can actually be seen. It would be overly time-consuming to automatically perform this after each call to the pixel-setting functions when many pixels are being changed together.

pmGetScreenSize()   Returns a tuple containing the width and height of the screen in pixels. For example, for a 1280-by-1024 screen, the returned tuple would be (1280, 1024).

pmGetWindowSize(windowNum)   Returns a tuple containing the width and height of the selected window in pixels. The parameter `windowNum` should be an integer that indicates the selected image window. For example, for a 128-by-64 image, the returned tuple would be (128, 64).

pmSetPolar()   Sets the calculator's coordinate system to be a polar one with origin in the center of the image. Values of rho range from 0 to its half the length of a diagonal of the image. Values of theta range from −pi to +pi, with 0 radians being the angle along the ray from the center of the image to the right.

pmSetCartesian()   Sets the calculator's coordinate system to be a Cartesian one with origin at the lower-left corner of the image. Values of *x* range from 0 to xmax, and values of *y* range from 0 to ymax.

pmSleep(millisec)   Pauses execution for the given number of milliseconds. This can be useful when playing through a timed presentation of images and their transformations.

pmHideProgress()   Suppresses the display of the progress bar during computations. This can be helpful if a computation is part of a transition effect during a presentation.

pmShowProgress()   Restores the display of the progress bar during computations.

pmZoom(windowNum, x, y)   Zooms the specified image window, using the point (*x*, *y*) as the focus of expansion.

pmUnzoom(windowNum, x, y)   Zooms out rather than in, using the specified window and focal point.

These functions can be typed into the listener as commands. They can also be used within program structures such as subprograms, loops, and branches. In the following chapters we'll learn to use these program structures as tools for setting up interesting effects and demonstrations.

11.7 An Example: Twin Monas

Let's create a sequence of commands that will set up the PixelMath environment to take the Mona Lisa image and create a larger image that contains two copies of it, one reflected so that the two Mona Lisas are facing each other. We'll call this the Twin Monas picture.

We'll assume that this script is run immediately after starting PixelMath, so that the first window created by the script will be the first image window opened during the session. If you try running this script, you'll find that it has a bug: the Monas don't face each other. Can you fix that? This script also assumes that the Mona Lisa image has width 423 and height 421. If you want to try this with a different image, you'll need to adjust the sizes in a couple of places. Also, note that if you need to run the script a second time, you'll need to restart PixelMath because the window numbers will not come out right. Later, we'll show a way to get around this restriction.

```
1   pmOpenImage(0, "mona-rgb.jpg")
2   pmNewImage(0, "Twin Monas", 846, 421, 0, 0, 0)
3   pmPositionWindow(2, 150, 250, 0, 0)
4   pmSetSource1(1)
5   pmSetDestination(2)
6   pmSetFormula("If (x < 423) Then S1(x,y) Else S1(845 - x,y)")
7   pmCompute()
```

11.8 References

Dawson, M. 2010. *Python Programming for the Absolute Beginner*, 3rd ed. Course Technology PTR.

Henstridge, J. 2006. GIMP Python documentation. www.gimp.org/docs/python/.

Van Rossum, G. 1996. Foreward for *Programming Python* by Mark Lutz Sebastopol, CA: O'Reilly. www.python.org/doc/essays/foreword/.

11.9 Exercises

1. Open up the Python interface to PixelMath and from the File menu create a new Python buffer. Then write a two-line program similar to that shown in figure 11.1 as follows: Write a `print` statement that prints your name followed by "presents a Python program." Using the `pmNewComputedImage` function and a formula such as `RGB(x,y,0)`, write a Python function call that creates a colorful image of size 256 by 256. Test your program.

2. Create a sequence of PixelMath commands that sets up four windows, each containing a 128-by-128 image representing a solid color. The first image should be red, the next green, and the third blue. The fourth should be gray. The windows should be arranged on the screen in a 2-by-2 grid. Use the `pmPositionWindow` function to locate the windows.

3. Develop a Python script that sets up some windows and creates a stereogram.

4. Develop a Python script that takes an input image and puts it in a circular frame, or better yet, an elliptical frame.

12 Basics of Python

12.1 Overview

In this chapter we cover the most essential features of the Python programming language, as well as how to interact with Python.

12.2 Interacting with Python

Python is a computer programming language that can be used in a great variety of settings, such as in an installation, separate from PixelMath, on a Windows computer, on a web server, or as a scripting language inside an application program. We will be using it mostly as a scripting language inside PixelMath. That means that if PixelMath is already running on your computer, you do not need to install anything extra to use Python.

To start working with Python in PixelMath, click on the Python button on the PixelMath launch pad window. Alternatively, from the calculator's Tools menu, select the Python programming window.

The Python programming window consists of a menu bar and three panes. The top pane is a "tabbed pane" that allows you to have buffers (like files) open for editing, running, or inspection. The middle pane is the history pane in which the session's inputs and outputs so far are shown. At the bottom is the input line, a small pane that holds the line of text being typed for input to Python.

You can use Python interactively a little bit like a printing calculator. If you enter "7 + 12" in the input line, the Python system will copy it to the history pane, interpret it, perform the addition, and print the answer in the history pane.

If you make a mistake and wish to modify the 12 to be 13, you can move the mouse cursor to the history pane's line containing "7 + 12", press the Enter key, and this line of text will be copied to the input line, where you can change the 12 to a 13 and enter it again.

12.3   Numbers

Let's start our technical coverage of Python with numbers. We'll see how we express numbers with some examples. The expression 7+12 involves two integers. The result of performing the addition is also an integer (see below).

Python also supports double-precision, floating-point numbers, which are appropriate when fractions and decimal points are needed. The expression 1.5 * 3 involves a floating-point number (float) and an integer. The result of this is a float.

```
1   >>> 7+12
2   19
3   >>> 1.5 * 3
4   4.5
```

Python also supports scientific notation for describing floats. A number in scientific notation, like 1.29E3, has two parts, separated by the letter E. The first part is an integer or float written in the normal way (not scientific notation) and the part after the E is an integer. This example represents the number equal to 1.29×10^3, or 1290.0. It becomes more convenient to use scientific notation as the power of 10 that we're dealing with gets higher. Here's an example that shows scientific notation involving negative numbers.

```
1   >>> -1.414213E-1
2   -0.1414213
```

Here's an example with Avogadro's number from physics.

```
1   >>> a = 6.02214179E23
2   >>> a * a
3   3.62661917388644e+47
```

Python supports integers of two sorts, normal and long. A normal integer is what Python calls an "int" and a long integer is what Python calls a "long." Longs are used automatically when a really large integer is computed. For example, the number 13!, known as thirteen factorial, can be computed in Python directly as follows:

```
1  >>> 13 * 12 * 11 * 10 * 9 * 8 * 7 * 6 * 5 * 4 * 3 * 2
2  6227020800L
```

The answer has the letter L at the end to indicate that this number is represented in Python's long format. (Note: future versions of Python will eliminate this use of L.)

By using a decimal point in at least one of the factors in our multiplication expression, we can see how Python produces its product as a float, and since it's such a large float, it's printed out in scientific notation.

```
1  # factorial(20.0)
2  >>> 20.0 * 19 * 18 * 17 * 16 * 15 * 14 * \
3      13 * 12 * 11 * 10 * 9 * 8 * 7 * 6 * 5 * 4 * 3 * 2
4  2.43290200817664E18
```

By the way, this last example shows how a line can be continued by using the backslash character at the end of each partial line. The continuation of the line can occur with any amount of indenting.

12.4 Variables

A variable is a symbol that is used to represent a value in a program or in a session. As in mathematics, a Python variable can take on many different values or, in a sense, represent a set of possibilities. A Python line such as

```
1  >>> x = 5
```

specifies an assignment. When this is evaluated, the variable x is assigned the value 5. This means the number 5 is stored in a memory location that goes with x. The association of 5 with x will be remembered for the rest of the session unless some other assignment to x changes it.

Here is an example of using variables in a session.

```
1   >>> x = 21
2   >>> 7 * x
3   147
4   >>> x * x
5   441
6   >>> x = 50
7   >>> y = 10
8   >>> x + y
9   60
10  >>> an_even_year = 2008
11  >>> x + an_even_year
12  2058
13  >>> X = 17
14  >>> x + X
15  67
```

As this example shows, once a variable has been assigned a value using the equationlike statement format, it can be used in arithmetic expressions like 7 * x. A variable can be reassigned and the new value replaces the old one. Subsequent instances of the variable in arithmetic expressions use the new value.

A variable need not be named by just a single letter like x or y but can be any string of characters involving letters, digits, and the underscore character, provided the string does not start with a digit. If a letter is capitalized in one variable name and uncapitalized in another, then these are separate variable names. In other words, the character case is significant in naming variables. At the end of the above example, the expression x + X has the value 67 because one variable, x, has a value 50, and the other variable, X, has a value 17.

There is more to say about variables, but that can wait until later. We've covered the most essential aspects.

12.5 Arithmetic Expressions

An arithmetic expression is a segment of Python code (some text) that represents a number. It is made up of numbers, variables, operators, function names, parentheses, and/or commas. Here are some examples.

```
5
5.0
1.234E-2
x
5 + sqrt(2) * pow(5, 3)
(7 % 4) / 100.0
```

These examples illustrate several different forms of numbers and use of functions. The first, 5, is an integer. Then 5.0 is a floating-point real number. Next is another floating-point real number written in scientific notation, where the number -2 following the letter E means that the 1.234 is multiplied by 10^{-2}. The expression x is really only valid as an arithmetic expression provided x will have been assigned a number by the time the expression is evaluated.

The function calls sqrt(2) and pow(5, 3) make use of mathematical functions that are defined in the Python module called math. The first takes the square root of 2 and the second computes the third power of 5, which is 5^3 or more simply 125.

The expression (7 % 4) takes 7 modulo 4, which means the remainder after dividing 7 by 4, which is 3. The expression (7 % 4) / 100.0 results in 0.03.

12.6 Strings

A sequence of characters, which is the same as a piece of text, is known as a character string, or simply a *string*. When represented in a program or in a Python session, strings are typically put in quotes. However, the quote marks themselves are not part of the strings. Several different forms of quoting are available in Python, for flexibility. Here are some examples:

```
1   >>> greeting = 'Hello there'
2   >>> who = 'friend'
3   >>> remark = "Isn't Python great?"
4   >>> full_greeting = greeting + ', ' + friend + ".\n" + remark
5   >>> print full_greeting
6   Hello there, friend.
7   Isn't Python great?
```

Short, single-line strings are typically surrounded by single quote marks. However, if the string itself must contain a single quote mark (the apostrophe), then it is convenient to use double-quote marks to delimit the string. Two strings can be put together via *concatenation*, which in Python is designated by a plus sign. Concatenation is a sort of string addition.

The effect of the example here is to create and print a two-line string. However, Python provides facilities for creating multiline strings that are even more convenient than those we have used.

```
1   >>> full_greeting = """Hello there, friend.
2   Isn't Python great?"""
3   >>> print full_greeting
4   Hello there, friend.
5   Isn't Python great?
```

A multiline string can be delimited either by a pair of triple-single quote marks or, as shown here, by a pair of triple-double quote marks.

Strings are essential in controlling PixelMath. Among other uses, they represent formulas, file names, and window titles. Here is an example of modifying the title of an image window that's already on the screen:

```
1   >>> newTitle = "My Image Window"
2   >>> pmSetTitle(1, newTitle)
```

Strings are sequences of characters. Particular parts of these sequences can be accessed using square-bracket notation, as the following examples show.

```
1    >>> s = 'abcde'
2    >>> s[0]
3    'a'
4    >>> s[1]
5    'b'
6    >>> s[1:3]
7    'bc'
8    >>> s[1:]
9    'bcde'
10   >>> s[:3]
11   'abc'
12   >>> s[:]
13   'abcd'
```

A colon is used to help establish ranges of elements from a sequence not only in strings but also in lists, which are the next topic.

12.7 Lists

A list is a sequence of elements, such as numbers, that are normally written with square brackets surrounding them. Here is a list of five values.

```
['A list of', 4, 'top-level', ['data', 'items']]
```

The last element of this list is itself a list, and so is in the role of a sublist.

Two lists can be put together, just as strings are concatenated, to form a longer list.

```
1   >>> L1 = ['a', 'b']
2   >>> L2 = [2, 3, 4]
3   >>> L1 + L2
4   ['a', 'b', 2, 3, 4]
```

An easy way to construct a list of, say seven items, is to use the built-in function range.

```
1   >>> range(7)
2   [0, 1, 2, 3, 4, 5, 6]
3   >>> range(3,7)
4   [3, 4, 5, 6]
5   >>> range(3,7,2)
6   [3, 5]
```

The second example shows that range can take, not only one argument, but two arguments: the first gives the starting value for the sequence and the second gives a value 1 greater than the last element. One can even give a third argument to range, which allows using step sizes other than 1.

A particular element in a list can be accessed using notation illustrated as follows:

```
1   >>> L = ['a', 'b', 'c', 'd', 'e']
2   >>> L[0]
```

```
3     'a'
4     >>> L[4]
5     'e'
6     >>> L[-1]
7     'e'
8     >>> L[-2]
9     'd'
```

Note that the first element of a list is at position 0. This is known as zero-based indexing, and it is common in computer programming languages. (And, as we have seen, strings are indexed the same way.)

Sublists and subsequences of a list can be accessed using the so-called slice notation.

```
1     >>> L = ['a', 'b', 'c', 'd', 'e']
2     >>> L[2:4]
3     ['c', 'd']
4     >>> L[2:]
5     ['c', 'd', 'e']
6     >>> L[:3]
7     ['a', 'b', 'c']
8     >>> L[::2]
9     ['a', 'c', 'e']
```

A slice is represented by including either a single colon or two colons in the list-indexing expression. If there is a single colon, e.g., as in L[m:n], the slice is a sublist beginning at the position m (or 0, if no number is given before the colon), and extending up to but not including the element in position n. If this argument is missing, then the end of the list is assumed. If there are two colons, then the value after the second colon is the step size.

Lists are often useful in scripts for controlling PixelMath. For example, we might want to set up a list of filenames for images to be processed or for a list of formulas to apply to an image.

```
1     >>> filenames = ["john.jpg", "tom.jpg", "vince.jpg"]
2     >>> pmOpenImage(0, filenames[0])
3     >>> pmOpenImage(0, filenames[1])
4     >>> pmOpenImage(0, filenames[2])
5     >>> formulas = ["s1(y,y)", "s1(w-x,y)", "s1(w,h-y)"]
```

Plate 1 (figure 1.1)
Chuck Close's "Emma," a woodcut completed in 2002, in which "pixels" are made up of colored lozenges and other shapes. Created in collaboration with Japanese woodblock artist Yasu Shibata, it is the woodblock with the world's most complex woodblock assemblage and printing process. Courtesy of Pace Editions, Inc. and the artist.

Plate 2 (figure 1.2)
A photomosaic image of a face composed of many small images of flowers using one of the methods described in this book.

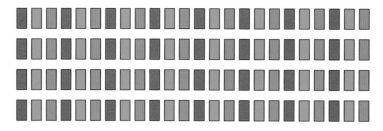

Plate 3 (figure 1.10)
How red, green, and blue photosites are arranged in the CCD array of a typical digital camera's sensor chip.

Plate 4 (figure 2.6)
Photograph of a scene with a picket fence (taken at the garden at the historic English Camp on San Juan Island, Washington State).

(a)

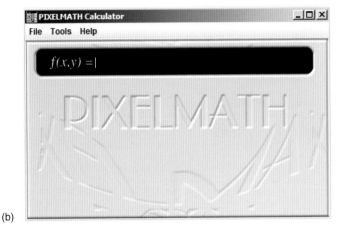

(b)

Plate 5 (figure 2.12)
PixelMath startup: (a) the launch pad and (b) the calculator with the cover still closed.

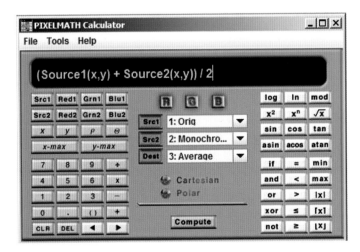

Plate 6 (figure 2.13)
The PixelMath calculator with cover open. It has a menu bar, a formula area, drop-down lists for selecting source images and destination, a Compute button, and additional buttons and controls.

Plate 7 (figure 2.15)
An image window after loading is complete.

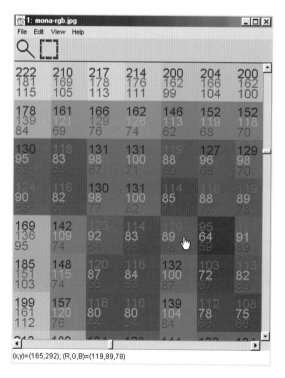

Plate 8 (figure 2.17)
A closeup of the Mona Lisa with RGB values of individual pixels showing.

Plate 9 (figure 4.1)
Spectrum of visible light. Wavelength markings are in nanometers.

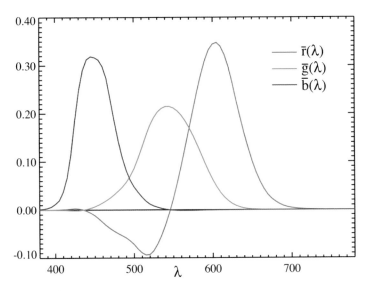

Plate 10 (figure 4.2)
Color-matching functions that show the relative amounts of red, green, and blue required to create a mixture that perceptually matches each spectral color. The curves also roughly indicate the sensitivity of each of kind of cone to light across the spectrum. The horizontal axis shows wavelength in nanometers and the vertical axis shows relative magnitude. The curves have been normalized so that the areas under them are equal. These functions correspond to the 1931 CIE standard observer.

Plate 11 (figure 4.3)
The enable-red, enable-green, and enable-blue toggles.

Plate 12 (figure 4.4)
Color gradients superimposed: red increases from left to right whereas green increases from bottom to top.

Plate 13 (figure 4.6)
Palette of colors constructed by superimposing a pattern of locally varying blue with a horizontal gradient of red and a vertical gradient of green.

Plate 14 (figure 4.7)
The Tree of Color photograph. Courtesy of Bruce Hemingway.

Plate 15 (figure 4.11)
A spectrum of colors created by varying the hue from 0.0 to 1.0 while the saturation and value are each maintained at 1.0.

(a)

(b)

Plate 16 (figure 4.12)
Effect of hue rotation by one-half. The original (a) shows the true colors, while (b) shows the complementary hues obtained by going 180 degrees around the gray axis in the HSV color space.

(a)

(b)

Plate 17 (figure 4.13)
Effect of hue rotation by one-third and two-thirds. In (a) the effect of rotation by one-third (i.e., 120 degrees) is shown and in (b) the amount of rotation is two-thirds (i.e., 240 degrees).

Plate 18 (figure 4.14)
Palette of colors with a horizontal gradient of hue values and a vertical gradient of saturation values. The value component of each color is 1.0 in this image.

(a)

(b)

Plate 19 (figure 4.15)
Results of boosting the saturation of an image, (a) by averaging the original saturation with 1.0, and (b) by replacing the original saturation by 1.0. The latter, representing maximum saturation, produces a somewhat garish effect.

(a)   (b)

Plate 20 (figure 4.16)
(a) The Mona Lisa and (b) the result of boosting the value of each color in the HSV system.

Plate 21 (figure 6.25)
Simulated effect of global warming on the Nisqually Glacier at Mt. Rainier National Park.

Plate 22 (figure 6.26)
Simulated effect of global cooling on the Earth.

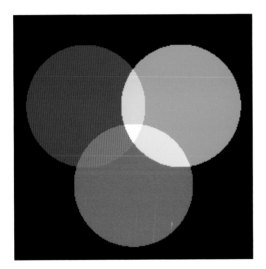

Plate 23 (figure 7.9)
A Venn diagram showing additive RGB color mixing produced using the circle formula.

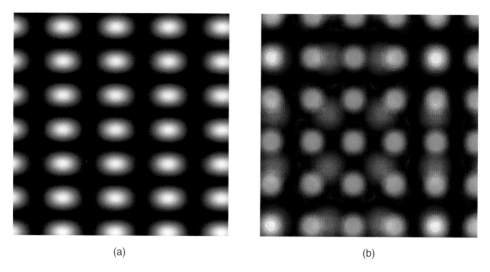

(a)   (b)

Plate 24 (figure 7.11)
Products of sinusoidal functions: (a) monochrome and (b) with different horizontal and vertical frequencies in each of R, G, and B.

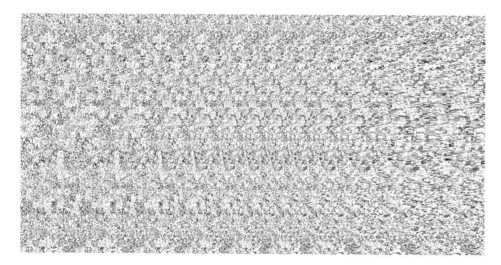

Plate 25 (figure 8.5)
Autostereogram resulting from the setup in figure 8.4.

Plate 26 (figure 9.2)
Photomosaic constructed with the single-tile method, with the Mona Lisa image used both for the subject and the tile.

Plate 27 (figure 9.3)
Detail of figure 9.2 in which we see the face made up of many small Mona Lisa images whose colors have been adjusted.

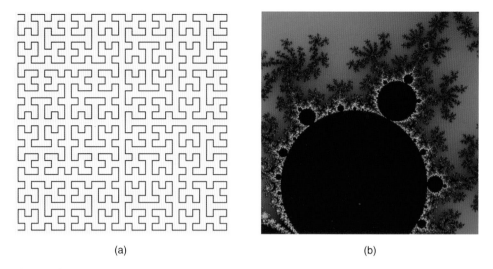

(a)   (b)

Plate 28 (figure 9.4)
(a) Approximation of the Hilbert curve fractal to five levels and (b) a portion of the Mandelbrot set.

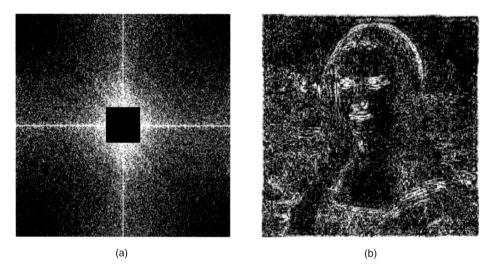

(a)   (b)

Plate 29 (figure 10.8)
High-pass filtering with the Mona Lisa image: (a) edited transform and (b) inverse of the edited transform.

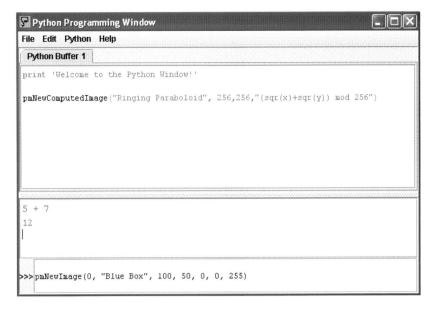

Plate 30 (figure 11.1)
The PixelMath Python window showing the buffer pane (just below the menu bar) and listener panes (lower half). The buffer pane shows what file (program) the user is currently editing or testing, in this case a two-line program beginning with a print statement. The history pane (here containing the two lines 5 + 7 and 12) contains a transcript of what the user has entered and what the responses from Python were. The input pane, at the bottom, holds the last line of the expression the user is currently typing in. In this case it is a call to the function pmNewImage.

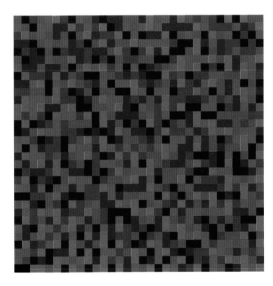

Plate 31 (figure 16.2)
The image produced by the PrimeNumbersImage.py program. The average density of prime numbers drops off slowly toward the top of the image. The locations of red pixels in the bottom row provide important clues about the correctness of the program.

(a)

(b)

(c)

(d)

Plate 32 (figure 19.1)
Example of input images and output image for high-dynamic-range imaging. (a) exposure for 1/60 second, (b) exposure for 1 second, (c) exposure for 15 seconds, and (d) tone-mapped result.

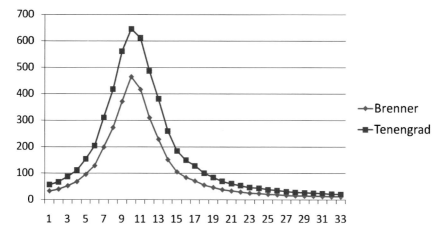

Plate 33 (figure 19.2)
Sharpness as a function of focus setting. The lower curve gives the Brenner sharpness and the upper curve gives the Tenengrad sharpness. The best focus is achieved in the tenth frame, where both types of sharpness are maximized.

(a)   (b)

Plate 34 (figure 19.3)
The first and tenth frames in the sequences of images used to demonstrate autofocus. Frame 10 achieves the best focus.

Plate 35 (figure 19.6)
(a) Normal photograph of eggs in a basket, (b) image representing only direct illumination, (c) image representing only global illumination, (d) normal photograph of grapes and cheese, (e) direct illumination only, and (f) global illumination only. Courtesy of Shree Nayar.

Plate 36 (figure 19.7)
Inpainting: (a) original damaged image, (b) inpainting with the average boundary color, (c) simple diffusion method, and (d) diffusion with barriers.

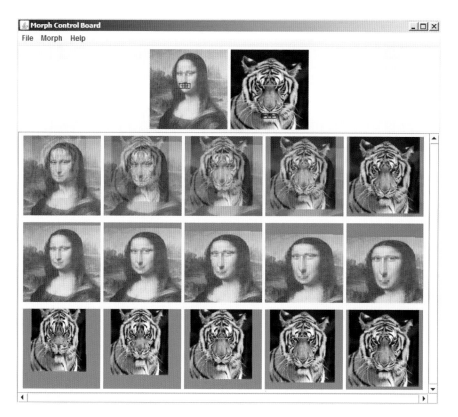

Plate 37 (figure 20.3)
Screen shot of the MorphingGUI program.

Plate 38 (figure 20.4)
Large database image that holds many tiles, prepared by MakePhotomosaicDBImage.py, ready for use in a photomosaic construction.

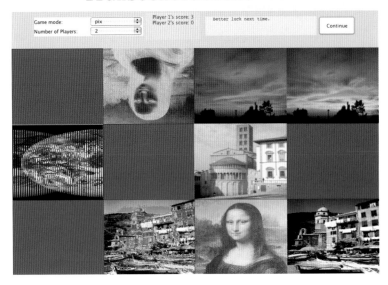

Plate 39 (figure 20.5)
Transcentration game screen shot. At this point in the game, four of twelve cards remain unmatched and face down (purple). Each of the others has been matched with its transform or inverse transform and is shown face up.

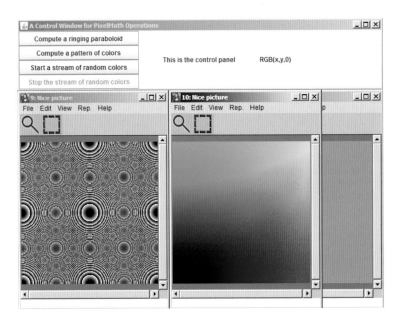

Plate 40 (figure E.1)
Screen shot of a program that computes PixelMath images from a graphical user interface. The interface uses buttons and labels.

12.8 Built-in Functions

Python has many functions available for use in programs. Some of these are immediately available and others must first be imported. Here are a few of the built-in functions that do not have to be imported: int, float, str, abs, pow. Some illustrations follow.

```
1   >>> int(2.5) + int('13')
2   15
3   >>> float(5)
4   5.0
5   >>> str(5.7)
6   '5.7'
7   >>> abs(-7)
8   7
9   >>> pow(5, 2)
10  25
```

12.9 Modules and Importing

Many other functions are available in external modules. Importing is usually just a matter of including a line such as one of the following before using the desired function.

```
import math
from math import sin
from math import *
import time, sys
```

If the math module has been imported with line 1 in

```
1   >>> import math
2   >>> math.sin(math.pi / 4)
3   0.7071067811865475
```

then its functions can be called, provided the module name is prefixed to each function using a dot. The symbol pi is also defined in the math module, even though it is not a function.

The need to prefix each function name with the module name disappears if one of the following forms is used.

```
1  >>> from math import sin
2  >>> sin(math.pi / 4)
3  0.7071067811865475
4  >>> from math import *
5  >>> cos(pi / 8)
6  0.9238795325112867
```

When working with large programs that have multiple modules or large modules, it is considered safe programming to avoid this form of importing if the functions might have the same names as functions from other modules being imported.

When exploring to find out what symbols (including functions) are defined in a module, the dir function (directory) can be useful.

```
1  >>> import math
2  >>> dir(math)
3  ['acos', 'asin', 'atan', 'atan2', 'ceil', 'classDictInit', 'cos',
4  'cosh', 'e', 'exp', 'fabs', 'floor', 'fmod', 'frexp', 'hypot',
5  'ldexp', 'log', 'log10', 'modf', 'pi', 'pow', 'sin', 'sinh',
6  'sqrt', 'tan', 'tanh']
```

Another useful module is the time module. Among other methods in this module are the asctime and localtime methods. Their use is illustrated in the following example.

```
1  >>> import time
2  >>> time.asctime()
3  'Sun Jan 20 23:04:07 2008'
4  >>> time.localtime()
5  (2008, 1, 20, 23, 4, 14, 6, 20, 0)
```

Here we can see that the asctime method returns a string that gives the day of the week, month, day of the month, time in hours, minutes, and seconds (hh:mm:ss format), and the year. Both the day of the week and the month are given using three-character abbreviations so that they can be easily extracted separately using fixed index values such as in

```
1   >>> dayOfWeek = time.asctime()[:3]
2   >>> dayOfWeek
3   Sun
4   month = time.asctime()[4:7]
```

12.10   Comments in Code

In a computer program, a *comment* is text that will be ignored during execution of the program but that might be useful to a person reading the program. Comments that are helpful in describing the workings or purpose of a program can be included in the program in two different ways. One way is to include multiline strings that are there only to carry textual documentation. Another way is to type a pound character # (sometimes known as the sharp sign) and then additional text after it on the same line. Here are two examples:

```
'''This multi-line string is just one kind
of comment.'''

year = 2008    # A nice even year.
```

12.11   Example

The following Python script illustrates many of the constructs presented in this chapter. First it imports the `time` module. It calls the function `asctime` to get a textual description of the current time and date. It prints this out. Then it calls the function `localtime` to get several separate pieces of information about the current time and date. These are returned in a tuple of integers. The seventh of these integers represents the day of the week. This is used to select a particular formula from a list of seven formulas. A string is created by concatenating a given string with the day of the week to create a title string. A new image window is set up with the new title and formula.

```
1   '''This example shows several Python constructs
2   working together to set up an image that depends on
3   the day of the week.'''
4   import time
```

```
5    today = time.asctime()
6    print "Today is " + today
7    formulas = ["x + y", "x * y", "x**y mod 256", \
8               "RGB(x,y,0)", "RGB(0,x,y)", "RGB(x,0,y)", \
9               "RGB(x,0,0)"]
10   timeInformation = time.localtime()
11   dayOfWeek = timeInformation[6]
12   title = "Image of the day for day: " + str(dayOfWeek)
13   todaysFormula = formulas[dayOfWeek]
14   pmNewComputedImage(title, 256, 128, todaysFormula)
```

12.12 References

Martelli, A. 2003. *Python in a Nutshell: A Desktop Quick Reference*. Sebastopol, CA: O'Reilly.

Miller, B., and Ranum, D. *Problem Solving with Algorithms and Data Structures Using Python*. (Wilsonville, OR: Franklin, Beedle.

12.13 Exercises

1. Write a Python expression for the Euclidean distance between two points, where the points are given as x0, y0, x1, y2.

2. Write a pair of Python expressions for the quadradic formula,

$$x = \frac{-b \pm \sqrt{b^2 - 4ac}}{2a}$$

3. Write an expression that concatenates three lists of words.

4. Write an expression that converts the square roots of the numbers 2 to 7 to integers and then adds them up.

5. What happens when you try to create a floating-point number that is too big for Python to process?

6. What happens if you type in the expression 1/0?

7. Give a concise expression that computes 2 to the 32nd power.

8. Write a Python expression that uses three variables—hours, minutes, and seconds—and expresses the total number of seconds represented by the variables. You should make some variable assignments to test the expression. For example, after typing

```
1   >>> hours = 4
2   >>> minutes = 30
3   >>> seconds = 15
```

your formula should produce the value 16215.

9. Develop a sequence of PixelMath Python commands that can be used to make "wall paper" from an image. A wallpaper image is a large image that has a smaller image repeated in it. We say that the small image tiles the large image. You may wish to consider using the array of miniatures approach described in chapter 5.

13 Control Structures: Conditionals and Repetition

13.1 Overview

In the preceding two chapters we saw examples of Python programs that involve sequences of operations. So far, these sequences have always followed a fixed order of the form, "step 1, step 2, step 3 . . .", etc.

In this chapter we'll cover two methods for making the order of execution more flexible. One is the use of "if", which can make some steps *conditional* upon something else. The other is the use of looping to cause some steps to be repeated a number of times.

13.2 Conditionals

A conditional statement or conditional block is one or more steps of a program that are executed only if some condition is true. The following is a simple example.

```
1   print "Have you visited the Art Institute of Chicago before?"
2   answer = raw_input("Y or N")
3   if answer=="Y":
4     print "Then a very special welcome to you!"
5   print "Now do come in."
```

In this example, a message is printed and then the program asks the user for input. If the user enters "Y", the program prints "Then a very special welcome to you!" Then, regardless of whether the user input "Y" or something else, the program prints "Now do come in." Notice that the part of the program that is executed conditionally, which is the printing of the special welcome message, follows a colon and is indented. The second print statement is not indented, and it is thus not conditional on the user's answer.

The next example is slightly more complex, having a so-called else clause in addition to what we call a then clause.

```
1   print "Do you like impressionism? (Y or N)"
2   answer = raw_input("Y or N")
3   if answer=="Y":
4     print "You'll love Claude Monet."
5   else:
6     print "You might like Rembrandt."
```

In this example, what is printed depends on whether the user types in "Y" or something else. If it's "Y", then the program prints "You'll love Claude Monet." Otherwise it prints "You might like Rembrandt."

13.3 Boolean Values

In each of these examples, the expression immediately following the word `if` is called the *condition* of the `if` statement. It must have a value that is either `True` or `False`. Such a value is called a *Boolean* value and the expression is called a *Boolean expression*. Boolean expressions are also called logical expressions.

The particular Boolean expression, `answer=="Y"` is a test for equality. The double equals sign is used for this purpose. If a single equals sign had been used, there would have been a syntax error, since a single equals sign denotes assignment, not a test for equality, and assignment would not be appropriate directly following the word `if`.

Boolean expressions can be as simple as `True` by itself, or `False` by itself. They can also simply be variables whose values are `True` or `False`. Here is an example:

```
1   sculpture = True
2   if sculpture:
3     nDimensions = 3
```

On the other hand, a Boolean expression can be built up of multiple parts, using the logical operators `and`, `or`, and `not`.

```
1    from random import randint, choice
2    n = randint(0, 100)
3    full_time_student = choice([True, False])
4    if n<14 or n>65 or (n<30 and full_time_student):
5        print "Discount applies."
6    else:
7        print "Full price required."
```

In this example, the `randint` function in the `random` module is used to obtain a random integer in the range of 0 to 100. The `choice` function gets a random member of the list [True, False], and then the value is assigned to `full_time_student`. Depending on how these values turn out, the condition (represented by the compound Boolean expression) is either True or False, and that controls what is printed.

The example also uses numeric comparison operators: $<$ and $>$. A variety of these operators are available in Python. Here are the possibilities, each as a part of a Boolean expression with a comment next to it:

```
x < y     # x less than y
x <= y    # x less than or equal to y
x > y     # x greater than y
x >= y    # x greater than or equal to y
x == y    # x equals y
x <> y    # x not equal to y
x != y    # x not equal to y (alternative formulation)
not x==y # x not equal to y (another alternative)
```

Here is another example of the use of a compound Boolean expression:

```
1    if style=="Impressionist" and \
2        (medium=="pastel" or medium=="watercolor") and \
3        not theme=="abstract":
4        print "This could be Edgar Degas."
```

Not only do we have a compound Boolean expression here, it is so large that we have to manage it in two ways. For one thing, we let it extend across three lines, but using a backslash character at the break. The continuation doesn't have to be indented in any special way, but we indent in an aesthetically pleasing manner. The second way in which we manage this large Boolean expression is by using parentheses to group the parts of a subexpression. Here, the subexpression communicates that the artistic medium can be either pastel or watercolor.

Another example of a Boolean expression involves an operator called `in`.

```
element in sequence
'a' in 'abc'  # True
'ab' in 'abc' # True
'ac' in 'abc' # False
'Arp' in ['Arp', 'Botero', 'Chase']   # True
['Arp'] in ['Arp', 'Botero', 'Chase'] # False
```

The `in` operator tests whether an element is a part of the sequence. In the case of the sequence being a string, the element can be a single character or a substring. In the case of a list, the element must be a list element in order for the result to be true; it can't just be a sublist. As we will see in chapter 15, it is possible for functions to return Boolean values.

Early versions of the Python language did not have Boolean values. Instead, the integer 0 was used to mean False in a condition, and a nonzero value was used to mean True. Even in recent versions of Python (e.g., 2.5), it is acceptable to use non-Boolean expressions as conditions with this understanding.

13.4 Multiple Cases

In the examples of `if` statements given here, we have seen that there can be one or more clauses (or cases) for a conditional. For example, we can handle three special cases by using `if` with an `elif` and an `else` clause as follows (continuing the previous example).

```
 1    if day_abbrev=='Sat' or day_abbrev=='Sun':
 2      hours = "10:00-5:00"
 3      free_admission = False
 4    elif day_abbrev=='Thu':
 5      free_admission = True
 6      hours = "10:30-8:00"
 7    else:
 8      free_admission = False
 9      is_weekend = 'No'
10      hours = "10:30-5:00"
11    print 'Admission' + 'free!' if free_admission else 'normal.'
```

This example uses just one `elif` clause, but it could have any number of them. Another feature in this example is multiple lines in each clause. In the first clause, the "then" clause, the variable `hours` is set to "10:00–5:00" and the variable `free_admission` is set to False. Generally, there must be at least one line in each clause, but there is no upper limit. Having at least one is not a problem because if there is nothing that you want the computer to do in a particular case, you can simply put in the word `pass`.

Another feature of this example is the use of a *conditional expression* in the last line. Such an expression has the form

value1 `if` *condition* `else` *value2*

Such an expression can be a component of a larger expression. Note that a conditional expression is not the same thing as a Boolean expression, although it is possible (but not usual) that the value of a conditional expression can be True or False. In the last line of the previous example, the conditional expression is used to select either "free!" or "normal." in the end of the message to be printed.

As a final example of an `if` statement with multiple cases, we have a tiny program that reports on the genre associated with various artists.

```
1   if artist=="Picasso":    genre = "Cubism"
2   elif artist=="Seurat":   genre = "Pointillism"
3   elif artist=="Mondrian": genre = "Modernism"
4   elif artist=="Calder":   genre = "Mobilism?";
5   print "very moving art"
```

This example involves four cases. The formatting of the code illustrates the use of the option, allowed by Python, to have a clause on the same line as the condition to which it corresponds. If a clause has multiple lines, the lines can be joined using the semicolon as a separator.

13.5 Loops

Once a sequence of instructions has been put in a form that a computer can understand, it's not difficult to make the computer do the instructions over and over again. Computers are good at repeating anything they know how to do.

Repetition is usually controlled with programming constructs called loops. Loops are extremely useful in programming. They provide a way to make a computer perform a lot of useful work with only a relatively small amount of programming effort. An easy way to set up a loop in Python is to use the `for` statement.

```
1   for artist in ['Whistler', 'Wyeth', 'Warhol']:
2     print "Who was "+artist+"?"
```

When this code is executed, we get

```
Who was Whistler?
Who was Wyeth?
Who was Warhol?
```

Here we have a list of three artists' names. The for statement goes through the list and for each element, assigns the element to the variable artist and then executes the indented statements on the following line(s). Such line(s) represent the *body* of the loop.

The following example uses a loop to print the cubes of the numbers 0 through 5.

```
1  for x in range(6):
2      print x*x*x
```

which produces

```
0
1
8
27
64
125
```

13.6   Nested Loops

Loops can be nested so that there is a loop within a loop. The following example shows this in the context of our museum cafe's daily menu generation.

```
1  for veggie in ['artichokes', 'broccoli', 'carrots']:
2      for sauce in ['dill', 'eggplant']:
3          print veggie + ' with ' + sauce + ' sauce'
```

which produces

```
artichokes with dill sauce
artichokes with eggplant sauce
broccoli with dill sauce
broccoli with eggplant sauce
```

```
carrots with dill sauce
carrots with eggplant sauce
```

The looping technique is indispensable in almost all serious programming with conventional languages such as Python, Java, C, and C++. The next section applies looping to controlling the magnification of an image in PixelMath.

13.7 Looping to Enlarge an Image

In the chapter that introduced programming, an example showed how to zoom an image until it filled the screen. That example consisted of a number of zoom steps that were each conditional upon the display needing still more zooming.

Let's show how a loop can shorten the code for this operation. To obtain the right number of zoom steps, we figure out how many doublings of the image width it would take to reach the screen width.

```
1    screenDimensions = pmGetScreenSize()
2    screenWidth = screenDimensions[0]
3    screenHeight = screenDimensions[1]
4    windowNum = pmNewImage(0, "Zoom-test", 64, 64, 0, 0, 255)
5    pmPositionWindow(windowNum, 0, 0, screenWidth, screenHeight)
6    (w,h) = pmGetWindowSize(windowNum)
7    zoomfactor = screenWidth / 2
8    nzooms = floor(log(zoomfactor, 2))
9    for i in range(nzooms):
10       pmZoomImage(windowNum, w/2, h/2)
```

Here *for* is used to repeat something. The value of *nzooms* gives the number of times to perform the repeated operation. It's determined by finding the logarithm to the base 2 of the *zoomfactor*, and so it represents the number of times the display size of the image has to be doubled before it begins to be partially hidden. The symbol *i* is used for counting the repetitions. *pmZoomImage* is used to enlarge the display of the image within its window. The expressions *w/2* and *h/2* specify that the zooming operation should be centered at the middle of the image, i.e., a point halfway across the width of the image and at half the height.

13.8 Loops Using *while*

Another way to construct a loop is to use Python's *while* command. This approach makes use of a Boolean expression, much as the *if* statement does. However, in a *while* loop, the condition is evaluated again and again, once when the loop begins, and once more for each time the loop body is completed. When the condition is found to be False, the loop terminates.

Here is an example of a `while` loop that generates random integers until the user doesn't want any more.

```
1   from random import randint
2   wants_more = True
3   while wants_more:
4       n = randint(0,100)
5       print "Here's a nice number for you: "+str(n)
6       answer = raw_input("Want another? (Y or N)")
7       if answer=="N": wants_more = False
8   print "OK, we're done."
```

Now let's consider a more involved program example using `while`, as well as various other Python features, such as programmer-defined functions, which are described in detail in chapter 15.

13.8.1 Mandelbrot Fractals: Iterating until Convergence

One of the most famous types of fractal images are pictures of the Mandelbrot set, which is a subset of the complex plane (each element of which is a complex number of the form $c = a + bi$, where i is the imaginary square root of -1). The following program computes a picture of part of the Mandelbrot set using three loops. Two of them cause the program to scan through the pixels of the image and the third one determines whether the pixel represents a point in the Mandelbrot set. The point is considered to be in the Mandelbrot set if, after being repeatedly transformed by a simple mathematical formula, its magnitude remains limited. The loop to test this condition is constructed using `while`, and as soon as the magnitude of the value being transformed exceeds a threshold, the iteration can stop. However, because the iteration might otherwise never stop for some points, the program also includes a limit on the number of iterations.

```
1   '''MandelbrotSet.py
2   This program computes a fractal image based on the Mandelbrot set.
3   The code below contains commented-out versions of various useful
4   settings.
5   '''
```

```
 6   #W=192; H=128 # For the region showing the whole Mandelbrot set.
 7   #W=64; H=64    # For quick evaluations of a region.
 8   #W=128; H=128
 9   #W=256; H=256
10   #W=512; H=512
11   W=1024; H=1024 # In some regions, this can take a long time.
12
13   # The initial range, showing the whole Mandelbrot set:
14   #REAL_RANGE = (-2, 1); IMAGINARY_RANGE = (-1, 1)
15
16   # Zooming in somewhat:
17   #REAL_RANGE = (0, 0.2); IMAGINARY_RANGE = (0.5, 0.7)
18
19   # One nice detail area:
20   #REAL_RANGE = (0.1, 0.15); IMAGINARY_RANGE = (0.6, 0.65)
21
22   # The following region contains a tree-like detail:
23   REAL_RANGE = [0.121, 0.128]
24   IMAGINARY_RANGE = [0.637, 0.644]
25
26   WIN = pmNewComputedImage("Mandelbrot Set within a in "+\
27           str(REAL_RANGE)+" and b in "+\
28           str(IMAGINARY_RANGE),\
29         W,H,"rgb(255, 230, 230)")
30
31   # The looping over the image is done in the next function.
32   def createMandelbrotImage():
33     ncols = pmGetImageWidth(WIN)
34     nrows = pmGetImageHeight(WIN)
35     rectWidth = float(REAL_RANGE[1]-REAL_RANGE[0])
36     rectHeight = float(IMAGINARY_RANGE[1]-IMAGINARY_RANGE[0])
37     for j in range(ncols): # Outer loop
38       for i in range(nrows): # Inner loop
39         real = REAL_RANGE[0]+j*rectWidth/ncols
40         imag = IMAGINARY_RANGE[0]+i*rectHeight/nrows
41         c = complex(real, imag)
42         count = iterate(c) # Call to a function with another loop.
43         (r,g,b) = getColor(count)
44         pmSetPixel(WIN, j, i, r, g, b)
45
46   NMAX = 2000      # Limit on now many iterations per pixel.
47   THRESH = 2000    # Threshold of divergence.
48
49   # Here's the definition of the function that tests
50   # a complex number c for membership in the Mandelbrot set:
51   def iterate(c): # We test the complex number c.
```

```
52     # Returns the num. of iterations needed to diverge.
53     n = 0
54     z = complex(0,0) # Start at the complex origin.
55     while n<NMAX:     # This starts the while loop.
56       z = z*z + c     # Here's the math formula for updating.
57       if abs(z)>THRESH: return n # Test for divergence
58       n += 1            # Count the iterations
59     return -1       # If no divergence in NMAX tries, return -1.
60
61   def getColor(count):
62     # Return an RGB triple based on the count value.
63     if count==-1: return (0, 0, 96)
64     else:
65       r = count
66       if count>255: g = (count*2) % 256
67       else: g = max(0,192-count*2)
68       b = int(count/8)
69       return (r,g,b)
70
71   createMandelbrotImage()
```

This program illustrates not only three loops but also the use of function definitions together with loops. The code in the function called `iterate` could have been embedded directly within the nested loops that scan the image. However, by separating it into a function, the program is arguably more readable and easier to debug without any significant loss in efficiency.

When running this program it's interesting to notice how the time it takes to compute different parts of the image depends on whether the pixels being computed are in the Mandelbrot set. The points in the Mandelbrot set take the most time because the `while` loop goes to the limit of NMAX iterations on those points. The Mandelbrot set image shown in figure 9.4b was computed with a variation of this program.

13.9 Setting up Multiple Windows

Some demonstrations require a lot of images on the screen at once. It is tedious to create all these windows manually with a mouse. With a small program that uses looping, lots of windows can be easily created and arranged. Here's an example:

```
1   w = 250
2   h = 200
```

```
3    windowNum = 0
4    for i in range(3):
5      for j in range(4):
6          windowNum = pmNewImage(0, "Test", 100, 80, 0, 0, 0)
7          pmPositionWindow(windowNum, j*w, i*h, w, h)
```

This program creates twelve new windows, each 100 pixels wide and 80 pixels high. It arranges them on the screen in three rows of four.

13.10 Building Convolution Formulas

In the previous example we used a pair of loops, one nested inside the other. The outer one ranged over values of a row index, taking on values 0, 1, and 2. The inner one ranged over a column index, taking on values in [0, 1, 2, 3]. The body of the inner loop created a new image window, and with all the iterations, twelve windows were produced.

Let's apply a similar programming structure to another task: creating a PixelMath formula to perform convolution using a kernel that is passed in as an argument. We will again use a pair of loops, with one handling rows and one handling columns (in this case, of the kernel array). However, the body of the inner loop will tack on a term to a growing formula string. Here is the Python code:

```
1    '''MakeConvolutionFormula.py
2    '''
3
4    def makeConvolutionFormula(kernel):
5      nrows = len(kernel)
6      ncols = len(kernel[0])
7      midx = ncols / 2      # (midx, midy) is the origin of the kernel.
8      midy = nrows / 2
9      f = ""                # The formula starts out empty.
10     dy = - midy           # Starting displacement for y
11     for row in kernel: # Loop over rows.
12       signdy = sign(dy)
13       dx = - midx         # Starting displacement for x
14       for elt in row:  # Loop over columns.
15         signdx = sign(dx)
16         if dx==0: dxExpression = ""
17         else: dxExpression = signdx+str(abs(dx))
18         if dy==0: dyExpression = ""
19         else: dyExpression = signdy+str(abs(dy))
```

```
20          if elt==0: continue   # if elt is 0, don't even
21                                 # include the pixel expression.
22          pixelExpression = "S1(x"+dxExpression+",y"+dyExpression+")"
23          if elt==1:
24            coefficientExpression = "+"
25          elif elt == -1:
26            coefficientExpression = "-"
27          else:
28            coefficientExpression = sign(elt)+str(abs(elt))+"*"
29          f += coefficientExpression + pixelExpression
30          dx += 1
31        dy += 1
32     if f[0]=='+': return f[1:]
33     else: return f
34
35  def sign(n):
36    if n < 0.0: return '-'
37    else: return '+'
38
39  def test():
40    sampleInput =\
41    [[-1,  -2,  -1],\
42     [ 0,   0,   0],\
43     [ 1,   2,   1]]
44
45    formula = makeConvolutionFormula(sampleInput)
46    print "The formula is:"
47    print formula
48
49  test()
```

In PixelMath, it is easy to specify a convolution formula by hand if the kernel is very small, such as 2 by 2. However, for larger kernels, creating the formula is a chore. This Python program takes a kernel as a list of lists and produces a PixelMath calculator formula that corresponds to it.

It takes advantage of certain values in the kernel to simplify formulas. Value 0 results in no corresponding term at all. This saves needless multiplication and addition in the formula. Negative values result in direct subtraction rather than addition of negative items. Factors of 1 are dropped. Similar tricks are used in the expressions for displacements (dx, dy). So instead of s1(x+-2, y+0) we would get s1(x-2,y). Running this code, which includes as a test case one of the two kernels used in Sobel edge detection, produces the PixelMath formula:

```
-S1(x-1,y-1)-2*S1(x,y-1)-S1(x+1,y-1)+
S1(x-1,y+1)+2*S1(x,y+1)+S1(x+1,y+1)
```

This program example shares with the previous (window-creating) example not only the use of nested loops but also the order in which the horizontal and vertical dimensions are treated by the nested loops. When working with arrays (or lists of lists), it is customary to have the outer loop control which row is being processed and the inner loop control which column is being processed. In a Cartesian coordinate system, this means that y is being varied slowly and x is being varied quickly. There is no requirement that programs work this way, but it is common practice.

The two programs differ in the way they accumulate the work done. In the window-creation example, the body of the loop calls PixelMath Python functions that create the windows, and then the program doesn't process them further; there is no variable defined in this code that remembers a list of the windows (although PixelMath has its own internal list of image windows). On the other hand, the convolution formula program keeps accumulating terms of the formula via string concatenation within the body of the inner loop. The line that begins with "f +=" causes the formula to be extended with another term. [Each term such as -5*S1(x-1,y+1) consists of a coefficient (−5) multiplied by a nearby pixel value, here S1(x-1,y+1).]

When constructing formulas such as convolution formulas, there is usually one term in the formula per iteration of the inner loop. (However, as mentioned earlier, this program takes notice when a coefficient is zero and drops the term.) If there are a total of k terms in a formula, then they are added or subtracted with a total of either k or $k − 1$ addition and subtraction signs: for example, 2*S1(x-2,y)+S1(x,y)-3*S1(x+2,y), which comes from the 1×5 kernel [[2, 0, 1, 0, -3]], has three terms and two signs (plus or minus). If the first coefficient were −2 instead of 2, then there would be three signs at the end. The way this program puts in the signs is to put them in front of each term. When the looping is finished, the program checks to see if there is an unnecessary + sign at the beginning of the formula, and if there is, it removes it. This might seem like undoing work done, and one can imagine putting a test into the body of the inner loop so that the plus sign would not be entered in the first place if the term is the first one in the formula. That solution would not be as good as fixing the formula at the end for the simple reason that the extra checking for a special case would have to be repeated for every term, adding up to a relatively large amount of extra work. This is an example of keeping loop bodies simple to save processing time.

13.11   Four-Level Nesting for Median Filtering

Often we need to process all the columns of an image, and for each column, we need to process all its pixels. We'll use one loop nested inside another, but the nesting might not end there. For each pixel, we may need to process all the pixels in its neighborhood, and the neighborhood itself, being two-dimensional, means we need two more levels of nesting. This is illustrated in the following program for median filtering of an image.

```
1    def medianFilter(source1, dest, k):
2      w = pmGetImageWidth(dest)
3      h = pmGetImageHeight(dest)
4      k2 = k/2
5      for x in range(w):
6        for y in range(h):
7          # Pull out vector to be sorted.
8          xstart = max(0, x-k2) # Be careful at the border
9          ystart = max(0, y-k2)
10         xend = min(w, xstart+k)
11         yend = min(h, ystart+k)
12         neighbors = []
13         for xx in range(xstart, xend):
14           for yy in range(ystart, yend):
15             neighbors.append(pmGetPixel(source1, xx, yy)[0])
16         index_of_median = len(neighbors)/2
17         neighbors.sort()
18         median = neighbors[index_of_median]
19         pmSetPixel(dest, x, y, median, median, median)
20
21   # An example call to filter the image in window 1,
22   # putting the result in window 2, using a 3x3 neighborhood:
23   medianFilter(1, 2, 3)
```

Note that this program not only uses four levels of looping, but the inner two (for obtaining the neighbors of a pixel) use a more interesting range construct than the usual range(n). The ranges used shrink down near the border of the image to avoid trying to access pixels outside the image. So if the width of the image is 100, our neighborhood size (k by k) is 13 by 13, and we are processing the pixel at $(x, y) = (98, 50)$, the neighborhood is limited to x values from 92 to 99, and not 92 to 104. Instead of 169 pixels in the neighborhood (the normal situation in the interior of the image), this neighborhood only has $9 \times 13 = 117$ pixels in it. The index of the median in this neighborhood is 58 and not 84.

13.12 Iterative Transformations

Some transformations can be applied over and over to an image, making it gradually change into something quite different. For example, darkening an image a little and then continuing to darken it will gradually make it become black.

Darkening in this repeated or iterative way does not really produce an image that couldn't have been produced in one big step. However, there are some transformations that are easier to describe and compute using the repeated gradual approach than one big step. Image smoothing is one of these. The following example illustrates this on the Mona Lisa.

```
1   win1 = pmOpenImage(0, "art/mona-rgb.jpg")
2   win2 = pmOpenImage(0, "art/mona-rgb.jpg")
3   pmSetSource1(win1)
4   pmSetDestination(win2)
5   pmSetFormula("(S1(x-1,y), +, S1(x,y))/2")
6   for i in range(5):
7     pmCompute()
8     pmSetSource1(win2)
9     pmSetDestination(win1)
10    pmCompute()
11    pmSetSource1(win1)
12    pmSetDestination(win2)
```

Each time this two-window transformation is applied, each pixel is averaged with its neighbor to the left, and so the differences between neighboring pixels are reduced, leading to a blending or smoothing effect. The more iterations used in the loop, the smoother and blurrier the image becomes. Try doing the same program but using the more complicated formula that averages, not only with the neighbor to the left, but also with the neighbor above.

```
(S1(x-1,y) + S1(x,y) + S1(x,y-1))/3
```

Another way to do this two-dimensional smoothing is to alternate the smoothing in the horizontal and vertical directions. Yet another variation is to do the averaging using both the left and the right neighbors (for horizontal smoothing) and the upper and lower neighbors (for vertical smoothing).

The different pixels can have different weights in the average, too. Here is a formula that smooths in both directions, giving greater weight to the center pixel of each neighborhood.

```
0.4 * S1x,y(), +, 0.15, *, (S1(x,y-1), +, S1(x-1,y)
+ S1x+1,y(), +, S1(x,y+1))
```

The weights associated with each neighboring pixel form a sort of blocky surface that has four pedestals and one central peak. Performing the iteration has an effect that is similar to what one could get by using a larger neighborhood in the formula, with the weights approximating a 2D Gaussian surface (that looks like a rounded mountain).

13.13 Dissolves

By using a loop to repeatedly blend two images in different proportions, we can easily create a dissolve effect. The first image will gradually fade away as a new image gradually fades in to take its place.

```
1  pmSetSource1(pmOpenImage(0, "landscape1.jpg"))
2  pmSetSource2(pmOpenImage(0, "mona-rgb.jpg"))
3  pmSetDestination(pmNewImage(0, "Screen", 512, 420, 0, 0, 0))
4  for i in range(10):
5    pmSetFormula(
6      "S1x,y()*" + str((10.0 - i)/10) + " + S2(x,y)*" + str(i/10.0))
7    pmCompute()
```

This example first opens up three windows and sets them up as Source1, Source2, and Destination. Then it goes into a loop in which a formula is created and applied to create the new destination image from the sources. The first formula is "S1(x,y)*1, +, S2(x,y)*0" because the string concatenation causes values to be placed in the string, and the values are 0 and 1 during the first iteration. We call these values *weights* since they are used as factors to control how much of each of the two images to take. In the second iteration, i has the value 1, and so the weights are 1/10 and 9/10. In the final iteration, i has the value 9, and so the weights are 9/10 and 1/10, and the final formula is "S1(x,y)*0.9, +, S2(x,y)*0.1".

13.14   Anatomy of a Loop

We have now seen several examples of using the `for` statement to make something be processed multiple times. Let's now consider a simple example in detail using `while`.

```
1   i = 0
2   while i < 5:
3       print (i*i)
4       i += 1
```

The symbol `i` is called the *loop variable*. The number 5 is the test value. The expression `print(i*i)` makes up the *body* of the loop. Before the loop begins in line 2, the symbol `i` gets a new *binding* or changeable value. This value is *initialized* to 0. Each time the loop is repeated, the value is increased by 1. We sometimes say that the value is incremented to mean that it is made a little larger. After the value has been incremented, it is compared with the test value, which is 5 in this example. If the incremented value is less than the test value, the body of the loop is processed. Otherwise the loop terminates.

The `for` operator gives a convenient way to evaluate some expressions a given number of times. It is also useful when a list of values is available, and some expressions need to be evaluated for each value in the list. Here's an example:

```
1   fruit = ['apple', 'banana', 'orange']
2
3   for f in fruit:
4       print 'A nice snack is ' + f + '.'
```

In this example, the symbol `fruit` represents a list of three items. The `for` operator causes the `print` command to be evaluated first with `f` bound to `apple`, then again with `f` bound to `banana`, and then a third time with `f` bound to `orange`. The following is printed:

```
A nice snack is apple.
A nice snack is banana.
A nice snack is orange.
```

Now let's apply `for` to an image setup problem. Suppose we want a program to open up three specific images. This could be done as follows:

```
1   for i in ['jack.jpg', 'jill.jpg', 'hill.jpg']:
2       pmOpenImage(0, i)
```

Here the symbol i will first be bound to the string "jack.jpg" and then pmOpenImage will be called to open that image in a new window. The same will then be done with the other two image files.

13.15 Progressive Scrambling

In this section we present a more complex example of looping. The effect here is to permute the pixels of the Mona Lisa in an almost random way and then unscramble the pixels to get back the original. The permutation is performed according to the method described in the chapter 9.

This example requires that we set up three 256-by-256 images with at least two of them containing the Mona Lisa. The following setup code has the effect of preparing PixelMath for the scrambling effect.

```
1    orig = pmOpenImage(0, "mona-rgb.jpg")
2    m256 = pmNewImage(0, "Reduced, Mona", 256, 256, 0, 0, 0)
3    pmSetSource1(orig)
4    pmSetDestination(m256)
5    pmSetFormula("S1(x*w1/w,y*h1/h)")
6    pmCompute()
7    windowA = pmNewImage(0, "Window, A", 256, 256, 0, 0, 0)
8    windowB = pmNewImage(0, "Window, B", 256, 256, 0, 0, 0)
9    pmSetFormula("S1(x,y)")
10   pmSetSource1(m256)
11   pmSetDestination(windowA)
12   pmCompute()
13   pmSetSource2(m256)
```

Now that the windows are set up, we can use the following program code to run the permutation sequence. In order to see this in action, arrange Window A and Window B so they are both visible on the screen and the Python window is available but very flat, so that the program code can be pasted into it without blocking your view of the image windows. Then paste the program code into the input pane of the listener. You should see eight steps of permutation that distort the image and then eight more steps that undo the distortion.

```
1    # First distort the image:
2    b = 2
3    c = 1
4    d = 256
5    e = 128
6    w1 = windowA
7    w2 = windowB
8    for i in range(8)
9      pmSetSource1(w1)
10     pmSetDestination(w2)
11     formula = "if (Red2(x band (255-" + e + "),y) mod " + b +
12       "<" + c + ") then if x mod " + d + "<" + e +
13       " then S1(x+" + e + ",y) else S1(x-" + e + ",y) else S1(x,y)"
14     print(formula)
15     pmSetFormula(formula)
16     pmCompute()
17     b = 2*b
18     c = 2*c
19     d = d/2
20     e = e/2
21     temp = w2
22     w1 = temp
23   # Then invert the distortion:
24   b = 256
25   c = 128
26   d = 2
27   e = 1
28   w1 = windowA
29   w2 = windowB
30   for i in range(8):
31     pmSetSource1(w1)
32     pmSetDestination(w2)
33     formula = "if (Red2(x band (255-" + e + "),y) mod " + b +
34       "<" + c + ") then if x mod " + d + "<" + e +
35       " then S1(x+" + e + ",y) else S1(x-" + e + ",y) else S1(x,y)"
36     print(formula)
37     pmSetFormula(formula)
38     pmCompute()
39     b = b/2
40     c = c/2
41     d = d*2
42     e = e*2
43     temp = w2
44     w2 = w1
45     w1 = temp
```

This program works by performing eight distorting permutations and then eight inverting permutations. These permutations are performed alternately from Window A to Window B and from Window B to Window A because it is important to use two windows for each step. The double-quoted strings used in the assignment to `formula` should be typed with no carriage returns inside them; they have been adjusted in the text here to make them more readable.

13.16 Handling Exceptions

Runtime errors typically fall into two kinds: semantic errors and program exceptions. A semantic error occurs when an otherwise correct program computes the wrong result because the programmer did not correctly express what computation was intended. A *program exception* (or more simply, exception) occurs when the Python runtime system detects a special condition. For example, an attempt to execute `range(5)[5]` is an attempt to access a sixth element of a five-element list, which is noticeably inappropriate, to the Python system. It causes an exception of type `IndexError`. If the programmer has set up, within the program currently running, a means to handle the exception, execution can continue. Otherwise the Python system prints an error message and a traceback, and stops the execution.

The following program example illustrates a way to handle the IndexError exceptions.

```
1    print 'This is your handy French weekday reminder.'
2    JOURS=['Lundi','Mardi','Mercredi','Jeudi',
3           'Vendredi','Samdi','Dimanche']
4    try:
5      while True:
6        i = int(raw_input('Enter 0 for Monday, or ..., 6 for Sunday'))
7        print JOURS[i]
8
9    except IndexError:
10     print 'That wasn\'t in range. Au revoir!'
```

In order to handle the exception, the program has both a `try` block and an `except` block. The `try` block contains the code that might cause the exception to occur. The `except` block contains what should be done if the exception does happen. For any one `try` block, there may be one or more `except` blocks set up to handle different types of exceptions. When an exception occurs, the first `except` block that can handle the exception does it. If there is an `except` block without any exception type (like `IndexError`) given, it will serve to handle any type of exception. Exception handling is a form of conditional execution in which the `except` block is executed only if the special condition arises during execution of the `try` block.

In the example here, if the user types '1000' in response to the prompt, the exception is handled by the program. However, if the user types "one thousand," then an exception is raised of type `ValueError`. Since a ValueError is not an IndexError, this exception is not handled by the program, and Python will print an error message and traceback, and halt the program. If the word Indexerror were dropped from the program, then all kinds of exceptions, including the ValueError, would be handled by the program. However, the message "That wasn't in range. Au revoir" might not be appropriate if the user simply mistyped a word or made an insult, etc. Python has a type hierarchy of exceptions. For details, see online references.[1]

It is especially recommended to provide in your programs explicit exception handling for situations involving file-system access or user interaction. In these situations errors are common. It is easy to predict the types of errors that will occur and have the program respond with useful information, and it can be frustrating to users (or yourself) when your program doesn't give any information about why it is failing to do what is expected.

Now that we've investigated the if-then, looping, and exception-handling features of Python, we have got control structures under control, and our next kind of structure is data structures these are discusse in chapter 14.

13.17 Exercises

1. Write Python Boolean expressions that are true in each of the following cases:

a. a variable m is even

b. a variable m is even or a variable n is a multiple of 3

c. a variable m is even or a variable n is a multiple of 3, but not both

d. a string (represented by a variable s) begins with the letter Z

2. Write short piece of Python code that takes the value of a variable s, which is assumed to be a string, determines its length, and prints one or the other of the following messages, depending on whether the string is shorter than five characters: `"You're being rather short with me."` or `"OK, OK, that's enough!"`.

3. Using `for`, write a loop in Python that prints out the fourth powers of the numbers 0 to 25.

4. Using `for`, write a loop that prints out the first twelve Fibonacci numbers. The first five numbers are 1, 1, 2, 3, and 5. The next number is obtained by adding the previous two.

---

1. Python exceptions are listed at http://docs.python.org/library/exceptions.html. Be sure you use exceptions defined in the version of Python you are using; the Jython implementation in PixelMath uses 2.5.1 as of 2011.

5. Using for, write a loop that takes the strings 'A', 'B', 'C', and 'D', and then prints out each one preceded by "The letter ".

6. Using for, create a nested pair of loops that prints out all ordered pairs of girls ['Ann', 'Barb', 'Carol'] with boys ['Dave', 'Eric', 'Fabio', 'Greg'].

7. Using for, create a program that wipes an image to black in a left-to-right sweep.

8. Using for, create a program that uses polar coordinates to make an image turn gradually black from the center outward.

14 Data Structures

14.1 Overview

We have already looked at several kinds of data in Python: integers, double-precision floating-point numbers, Booleans, strings, and lists. In this chapter we go deeper into data structures in two ways. One is by discussing more of the techniques available for strings and lists. The other is by presenting additional kinds of data: tuples, dictionaries, and objects. Finally, we briefly consider the Python module `array`, which offers efficient access to large, homogeneous collections of simple data, such as the pixels of images.

14.2 Strings

Strings are such an important kind of data that lots of special facilities are available to work with them in Python. Strings are sequences of characters. As sequences, strings and lists both benefit from special syntax for accessing their parts. Particular parts of sequences can be accessed in Python using square-bracket notation, as the following examples with strings show.

```
1    >>> s = 'abcde'
2    >>> s[0]
3    'a'
4    >>> s[1]
5    'b'
6    >>> s[1:3]
7    'bc'
8    >>> s[1:]
9    'bcde'
10   >>> s[:3]
```

```
11   'abc'
12   >>> s[:]
13   'abcd'
```

As can be seen, one effect of evaluating the expression s[1:3] is that the value 'bc' is returned. Not necessarily obvious is that this part of the string is copied in the course of this evaluation. The last example above, s[:] illustrates how, by using the colon notation, we can request that an entire string be copied. (Copying of whole strings is not common in Python, due to string "immutability." Python lists are another story.) Later we'll see the use of the colon again to help establish ranges of elements from a list rather than a string.

There are a number of operations on strings that should be mentioned because they are needed frequently. The first is concatenation. The plus sign, used for addition of numbers, is used to denote concatenation when the data consist of strings.

```
1   >>> s1 = 'abcde'
2   >>> s2 = 'fghij'
3   >>> s3 = s1 + s2
4   >>> s3
5   'abcdefghij'
```

To make sure that a data item is a string, we normally use the function str, which converts its argument to a string if it is not already a string. The following example shows its use.

```
1   >>> n = 5
2   >>> n + n
3   10
4   >>> m = str(n)
5   >>> m
6   '5'
7   >>> m + m
8   '55'
```

Here the value of n is added to itself producing 10, and then the value of m is concatenated with itself, producing the string '55'. Multiplying a string by an integer n greater than 1 returns a new string that consists of n copies of the string, concatenated together.

The function `len` is used to obtain the length of a string. The method `lower` is used to convert any uppercase letters in the string to their corresponding lowercase versions. Note that methods are called with the object-oriented style, following the name of the argument (known as the object) rather than with the functional style.

```
1   >>> s = 'aBcDeF'
2   >>> len(s)
3   6
4   >>> 3*s
5   'aBcDeFaBcDeFaBcDeF'
6   >>> len(3*s)
7   18
8   >>> s.lower()
9   'abcdef'
10  >>> s.upper()
11  'ABCDEF'
12  >>> s
13  'aBcDeF'
```

The last line shows that the operations we performed on s were nondestructive. The original value of s is maintained in spite of the multiplication by 3 and the calls to upper and lower.

The empty string `''` is a legal string having no characters. Its length is 0. Concatenating it with another string, we obtain the other string's value unchanged. On the other hand, a string consisting of a single-spaced character is a string of length 1, even though the space is not directly visible.

```
1   >>> s1 = 'abc'
2   >>> s2 = ''
3   >>> s3 = ' '
4   >>> len(s2)
5   0
6   >>> len(s3)
7   1
8   >>> len(3*s1+3*s2+3*s3)
9   12
```

Strings have several methods for matching. Some simply report on whether a given substring occurs in a certain way. Others tell where a character or substring occurs or make changes.

```
1    >>> ms = 'MISSISSIPPI'
2    >>> ms.startswith('MISS')
3    True
4    >>> ms.endswith('IPP')
5    False
6    >>> ms.index('IS')
7    1
8    >>> ms.index('IS', 2)
9    4
10   >>> ms.index('IS', 5)
11   Traceback (most recent call last):
12     File "<stdin>", line 1, in <module>
13   ValueError: substring not found in string.index
14   >>> ms.find('IS')
15   1
16   >>> ms.find('IS', 2)
17   4
18   >>> ms.find('IS', 5)
19   -1
20   >>> ms.replace('IS', 'AAZ')
21   'MAAZSAAZSIPPI'
```

These examples show that matching comes in several varieties. Testing whether a string starts or ends with some other string works as one might expect, returning True or False. The `index` method reports the next place where some string occurs in the main string, but it throws an exception if it doesn't find the string. On the other hand, the `find` method has similar behavior, but instead of throwing an exception when there is no such substring in the string, it returns −1. The `replace` method looks for all occurrences of the first argument in the main string and it replaces them by the second argument. The original string is not modified and a new string is returned. More sophisticated matching is possible using a Python module called `re`, which means "regular expressions." That's a fairly substantial subtopic on its own, and we don't cover it in this book.

Sometimes strings contain several items of data separated by a particular character. For example `"11:15:00"` describes a time of day in hh:mm:ss format (hours, minutes, and seconds). In this case, the colon is the separator. There is a handy method for strings that can be used to split up a string like this into a list of substrings. Here's a demonstration:

```
1    >>> time = "11:15:00"
2    >>> time.split(":")
3    ['11', '15', '00']
```

This is also an example of type conversion, in this case from a string to a list. This list happens to be a list of strings.

Whereas the `split` method provides a way to take strings apart, sometimes we wish to put strings together. We've already seen how "+" can be used to concatenate strings. Another operator for building strings is the "format" operator: `%`. This is an "infix" operator, like +, that goes between a string and some data. It tells the computer to use the data to fill in certain places in the string. The places in the string to be filled in are indicated by special character sequences called *conversion specifiers*. The following examples show how formatting can be done in this manner.

```
1   >>> from math import pi
2   >>> print "The value of pi is about %1.4f." % pi
3   The value of pi is about 3.1416.
4   >>> s = 'Yesterday's low was%3d, and the high was%3d.' % (67, 85)
5   >>> print s
6   Yesterday's low was 67, and the high was 85.
7   >>> wavelengths = {'B': 475, 'G': 510, 'R': 650}
8   >>> s = 'Wavelengths for red, green, and blue '+\
9   >>> 'are %(R)3d nm, %(G)3d nm, and %(B)3d nm.' % wavelengths
10  >>> print s
11  Wavelengths for red, green, and blue are 650 nm, 510 nm, and
12  475 nm.
13  >>> for (planet, diam) in [['Mercury',3031], ['Venus',7520],
14                             ['Mars',4221]]:
15  >>>     print "*** %-10s%1.3E ***" % (planet, diam)
16  *** Mercury    3.031E+03 ***
17  *** Venus      7.520E+03 ***
18  *** Mars       4.221E+03 ***
```

The first example shows how to format a floating-point number such as `math.pi`. The conversion specification `%1.4f` indicates that there is a floating-point number that should be converted with one digit to the left of the decimal point and four digits to the right of the decimal point. In line 4, the format string contains two conversion specifications, both for decimal integers with room for three digits. The data are given as a tuple, with items in the order in which they should be converted. In line 7, a dictionary is prepared with three entries, one for each of R, G, and B. (Dictionaries are discussed later in this chapter.) The format string in lines 8 and 9 references the dictionary items using the keys in parentheses. For example, `%(R)3d` indicates that the value corresponding to `R` in the `wavelengths` dictionary should be converted as a three-digit decimal integer. In line 13, a loop begins in which successive pairs of data are printed out. Each pair has the name of a planet and its diameter in miles. The date is given as a list of lists. It could just as well have been a tuple of tuples (we'll describe tuples later in this chapter), a list of tuples, or a tuple of lists. The conversion specification `-10s` tells the Python system that a string is to be converted in such a way that it occupies a ten-character field, and the minus sign means that it should be left-justified in the field. The rest of the field is automatically set to blank characters. The conversion specifier `%1.3E` means that a floating-point number is to be expressed in scientific notation, with one digit before the decimal point, three to the right of it, and then the letter E followed by the exponent. In the resulting printout, we see that using the fixed field width of 10 for the strings leads to a nice, tabular format, with both columns lined up. Python provides additional options for conversion specifiers, and if you need them, the online documentation for string formatting operations will answer most questions.

To learn what methods are automatically available for strings in Python, one can simply type `dir('')`, or `dir` with any string as its argument. Let us next consider the other type of sequence in Python: lists.

14.3 Lists

A list is a sequence of Python data elements written between square brackets and separated by commas. The elements of a list might all be of the same type (say all integers), but they don't have to be. The types can vary. Lists can contain elements that are also lists.

Many of the methods available for strings also apply to lists. Access to parts of lists can be obtained using the colon notation. Concatenation works in a similar fashion. Here are some examples of lists:

```
 1   >>> lst = range(5)
 2   >>> lst
 3   [0, 1, 2, 3, 4]
 4   >>> lst[1:3]
 5   [1, 2]
 6   >>> lst[0:5:2]
 7   [0, 2, 4]
 8   >>> len(lst)
 9   5
10   >>> lst[:]
11   [0, 1, 2, 3, 4]
```

In the first example, we make a call to the `range` function to get a list of the first five non-negative integers. Then, using the expression `lst[1:3]`, we request a slice of the list starting at the element having index 1 and going up to, but not including, the element having index 3.

The expression lst[0:5:2] specifies that we want a slice that starts at position 0, ends right before position 5, and takes every second element. We could get the same result with the expression lst[::2] because if the first index is omitted, it defaults to 0, and if the second element is omitted, it defaults to the length of the list (which is 5 in this case).

The last example illustrates how to request a copy of a list using the slicing notation. Note that if the list contains sublists, then references to the sublists are copied, but the sublists themselves are not duplicated. If there is a need for a copy of a list in which sublists are also copied, then care must be taken to explicitly accomplish this, say by either by writing a new method or by using the Python module copy and calling its deepcopy method.

Some other methods that are available for lists include append, index, insert, remove , reverse , and sort. The following examples illustrate the use of these methods.

```
1   >>> lst = ['a', 'b', 'c']
2   >>> lst.reverse()
3   >>> lst
4   ['c', 'b', 'a']
5   >>> lst.append('a')
6   >>> lst
7   ['c', 'b', 'a', 'd']
8   >>> lst.index('a')
9   2
10  >>> lst.remove('b')
11  >>> lst
12  ['c', 'a', 'd']
13  >>> lst.sort()
14  >>> lst
15  ['a', 'c', 'd']
16  >>> lst.insert(2, 'z')
17  >>> lst
18  ['a', 'c', 'z', 'd']
```

Note that all these particular operations, except for index, are destructive in the sense that they modify the list. Also, they only return None, so that we have to evaluate lst each time to see the effect. The append inserts an element at the end of the list. On the other hand, insert puts the element at an arbitrary place in the list, according to the first argument. The method index determines where, if at all, a particular value occurs in the list. If the element does not occur in the list, then a ValueError exception is raised. The remove method also raises the `ValueError` exception if the element is not in the list. The `sort` method reorders the list. It can take various options, but these are beyond the scope of this presentation.

14.3.1 Multiple Assignment

Python supports a feature called *multiple assignment*. It can be used with lists, with comma-separated variable sequences, and with tuples (which are described later). Whereas a single assignment has the form *variable = value*, a multiple assignment has the form *variable sequence = value sequence*. Python is quite flexible about what kinds of sequences can be used in multiple assignments. The following examples indicate some of the forms available.

```
1   >>> x, y = 5, 10
2   >>> [a, b] = 6, 11
3   >>> c, d = [a, b]
4   >>> (e, f) = [c+1, d+1]
5   >>> [g, [h, i]] = 0, (1, 2)
6   >>> j, k = [3, [4, 5]]
7   >>> print x,y,a,b,c,d,e,f,g,h,i,j,k
8   5 10 6 11 6 11 7 12 0 1 2 3 [4, 5]
9   >>> (z, w) = 1
10  TypeError: 'int' object is not iterable
```

A form of multiple assignment can be used with the `for` construct. An example was shown in the string formatting discussion earlier, when the pairs (`planet`, `diam`) were given values from sublists.

14.3.2 Mutability

As we have seen in the examples given here, a list can be modified by various operations. A data object that can be modified is said to be *mutable*. In some situations, we need a data object equivalent to a list, but which is not mutable. Such a data type is a tuple.

14.4 Tuples

A tuple is like a list except that it is written differently and it is not mutable. The main benefit of an immutable data object is that it can be used as a key in another type of data object called a dictionary. We'll examine dictionaries shortly, but before that, we consider some examples of tuples. Tuples are written like lists, except that instead of using square brackets to surround the elements, we use parentheses. However, when accessing the elements of a tuple using indexes, we still use square brackets, just as with lists and strings.

```
1    >>> t1 = ('a', 'b', 'c')
2    >>> t1[0]
3    'a'
4    >>> lst = range(5)
5    >>> lst
6    [0, 1, 2, 3, 4]
7    >>> t2 = tuple(lst)
8    >>> t2
9    (0, 1, 2, 3, 4)
10   >>> type(t2)
11   <type 'tuple'>
12   >>> type((0))
13   <type 'int'>
14   >>> type((0,))
15   <type 'tuple'>
```

In the third and fourth input lines in this example, we create a list and then convert it into a tuple. In the following lines we see that while we normally put a sequence of elements in parentheses to create a tuple we must be careful in the case when there is only one element. In that case, to get a tuple, we must put a comma right after the element. Otherwise, Python will consider the parentheses as ordinary, non-tuple-creating parentheses, such as those used in grouping arithmetic subexpressions.

As mentioned earlier, tuples can serve as keys in data structures called dictionaries. Let's now consider dictionaries.

14.5 Dictionaries

A dictionary is a Python data structure for representing collections of pairs. The pairs follow a convention commonly known as attribute-value pairs. In each pair, the first item represents some attribute (such as color), and the second pair represents a value of that attribute (such as red). In a Python dictionary, the first element of each pair must be an immutable data object, such as an integer, string, or tuple. (It may not be a list). On the other hand, the second element of each pair is not restricted in its type, and it may be of any type, including a list. A Python dictionary can be specified in a variety of ways. The following examples show, first, a literal expression for a dictionary and then a dictionary built up using separate assignments for each pair.

```
1    >>> age = {'Adam':21, 'Barb':22, 'Carl':19}
2    >>> birthmonth = {}
```

```
3    >>> birthmonth['Adam'] = 'April'
4    >>> birthmonth['Barb']='June'
5    >>> birthmonth['Carl']='January'
6    >>> birthmonth
7    {'Carl': 'January', 'Barb': 'June', 'Adam': 'April'}
8    >>> for name in birthmonth.keys():
9            print name + " was born in the month of " + birthmonth[name]
10
11   Carl was born in the month of January
12   Barb was born in the month of June
13   Adam was born in the month of April
```

The last example here shows how dictionary items can be accessed and how to retrieve the keys of a dictionary. The keys are returned as a list, and we are using a `for` loop to iterate over the elements of this list.

Dictionaries have countless uses in writing programs. We can use them as simple databases as in the examples here. (A real database would also provide longer-term storage for persistence from one run of a program to another.) We can use them to organize images by associating them with filenames or other properties. A dictionary can be thought of as an array whose indexes are not confined to being integers, but which can be strings or other (immutable) data objects.

From a mathematical point of view, a dictionary provides a convenient way to represent a function whose domain is a finite set. Each domain element is represented by a key in the dictionary, and its corresponding range element is the value associated with the key in the dictionary.

14.5.1 Counting Colors

A dictionary provides a convenient data structure for counting members of a population when the population is divided into groups. For example, the population of pixels of an image can be divided into all the black pixels or all the pixels with RGB values (0,0,1). As will become clear, with a dictionary, we end up with information organized so that it's easy to answer such questions as "How many black pixels are in the image?" or "What is the most frequently occurring color (RGB triple) in the image?"

Our method uses a dictionary whose keys are tuples. Each tuple is of the form (R, G, B). The value associated with a tuple will be an integer greater than or equal to 1. If a color does not occur at all in the image, then there will simply be no entry in the dictionary for it. This is good, because in most cases an image does not contain pixels of all possible colors; in fact, a typical image uses only a small fraction of the 2^{24} possible colors afforded by the 8-bits-per-pixel RGB representation scheme.

The following program counts the occurrences of each RGB triple and then prints out the results sorted according to their frequencies of occurrence.

```
1   '''CountColorOccurrences.py
2   '''
3   IMG = pmOpenImage(0, "Earth.jpg")
4
5   colorCounts = {} # Create an empty dictionary
6   # Now use it to count the number of pixels of each color.
7   for y in range(pmGetImageHeight(IMG)):
8     for x in range(pmGetImageWidth(IMG)):
9       color = pmGetPixel(IMG, x, y) # Get the pixel's color.
10      try:
11        count = colorCounts[color] # Retrieve current count.
12      except KeyError:
13        count = 0 # No count yet, make it zero.
14      colorCounts[color] = count + 1 # Add one.
15
16  itemList = colorCounts.items()
17  print "This image has "+str(len(itemList))+" unique colors."
18  itemList.sort(key=lambda item: -item[1])
19  print "The most common color is "+str(itemList[0][0])
20  print " which occurs "+str(itemList[0][1])+" times."
21  print "Here is the complete list of colors and their counts:"
22  print itemList
```

First, the dictionary is initialized on line 5. In line 11, an attempt is made to access a dictionary item using the value of color as the key. If an entry exists for this color, then getting the count value works, and it is assigned to the variable count. If there is no item having a key that matches the value of color, then an exception of type KeyError is raised, and execution jumps to line 13. When that happens, it means that we have not seen this color previously in the image, and so we want the count to be zero. Once we have the count value (whether nonzero or zero), we can now add 1 for the pixel just considered. The updated count value is stored back in the dictionary in the assignment part of line 14.

After the loop is complete, we can get a list of all the (key, value) pairs by calling the items method of the dictionary. The length of this list corresponds to the number of distinct colors in the image. [We could also obtain this number via the expression len(colorCounts).] Next, we sort the list. We have to tell the sorting method that we want the list sorted according to the counts. The count for each item is in item[1]. We want the most frequently occurring item to be first in the list, and this means sorting in descending order. That's why there is a minus sign in the key function.

14.6   Classes

Many programmers organize the data in their programs by categories called classes. Some of these classes are predefined in the Python language, such as ints, lists, strings, and dictionaries. However, Python makes it possible for the programmer to set up new classes. There are a number of benefits of organizing one's data into classes. Here are a few: (1) The programmer can specify once and for all how to represent the many parts of a possibly complicated kind of data, such as an airline reservation record or a curation record for an old painting. (2) The various methods for creating, querying, and transforming the data can be tightly integrated with the data definition, simplifying the specification and use of the methods. (3) It becomes easy to create variations on the class for special kinds of data having additional properties or specialized methods; for example, the class of employees of a company might have a subclass for managers in which extra information and methods are needed that deal with the employee they supervise. (4) One tends to get more reliable software, owing to well-defined development methodologies for object-oriented (i.e., class-oriented) software.

Python supports object-oriented programming by providing the following features: having each data object belong to a class, whether or not it is explicitly defined by the programmer; making the `class` feature available so that the programmer can define new classes; providing method-invocation syntax, so that class-oriented functions can be called using a traditional form: `dataObject.methodName(argument1, ..., argumentK)`; and supporting inheritance so that one class can be defined as a subclass of another and inherit its methods and data members.

There are many books about object-oriented programming. Our coverage is very basic. It's sufficient to provide a better understanding of how some of Python's built-in classes work and support some of the program examples in the rest of this book.

14.6.1   Defining a New Class

Suppose we want to write a program that will answer questions about works of art. Then we might want to consider defining a class called `artWork`. Each work of art has an artist, a title, and a medium (e.g., oil on canvas). We'll need a method to create new instances of this class. Such a method is called a *constructor*, and in Python, we specify the details of construction by defining a method (actually just a function associated with the class) having the name `__init__`. The underscore characters are an important part of the names; there are two underscores at the beginning of the name and two at the end. This convention for the names of special methods makes it clear that Python will handle such methods in certain

predefined ways. In this case, the `__init__` method is called immediately after the memory
has been allocated for a new instance of the class.

Suppose there is a particular type of question that we want our artwork advisor to be
able to answer and that it is about the number of dimensions of the artwork (2 for graphic
works, 3 for sculptures, 4 for moving sculptures). We'll create a method called `dimension`
for this purpose. The method will be defined as part of the class `artWork`, and we ensure this
by using appropriate indentation of the code.

```
1   class artWork:
2     def __init__(self, artist_name, title, medium):
3       self.artist = artist_name
4       self.title = title
5       self.medium = medium
6
7     def dimension(self):
8         if self.medium == 'moving sculpture':
9           return 4
10        if self.medium == 'sculpture' or\
11            self.medium == 'film':
12          return 3
13        else: return 2
14
15    def report(self):
16      return '"'+self.title+'"\n ('+self.medium+" by "+\
17        self.artist+" having dimension "+str(self.dimension())+")"
```

Notice that each method defined in a class has a first argument named `self`. Python requires
this for any method that will support the standard object-oriented method-invocation syntax:
`dataObject.methodName(argument1, ..., argumentK)`. When a call happens during execution,
the data object itself is prepended to the argument list, which is passed to the function. Thus,
if the method will be invoked with k arguments, it must be defined with $1 + k$ arguments
(including `self`). Within the body of such a method, the identifier `self` is used as a reference
to the class instance (the object) whose data are being manipulated.

14.6.2 Using the New Class
Outside the class, the data could be referenced in a similar style, but with an identifier other
than `self` for the object. Here's an example of a short session in which an instance of our
`artWork` class is created and manipulated. The creation is caused by a call to `artWork` itself. In
other words, the name of the class is the name of its constructor. The initialization defined
in `__init__` then takes care of the details specified by the programmer.

```
1   >>> mona = artWork("Leonardo da Vinci", "La Joconde",
2                      "oil painting")
3   >>> mona.dimension()
4   2
5   >>> mona.location = "Louvre" # new fields can be added later.
6   >>> print mona.report()
7   "La Joconde"
8    (oil painting by Leonardo da Vinci having dimension 2)
```

After the new instance of artWork has been constructed, it is assigned to the variable mona in this example. The dimension method is invoked in line 2, which returns 2, telling us that the Mona Lisa is a two-dimensional piece of art. Line 4 shows that we can attach another attribute to the artWork object even though it was not specified in the class definition. In this case we are giving the mona instance an additional data member called location with a value of "Louvre". The invocation of the report method in line 5 causes various strings to be concatenated and returned. That result is printed. Notice that there is no mention of the Louvre, since the report method does not involve a location data field.

14.6.3 Subclasses

One of the reasons that object-oriented programming is attractive is that there is a straightforward way to build new functionality from existing classes. It not only lets one programmer make things out of components developed by others, it also lets the programmer modify the components without having to redefine them from scratch. The key to this is the concept of subclasses. A *subclass* B of a class A is a specialized type of A that may have different behavior and different data members. However, as a subclass of A, it *inherits* the data members and methods of A unless the programmer specifies otherwise. All the features that B needs that are already in A do not have to be redone.

Let's consider an example. In the following code, two subclasses of artWork are defined: sculpture and painting. In order to illustrate several of Python's options related to subclassing, these two subclasses have been defined more differently from each other than they might otherwise have been.

```
1   class sculpture(artWork):
2     def __init__(self, artist_name, title, material="bronze"):
3       artWork.__init__(self, artist_name, title, 'sculpture')
4       self.material = material
```

```
5
6      def report(self):
7        return artWork.report(self)+" made in "+self.material
8
9    class painting(artWork):
10
11     def dimension(self): return 2
12
13     def setBrushStyle(self, style):
14       self.brushStyle = style
15
16     def report(self):
17       return artWork.report(self)+" with the "+\
18         self.brushStyle+" brush style"
19
20   Thinker = sculpture("Rodin", "The Thinker")
21   print Thinker.report()
22
23   GrandeJatte = painting(
24    "Seurat",
25    "Un dimanche apre-midi a l'Ile de la Grande Jatte",
26    "oil")
27
28   GrandeJatte.setBrushStyle("dots")
29   print GrandeJatte.report()
```

This would result in the following printout:

```
"Rodin"
 (sculpture by The Thinker having dimension 3) made in bronze"
"Un dimanche apres-midi a l'Ile de la Grande Jatte"
 (oil by Seurat having dimension 2) with the dots brush style
```

In order to define `sculpture` as a subclass of artWork, in line 1, the name of the class being defined (sculpture) is followed by `(artWork)`. That establishes a parent-child relationship among `artWork` and `sculpture`. The child class then inherits the three methods of `artWork`: `__init__`, `dimension`, and `report`. It also inherits the three data members of `artWork`: `artist`, `title`, and `medium`.

However, `sculpture` has some differences. Its `__init__` method is different from that of `artWork`; it takes either two or three arguments, and the third, if used, has a different meaning (material) instead of medium. The definition of this `__init__` method includes a call to the parent class's method. The call is expressed by writing the parent class name (`artWork`) followed by the dot and `__init__`, followed by the desired arguments. We say that the __init__ method of sculpture *overrides* that of artWork, because without its explicit definition, calling the class sculpture to create a new instance of it would use the parent's __init__ method alone.

There is a second method defined in the class sculpture that overrides a parent method, and that is report. The child version calls the parent version and then appends more text to the result, so that not only will the standard description of an artwork be returned, but some additional information about the sculpture's material (e.g., wood or bronze) will be given.

Although there is no explicit definition for dimension given in the class sculpture, the method is still available to any instance of the class sculpture, because as a subclass of artWork, sculpture inherits dimension. Here dimension is the one method of artWork that is inherited but not overridden by a more specific version.

In the definition for the class painting, which starts on line 9, the __init__ method is not overridden, but the dimension method is. The report method is also overridden, with yet a different definition from that of artWork or sculpture.

14.6.4 Subclassing Built-in Classes

Taking advantage of built-in classes by subclassing them and adding new functionality is not difficult. As an example, consider the following new subclass of the built-in dictionary type dict.

```
1   class countKeeper(dict):
2     def __getitem__(self, key):
3       if not self.has_key(key):
4         return 0
5       return dict.__getitem__(self, key)
6
7     def increment(self, key):
8       temp = self.__getitem__(key)
9       self.__setitem__(key, temp+1)
10
11  fruitCounts = countKeeper()
12  fruitCounts["orange"] = 5
13  fruitCounts.increment("orange")
14  fruitCounts.increment("banana")
15  print "There are "+str(fruitCounts["orange"])+" oranges."
16  print "There are "+str(fruitCounts["apple"])+" apples."
17  print "There are "+str(fruitCounts["banana"])+" bananas."
```

Executing this code results in the following being printed out:

```
There are 6 oranges.
There are 0 apples.
There are 1 bananas.
```

In line 11, an empty countKeeper object is created. In line 12, the assignment-like syntax involving square brackets causes a call to the __setitem__ method of class dict, whose definition is not seen here, but which is inherited by the class countKeeper. The value 5 is stored under the key "orange". In line 13, the increment method is invoked, causing the count for "orange" to go up by one to 6. In line 14, a similar call is made with the key "banana"; however, there is no entry yet for banana. In the definition of increment, a call is made to __getitem__, which we defined to handle this case by returning 0. So the incrementing results in a count of 1 for banana. In line 15, we have the first of three print statements. The important thing to notice here is how the count for "orange" is retrieved. Here we get to use the square-bracket syntax used by dictionaries once again because we overloaded the class dict method __getitem__, which is automatically called as a result of the square-bracket syntax. However, as a result of the overloading, we get to have countKeeper have the special behavior of not throwing an exception if the key (i.e., "apple" in line 16) isn't there.

Subclassing built-in classes is especially useful when creating graphical user interfaces using existing component classes such as those for windows, buttons, or panels. Examples of such subclassing can be found in the implementation of the Transcentration game in chapter 20.

14.7 Trees

A *tree* is kind of data structure that organizes the data into a hierarchy. It is, in general, a branching structure made up of points called *nodes* and segments (or arcs) called *edges*. The most common way to draw a tree in computer science is starting at the top of the diagram with a point called the *root* that is the starting point for all the branches in the tree. The root is a node of the tree—a special node. There may be edges leading down from the root (computer-science trees grow down from the root, rather than up, like biological trees). The relationships among nodes are modeled roughly after family relationships, and so perhaps trees in computer science are more closely aligned with kinship diagrams known as family trees than with botanical trees that have bark on their trunks and birds' nests in their branches. When an edge leads down from one node to another, the upper one is a parent of the lower one, and the lower one is a child of the upper one. Two children of the same parent are called siblings. Unlike family trees that show two parents per child, our trees always have one parent per child (except for the root, which has no parent). But again using the botanical metaphor, any childless node is called a *leaf*. Each node of a tree is in a *level* according to how many edges away from the root it is. The root itself is in level zero, its children are in level one, and so on. The level of a node is also known as the *depth* of the node in the tree.

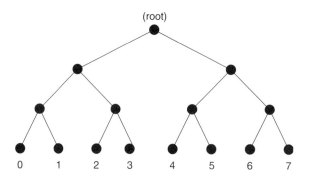

Figure 14.1
A perfect binary tree.

Trees are used for numerous things in programming. Very, very often, a data object has a hierarchical structure without even being called a tree, but it can almost always be viewed as a tree. For example, a list [0, 1, 2] can be considered to be a tree with four nodes: the root represents the whole list, and it has three children, one for 0, one for 1, and one for 3. A list with sublists is a more interesting example because its tree will be deeper. The list [[[0, 1], [2, 3]], [[4, 5], [6, 7]]] corresponds to a tree whose nodes (including the root) occur on four levels. The tree shown in figure 14.1 is an example of a *binary* tree. Every one of its nodes has either no children, one child, or two children. (In this example, there aren't any nodes with one child, and all leaves are at the same level, and so we say it is a perfect binary tree.)

14.7.1   Folder Structures as Trees

Just as lists can contain sublists, which gives rise to a multilevel hierarchical structure, so can file folders on a computer hard drive. Folders can contain folders themselves, and they can be nested arbitrarily deeply. The structure showing what's inside of what is best shown as some kind of tree. The Windows Explorer (file browser) that comes with Microsoft Windows divides the display into two panes, with a tree view on the left and a display of the contents of the current folder on the right. That tree view is shown as a long list of files and folders. The items contained within a folder are shown directly under it, indented a little more than the folder is.

When we design a program to work with a folder structure, we'll often use the tree terminology to describe some of the steps. For example, a comment on a program that traverses a folder structure might read, "Now let's visit the first child folder of the current folder . . . finally move back up to the parent . . . when we arrive back at the root, we are done."

Programs that traverse folder structures (or any tree structure for that matter) are often organized in terms of a recursive function. We'll consider recursion in chapter 15 and see how it can facilitate processing tree-structured data.

14.7.2 Images as Trees

Images in a computer are normally considered to be two-dimensional arrays. However, there are many times when images are described or processed as trees. Let's consider three particular examples that show how an image can be organized as a tree. In each case, the root of a tree represents the image as a whole and other nodes represent parts of the image. The first example easily applies to just about any image. If we consider each row of pixels in an image (e.g., the image array shown in figure 14.2a) to be a part of the image, and the individual pixels are parts of their rows, then we have the regularly structured tree shown in figure 14.2b.

Another method of treating or representing an image as a tree is based on a subdivision scheme that works with quadrants. Assuming that the image has equal width and height and that this number is a power of 2, such as 512, then an image can be considered to be either a square region having a single color or a collection of four quadrants, each of which is either a single color or a collection of four subquadrants, etc. The tree that corresponds to this structure is called a *quadtree* and an example is shown in figure 14.3b for the subdivision in figure 14.3a. Quadtrees find uses in applications in which the images have substantial blank areas or areas of constant color, such as with some maps and graphic art.

In computer vision, the objective is often to create, from a digital photo, a structural model of the scene depicted in the photo. figure 14.4b shows an example of a tree that expresses the structure of the scene sketched in figure 14.4a.

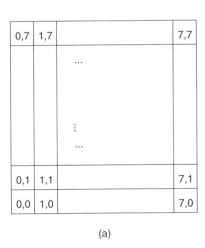

(a)

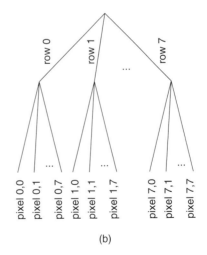

(b)

Figure 14.2
(a) An image array and (b) its representation as a tree organized by rows of the image.

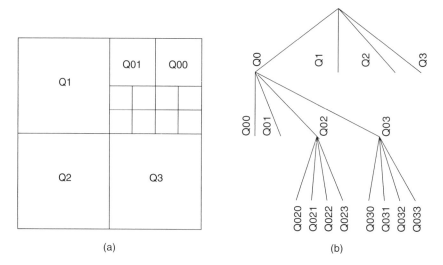

Figure 14.3
(a) An image subdivided into quadrants and subquadrants and (b) its corresponding quadtree.

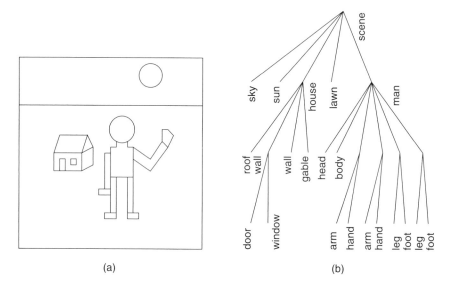

Figure 14.4
(a) Outlines of scene components in an image and (b) a tree representing the structure of the scene.

14.8 Graphs

A more general category of structures that includes trees is *graphs*. A graph consists of a set of nodes and a set of edges. However, there may be cycles in a graph, and there is no required notion of a root, of parents, of children, or of siblings. Whereas any tree is a graph, it is not true that any graph must be a tree.

An example of a graph based on an image is a *region adjacency graph*. Consider the image in figure 14.5a. If we consider the pixels of this image with value 1 to form a region, and the pixels with value 2 to form another region, etc., then we see that there are seven regions in this image. Each of these regions consists of a set of contiguous (connected) pixels having a single value.

Let us make a node in a graph for each region of the image. There must be seven nodes in the graph for this image. Then let us draw an edge from one node to another, provided the regions that correspond to those nodes touch each other in the image. They should touch along at least one side of one pixel. The resulting graph is shown in figure 14.5b.

One can think of this image as a representation of a map having seven countries, each of which borders other countries. The well-known map-coloring problem is to assign to each country a color from a short list (such as red, yellow, green, and blue) in such a way that no adjacent countries receive the same color. The problem of coloring the countries is equivalent to assigning colors to the nodes of the region-adjacency graph in such a way that no two nodes connected by an edge receive the same color.

A graph can be represented in a computer in a variety of ways. One way is by having a set of lists, with one list for each node, where each list tells what other nodes a node is linked to by an edge. This is called the *adjacency list* representation of the graph. Here is an adjacency-list representation for the graph of figure 14.5b.

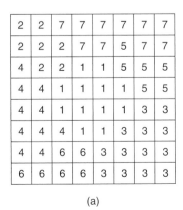

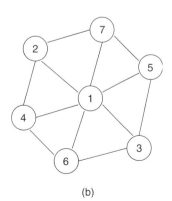

(a)   (b)

Figure 14.5
(a) An image whose pixels identify regions, and (b) its corresponding region-adjacency graph.

```
[[1, [2, 3, 4, 5, 6, 7]],
 [2, [1, 4, 7]],
 [3, [1, 5, 6]],
 [4, [1, 2, 6]],
 [5, [1, 3, 7]],
 [6, [1, 3, 4]],
 [7, [1, 2, 5]]]
```

Here the list for node 1 has six entries in it, since 1 is connected by an edge to every other node. Notice that just as node 1 is connected to, say node 2, the list for node 2 shows that node 2 is connected to node 1. This shows that each edge of a graph (as we have defined it) is bidirectional. This kind of graph is also called an *undirected graph*.

By contrast, a *directed graph* has a set of edges, each of which is considered to go in only one direction. An edge can be specified by a pair of nodes; for example (1, 2) represents the edge going from node 1 to node 2. This is an ordered pair, and it corresponds to the directed edge. A directed graph is allowed to have undirected edges as well as directed edges in it, but any undirected edge in a directed graph would have to be represented by *two* directed edges, for example (1, 2) and (2, 1). A directed edge can express a one-way relationship. For example, in an image, two adjacent regions probably have differing average brightness levels. Using a variation of the region-adjacency graph, we could have a directed edge from node A to node B provided that the regions corresponding to A and B are not only adjacent, but that B, on average, is lighter in color than A.

The theory and application of graphs is a significant subject in its own right, and it applies not only to image processing and computer science more broadly, but also to such diverse areas as transportation networks, social networking, system simulation, and games.

14.9   References

Samet, H. 1990. *The Design and Analysis of Spatial Data Structures*. Reading, MA: Addison-Wesley.

Shaffer, C. 2001. *A Practical Introduction to Data Structures and Algorithm Analysis*, 2nd ed., Upper Saddle River, NJ: Prentice Hall.

Zachmann, G., and Langetepe, E. 2006. *Geometric Data Structures for Computer Graphics*. Wellesley, MA: A. K. Peters.

Zelle, J. M. 2002. *Python Programming: An Introduction to Computer Science*. Wilsonville, OR: Franklin, Beedle.

14.10   Exercises

1. Using the `find` method for strings, show all the positions where the string "AM" occurs in `"MADAM I'M ADAM."` You'll need to use two calls, with slightly different arguments.

2. Some encryption methods are called substitution ciphers, and involve replacing each letter of the alphabet with some other in a consistent manner.

a. Write down the encryption of the word "mystery" using a code in which each character is replaced by its successor in the alphabet. The first letter of it will be "n" and so on. Note that if there were a "z" in the word, it would translate to "a", thereby "wrapping around" the end of the alphabet.

b. Starting with the following line of code and then using the index method for strings, find, character by character, the encryption of the word "mystery" using a code in which each character is replaced by a letter k steps down in the alphabet, where $k = 5$.

c. Describe how to do the encryption in the general case for any value of k. Note that Python has an arithmetic operator called the modulo operation (or simply mod) for taking the remainders of division.

```
1   >>> 33 % 26     # This means 33 modulo 26
2   7
```

3. Give an example of using the split method of strings for separating the two parts of a filename (the name and the extension).

4. Give an expression involving range that will return a list of integers starting with 100 and ending with 109.

5. Give an expression involving range that will return a list of odd integers starting with 25 and ending with 39.

6. Why is nothing printed out when you type the following into Python?

`print range(10).reverse().`

7. There is a method reverse to reverse a list. There is not a built-in method to reverse a string. What might this have to do with the mutability of these types?

8. Write a short program involving a loop that can take a list of five girls' names, and list of five boys' names, and return a list of girl/boy pairs. For example, the input lists might be `['Ann', x'Barb', 'Carrie', 'Deb', 'Elise']` and `['Al', 'Bob', 'Cal', 'Don', 'Eric']` and the output would be `[['Ann', 'Al'], ['Barb', 'Bob'], ['Carrie', 'Cal'], ['Deb', 'Don'], ['Elise', 'Eric']]`.

9. Consider the list `[0, [1], [[2]], [[[3]]]]`. Give an expression that will create a tuple that has the same nested structure and the same numbers in it.

10. Write down four lines of code that will create a dictionary and then enter information about three holidays into it. The information should associate with each holiday name (e.g., `"Easter"`) the date on which it is occurring this year (e.g., `[8, 'April', 2012]`). Suppose you wanted the date to be the key and the holiday name to be the associated value. What

thing(s) would you have to do differently to make your code handle the relationships in that direction?

11. In the definitions of the classes `artWork`, `sculpture`, and `painting` in sections 14.6.1 to 14.6.3, (a) how many methods of `artWork` override those of a parent class? (b) How many methods of `sculpture` override those of a parent class? (c) How many methods of `painting` override those of a parent class?

12. Once we have defined a class such as `artWork`, is there a limit to how many instances of it there are during the execution of a program that uses that class?

13. The two subclasses, `sculpture` and `painting`, of the class `artWork` suggest that there could be a separate subclass for each possible art medium. Discuss the pros and cons of having separate subclasses for many media in one computer program. (Some additional media are cartoons, pencil sketches, pastels, watercolors, crayon etchings, lithographs, woodblock prints, collages, mobiles, stabiles, movies, 3D movies, plays, operas, concerts, happenings, and installations.)

14. Create a new method for the class `artWork` called `recordSale`. It should take as arguments, not only the `self` argument, but something called `details`, which will correspond to a list of the form `[year, buyer, price]`. It should register the sale by assigning to a new member variable `sales` a list containing this list of details. If there is already a list of recorded sales, the new sale should be put at the end of the existing list. Then create a method `reportSales` that will return a string describing any sales of the item that have been made.

15. Write a Python class definition for a new class called `PixelMathFormula`, so that a new instance could be created as follows:

```
flip = PixelMathFormula("S1(y,x)", "cartesian").
```

Create a method `apply` that when invoked will cause the formula to be applied to an image. For example, `flip.apply(5)` should create a new window of the same dimensions as window 5 and then apply the formula using window 5 as the source and the new window as the destination.

16. Using the `countKeeper` class defined on in section 14.6.4, instead of an ordinary dictionary, reimplement the `CountColorOccurrences` program in section 14.5.1.

17. Suppose that an image of size 128 by 128 is to be represented as a tree.

a. Using the tree-of-rows scheme illustrated in figure 14.2b, how many siblings will each leaf node have? How many distinct levels will be in the tree? What will be the maximum depth of a node in this tree?

b. Using the quadtree scheme illustrated in figure 14.3b, what will be the maximum number of siblings that a single node can have? What will be the maximum possible depth of a node in the tree? What will be the minimum number of colors in the image that will still require the maximum number of nodes in the tree? Why?

18. Suppose that we have an image of size 8 by 8. What is the minimum number of nodes that there can be in the region-adjacency graph for this image? What is the maximum number of nodes? What is the minimum number of edges? What is the maximum number of edges? What is the maximum number of edges that a single node could have in a region-adjacency graph for the image?

19. Write a Python program that could take as input an image and output its region-adjacency graph. Assume that the input format is a list of lists of integers and that the output format is as shown for the region-adjacency graph example in section 14.8. The program should scan the image, starting at $(1,1)$, considering at each pixel p its south and west neighbors p_s and p_e. First it should make sure there is a node in the graph for the region to which p belongs. Then for each of the two neighbors it should check to see if (a) p is in a different region from the neighbor, and if so, (b) whether an edge has already been registered between the region for p and the neighbor's region, and (c) if not, creating the edge.

15 Creating Functions

15.1 Encapsulating Sequences of Operations

In chapter 13 on control structures, we found a wonderful way to make a computer do a lot of work without our having to do much work ourselves: we use a loop that has the computer repeat a sequence of steps over and over again, typically processing different data each time. This chapter discusses another good way to get computers to do a lot of work with relatively little programming: the use of user-defined functions. The idea here will be for us to write a piece of a program called a function definition, and then tell the computer to execute this function not just once, but a number of times. This can be done with or without using the looping idea at the same time.

There is another important purpose of a function. A function in a programming language serves as a way to package some operations in a single logical unit. That unit can be used as a building block for more complex programs. Once the functional unit is defined and working reliably, it can be used without anybody having to remember exactly how it works. This is helpful in simplifying the development of software. Without functions, programmers would have to keep many more things in mind at the same time, and that would most likely lead to buggier programs, or failure to complete a programming project at all.

In mathematics, the word "function" has a special meaning. It refers to a relation between two sets of values. It's often described as a mapping or rule that says, "If we're given a particular value as an input to the function, here is the corresponding output." The output of the function depends on what goes in. For example, the squaring function, $f(x) = x^2$, maps the number 5 to the number 25. Five goes in and 25 comes out. The two sets of values involved are called the *domain* and the *range*. They can be the same set or different sets. The domain of the squaring function consists of the real numbers. The range of the squaring function could be declared to also be the real numbers (although only the non-negative ones will actually participate in the function). The range of the squaring function could also be declared to be only the non-negative real numbers.

In programming, a function works in much the same way except that it is usually possible to create "impure" functions for which the output might not depend completely on the input.

An example of such an impure function is a random-number function that doesn't take any input, but returns a random number. A function in a program could also return a value that depends on some variable that's not established as one of the function's inputs but is established outside the function. This is another example of an impure function. One more kind of impure function is one that does something to the state of the programming environment that is separate from any value it returns. For example, a function that changes the value of a global variable X (one defined outside of all the functions in the session) is an impure function.

There are situations in which we desire pure functions as well as situations in which impure functions are just fine. We'll have more to say about pure and impure functions later on.

This chapter starts with simple function definitions and moves toward more sophisticated styles and uses. By the end of the chapter we will be combining techniques of recursion; functional programming constructs such as `lambda`, `map`, and `reduce`; and handling argument passing in a variety of ways. Throughout the discussion of these features, it should be kept in mind that functions are essential chunks of programs and that learning how to define them well and use them well is one key to successful programming.

15.2 Defining Simple Python Functions

Before we go about creating our own functions, we should point out that Python already comes with lots of functions. An example is the function `math.log`, which returns the logarithm of a number. The function call `log(1000)` takes the logarithm of 1000 (using base 10). The value 1000 is an argument to the function; it's the input to the function. (Arguments will be discussed in section 15.3) Notice that math.log is a pure function because its returned value depends only on its argument, and it does not alter the state of the environment.

Let's begin by defining a function that simply encapsulates a sequence of operations and doesn't take any arguments.

```
1    def getMona():
2        monaWindow = pmOpenImage(0, "art/mona-rgb.jpg")
3        pmPositionWindow(monaWindow, 300, 600, 0, 0)
```

Once this has been entered into the Python interpreter, it is possible to type in the expression `getMona()` to set up a new window with the Mona Lisa image and move it into the central part of the screen. Typing the expression again sets up another window with another copy of that image. In other words, once the function `getMona` has been defined, it's easy to make the computer do all the work of opening up the image and doing it multiple times, if desired. Notice that this is an example of an impure function, since it alters the environment (i.e., the image windows).

One of the key steps in creating such a function is choosing an appropriate name for it. The name we chose here, `getMona`, is a mixed lowercase and uppercase one. Using this "camel case" capitalization scheme (with "humps") in function names can help to create names that are easily readable and self-descriptive. The capital M is like the hump in a camel's back, and it shows where the second word of the name starts. The other popular scheme for creating multiword function names (or multiword identifiers for any purpose) is connecting the words with underscores. With the underscore method, our name would be `get_mona`. Some programmers simply concatenate words without any special indication of their separation, as in `getmona`.

15.3 Functions with Parameters

In addition to grouping several operations into a unit with a single name, functions can be useful in permitting one sequence of operations to be used on multiple pieces of data. In order to do this, we define a function with one or more parameters. Each parameter represents a value that will be passed to the function when it is called. These values passed at runtime to functions are called *arguments*. We saw an example of an argument, 1000, to the function `math.log`, near the beginning of section 15.2. Here's an example of a function with one parameter: x. This function will accept one argument when called.

```
def double(x):
    return x*2
```

When this function is called using the expression `double(7)`, the body of the function is evaluated after the parameter x has been temporarily given the value 7. The result of the call is 14. By calling the same function again with a different argument, say 11, we are able to reuse the same function to compute with different data.

In this function, `double`, we assumed that the parameter x will represent a number. In general, the parameters of a function can be used to represent any type of Python data value. For example, the following function will accept a string as an argument. It assumes the string represents the name of a file.

```
1    def getImage(filenameString):
2      imageWindow = pmOpenImage(0, filenameString)
3      pmPositionWindow(imageWindow, 300, 600, 0, 0)
```

An appropriate call to this function might be

```
getImage("art/mona-rgb.jpg")
```

To define a function with more than one parameter, we use one identifier for each parameter and they are separated by commas. Here's an example:

```
def distanceFromOrigin(x, y):
   return Math.sqrt(x*x + y*y)
```

We would then call the function with two arguments, as in, for example, distanceFromOrigin(3, 4). The value returned here would be 5.

15.4   Software Engineering with Functions

As mentioned earlier, we can think of functions as kinds of building blocks. Different functions give us different shapes of blocks, metaphorically speaking. By using a variety of blocks, we can build a house. If we glue two or more blocks together, we have a new, larger kind of block. Just as blocks can be made out of blocks, functions can be made out of functions.

To illustrate this, suppose we have two functions, one to make some new windows and another to create a rotation formula. We can combine them to obtain a new function that first makes some new windows and then fills each window with a different rotation of a given image. Here is one example of doing this. Our first building-block is the function makeNWindows. It takes two arguments. The first should be the window number of some existing image window. It will use this window to determine the width and height for the new windows. The second argument is the number of new windows desired. This function makes the new windows and returns a list of their window numbers. The second building-block function is makeRotationFormula. It takes one argument, which should be a number representing the angle for rotation, in radians. There is a third function defined here. It's called makeRotatedCopies, and it is built out of the other two functions to show how this building-block idea works. The final two lines of the example show how these functions can be applied to an image such as the Mona Lisa.

```
1   def makeNWindows(origToCopy, n):
2     windowList = []
3     dimensions = pmGetImageSize(origtoCopy)
4     width = dimensions[0]
5     height = dimensions[1]
6     delta = 200/n
7     origTitle = pmGetWindowTitle(origToCopy)
8     for i in range(n):
9       title = origTitle + ' Version ' + str(i+2)
10      windowNum = pmNewImage(0, title, width, height, 0, 0, 0)
11      pmPositionWindow(windownum, i*delta, i*delta, width, height)
12      windowList.push(windownum)
13    reverse(windowList)
14
15  def makeRotationFormula(angle):
16    return "Source1(rho, theta+" + angle + ")"
17
18  def makeRotatedCopies(orig, n):
19    windows = makeNWindows(orig, n)
20    angle = (2*3.14159) / n
21    pmSetPolar()
22    pmSetSource1(orig)
23    i = 0
24    for w in windows:
25      i = i+1
26      pmSetDestination(w)
27      pmSetFormula(makeRotationFormula(angle*(i+1)))
28      pmCompute()
29    pmSetCartesian()
30
31  s1 = pmOpenImage(0, "art/mona-rgb.jpg")
32  makeRotatedCopies(s1, 3)
```

Notice that in defining makeNWindows, we can use any of Python's programming constructs, including assignment to new variables, loops, and conditionals, as well as calls to other functions.

Software design is often done in terms of functions. When somebody writes a computer program to solve a problem, we can think of the program as a large function: you input the problem to it and the solution comes out. The challenge of creating such a function is to find the right way to build it out of other functions, and how to make those functions out of other functions, etc., until we're using functions that are already provided by the Python language.

Although most programming involves defining functions, the practice of programming by defining functions and using functions that themselves create and apply functions is called *functional programming*. This is an important methodology for computer programming and we'll address it later.

15.5   Returned Values versus Side Effects

A mathematical function such as $f(x) = x^2$ is simply a relation between the possible input values and their corresponding output values. A Python function, however, can be more than a relation between inputs and outputs. Python functions can have side effects. The example functions `getImage`, `makeNWindows`, and `makeRotatedCopies`, discussed earlier, have side effects.

A good example of a PixelMath Python function with a side effect is `pmOpenImage`. When this function is called, the state of the computer screen is changed by the displaying of an image.

Another difference between a Python function and a mathematical function is that the result of a mathematical function must not depend on any system state, but must be completely determined by the values of the input argument. This property is known as referential transparency. A mathematical function is always referentially transparent. On the other hand, a Python function may or may not be referentially transparent. The output value of the `pmOpenImage` function, its return value, is simply the window number for the image that was displayed. That number doesn't really depend much on the arguments to `pmOpenImage` in the way that x^2 depends on x. This Python function is not referentially transparent.

If a Python function has no side effects and is referentially transparent, then it is called a pure function. The Python function `double`, defined earlier, is a good example of a pure function. Its value depends only on the value of its input argument, and it doesn't have any side effects, such as displaying a new window on the screen.

Note that a Python function that does not explicitly return a value will by default return the special value called `None`. Unless `None` is specifically printed, it is not shown. The function `sleepOneSec` defined as follows waits a second and then returns `None`. A function such as this that always returns `None` is of no value except for its side effects, which here consist of the passage of a certain amount of time.

```
1   def sleepOneSec ():
2     from time import sleep
3     sleep (1)
4
5   x = sleepOneSec (); print x # None
```

A typical program using Python will have some pure functions and some functions that have side effects and/or dependencies on the state of execution (or state of the system or environment). It's considered good software engineering practice to be aware of these properties during the design process and to try to use mostly pure functions rather than impure ones when it can be done without complicating the program. Programs built with pure functions tend to be easier to debug.

15.6 Parameter List Options

When we define a function like cube below, we are using the simplest kind of parameter specification—a named parameter that is required. Another way to specify a parameter is to make it optional for the caller to provide the argument and to give the parameter a default value.

```
1   def cube (x):
2     return x**3
3
4   def nextOdd (n=0):
5     if n % 2 == 0: return n+1
6     else: return n+2
```

We have thus defined the function nextOdd to take either no argument or one argument. Now let's consider the different calling styles that we may use.

```
1   >>> nextOdd ()
2   1
3   >>> nextOdd (1)
4   3
5   >>> nextOdd (2)
```

```
6    3
7    >>> nextOdd(n=2)
8    3
```

With no argument, the default value of 0 is used for n, and so 1 is returned. With one argument, the function does what we expect from our experience with other function definitions. When the argument has the form identifier = value, we see that it is allowed, and it has the same effect here as the previous call.

The reason that it might be important to use this last form of calling is that a function can have more than one optional argument, and then there is a real ambiguity about how to specify the value of one parameter but not the other and have the computer know which one you are specifying. Without the use of the n=2 form, the Python system has to assume that the value being passed is intended as the value of the next parameter, whether or not it is a required parameter. This last form of argument passing is sometimes called the keyword format because n serves as a keyword to tell Python how to use the value 2.

One more facility for parameter specification in Python is worthy of mention. This is a way to allow a function call to contain arbitrarily many arguments. Consider the following example in which we define a function mean that computes the average of some numbers.

```
1    def mean(*vals):
2        total = 0.0
3        if len(vals)==0:  return 0
4        for val in vals:
5            total += val
6        return total/len(vals)
7
8    print mean(1, 10, 100, 1000) # 277.75
```

In the call shown here, four arguments are passed and their mean is 277.75. What allows us to do this is the fact that the parameter vals is preceded by an asterisk (*). This causes the calling mechanism to assign to the parameter vals all remaining arguments in the call. This sequence of values is then accessible by standard methods, such as done here with the for loop. If we wanted only the first argument's value, we could write vals[0] and get it. Another example using this argument sequence construct is the definition of average_color in section 15.8.4.

15.7 Recursive Functions

A definition for a (pure) Python function tells a computer how to come up with an output value on the basis of one or more input values. It's allowable for such a definition to be circular in some situations. A definition of a function that makes use of itself (the same function) is called recursive.

Let's consider the problem of determining the number of elements in a list. One way of doing this might be to establish a loop in which a counter is first set to 0, and then 1 is added for each element of the list. Here's a solution using a loop:

```
1    def listLength(theList):
2        length = 0
3        for elt in theList:
4            length = length + 1
5        return length
```

An alternative and possibly simpler definition is possible using recursion. The idea is to test the input list to determine if it is empty, and if so, return the answer 0. Otherwise, it adds 1 to the result of calling the listLength function on the rest of the list (without the first element).

```
1    def listLength(theList):
2        if theList == []: return 0
3        else: return 1 + listLength(theList[1:])
```

Either way, when listLength has been defined, we could use it to find the number of elements in a list.

```
listLength(['a', 'b', 'c', 'd', 'e']) # 5
```

(Since there is a built-in function len for sequences, we don't really need this new function, but it's a nice, simple illustration of recursion.)

Another example of a recursive function is a Python implementation of the well-known factorial function of mathematics: $n! = n \times (n - 1) \times \ldots \times 1$.

```
1   def factorial(n):
2     if n==1: return 1
3     else: return n * factorial(n-1)
```

If we call this function with the expression `factorial(5)`, a version for the symbol `n` is established with value 5. This value is compared with 1. Since it's not 1, the value 1 is skipped, and the expression `factorial(n-1)` is evaluated. After the evaluations of `n` and `n-1` are completed, the expression remaining to be evaluated is `5 * factorial(4)`. In order to proceed, Python must then obtain the value of `factorial(4)`. This causes a new version of `n` to be created (shadowing, but not canceling, the old version of `n` with value 5), with value 4. The evaluation will proceed and it will have to process `factorial(4)`, then `factorial(3)`, etc., until it gets to `factorial(1)`. When it handles this last case (with all the other cases still pending), the condition `(n==1)` is true, and the answer 1 is returned at that level. The 1 is used in computing `2 * factorial(1)` at the next level, resulting in 2. That's used at the next level, resulting in 6, and then 24 is used as the value of `factorial(4)` in the computation of `5 * factorial(4)`, and the final value, 120, is found. From the top-level call, this value, 120, is returned.

It's important to realize that with these many slightly different calls to the same function, there are many separate versions or copies of the variable `n` and these copies have different values (at least in this case). A call from within `factorial` to itself does not cause the current value of `n` to be lost. Rather, it causes a new version of `n` to be created, and that version lasts until the inner call to `factorial` is complete. This is part of what makes recursion so powerful. The function we define to solve the main problem is allowed to call itself to solve subproblems, without any worry that the subproblems will interfere with the main problem.

15.7.1 Recursive Traversal of a Folder Tree

As mentioned in chapter 14, a collection of file folders, some nested inside others, can be considered to be a tree. Recursive functions are ideal for processing such trees. The following program defines several functions, one of which is recursive: `reduce_all_in_folder_tree`. What the program does is search a folder and all its subfolders for image files having the ".JPG" file extension. It makes a reduced version of each of these and stores it in a parallel folder structure that it creates. All the new folders and image files are given names that consist of the corresponding original name and a suffix `_reduced_by_0.1`.

A program like this comes in handy when one has just transferred many high-resolution images from the flash-memory card of a digital camera, but wants small (low-resolution) versions to work with. Rather than manually going through the main folder (and its subfolders) looking for images and painstakingly resizing each one, we can leave it to this program to find all the images and do the right thing. Of course, if you want it to work with

".PNG" images or the lowercase ".jpg" filename extensions, you'll need to make a minor modification to the program.

```
1   '''MakeReductions.py
2   Copy a folder tree containing .JPG image files,
3   making reduced-resolution copies of the images found,
4   and naming the new folders slightly differently.
5
6   SF is the reduction, scale factor with default of 0.1
7   '''
8
9   SF = 0.1    # scale factor
10  RF = 1.0/SF # resampling factor
11  import os   # operating system functions
12
13  def list_JPGs(folder):
14    files = os.listdir(folder)
15    return filter(lambda f: f[-4:]==".JPG", files)
16
17  def list_folders(folder):
18    files = os.listdir(folder)
19    return filter(\
20      lambda f: os.path.isdir(os.path.join(folder,f)),
21      files)
22
23  def reduce_image(source_path, destination_path):
24    print "Preparing to  reduce the image: "+\
25          source_path+" to get: "+destination_path
26    pmOpenImage(1, source_path)
27    width = pmGetImageWidth(1)
28    height = pmGetImageHeight(1)
29    w1 = int(SF*width)
30    h1 = int(SF*height)
31    pmSetSource1(1)
32    newWin = pmNewImage(2, destination_path, w1, h1, 255, 0, 0)
33    pmSetDestination(newWin)
34    pmSetFormula("S1("+str(RF)+"*x,"+str(RF)+"*y)")
35    pmCompute()
36    pmSaveImageAs(newWin, destination_path)
37
38  def reduce_all_in_folder_tree(source_path,
39                                source_folder_name,
40                                destination_path):
```

```
41    # create destination folder.
42    new_destination_path =\
43      os.path.join(destination_path,
44                    source_folder_name+"_reduced_by_"+str(SF))
45    print "new_destination_path = "+new_destination_path
46    os.makedirs(new_destination_path)
47    # go into the source folder and reduce all the JPGs there.
48    new_source_path = os.path.join(source_path, source_folder_name)
49    print "new_source_path = "+new_source_path
50    JPGs = list_JPGs(new_source_path)
51    for fn in JPGs:
52      new_fn = fn[:-4]+"_reduced_by_"+str(SF)+".JPG"
53      reduce_image(os.path.join(new_source_path, fn),
54                    os.path.join(new_destination_path, new_fn))
55    # Process subdirectories recursively:
56    print "Requesting list of folders in "+new_source_path
57    folders = list_folders(new_source_path)
58    print "Folders to be processed: "+str(folders)
59    for f in folders:
60      # Now here is the recursive call, made once per subfolder:
61      reduce_all_in_folder_tree(new_source_path, f,
62                                new_destination_path)
63
64  # Now let's initiate the whole operation:
65  reduce_all_in_folder_tree('.', 'My-Images', '.')
```

15.7.2 Recursion for Making Fractals

One way to describe a fractal is as a recursive image. Just as a recursive function has one or more calls to itself embedded in its own definition, a fractal image often has copies of itself (at a smaller scale) inside it. The connection between fractals and recursive functions isn't just one of appearance; we can make fractal images using recursive functions. A good example of this is plotting an approximation of the Hilbert curve (sometimes called the Peano curve). The following program does the job.

```
1    '''HilbertCurve.py
2    Demonstrates the use of recursion to produce an image that
3    represents an approximation of the fractal Hilbert curve.
4    '''
5
6    WIN = pmNewComputedImage('Hilbert Curve',
7                              256,256,'rgb(255, 200,200)')
```

```
 8
 9    XPEN = None; YPEN = None
10    PENCOLOR = (0,0,128) # Dark blue
11
12    # First we define two graphics primitives: moveTo and lineTo.
13    def moveTo(x,y):
14      global XPEN, YPEN
15      XPEN = x; YPEN = y
16
17    def lineTo(endX,endY):
18      if XPEN==None or YPEN==None: moveTo(endX, endY); return
19      (R,G,B)=PENCOLOR
20      dx = endX-XPEN; dy=endY-YPEN
21      if abs(dx)>abs(dy):
22        if dx>0: xstart = XPEN; ystart = YPEN
23        else: xstart = endX; ystart = endY
24        for i in range(abs(dx)+1):
25          x = xstart+i
26          y = ystart+int(i*dy/dx)
27          pmSetPixel(WIN, x, y, R, G, B)
28      else:
29        if dy>0: ystart = YPEN; xstart = XPEN
30        else: ystart = endY; xstart = endX
31        for i in range(abs(dy)+1):
32          y = ystart+i
33          x = xstart+int(i*dx/dy)
34          pmSetPixel(WIN, x, y, R, G, B)
35      XPEN=endX; YPEN=endY
36
37    def hilbert(x, y, ux, uy, vx, vy, k):
38      if k==0: lineTo(x + (ux+vx)/2, y + (uy+vy)/2)
39      else:
40        hilbert(x, y, vx/2, vy/2, ux/2, uy/2, k-1)
41        hilbert(x+ux/2, y+uy/2, ux/2, uy/2, vx/2, vy/2, k-1)
42        hilbert(x+ux/2+vx/2, y+uy/2+vy/2, ux/2, uy/2, vx/2, vy/2, k-1)
43        hilbert(x+ux/2+vx, y+uy/2+vy, -vx/2, -vy/2, -ux/2, -uy/2, k-1)
44
45    hilbert(0, 0, 256, 0, 0, 256, 7)
```

Although most of the code in this example is dedicated to the process of drawing a line segment, the real logic of creating the fractal pattern is in the recursive function hilbert. If called with $k=0$, it simply draws a line segment from wherever the pen is currently located to the point obtained by adding some amount to each of x and y, which represent

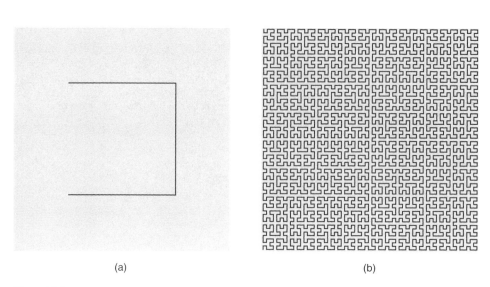

(a)   (b)

Figure 15.1
Images produced by calling hilbert with (a) $k = 1$ and (b) $k = 6$.

the coordinates of the lower-left corner of a square region of the smallest size considered by the program. The parameters ux and uy give the x and y components of a unit vector representing one side of the square, while vx and vy describe a unit vector perpendicular to (ux,uy). The parameter k gives the number of levels up from the most detailed level. Calling the hilbert function with $k=1$ results in the basic U-shaped curve that constitutes the prototype from which all subcurves are derived. This is shown in figure 15.1a, whereas the call with $k=6$ produces the picture shown in figure 15.1b. The result for $k = 5$ is shown in chapter 9 in the discussion of fractals.

15.7.3 Fast Fourier Transforms
Recursion plays an important role in the design of efficient algorithms. Many problems can be solved efficiently using a strategy known as divide-and-conquer. In this strategy, the problem is first partitioned into parts called subproblems, and these subproblems are then solved. Then the solutions to the subproblems are combined, giving a solution to the original problem. Recursion is used at the step where the subproblems must be solved, and it greatly simplifies the expression of the whole process.

In chapter 10 we introduced the discrete Fourier transform and showed how it could be applied to problems such as smoothing or sharpening an image. In the exercises, a short Python program was given that can be used to compute the DFT. However, that program is so inefficient that it could take minutes or hours to compute the DFT of a sequence of a few thousand elements. Because it works by simply looping to add up the n terms of each of n output values, it must perform n^2 multiplications and $n(n-1)$ additions. If we double the size of the input vector, then the time required goes up by roughly a factor of 4.

If we apply the divide-and-conquer approach to computing the DFT, we can get a big speedup. There is a family of algorithms called fast Fourier transforms (FFT) that are all based on the general idea of factoring and reordering the multiplications and additions of the DFT so that instead of about n^2 of them being needed, only about $n \log_2 n$ of them are needed. We'll illustrate one of these FFTs with an intuitive, recursive approach.

The first thing to notice about the DFT is that it's equivalent to evaluating a polynomial $P(x)$ at each of a list of points. If the input data to the DFT are $[f_0, f_1, \ldots, f_{n-1}]$, then the polynomial is this:

$$P(x) = f_0 x^0 + f_1 x^1 + \cdots + f_{n-1} x^{n-1}$$

This polynomial is to be evaluated at the points (complex numbers):

$$1, \omega, \omega^2, \ldots, \omega^{n-1}$$

where $\omega = e^{-2\pi i/n}$. (For a review, refer back to the DFT definition in chapter 10.) Now we divide the polynomial P into two parts consisting of the even and odd terms.

$$P_{\text{even}}(x) = f_0 x^0 + f_2 x^2 + \cdots + f_{n-2} x^{n-2}$$

$$P_{\text{odd}}(x) = f_1 x^1 + f_3 x^3 + \cdots + f_{n-1} x^{n-1}$$

Naturally, the whole polynomial can be evaluated at a point x by computing each smaller polynomial and adding the results.

$$P(x) = P_{\text{even}}(x) + P_{\text{odd}}(x)$$

Now, because the powers of x in P_{even} are all even, evaluating $P_{\text{even}}(x)$ is equivalent to evaluating

$$Q_{\text{even}}(y) = f_0 y^0 + f_2 y^1 + \cdots + f_{n-2} y^{n/2-1}$$

where $y = x^2$. Also, evaluating $P_{\text{odd}}(x)$ is equivalent to evaluating $x\, Q_{\text{odd}}(y)$, where $y = x^2$, and

$$Q_{\text{odd}}(y) = f_1 y^0 + f_3 y^1 + \cdots + f_{n-1} y^{n/2-2}$$

That's just saying

$$P(x) = Q_{\text{even}}(x^2) + x\, Q_{\text{odd}}(x^2)$$

We now have a way to split a polynomial in half [getting $P_{\text{even}}(x)$ and $P_{\text{odd}}(x)$], and make some minor modifications so that we have normal polynomials [rather than the sparse polynomials that $P_{\text{even}}(x)$ and $P_{\text{odd}}(x)$ are], but now of degree $n/2$: (Q_{even} and Q_{odd}). This allows us to use the divide-and-conquer approach for evaluating one polynomial on one given value. This does not lead to any savings in time, however. To obtain savings, we take into consideration two ideas. First, we'll evaluate the polynomial at multiple input points so that we can share partial results and second, we'll use the n complex n-th roots of unity as our points both because they are what we need for the DFT definition and because they in particular allow the sharing of partial results very well.

Our job is to evaluate $P(x)$ at each element of the sequence $[1, \omega, \omega^2, \ldots, \omega^{n-1}]$. This is computed recursively. We'll assume n is a power of 2 for convenience, as is commonly done. If $n = 1$, then $k = 0$, and the answer is f_0, the only term in P. When $n > 1$, then we make two vectors of length $n/2$, one of even coefficients and the other of the odd coefficients from P. We recursively have these two polynomials evaluated at the $n/2$ "half-n-th" roots of unity (which are the even powers of ω). Then we use our recurrence formula above to get $P(\omega^k)$ for $k = 0, 1, \ldots, n/2 - 1$. This gives us half of the values we need. For the other half (where $n/2 \leq k < n$), we make use of the fact that $\omega^{k+n/2} = -\omega$, which means $Q_{\text{even}}(-\omega) = Q_{\text{even}}(\omega)$, so the even part doesn't change. Furthermore, $Q_{\text{odd}}(-\omega) = -Q_{\text{odd}}(\omega)$. This allows us to compute $P(x)$ for the other n-th roots of unity (with no further recursive calls) using the same partial results as we used to obtain the first half of the answer sequence:

$$P(\omega^{k+n/2}) = Q_{\text{even}}(\omega^{2k}) - \omega^k Q_{\text{odd}}(\omega^{2k})$$

The following Python program implements this method and achieves a running time proportional to $n \log_2 n$.

```
 1    from cmath import exp , sqrt , pi
 2
 3    def FFT(f):
 4        n = len(f) # How many elements in the input?
 5        print "Entering FFT with n="+str(n)
 6        if n==1: return [f[0]] # sequence with one element.
 7        F = N * [0]      # space for the answers.
 8        f_even = f[0::2] # every other element , starting at 0
 9        f_odd  = f[1::2] #   "      "        "        "      " 1
10        print "f_even: "+str(f_even)
11        print "f_odd:  "+str(f_odd)
12        F_even = FFT(f_even) # first recursive call.
13        F_odd  = FFT(f_odd)  # second recursive call
14        # Now combine:
15        n2 = int(n/2)
16        for i in range(n2):
17            twiddle = exp(-2*pi*1j*i/n)
18            oddTerm = F_odd[i] * twiddle
```

```
19              F[i]    = F_even[i] + oddTerm
20              F[i+N2] = F_even[i] - oddTerm
21          return  F
22
23      # Now for a test:
24      f8 = [1, 2, 0, -2, 3, 0, -4, -2] # sample data
25      F = FFT(f8)
26      print F
```

As shown in figure 15.2, our recursive FFT program divides an 8-element input vector $[f_0, f_1, \ldots, f_7]$ into even and odd lists and then makes recursive calls to further subdivide the lists until level 0 is reached. At this level, the DFT of a single number is that number itself. After level 0, we see the "conquer" parts of the algorithm happening back in levels 1, 2, and ending back in 3. Except at level 0, there is a result list for each even subproblem and one for the corresponding odd subproblem. One of each is combined in one "butterfly" step, producing two outputs. At the end of the process, the DFT values $[F_0, F_1, \ldots F_7]$ are ready.

This particular fast Fourier transform method is one of many related algorithms for computing the DFT. It shows the power of recursion and it is about as simple as an FFT program gets. There are various optimizations that programmers would normally make before using something like this in an application: (1) Precompute the "twiddle factors" and pull them out of a table instead of recomputing them within the FFT loop. (The powers of ω used to multiply the odd terms in line 18 of the program are known as "twiddle factors.") (2) Set up the program to compute in-place so that it doesn't consume an amount of memory proportional to $n \log n$; that optimization does require permuting the results according to a bit reversal ordering, though. This FFT is of the variety known as decimation-in-time, as opposed to decimation-in-frequency or a combination of the two. We assume here that n is a power of 2, but other values of n, in general composite (nonprime), can also be used in FFT algorithms. Many FFTs are implemented without recursion, using more looping, but they are typically more complicated to express and understand than recursive versions.

Recursion is very useful. As we've seen, it can help in traversing tree data structures such as file hierarchies, and it's very good for fractal construction. It's also valuable in programs that process mathematical formulas in which expressions can be embedded within other expressions. Naturally, it's used in systems such as Mathematica and Maple that perform symbolic algebra manipulations. Finally, we've seen how recursion is a convenient tool for implementing algorithms (such as the FFT) that use the divide-and-conquer strategy.

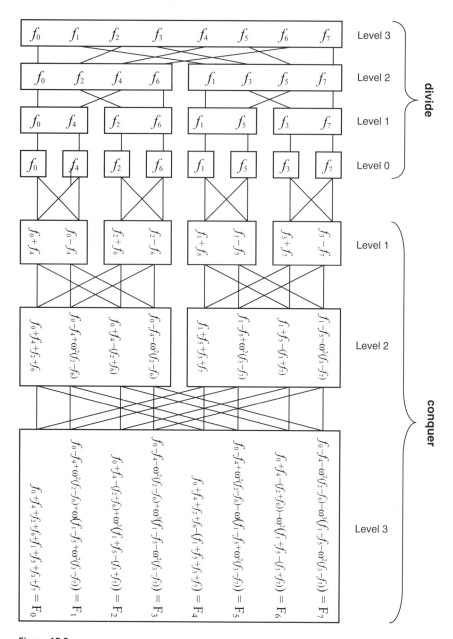

Figure 15.2
Fast Fourier transform computation diagram for the recursive, divide-and-conquer method when $n = 8$. The final expressions in level 3 have been left unsimplified to better show how they are computed from those in level 2.

15.8 Functional Programming Techniques

As we have seen, functions are typically used to process and return data. We have also seen them used for their side effects, the messages that they print, or the values of variables in the environment that they change. However, functions can themselves be treated like data. For example, they can be passed as arguments to other functions and they can be returned as results from other functions. This ability to be treated like data can be quite handy when programming more complicated behavior. In this section we consider four typical patterns of functional programming: (1) anonymous function creation with `lambda`, (2) functions that create functions, (3) mapping functions onto argument lists, and (4) reductions.

15.8.1 Lambda Expressions

Although `def` is the usual way of defining a function, another way is to simply create a function with a `lambda` expression and then either use it directly or assign it to a variable. In the `Makereductions.py` program in section 15.7.1, the lambda expressions on lines 15 and 20 are used directly as arguments to the built-in function `filter`. The following example illustrates the two ways of defining a square function.

```
1   # standard method using def:
2   def square(n): return n*n
3
4   square(7) # produces 49
5
6   # alternative method using lambda:
7   square = lambda n: n*n
8
9   square(7) # also produces 49
10
11  (lambda n: n*n)(7) # This, too, produces 49.
```

In the last line, the lambda expression is applied directly to the argument 7, without being first stored as the value of `square`. This illustrates that it is possible to create and use functions that are never associated with a name (i.e., with a variable such as `square`).

A good reason to use a lambda expression to create a function, rather than using `def`, is because the function needs, as part of its body, to reference a variable whose value is computed just outside of it. For example, in line 20 of the `makeReductions` program, the variable `folder`, which is the parameter of the surrounding function, `list_folders`, obtains its value when `list_folders` is called. The function created by the lambda expression will be different each time `list_folders` is called with a different argument.

The built-in function `filter` is one of many Python functions that accept functions as arguments. The effect of calling `filter` with a function f and a list *lst* is to return a new list containing only those elements which, having f applied to them, produce `True`. The example in line 20 of the `MakeReductions` program shows a way to obtain only the directory entries that are folder names (and not ordinary file names).

The `sort` method of the `list` class takes an optional `key` argument, which should be a function. It's common to use a lambda expression to specify such a function. Here is an example of how to sort a list of (R,G,B) triples into increasing order of the G component:

```
1    colorList = [(0, 255, 127), (200, 50, 255), (127, 0, 127)
2    colorList.sort(key = lambda rgb: rgb[1])
3    colorList #displays [(127, 0, 127), (200, 50, 255), (0, 255, 127)]
```

Here the special function merely selects the G component (which is in position 1) of its argument. If we wanted to sort on, say brightness, the lambda expression would need to do some computation. Note that there is no need to divide the RGB sums by 3, since the orderings after sorting would not be affected by that.

```
1    colorList.sort(key = lambda rgb: rgb[0]+rgb[1]+rgb[2])
2    colorList #displays [(127, 0, 127), (0, 255, 127), (200, 50, 255)]
```

15.8.2 Functions Creating Functions

Having the ability to create functions at runtime using `lambda` expressions means that we can build functions that create functions. A simple example is the function `make_incrementor` shown here. It takes an integer as its argument and returns a function that when called adds that much to its own argument.

```
1    def make_incrementor(increment):
2        return lambda n: n+increment
3
4    add13 = make_incrementor(13)
5
6    add13(21) # returns 34
```

```
7
8    subtract1 = make_incrementor(-1)
9
10   subtract1(10) # returns 9
```

In the realm of color mixing, we could use this idea to create functions at runtime that take any RGB color and then mix in some percentage of a special color, like light blue.

```
1    def make_mixer(s, percent): # s = special color
2      return lambda rgb:\
3        ((rgb[0]*(100-percent)+s[0]*percent)/100,
4         (rgb[1]*(100-percent)+s[1]*percent)/100,
5         (rgb[2]*(100-percent)+s[2]*percent)/100)
6
7    dull_it_down =\
8    make_mixer((128,128,128), 50) # mix in equal amount gray.
9    pure_red = (255,0,0)
10   dull_red = dull_it_down(pure_red)
11   print dull_red # (191,64,64)
12
13   give_it_the_blues =\
14   make_mixer((0, 0, 255), 25) # 75% orig. color + 25% blue.
15   red_with_the_blues = give_it_the_blues(pure_red)
16   print red_with_the_blues # (191, 0, 63)
```

These demonstrations show that Python's facilities for defining functions are flexible both in terms of format and the point in time when the functions are created. Normally, with def this time is when the program is started, and even if it were done twice, we'd simply get the same function with the (wasted) second evaluation. But with lambda, it is when the expression is evaluated, and it can be evaluated many times during the execution, producing potentially different functions each time.

Let's now use this technique to create functions for transforming images in PixelMath.

```
1    def make_transformer(formula):
2      return lambda wn: helper(wn, formula)
```

```
3
4    def helper(wn, formula)
5      new_win = pmCloneImage(wn)
6      pmSetSource1(wn)
7      pmSetDestination(new_win)
8      pmSetFormula(formula)
9      pmCompute()
10     pmSetTitle(new_win,"Image "+str(wn)+" transformed by: "+formula)
11     return new_win
12
13   upsidedown = make_transformer("S1(x, ymax-y)")
14   photoneg   = make_transformer("255-S1(x, y)")
15
16   mona = pmOpenImage(0, "mona-rgb.jpg")
17   upsidedown(mona)
18   photoneg(mona)
19   upsidedown(photoneg(mona)) # these functions are composable.
```

The function make_transformer takes a single argument, which should be a string containing a PixelMath calculator formula. It returns a new function whose behavior is defined as that of the helper function working with the particular formula. The helper function is needed to encapsulate the multiple steps involved in setting up for the image transformation. The lambda expression is not permitted to contain its own statements—only an expression, which in this case is the call to helper.

Notice that since helper returns the window number of the new image (the transformed image), it becomes possible to compose multiple calls to functions created by make _transformer. The last line of the example illustrates how upsidedown can be called on the result of photoneg(mona) to produce the upside-down version of the negative of the Mona Lisa.

15.8.3 map

Python provides another way to specify repeated computation other than using loops or recursive functions. It's called mapping a function onto a list of arguments. It is similar to using a loop (e.g., with for) in that it repeats something for each element of a list. The map function differs, however, from for in several ways. For one thing, map returns a list of the values generated by the repeated calls. Another difference is that there is no explicit loop variable and no explicit loop body. Instead of a loop body, a function is used to specify what happens to each element of the input list. Here is an example:

```
1   def add1(n): return n+1
2
3   map(add1, [1, 2, 3, 98.6])
4    # returns [2, 3, 4, 99.6]
```

In this example, the map function causes add1 to be applied first to 1, then 2, then 3, then 98.6. The results are collected into a list and returned as the value.

One of our examples in an earlier chapter used for to open up three images. Let's do the same with map, but also collect the window numbers returned by pmOpenImage. It would be nice to have a function like pmOpenImage that takes just one argument, the name of the file to open, and does not need the window number 0, which tells pmOpenImage to use a new window. The new function, named f, is created in the first line of the following example.

```
1   def f(filename):    pmOpenImage(0, filename)
2
3   map(f,                              # function to be applied
4      ["jack.jpg", "jill.jpg", "hill.jpg"]) # list of file names
```

The result is a list of consecutive integers such as [1, 2, 3] or [15, 16, 17]. PixelMath numbers a new image window with the next available number.

15.8.4 Reducing Sequences

When one function has to be applied many times in order to obtain one overall value, there is a convenient shortcut for expressing that. It's a special function called reduce that takes another function f and a sequence of values and combines all the values using f as many times as needed. Here are two examples of using reduce:

```
1   product = reduce(lambda x,y:x*y, [5, 4, 3])
2   print product # 60
3
4   def average_color(*rgb_triples):
5       n = len(rgb_triples)
6       if n==0: return ((0,0,0))
7       totals = reduce(add_colors, rgb_triples)
8       return map(lambda c:c/n, totals)
```

```
 9
10   def add_colors((r1, g1, b1), (r2, g2, b2)):
11       return (r1+r2, g1+g2, b1+b2)
12
13   ac = average_color( (100,100,0), (0, 0, 255), (10, 0, 127) )
14   print ac
```

15.9   References

Breinholt, G., and Schierz, C. 1998. Algorithm 781: Generating Hilbert's space-filling curve by recursion. *ACM Transactions on Mathematical Software*, Vol. 24, No. 2, p. 184-189.

Kleinberg, J., and Tardos, E. 2005. *Algorithm Design*. Reading, MA: Addison-Wesley.

Programming-guides.com. 2010. Python Functions. http://programming-guides.com/python/functions.

Saha, Amit. 2009. A primer on recursion. http://amitksaha.files.wordpress.com/2009/05/-recursion-primer.pdf.

15.10   Exercises

1. Create a Python definition for a function f that takes a number (call it x) and returns the value of $3x + 5$.

2. Define a function `complement` that takes an HSV triple as its argument and returns an HSV triple for a color that is complementary to it. You can assume that in finding the complement only the hue needs to change, and that it changes by adding 0.5 and wrapping the value around if it exceeds 1.0.

3. Create definitions for two functions f1 and f2, each of which takes as input an integer and returns a string that is somehow related to it. However, you should design f1 to be referentially transparent and f2 to be not referentially transparent. Put a comment in your code explaining why f2 is not referentially transparent.

4. Create a function `newRedSquare` that takes a number n and uses `pmNewImage` to create a new window containing a red square image of width and height n. If you then call `newRedSquare(50)`, you should get a new window and image containing a 50-by-50 square of red pixels.

5. Create a function `fadeOut` that takes one argument representing a window number and then causes the image in that window to gradually turn black in a sequence of ten steps.

6. Define a function `myNewImage` that takes three optional arguments (width, height, and color) and opens a new window with the specified dimensions and color. The default width should be 572, the default height should be 256, and the default color should be (0, 127, 192). Show how to call the function as concisely as possible for each of six cases, where in each case either none, one, two, or three of the arguments are omitted.

7. Define a function `checkerboard` that has five optional parameters: `nrows`, defaulting to 8; `ncols`, also defaulting to 8; `lightColor`, defaulting to white; `darkcolor`, defaulting to black; and `squareSize`, defaulting to 50. It should use whatever values of these parameters it has after each call to create a PixelMath image containing a checkerboard pattern of the specified dimensions (in rows and columns), colors, and size (in pixel widths) of each square.

8. Using the same program structure as in `makeReductions.py`, write a program that will make supersaturated versions of all the images in a folder tree. A supersaturated image is one whose pixel saturation levels have all been set to 1.0, with their hue and value levels unchanged.

9. Using the same program structure as in `makeReductions.py`, write a program that will make transformed versions of all the images in a folder tree. You may decide what the featured transformation will be. Some possibilities include creating sepia-tone versions, monochrome versions, upside-down or mirrored versions, framed versions, or versions that have a signature added to them.

10. Modify the program called `makeReductions.py` so that it not only reduces each image, but if the width of the original image is greater than its height, the rightmost column of pixels is predominately blue, and the leftmost column of pixels is not predominately blue, then the program also rotates the image 90 degrees counterclockwise. Similarly, if there is a predominately blue column of pixels at the left edge and not at the right edge, then the image is rotated 90 degrees clockwise. Whatever criterion you decide to use for your choice on rotation, test it out on some trial images and give a rationale for it as a comment in your program.

11. Compare the performance of two different methods for computing the discrete Fourier transform as follows. Create a single Python file that contains (a) the DFT function from the DFT exercise in chapter 10, (b) the FFT function in this chapter (but with the `print` statements commented out), and (c) the following code. Run the test and then if it does not take too long on your computer, try increasing M by 1 or 2 at a time until it takes longer than you have patience for. Note the timing values printed out and draw a graph that shows the time taken by each of DFT and FFT as a function of M. (This program can be run either within PixelMath or in a standalone implementation of Python 2.6 or 2.7.)

```
1    # Do a performance comparison between the straight DFT and the FFT
2
3    import time
4
5    def startClock():
6        C = time.clock()
7        return C
```

```
8
9     def reportTime(C):
10        now = time.clock()
11        print "Time used: "+str(now-C)
12
13    def runTest(M):  # m controls how long the input gets. n = 2 M.
14        n = 1
15        inputData = [1] # Start at n=0.
16        for k in range(M):
17            print "When n = "+str(n)+":"
18            Cdct = startClock()
19            Ddct = DFT(inputData)
20            print "    DFT used ",
21            reportTime(Cdct)
22            Cfft = startClock()
23            Dfft = FFT(inputData)
24            print "    FFT used ",
25            reportTime(Cfft)
26            # Now lengthen the data for the next iteration
27            # by concatenating it with a multiple of itself (by 2)
28            inputData += [2*e for e in inputData]
29            n *= 2 # Update n.
30
31    runTest(15)
```

12. Modify your program from the previous exercise so that it calls only the FFT and not the DFT. (Comment out the lines 18–21 in runTest.) Experiment with increasing values of M to determine what the largest values of M and n are that you can use before the time required for the FFT exceeds 1 minute on your computer.

13. Using the example function make_mixer as a guide, define a function make_filter that creates new functions that modify colors, not by weighted averaging, but according to the physics of color filtering. Suppose that color $C_1 = (R_1, G_1, B_1)$ is to be filtered through a color filter whose transmittance is represented by $C_2 = (R_2, G_2, B_2)$. Each component of C_2 tells what fraction (when the component is divided by 255) of the corresponding component from C_1 passes through the filter. For example, if $C_1 = (100, 100, 50)$ (a dark yellow), and $C_2 = (200, 63, 200)$ (a magenta filter with some loss of intensity even in red and blue and some leakage through of green), the resulting filtered color would be $C_3 = (100 \cdot \frac{200}{255}, 100 \cdot \frac{63}{255}, 50 \cdot \frac{200}{255})$, which is redder and darker than C_1. You can drop the percent parameter for this exercise.

14. Rewrite the definition of mean shown in section 15.6 so that it does not use a loop or any new local variable (like total), instead making use of reduce and a lambda expression.

15. Design a recursive function `all_bit_strings(n)` that will return a list of all bit strings of length *n*. For example, `all_bit_strings(3)` should return the list

```
['000', '001', '010', '011', '100', '101', '110', '111']
```

Note that if $n = 0$, then a list containing one string (the empty string `' '`) should be returned. Show your function's results for the following cases: $n = 0$, $n = 1$, $n = 2$, $n = 3$, $n = 4$, $n = 5$, and $n = 6$.

16. Write a (recursive) definition for a Python function `bead_strings` that takes one argument: a list that represents what beads are available and outputs a list of all the possible strings of beads that can be constructed using all the available beads. An example input list is `[['R',2],['Y',3]]`, which means that there are two red beads and three yellow beads. The possible strings of beads for this input are the following:

```
['RRYYY', 'RYRYY', 'RYYRY', 'RYYYR', 'YRRYY',
 'YRYRY', 'YRYYR', 'YYRRY', 'YYRYR', 'YYYRR'].
```

Note: Using `map`, as well as `lambda`, and a loop over positions in the input list may be helpful here. It also helps to think recursively; what is a way to get the answer required that involves making recursive calls?

17. Write a PixelMath Python function that takes a list of strings, such as that output by the `bead_strings` function of the previous exercise, and synthesizes an image that illustrates the strings. The image should be wide enough for all the strings and high enough so that all the elements of each string can be shown. Show each element (such as 'R') as a colored (such as red) circle in the image, on a neutral gray background. Separate the strings of beads by a few pixels so that they are graphically distinct. To plot a circle, you can use the techniques described in chapter 7.

18. Write a recursive function that takes a square image having dimensions $2^k \times 2^k$ and performs the following method for rotation by 90 degrees. If the region to be rotated is 1 by 1, do nothing. Otherwise, divide it into quadrants (see the discussion on quadtrees in section 14.7 of chapter 14), save quadrant 0 in a buffer, copy quadrant 3 to quadrant 0 (without any rotation), quadrant 2 to quadrant 3, quadrant 1 to quadrant 2, and the saved quadrant 0 to quadrant 1. Then recursively call the rotation method separately on each of the four quadrants.

a. For simplicity, assume the image is represented as a list of a list of integers and is quite small, say 16 by 16.

b. For a more amusing demonstration, but at a cost of some extra design work to get the formulas right for copying quadrant-oriented blocks of pixels in PixelMath, implement the method using PixelMath image windows and commands. When performing each copy operation in PixelMath, you should make use of the function `pmSetRectangle` to limit the set of pixels in the destination that are affected. This not only simplifies the formulation of the copy step, but saves time. It also means that three of the five copy operations (those not involving the buffer) can use the main image for both Source1 and Destination. For the buffer, simply use another PixelMath image window large enough to hold whatever might need to be copied (i.e., the size of the largest quadrant to be copied). By delaying the recursive calls until all four quadrants at the current level have been moved, the same buffer image can be used at all levels of recursion. Before trying your algorithm on a medium-sized image, make sure it works correctly on a very small image (e.g., 8 by 8 or 16 by 16). Although it may be entertaining to watch for a while, it might be very slow with a large image.

16 Programming Techniques

16.1 Overview

Having now covered many basic techniques of computer programming, the purpose of this chapter is primarily to present some fundamental philosophical, organizational, and design ideas (related mainly to software engineering), and secondarily, to further enrich our vocabulary about ways to program, including a few additional mechanisms available in Python. To illustrate some of the concepts, a number of examples are discussed that are all related to one application: making presentations.

16.2 Concepts and Paradigms

As we cover each of several programming paradigms, we'll discuss how each one relates to several key concepts. Here are the concepts.

Encapsulation refers to the wrapping up of a piece of code in such a manner that several items of data and the functions related to them can be combined and considered as a unit.

Abstraction is a combination of generalization and simplification. One method is more general than another if it can handle more cases or perform a wider variety of operations. One method is simpler than another if its description is shorter than another's; for example, if it does not require descriptions of more special cases. Abstraction allows the expression of widely applicable ideas without having to explain their details.

Reuse is taking advantage of code already written to serve a similar purpose or a completely new purpose.

Defensive programming is the use of programming discipline and strategies that reduce the likelihood of errors and the time needed to achieve a satisfactory program.

Now let's say more about encapsulation, particularly with regard to Python. Encapsulation is supported at many scales and in several styles in Python. At the file level, modules are a key tool for encapsulating functions and data with related capabilities. There is also the class level and below that, the function (and method) level. Then there is the code-block level. Encapsulation of data happens not only with modules and classes but also in data structures for collections, including tuples, lists, and dictionaries. Encapsulation helps to support abstraction as well as reuse, both of which we will discuss shortly.

Abstraction is essential when creating programs that solve complex problems. It is a fundamental tool for managing complexity. Not only does encapsulation directly support abstraction, but the ability to call a function with different arguments means that the essential transformation can be abstracted from the particular domain-range pairs involved. The definition of classes of objects abstracts from the instances all the common structure, helping to manage what would otherwise be too many different objects. An important aspect of both encapsulation and abstraction is *information hiding*. A programming language makes it possible to hide the details of the implementation of a method from a programmer by putting the details into a module, a class, or a function. The module, class, or function can be used without any need for seeing the details. This helps a programmer think at a higher level of abstraction than would be possible if all the details had to be kept in mind.

Reuse makes programs both more economical and much easier to create and maintain. The development and use (and reuse) of building blocks is, along with encapsulation and abstraction, essential in constructing software for complex problems. Python supports reuse at many levels. At one level, the language itself is reused every time a program is developed in it. A library (module) is usually designed explicitly for reuse. A function is reused every time it is called, whether with the same arguments or different arguments. A class is used or reused when it is instantiated and when it is subclassed.

Defensive programming is about using methodologies that help avoid bugs and misconceptions about how the program works, and that facilitate testing and maintenance. Part of it is about good design. Other aspects are clean interfaces between components, incremental development, design for testability, and built-in safety checks. A programmer who is aware of these concepts and their importance will code carefully to take full advantage of the benefits that these ideas offer.

A programming *paradigm* is an overall approach to programming that emphasizes a particular mode of communication or method of thinking about computation. For example, the imperative paradigm treats programs as sequences of commands to the computer. The declarative paradigm, which we will not discuss further, considers a program to be a collection of factual statements and statements of "if-then" rules; the computer's job is then to answer questions by making chains of inferences. The data-flow paradigm considers computation to be a network of processing elements connected by data-transport channels, so that the task of programming becomes one of designing the data-flow network.

A computer program is always a specification to a computer for a task to be performed, how to go about a task, how to respond to input, or simply what to do. However, a program can be expressed in multiple, quite different ways, depending upon the language being used, the paradigm being followed, and the programmer's style. In the following sections we examine the three most important paradigms: imperative, object-oriented, and functional. Python supports all three of these.

16.3   Imperative Programming

Programming in the imperative paradigm consists of giving sequences of commands. Within this general structure we can have conditionals, loops, location transfers called go-to statements (but not in Python), and function calls. Yet the overall feel of an imperative program is similar to that of a cookbook recipe; the program consists primarily of step-by-step instructions.

One advantage of the imperative paradigm is the simplicity of its concepts and constructs. A sequence of steps is structually straightforward. If the steps are clear, then the whole program can be clear. Another advantage of the step-by-step kind of programming is that it maps relatively closely onto a standard conceptual model of a computer. Machine-language programs are often mostly sequences of low-level instructions about obtaining values from memory, adding them, storing them, etc. If the task to be performed is simple, an imperative program is often not only the simplest way to express the task to a computer, but also to express it to a human. Where imperative programming's weaknesses show up is in handling complex processes and systems when we really have a need for encapsulation and abstraction.

16.4   Object-Oriented Programming

A program that strictly follows the object-oriented paradigm consists only of object method calls, including the construction of objects, and the invocation of methods via message passing. For example, to print out the number 7, an object-oriented program would first construct a numerical object for 7 and then send it a "print yourself" message. That would cause the seven object's print method to be invoked. Then the printing would take place.

In order to facilitate the definition and construction of objects, languages that support the object-oriented paradigm allow programmers to specify classes and subclasses. They provide automatic inheritance by subclasses of their parent classes' features, including data fields and functional methods.

Object-oriented programs can also take advantage of powerful encapsulation facilities. However, programs that adhere very strictly to the paradigm may be verbose, owing to the need to manipulate even the simplest kinds of data (numbers, Booleans, characters, and strings) by sending them messages rather than treating them as special-purpose, simple data types. Consequently, most object-oriented languages, such as Java, make a compromise between the use of specialized data types (e.g., integers, floating-point numbers) and bona-fide objects, which require more overhead in terms of data storage and program code.

16.5   Functional Programming

A purely functional program works without assignment statements, using only parameter-to-argument binding within function calls to achieve associations between variables and values. Each function in a program that strictly follows the functional paradigm must be a pure function; it must not have any side effects, and its returned value must depend only on the values of its arguments and not on any global variable or other environmental values. Input, output, and persistent file storage are outside the scope of a purely functional language, and yet they are essential to real computing. Consequently, languages such as Haskell and ML that support functional programming make exceptions for them in order to be practical. Purely functional programs may be easier to write, debug, and make assurances for their correctness than programs that allow impure constructs.

Common features of functional programs are the following: Nearly all the code consists of function definitions. Functions may be passed as arguments to other functions. Functions may be created at runtime via the `lambda` construct. Explicit application of functions may be performed with `map` and `reduce`. Recursive functions are used. Many of the functions are either pure or at least referentially transparent or side-effect free.

Python is a multiparadigm language, which means it supports more than one paradigm. It can be easily used for imperative programming, object-oriented programming, or functional programming. Some examples of Python used in each of these styles are given later in the chapter.

16.6 Callable Objects

A powerful feature Python provides that is not commonly found in other programming languages is a combination of object-oriented and functional programming ideas called callable objects. With this technique, any class of objects can be made into a class of functions simply by adding a new method to the class. That method must have the name `__call__`.

As an example of callable objects, consider the following class of linear functions.

```
 1   class linearFunction:
 2     def __init__(self, a, b):
 3       self.a = a
 4       self.b = b
 5
 6     def report(self):
 7       return "y = "+str(self.a)+"x + "+str(self.b)
 8
 9     def __call__(self, x):
10       return self.a*x + self.b
```

To create an instance of this object, we construct it in the usual way. We can invoke its report method and get a message. However, we can also use the object as a function. The following session shows this.

```
>>> d = linearFunction(2, 0)
>>> d.report()
y = 2x + 0
>>> d(7)
14
```

This construct can be very useful, especially when the function needs to depend on a certain amount of state internal to the object. Although this kind of function is, in general, not referentially transparent, it can be convenient when functions with possibly complex behavior are needed as arguments to other functions, such as map, reduce, sort, or filter. Lambda expressions are fine when the functions to be expressed are simple, and callable objects can do the job when the functions are more involved.

16.7   A Three-Paradigm Presentation

The following code example serves two purposes. First, it illustrates each of the three paradigms discussed earlier. Second, it gives some techniques that facilitate using Python and PixelMath for making presentations. These techniques might be useful in a project that involves explaining and then demonstrating an image-processing technique or introducing and then showing a portfolio of images constructed with formulas or programs.

```
'''ParadigmShow.py
A multi-paradigm presentation.
'''
from PMGraphics import drawStringInPMImage, getPMGraphics,\
   isValidWindow, updatePMImageNumbers
from java.awt import Color

W = 800; H = 600 # The image dimensions

temp = pmNewImage(0, "Temporary", W, H, 128,128,192)
pmMaximizeWindow(temp)

drawStringInPMImage("Imperative Programming", wn=0, fontSize=24,
```

```
14                           y=200, color=(128,0,255))
15   drawStringInPMImage("is")
16   drawStringInPMImage("pretty basic.")
17
18   pmMessage("That's imperative programming.", "Do it!",
19              600,700, 300,100)
20
21   class slide(object):
22     def __init__(self, title, bg=(225,225,200)):
23       self.title = title
24       self.backgroundColor = Color(bg[0],bg[1],bg[2])
25
26     def renderOn(self, wn):
27       self.wn = wn
28       if not isValidWindow(wn):
29         wn = pmNewImage(wn, self.title, W, H, 128,128,128)
30         pmMaximizeWindow(wn)
31         self.wn = wn
32       g = getPMGraphics(wn)
33       g.setColor(self.backgroundColor)
34       g.fillRect(0, 0, W, H)
35       drawStringInPMImage(self.title, y=100, color=(192,0,0))
36       updatePMImageNumbers(wn)
37       return self.wn
38
39   a = slide("Object-oriented Programming")
40   mainWin = a.renderOn(0)
41
42   class fancySlide(slide):
43     def wipeTo(self, temp, wn, n=5):
44       # first render on the temporary slide.
45       self.renderOn(temp)
46       # make sure wn exists
47       if not isValidWindow(wn):
48         pmNewImage(wn, self.title,W, H, 128,128,128)
49       pmSetSource1(temp)
50       pmSetSource2(wn)
51       pmSetDestination(wn)
52       pmHideProgress()
53       pmHideSelections(wn)
54       for i in range(n):
55         bar = W * (i+1) /n
56         pmSetFormula("if x<"+str(bar)+" then s1(x,y) else s2(x,y)")
57         pmSetRectangle(wn, int(W*i/n),0,int(W/n)+1,H)
58         pmCompute()
```

```
59        pmSleep(1000/n)
60      pmSetRectangle(wn,0,0,W,H)
61
62   b = fancySlide("This uses ... Inheritance!",bg=(128,128,100))
63   b.wipeTo(temp, mainWin, 50)
64
65   pmMessage("That slide was an object!", "Being objective",
66            600,700, 300,100)
67
68   # Now for a recursive function to help generate "content".
69   def funfun(n):
70     if n==1: return 'fun'
71     else: return 'fun '+funfun(n-1)
72
73   # And a recursive function to handle transition...
74   def zoomzoom(n, sourceSlide, destSlide):
75     if n<0: return
76     else:
77       denom = 1.1**n
78       wd = int(W/denom); hd = int(H/denom)
79       x1 = (W-wd)/2; y1 = (H-hd)/2
80       pmSetSource1(sourceSlide.wn)
81       pmSetDestination(destSlide.wn)
82       pmSetRectangle(destSlide.wn, x1, y1, wd, hd)
83       pmSetFormula("S1(x,y)")
84       pmCompute()
85       zoomzoom(n-1, sourceSlide, destSlide)
86
87   c = slide("Functional programming is\n "+funfun(10))
88   c.renderOn(temp)
89   zoomzoom(25, c, a)
90
91   pmMessage("End of fun.", "No more fun", 600,700, 300,100)
92
93   # Finally, functional (callable) objects:
94   class selfTransitioningSlide(fancySlide):
95     def __call__(self, temp, wn):
96       self.wipeTo(temp, wn, 20)
97
98   sts = selfTransitioningSlide("Callable objects are lovable!")
99   sts(temp,a.wn) # The call.
```

This program begins by importing four functions from a module called PMGraphics. This module is shown in the next section, and it primarily provides a means to expose the

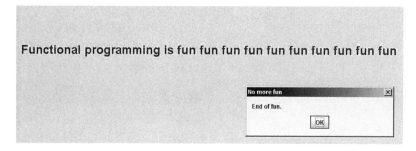

Figure 16.1
Portion of a screen shot showing the slide show after the slide on functional programming has been displayed.

underlying Java `Image` object of a PixelMath image, so that graphics calls can be made on it from Python. Also, the class `Color` is imported from the `java.awt` package, so that the Python program can construct color objects to use in graphics calls. In line 8, the width and height of most of the images to be used for the slide show are set, and in lines 10–11 one image (`temp`) is set up and maximized to fill the screen.

The imperative part of the presentation is created by three calls to `drawStringInPMImage`, one after the other, and they are followed by a dialog box that the user (the viewer of the presentation) must click on to proceed.

The object-oriented part of the presentation uses a class called `slide` to define a unit of text that can be shown on an image window. A background color is defined for each slide, with beige being the default. A subclass of `slide`, called `fancySlide`, is defined that adds a method called `wipeTo` that can display a gradual transition from a previous slide to the current one.

The functional-programming portion involves one more slide. The contents of this slide consist of a sentence with the word "fun" repeated a number of times. This is accomplished with a recursive function called `funfun`. A second recursive function, `zoomzoom`, performs a transition involving gradually enlarging the rectangular region of the destination image that is allowed to receive pixels copied from the source. Part of a screen shot taken at this point in the presentation is given in figure 16.1.

In producing the last slide, a combination of object-oriented and functional programming is used. The class `selfTransitioningSlide` is a subclass of `fancySlide`. Its only additional capability is being able to perform the wipe transition via the object itself being called (as a function) rather than the wipe method of the object being called directly.

16.8   Some Details About the Example

The presentation described here cannot be run without the following module. This module is presented here, not only because it would otherwise be a missing link, but also because it demonstrates, more clearly than any other example, an exploitation of the integration of Python, Java graphics components, and PixelMath. Although some of the programs in the final chapters of this text integrate Python, PixelMath, and Java graphics, they do not call PixelMath's internal Java-defined methods as done here.

```
1    ''' PMGraphics.py
2
3    Functions to permit using AWT graphics in PixelMath. The
4    functions here allow and demonstrate how to draw directly onto
5    PixelMath images from Python programs by taking advantage of
6    Jython's integration with Java.  There are three parts to the
7    process:
8
9    1. Getting a Graphics object from a PixelMath Image Frame.
10       The function getPMGraphics makes this easy.
11
12   2. Drawing with the Graphics object g.
13      This is simply a matter of using Java methods and classes,
14      with Python syntax.
15
16   3. Updating the Image Frame so the numbers are consistent with
17      the image. The function updatePMImageNumbers makes this easy.
18
19   '''
20   from java.awt import Color, Font
21   from java.awt.image import BufferedImage
22   from JythonPixelMathInterface import *
23
24   G = None
25   WN = None
26   FONTSIZE = 18
27   FONT = Font("Helvetica", 2, FONTSIZE)
28   X=50
29   Y=50
30   COLOR=Color(127,0,192)
31   LASTY=0
32
33   def getPMGraphics(wn=1):
34     from pmpython.pixelmath import CalcPane
35     tcp = CalcPane.theCalcPane
36     imf = tcp.getImageFrame(wn)
37     try:
38       g = imf.theImage.getGraphics()
```

```
39      except:
40        w = imf.theImage.getWidth()
41        h = imf.theImage.getHeight()
42        bi = BufferedImage(w, h, BufferedImage.TYPE_INT_RGB)
43        g = bi.getGraphics()
44        g.drawImage(imf.theImage, 0, 0, None)
45        imf.theImage = bi
46      global G, WN
47      G = g; WN = wn
48      return g
49
50    # After drawing on the Java image belonging to a
51    # PixelMath Image Frame, you should call the following
52    # to make sure that the numbers (stored separately) that
53    # correspond to the image are updated to be consistent
54    # with the image.
55    def updatePMImageNumbers(wn=1):
56      from pmpython.pixelmath import CalcPane
57      imf = CalcPane.theCalcPane.getImageFrame(wn)
58      imf.getImageCanvas().recalcPixels()
59
60    # The following is a convenient way to draw text into a
61    # PixelMath image. The string must always be specified.
62    # The other arguments are optional and if not specified,
63    # you get either the default or what was specified most recently.
64    # In the case of y not specified, you get the last value of
65    # y plus an increment that is 1.7 times the FONTSIZE.
66    def drawStringInPMImage(theStr, wn=-1, fontSize=-1,
67                            x=-1, y=-1, color=None):
68      global G, WN, FONTSIZE, FONT, X, Y, COLOR, LASTY
69      if (wn>0 and not isValidWindow(wn)) or\
70         (wn==0 or (wn==-1 and not isValidWindow(WN))):
71        if wn>0: WN=wn
72        WN=pmNewImage(0,"PixelMath Image Frame", 800, 600, 0, 0, 0)
73        pmMaximizeWindow(WN)
74      G = getPMGraphics(WN)
75      if fontSize > -1:
76        FONT = Font("Helvetica", 1, fontSize)
77      G.setFont(FONT)
78      fm = G.getFontMetrics()
79      sw = fm.stringWidth(theStr)
80      imageW = pmGetImageWidth(WN)
81      imageH = pmGetImageHeight(WN)
82      if x==-1: # find x that centers the string in the window.
83        x = int((imageW - sw)/2)
```

```
84       if  y==-1:
85          y  =  LASTY  +  int(1.7*FONTSIZE)
86       LASTY  =  y
87       if  color!=None:
88          COLOR  =  Color(color[0],color[1],color[2])
89       G.setColor(COLOR)
90       G.drawString(theStr,  x,  y)
91       updatePMImageNumbers(WN)
92
93    def  isValidWindow(wn):
94       vwn  =  pmGetValidWindowNumbers()
95       return  wn  in  vwn
96
97    def  test1():
98       drawStringInPMImage("Imperative  Programming",\
99          wn=0,  fontSize=24,  y=200,  color=(128,0,255))
100      drawStringInPMImage("is")
101      drawStringInPMImage("pretty  basic.")
102
103   def  test2():
104      pmNewImage(1,  "A  PixelMath  Image  Window",  600,  400,  128,  0,  192)
105      g  =  getPMGraphics(1)
106      g.setColor(Color(0,  0,  255))
107      timesFont  =  Font("Helvetica",  1,  24)
108      g.setFont(timesFont)
109      g.drawString("Text  on  an  Image",  250,  200)
110      updatePMImageNumbers(1)
111
112   if  __name__  ==  "__main__":
113      test1()
```

The function getPMGraphics makes it possible to draw onto a PixelMath image using the drawing methods of Java's abstract windowing toolkit (AWT). This function returns a "Graphics" object whose various drawing methods can then be called. The methods are described in the Java documentation for the awt package, under the Graphics class. If all you want to do is draw text, then drawStringInPMImage may be all you need after that. However, if you wish to draw rectangles, ovals, or use other graphics calls, then they can be used, but they should be followed by a call to updatePMImageNumbers so that any subsequent transformations of the image use the values created by the graphics calls rather than the old values.

If you are creating a PixelMath project involving multiple Python files, note the following point. Any "PixelMath Python" function (a function such as pmSetDestination, whose name starts with the letters "pm") is known to the Python interpreter only if (1) a module named

JythonPixelMathInterface has its functions imported by your module or (2) the use of the function occurs in the main module, which is the Python buffer or file that you run to start your program. You don't have to import the functions of JythonPixelMathInterface in the main module because it is done automatically.

Note that this program imports in line 22 all functions from JythonPixelMathInterface. The importing is done there in case the module is loaded by another module and therefore is not itself the main module. That is the case when the "ParadigmShow" program is run. However, the module PMGraphics can also be run as the main module, in which case it performs a test. The test is not performed if this module is imported by another module because in that case it is not the main module, and the check on the next-to-last line for __name__ being equal to "__main__" will fail.

16.9   Scaffolding, Testing, and Debugging

Creating a piece of software that works can be challenging for many reasons. A common reason is a lack of clarity in the designer's mind about what the program should do. Another is lack of clarity in how the behavior should be achieved. However, another is that keeping track of many details can be difficult and confusing. Finally, when something doesn't work as expected, it can be difficult to find out why.

Here are some general rules of thumb to avoid spending long periods of time debugging. (1) Spend extra time deciding exactly what the program should do and try to keep the requirements simple, avoiding special cases if possible. (2) Break down the process that the program must follow into clear, logical parts, and describe the relationships among them. If they are steps in a sequence, make the order very clear. If they are components that work together (for example, one component managing data in files and another component interacting with the user), specify what information must flow between them and then give that information a format. (3) Don't expect any but the smallest components of your program to run correctly the first time you test them. Even then, be prepared for errors. It's very easy to make typing mistakes as well as to forget the spellings of variable names and built-in methods. (4) Code defensively by building scaffolding and debugging features into your first version of each program component.

16.9.1   Scaffolding
Scaffolding refers to temporary program code that serves as a support while some other part of the program or the overall structure of the program is being built. One example is the definition of a function that is to perform something complicated (eventually), but a simple version of it is sufficient to allow some other function to be tested. For example, suppose two functions are to be written. One, createFiveWindows, should create and place five PixelMath image windows on the screen and then it should return a list of the new

window numbers. The other, `createAndPlaceOneWindow`, should create a new window and put it in a particular location on the screen, returning the number of the new window. The programmer may write the definitions for these functions in either order. Logically, the one-window function might come first, since it will be called by the other. However, the programmer may wish to write the caller first for some reason, such as allowing some other part of the program to be tested as soon as possible, or simply because the idea for `createFiveWindows` is clear in the programmer's mind. The programmer can do this and then use a scaffolding version of the single-window function that takes the right number and kinds of arguments and returns the right kind of value, without actually doing what it will eventually need to do. Here's a scaffolding version of this function:

```
1   def createAndPlaceOneWindow(width, height, x, y):
2       print '''This function should eventually create an image
3   window and place it on the screen.'''
4       return 1
```

This example uses a printed string as a reminder of what the function should, but doesn't do. It's reasonably readable in the code and it also shows up on the screen when the function is called. Comments that can be read in the code, but that do not show up when the function is called, can indicate the intent and current status of a function under development. The extent to which comments are used is usually a matter of personal preference. Comments are usually much easier to read than the code itself, particularly if a complex explanation is needed. However, many programmers feel that comments can clutter code that is otherwise clear enough. A good rule of thumb is to provide comments that (1) summarize the operation of a function and how it needs to be called and (2) briefly explain small details within the code, when the code might be difficult for a reasonably proficient Python programmer to interpret.

16.9.2 Reporting Progress

The simplest and often most effective debugging method is to insert `print` statements in one's code, so that two kinds of information can be revealed: (1) whether execution has reached a particular part of the program and (2) the values of local variables at the time.

However, if a program is complicated, if it produces other printed output, or if it involves loops with many iterations or recursion with many levels, then the output produced by simple print statements can be too much to efficiently analyze. There are two approaches to scaling up the reporting methodology: (1) write one or more simple reporting functions that control the volume of output or (2) use the `logging` module available for Python. Writing your own reporting function means you can specify precisely what you want, and you don't have to be familiar with the ins and outs of a particular module such as logging. On the other hand, a module such as logging provides certain services and a structure that may lead to more systematic debugging, particularly for large projects.

The following program illustrates the self-written reporting approach. It has the following features: (1) The printing of debugging information only occurs if DEBUG is set to True. (2) The number of times information about calls to a particular function is printed is limited by the value of MAX_REPORTS_PER_FUNCTION. (3) The calls to the report function fit on one line (at least in the examples here).

This program contains a pair of nested loops. The information reported is about calls to a couple of functions that occur within the body of the inner loop. Without the limits on the number of times the reporting prints information, a massive amount of debugging information could be printed. That potential mess is avoided, and yet enough information is printed that the programmer can see a pattern and be assured that the functions are getting called with the right arguments.

```
1    '''PrimeNumbersImage.py
2    Create a PixelMath image that shows where the primes are.'''
3
4    W = None; H = None
5    def build_prime_image(width, height):
6      global W, H
7      W = width; H = height
8      wn = pmNewImage(0, "Where the Primes Are", W, H, 0,0,0)
9      pmSetDestination(wn)
10     nprimes_so_far = 0
11     for y in range(height):
12       for x in range(width):
13         number = y*width+x
14         if number >1:
15           (r,g,b)=pmGetPixel(wn,x,y)
16           if r+g+b==0:
17             pmSetPixel(wn,x,y,255,0,0) # prime
18             colorMultiples(number, getColor(nprimes_so_far))
19             nprimes_so_far += 1
20
21   def colorMultiples(n, color):
22     if DEBUG: report("colorMultiples", "n="+str(n))
23     f = "if   (y*"+str(W)+"+x)>"+str(n)+\
24         " and (y*"+str(W)+"+x) mod "+str(n)+\
25         "=0 then rgb"+str(color)+" else d(x,y)"
```

```
26      pmSetFormula(f)
27      pmCompute()
28
29    def getColor(i):
30      if DEBUG: report("getColor", "i="+str(i))
31      return [(0,128,0),(0,0,128),(96,128,0),(96,0,128),(0,96,128)]\
32               [i % 6]
33
34    DEBUG = True
35    CALL_COUNTS = {}
36    MAX_REPORTS_PER_FUNCTION = 10
37    def report(functionName, message):
38      try: c=CALL_COUNTS[functionName]
39      except KeyError: c=0
40      CALL_COUNTS[functionName]=c+1
41      if c<MAX_REPORTS_PER_FUNCTION:
42        print "In "+functionName+", "+message
43
44    build_prime_image(32,32)
```

The program itself creates a display using an interesting form of the Sieve of Eratosthenes for finding prime numbers. First it creates a PixelMath image window of black pixels. Each pixel represents a natural number in the range from 0 to width×height−1. The number depends on the pixel's coordinates: $n = y * $ width $+ x$. The program scans the array in a way that corresponds to considering the numbers in order. It does nothing when $n = 0$ or $n = 1$ because those are not candidates for being primes. Then at each n after 1, it checks to see if the pixel has already been colored as a multiple of some prime. If not, it must be prime itself. In that case it is colored red, and all its multiples greater than itself are colored with some color selected from a list. As the program runs, although the red values are colored in a somewhat slow process, one can see the coloring of all multiples of each prime happen nearly instantaneously. The filtering caused by the "sieve" therefore is quite visible as a kind of animation. The final image provides a graphic illustration that the density of the prime numbers near n, on average, decreases very gradually as n increases. This is a consequence of the prime number theorem, which states that the average density of prime numbers near n is approximately $1/\ln(n)$, for a large n.

In image processing and graphics, the end result produced by a program is often a visual object, and this object can serve nicely in the debugging process, assuming that the program works well enough to produce something visible. The program discussed here produces a display (see figure 16.2—plate 31) that is related to prime numbers. If the logic in the program were flawed or carelessly implemented, we might see red pixels at non-prime-number locations, or we might see no red pixels at all. Understanding that the pixels

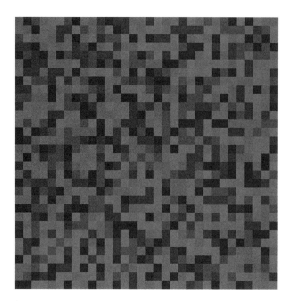

Figure 16.2 (plate 31)
The image produced by the PrimeNumbersImage.py program. The average density of prime numbers drops off
slowly toward the top of the image. The locations of red pixels in the bottom row provide important clues about
the correctness of the program.

at positions (0, 2), (0, 3), and (0, 5) should be red, but at (0, 4) should not be red is important
information for debugging. One inequality, turned the wrong way, could easily cause such a
bug. Also, if we saw the average density of red pixels increasing toward the top of the image,
we should realize that something is amiss. The lesson is that the image being produced is
often the best evidence of a bug or of correct behavior. It can sometimes be helpful to
create additional images along the way to provide clues to an image-processing program's
behavior when the final result either is wrong or is not produced at all.

16.9.3   Testing
The ideal time to test a new component is during and immediately after its development.
A test method can be created *before* the component is written, as part of the specification
process for the component. The testing during its development can consist of a call with
values that should lead to predictable behavior of the component, even if the expected
behavior consists only of reporting, so far.

   A testing function that aims for *coverage* serves the purpose of determining what part of
the domain of reasonable input values is handled properly by the component. Extreme values
such as 0, negative numbers, and very large numbers can be used if they cover important
use cases.

A *regression test* is used to test a system or component whenever something in the system is changed. A component that has checked out in the past as working properly could, in theory, break if some other component on which it depends has been changed. A regression test can catch such an error.

A *unit test* is a test that is created specifically for one component, often as a part of the component itself. For example, an object-oriented class definition for colorMixer could have a method unitTest defined as follows:

```
1    class colorMixer:
2      def unitTest(self):
3        assert(self.add((0, 0, 0), (0, 93, 0))==(0, 93, 0))
4        assert(self.add((255, 128, 0), (0, 255, 0))==(255, 255, 0))
5        assert(self.negative((255, 128, 255))==(0, 127, 0))
```

When this unit test is run, it causes the add and negate methods to be run, and it checks their output for consistency with the input. The built-in function assert does nothing if its argument is True. However, if it is False, it throws an exception of type AssertionError.

Python has a module unittest that supports more elaborate testing frameworks. With the help of this module, the programmer can set up an automatic testing process that can be used for testing individual units and regression testing an entire project.

The importance of systematic testing grows with the complexity of a program. Also, when multiple programmers are expected to contribute to the same project, testing becomes part of the coordination process.

Programming can be done in many styles, languages, and for many purposes. It can be done informally as a means to test one's own ideas. It can be done to provide a simple tool to others. It can also be done to create complex services and systems. Because of the complexity of such systems and the need to involve multiple programmers, rigorous development disciplines are then required. The field of software engineering encompasses such methodologies.

16.10   Considerations for Large Projects

If a program must do many things, or if it must do complicated things, then it could be a large program, and it could be very difficult to develop. The difficulties of constructing large programs arise as a result of several factors: (1) possible lack of clarity in what the program is supposed to do, (2) changes in the specifications during the development process, (3) inconsistencies between parts of the program, (4) challenges of testing some parts of the program when others are not ready, and (5) challenges arising from having many people working on the project. Special discipline is needed for large projects. The famous book by Brooks, *The Mythical Man-Month*, explains how a programming team at IBM learned some software-engineering lessons the hard way.

16.11 References

Brooks, F. P. 1975. *The Mythical Man-Month: Essays on Software Engineering*. Reading, MA: Addison-Wesley.

Hourieh, A. 2009. Python debugging techniques. aymanh.com/python-debugging-techniques.

Oracle Corp. 2010. Java Platform standard edition 6 API documentation. download.oracle.com/javase/6/docs/api /index.html. (see java.awt.Graphics).

Sebesta, R. 2010. *Concepts of Programming Languages*, 9th ed. Upper Saddle River, NJ: Pearson.

16.12 Exercises

1. Using the imperative style, create a slide show consisting of three textual slides and three image slides (with the images either loaded from files or generated by formulas). Display a dialog box after each slide prompting the viewer to click to continue the presentation.

2. Using the object-oriented style, create a slide show consisting of four images. Add a new kind of wipe transition to the `fancySlide` class that performs the wipe effect in the vertical direction. Use both vertical and horizontal effects in your presentation.

3. Explore the use of the `java.awt.Graphics` class to draw graphics on top of a Pixel-Math image. (a) Use either `drawRoundRect` or the `fillRoundRect` or the `fill3DRect` method. (b) Create an image containing text of at least three different colors and two different fonts or font styles. After the text has been drawn, verify by zooming in on the image that the numeric pixel values have been updated properly. (Use the online Java documentation to learn what arguments are required by these methods. In most cases it is easy to guess what Python data types are needed from the Java-oriented documentation.)

4. Complete an implementation of the class `colorMixer` started in the example in section 16.9.3. Your `add` and `negate` methods should pass the unit test.

5. Write a test method for the `countColorOccurrences` program in chapter 14 that separately counts the number of occurrences of one particular color (the color of the first pixel in the image) and compares the count for that color to the count computed by the `countColorOccurrences` program.

17 Image Analysis

17.1 Overview

Whereas much of the field of image processing is about enhancing images, including filtering out noise, improving contrast, etc., image *analysis* and *pattern recognition* are concerned with answering such questions as "What shapes and textures occur in the image?" "Is this chest X-ray normal, or might the patient have a lung tumor?" "Is there a person in this picture?" "Who is it?" Image analysis puts the emphasis on extracting and measuring features of images, whereas pattern recognition emphasizes the classification step, using the features to make a decision about the contents of the image.

Figure 17.1 shows a typical sequence of steps for image analysis. Image information is acquired in the capture step and then is processed in various ways until we reach the classification step. It's conventional to describe this flow as "bottom-up" because the data involved represent information at higher and higher levels of abstraction. At the lowest level, we have raw pixel data. By the time we're done with classification, we have a name (e.g., John Smith) or a yes-no decision. Although all these steps are typically involved in an image analysis application, the first two of them (capture and preprocessing) are needed not only for analysis but for nearly any kind of image processing. The classification step involves techniques that are not particular to image analysis, but are important in any kind of pattern recognition (such as speech recognition, sonar signal analysis, or earthquake prediction from seismic wave measurements).

This chapter focuses on the remaining steps: segmentation and feature extraction. It includes building structural descriptions in terms of regions and contours and their properties, as well as key geometric features such as lines and corners. The measurement of shape and texture is also covered. Our brief exploration of these parts of image analysis covers these specific aspects: detecting edges, following contours; finding lines; segmenting images into regions; morphological operations; and finally, computing statistical, shape and texture features. Then, in chapter 18 we'll see how such features can be processed into decisions about the contents of images.

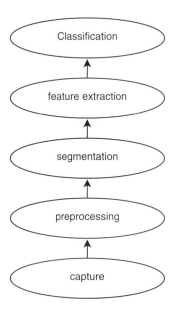

Figure 17.1
The typical steps in image analysis, organized as a bottom-up information flow from raw input to abstract description.

17.2 Applications of Image Analysis

Image analysis has many important applications. Optical character recognition is important in machines to help blind people read, as well as document scanning and archiving. Finger-print and retinal fundus recognition are important biometric technologies used in verifying personal identity. Microscope image analysis is an important part of medical laboratory work, and it includes automatic cancer screening with Pap smears and other types of lab tests. Robots use image analysis for industrial inspection of bottle labels, for autonomous vehicle navigation, and playing robot soccer. Web search engines analyze images so that they can be retrieved with content-based image search tools. Image analysis is also an impor-tant part of land-use analysis from aerial and satellite imagery. In the future, image analysis is likely to be a part of green technologies, contributing to monitoring energy systems, smart buildings, sustainable farming, and efficient recycling.

17.3 Boundary Finding

Image analysis often begins with an attempt to find the boundaries of objects in a scene. A standard approach is to apply some kind of edge detector. An edge detector is an operator that transforms a given image into an edge image. Each pixel of an edge image typically represents the strength of any (the strongest) edge passing through the corresponding location in the original image. In some applications it may also represent the direction of such an edge (with an angle value in the range of 0 to 2π).

17.3.1 Roberts Cross Edge Detector

The *Roberts cross* operator is a simple and popular edge detector. It is defined as follows, where $I(x, y)$ is the original (monochrome) image and $E(x, y)$ is the edge image:

$$E(x, y) = \sqrt{(I(x, y) - I(x + 1, y + 1))^2 + (I(x + 1, y) - I(x, y + 1))^2}$$

The operator is named after its inventor, Larry Roberts, and the shape of the pattern of differences used to compute it. In each 2-by-2 neighborhood of the image we have the pattern of values shown in figure 17.2, and the Roberts operator is based on the differences of diagonally related pixels. An example of applying the Roberts cross operator to a photograph can be seen in figure 17.3. This operator is popular for several reasons: it is simple; it is efficient if one drops the step of computing square roots; and it provides reasonably precise location of edges.

However, it has these disadvantages: it is quite sensitive to noise, since each gradient estimate (one along each diagonal) is based on the values of only two pixels; and its results do not take context into account, such as the presence of other edges nearby. Other operators improve on the Roberts operator in some ways although they may be more complex or computationally costly.

17.3.2 Sobel Operator

The edge-detection method known as the Sobel operator uses a 3-by-3 neighborhood of each pixel to arrive at its edge value, and it is less sensitive to noise than the Roberts operator. On the other hand, it doesn't locate edges quite as accurately, which means that the resulting edges tend not to be as sharp.

The Sobel operator, like the Roberts cross operator, computes estimates of gradients in each of two perpendicular directions. However, they are computed differently, and they are

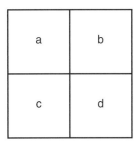

Figure 17.2
Neighborhood arrangement for computing the Roberts cross operator. $E = \sqrt{(a - d)^2 + (b - c)^2}$.

Figure 17.3
(a) Original and (b) results of applying the Roberts cross operator to an image of Heidelberg, Germany.

in the vertical and horizontal directions instead of diagonal directions. The gradients for the Sobel operator are computed using convolution with the following two masks, the first for detecting differences along the horizontal direction and the second for the vertical.

$$S_x = \begin{bmatrix} -1 & 0 & 1 \\ -2 & 0 & 2 \\ -1 & 0 & 1 \end{bmatrix} \text{ and } S_y = \begin{bmatrix} -1 & -2 & -1 \\ 0 & 0 & 0 \\ 1 & 2 & 1 \end{bmatrix}$$

Which means that

$$G_x(I, x, y) = I(x+1, y+1) + 2I(x+1, y) + I(x+1, y-1) +$$
$$- I(x-1, y-1) - 2I(x-1, y) - I(x-1, y-1)$$

and

$$G_y(I, x, y) = I(x-1, y-1) + 2I(x, y-1) + I(x+1, y-1) +$$
$$- I(x-1, y+1) - 2I(x, y-1) - I(x+1, y-1)$$

The Sobel edge value at each pixel is given by the formula

$$E(I, x, y) = \sqrt{G_x(I, x, y)^2 + G_y(I, x, y)^2}$$

The results of applying the Sobel operator to the Heidelberg image in figure 17.3a are shown in figure 17.4.

17.3.3 Laplacian of Gaussians
The Laplacian of Gaussians (LoG) method applies a filter kernel to the image that combines smoothing (with a Gaussian filter) and determination of acceleration (change in the rate of

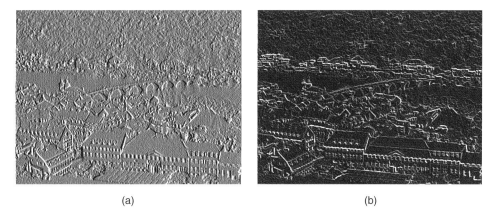

(a)   (b)

Figure 17.4
Sobel edges for figure 17.3a: (a) horizontal differences component alone (which responds to vertical edges) and (b) combined horizontal and vertical components.

change of intensity via the Laplacian filter). Then it is common to determine the locations in the image at which this value goes from positive to negative (or vice versa). In a cross-section of the image, these locations correspond to the inflection points in a continuous version of the image. These locations are known as the zero-crossings of the Laplacian-of-Gaussians. This approach has two advantages: (1) the scale at which edges are detected is controlled by the parameter σ of the Gaussian, and so it can be tuned; and (2) the located edges tend to be very precise, especially if the zero-crossings are detected by using interpolation to get subpixel accuracy.

One disadvantage of the zero-crossings of the LoG, however, is that typically there are many detected edges that are far away from the real edges of interest, such as object boundaries. An example of the Laplacian-of-Gaussians result and its corresponding zero crossings are shown in figure 17.5.

17.3.4   Additional Edge Operators

Without giving their details here, we mention several other important edge-detection methods. They are typically more complicated than those we have discussed, but they provide results that tend to be cleaner, more precise, or more tunable to the expected features in the images to be treated.

Because many natural scenes involve edges that are not completely sharp (or are blurred by the photographic process), the analysis of contours in an image can be impaired by having wide, imprecise edges. An operator developed by John Canny has explicit steps to counteract this tendency. The detection of edges based on gradient information is followed by a step known as nonmaximum suppression. The idea behind this is that a blurry edge tends to have a maximum value across it (in a direction normal to the direction of the edge).

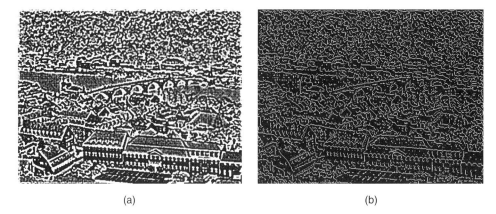

(a)   (b)

Figure 17.5
(a) The Laplacian-of-Gaussian result for figure 17.3a using $\sigma = 1.4$ and a 9-by-9 kernel and (b) its zero-crossings.

By detecting the maximum and lowering the values of pixels on each of its two sides, the resulting edge becomes sharper and the edge image less cluttered. Many image-processing systems include the Canny operator among the tools they provide.

Another notable method of edge detection is based on the idea that each 3-by-3 neighborhood of a pixel in an image can be thought of as a point in a nine-dimensional vector space. The Frei and Chen method performs a linear mapping of the nine-dimensional vector into another nine-dimensional space, one of whose subspaces is an edge subspace. The mappings can be easily computed, and the results can be well understood from a mathematical point of view.

17.4   Contour and Line Finding

Whereas edge detection seeks to determine, at each location of the image, the extent to which an edge passes through the location, it is not much concerned about how multiple edges connect to each other or line up.

17.4.1   Contour Following
Rather than scan an image in a completely fixed order, as edge-detection methods typically do, a contour-following algorithm might scan until it finds a contour, and then move through the image along the contour. An advantage of this approach is that the result is typically some representation of one or more contours (connected chains of edge elements) rather than just an array of edge values that are not organized into chains or contours.

Here is a simple, "greedy" contour-following algorithm. It first scans the image left-to-right and top-to-bottom until it finds a (significant) difference in brightness between two adjacent pixels that indicates the presence of a contour. From there, it moves in the direction of the contour, keeping the darker side of the contour on the same side as it goes. It keeps track of its progress by marking where it has been in the image, and it outputs a list of the contour segments it finds. At each step it takes, it checks to see if it has reached a marked location, and if so, it closes the contour and goes back to start looking for the next contour. It reaches a dead end when there is no longer sufficient contrast for it to extend a contour. In that case, it also terminates the contour and goes back to search for the next contour. We call it "greedy" because (1) at each step of extending the contour, it maximizes the contrast there without considering the contrast further along and (2) it doesn't ever retract any of its decisions about which way to go.

Greedy algorithms typically work efficiently, but they usually produce nonoptimal results. A set of contours found by this method with a detail of the Heidelberg image is shown in figure 17.6. For this example, a contour is started if the local contrast exceeds 50 and is permitted to continue as long as the local contrast remains above 6. Although these contours are terminated if they close upon themselves, they have not been prevented from changing direction quickly, and that can lead to an appearance of thickness, when the contours are rendered as sets of pixels, as they are here. More sophisticated contour-following algorithms permit backtracking and use multiple criteria to decide which direction is best for extending a contour: not just local contrast, but some more global contrast, curvature, and application-specific information about the image, such as expected foreground and background colors.

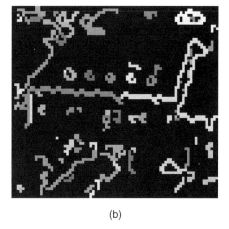

(a)   (b)

Figure 17.6
(a) A detail of the Heidelberg image and (b) a display of the contours found with the simple greedy method described in the text. The contours have been shaded randomly.

17.4.2   Chain Codes

In order to efficiently represent contours of the type produced by the algorithm discussed here, H. Freeman developed a "chain code." The simplest version of the chain code uses four "elementary vectors" and assigns a 2-bit code to each one. Figure 17.7 shows the elementary vectors and a sample contour. Its basic chain code is given in the caption. Note that 2 bits per element does not by itself provide a way to know where the end of a contour lies. One means of indicating the end of a contour requires the use of 3 bits per element, so that additional symbols can be accommodated: "end of current contour" and "end of last contour." Rather than incur this 33 percent increase in size, an alternative may be preferable: for each contour, represent its length separately as an integer. Then, under the assumption that contours tend to be long, one can obtain an efficient representation of lists of contours. Chain codes are examples of data structures that are specially designed for the needs of image processing. Particular applications may warrant the development of new variations of these codes to meet the space, performance, and transparency needs of the application.

17.4.3   The Problem of Line Finding

Many types of scenes contain straight lines. For example, buildings, documents, some landscapes, and machinery often have straight line segments as boundaries between regions. It is often useful in analysis to have a concise representation of the lines or segments as part of a description of the scene.

In high school we are taught to work with the standard line equation, $y = ax + b$. Here a represents the slope of the line and b represents its y-intercept, the point on the y-axis where the line crosses it. In image analysis, this representation of lines is usually avoided

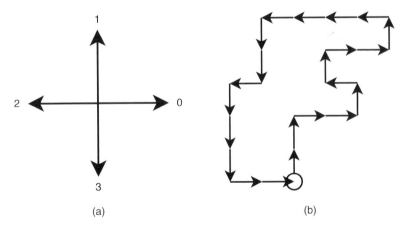

(a)   (b)

Figure 17.7
Freeman chain code: (a) elementary vectors and (b) example contour whose representation is "1100121001222233233300". Using a 2-bit code for the vectors, this is equivalent to the following (where the spaces have been added for readability): 01 01 00 00 01 10 01 00 00 01 10 10 10 10 11 11 10 11 11 11 00 00.

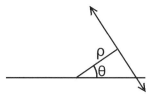

Figure 17.8
Relation of a line to its parameters θ and ρ. A normal to the line (i.e., a perpendicular to the line) forms an angle of θ radians with the x-axis, and the line is at a distance ρ from the origin.

because it has a serious limitation: it cannot represent any vertical line. This is bad because vertical lines are very common in images. For example, the left edge of a building in a cityscape probably shows up as a vertical line. The slope of a vertical line is infinite, or if you prefer, undefined.

There are ways around this, of course. One way is two use two coordinate systems, effectively interchanging x and y for lines that are steep (and would have a slope with an absolute value greater than 1 in the original coordinate system). However, this is generally considered to be an awkward solution.

The standard way of handling the matter is to use a polar form of line representation. Instead of specifying a line by a slope and an intercept, the polar approach uses an angle (theta) and a distance from the origin (rho). A point (x, y) lies on the line specified by (θ, ρ), provided the following equation is satisfied:

$$\rho = x \cos \theta + y \sin \theta$$

As one example, consider the line $(\theta, \rho) = (0, 0)$. Since $\sin 0 = 0$, there is no effect from changing the value of y. And because $\cos 0 = 1$, the only way to make the right-hand side equal to zero is to have x be zero. Thus the equation is satisfied by all points (x, y) where x is zero. So, it's a vertical line through the origin; it's the y-axis. The general case is illustrated in figure 17.8.

17.4.4 The Hough Transform

In order to detect the presence of straight lines in an image, one approach would be to follow contours and check whether they approximate straight line segments. However, that approach would have difficulty if the contours were broken up by gaps in the lines or noise in the image.

A technique called the Hough transform overcomes the problem by combining evidence for each line from all over the image, gaps or no gaps. The technique is important, not only because it is a practical means to find lines, but also because its approach is often adapted for other problems, such as finding higher-dimension shapes or arrangements of points.

There are many variations on the Hough transform, but the basic one takes an input image (usually assumed to be an edge image) and transforms it into an array of values (the Hough transform of the image), each of whose elements is associated with a particular pair of (θ, ρ) values and corresponds to a possible line in the image. The value for (θ, ρ) represents the strength of evidence for the line having these parameters. The Hough transform is defined as follows:

$$H(\theta, \rho) = \sum_x \sum_y E(x, y) \delta(x, y, \theta, \rho)$$

where

$$\delta(x, y, \theta, \rho) = \begin{cases} 1, \text{ if } |x \cos \theta + y \sin \theta - \rho| < \epsilon \\ 0, \text{ otherwise.} \end{cases}$$

This means that the Hough transform can be computed by considering each pair of values (θ, ρ) for each pair performing a summation over all pixels of the edge image. The summation takes one product for each pixel position: the edge value multiplied by a number that represents the extent to which the point (x, y) lies on (or very close to) the line specified by (θ, ρ). An example of the Hough transform is shown in figure 17.9.

After a Hough transform array $H(\theta, \rho)$ has been computed, the next big step is to find the peaks (locally or globally maximum values) in that array. This step can be tricky because what is or is not a peak has to be carefully defined. One possibility is that an array position represents a peak if all the values within a radius of (some value) d are strictly lower than the value at the array position. However, if there is a tie for maximum and the two (or more) maximal entries are within d of each other, then none of these maxima are reported

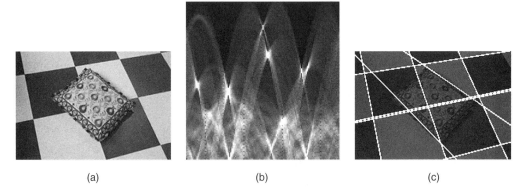

(a)   (b)   (c)

Figure 17.9
(a) Original image, (b) its Hough transform, and (c) its detected lines overlaid on the original, which has been darkened to make the lines more visible.

as a peak. One way around this is to allow ties, but only take the first peak within the area, suppressing the other occurrences within distance d. Once the peaks have been chosen, further processing might involve processing the pixels of the original image in the vicinity of each strong line to find segment endpoints.

17.5   Connected Components

So far, our approach to finding the parts of an image has focused on linear features: lines, contours, and small pieces of boundary contours (edges). There is another important approach, and that is finding the regions of the image directly, without first looking for their boundaries. This can work when the pixels that belong to a region are all the same color or all share some other easily computable property.

In the case of a grayscale image, it is often possible to separate important regions from the background by simply thresholding (see chapter 3). With color images, one can consider thresholding on the basis of hue or saturation, as well as value.

17.5.1   4 and 8 Connectivity

Once some thresholding has been performed, there may be multiple regions of ones or zeros or both in the image. What exactly is a region and how do we decide whether or not a pixel belongs to a particular region? Part of the answer is based on the concept of connectivity. If two pixels have the same color (or other attribute that we agree on) and they are adjacent (touching), then we say they are connected. However, there are two subtle aspects of this idea. One is that "adjacent" is ambiguous, since two pixels might touch along an edge or only at a corner. The other is that two pixels can be connected through other pixels, and so they don't have to be adjacent. Let's first address the ambiguity about adjacency. We'll define two kinds of adjacency.

We say that two pixels P_1 and P_2 are *4-adjacent* provided they share a common side. Suppose the coordinates of P_1 are x_1 and y_1 and that the coordinates of P_2 are x_2 and y_2. Then P_1 and P_2 are 4-adjacent if and only if $|x_1 - x_2| + |y_1 - y_2| = 1$. To get from P_1 to P_2, we take one step in any of the four directions: north, east, west, or south.

Similarly, we say that two pixels P_1 and P_2 are *8-adjacent* provided they share at least one common corner. If P_1 and P_2 are 4-adjacent, then they are certainly 8-adjacent also, because they actually share two common corners (and a whole side). However, two pixels that are separated by one horizontal step followed by one vertical step are also 8-adjacent. Thus to get from P_1 to P_2 we can now take a step in any of eight directions: north, east, west, south, northeast, northwest, southeast, or southwest. Figure 17.10 shows the 4-adjacent and the 8-adjacent neighbors of the center pixel.

Suppose we have a set of pixels S, which is some subset of the pixels of an image. Two particular pixels, P_1 and P_2, both in S, are said to be *4-connected* in S provided there is a

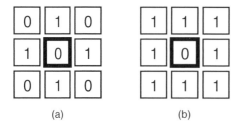

Figure 17.10
The pixels adjacent to a center pixel: (a) 4-adjacent neighbors and (b) 8-adjacent neighbors.

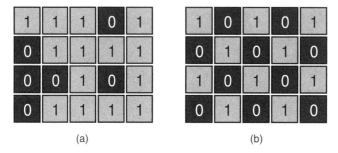

Figure 17.11
Binary images with varying numbers of 4-connected and 8-connected regions of ones and zeros.

sequence of pixels P_{i_0}, P_{i_1}, P_{i_2}, ..., P_{i_n}, such that all the P_{i_k} are in S, and $P_1 = P_{i_0}$, and $P_{i_n} = P_2$, and for each pair $(P_{i_j}, P_{i_{j+1}})$ it is true that P_{i_j} is 4-adjacent to $P_{i_{j+1}}$. The whole set S is said to be 4-connected provided every pair of pixels (P_1, P_2) in it is 4-connected.

We can also define an *8-connected* pair of pixels in a similar fashion, where each successive pair in the sequence of pixels connected P_1 to P_2 must be 8-adjacent instead of 4-adjacent. Then we can say that the whole set S is 8-connected under the condition that every pair of pixels in it is 8-connected.

Figure 17.11 shows two binary images. In the first image, the ones form a region, and it's the same region whether we consider 4-connectedness or 8-connectedness. The zeros form three regions, again, regardless of the type of connectedness. However, in figure 17.11b, there is a big difference in the number of regions when we consider 4-connectedness versus 8-connectedness. Here, the ones form ten separate 4-connected regions, each of size 1. The zeros also form ten separate 4-connected regions, each of size 1. However, the ones form just a single 8-connected region, as do the zeros.

17.5.2 Connected Components

A *4-connected component* of an image I is a 4-connected set of pixels S, all having the same color (e.g., all 1 or all 0, in the case of a binary image), such that no additional pixels of I of the same color can be added to the set without breaking its 4-connectedness. Thus, a 4-connected component of an image is not only a 4-connected set of pixels having the same color, but it is maximal. It can't be extended, since extending it would mean either losing connectedness, losing uniformity of color, or changing the image. In similar fashion, we define an *8-connected component* of a binary image.

The set of all the 4-connected components of a given image form a partition of its pixels. (A *partition* of a set Q is a set of subsets of Q such that the subsets are pairwise disjoint, and the union of all the subsets is Q itself. Two sets are disjoint provided their intersection is empty; i.e., they have no elements in common.)

A well-known image-processing problem is the following: given an image, identify all its 4-connected components. The identification may be represented in any of three ways: (1) an image of positive integers n, where any pixel having value n belongs to the nth connected component; (2) a list of connected components in which each entry consists of an (x, y) coordinate pair that identifies the first pixel (in raster-scan order) of a component; the other pixels of the component, if needed in an application, then need to be extracted using a search process; and (3) a list of binary images in which the ones of the first binary image identify the first connected component, etc.

17.5.3 An Efficient Algorithm

There is an efficient algorithm for determining the connected components of an image. Let's assume that two 4-adjacent pixels belong to the same component provided they have the same color (pixel value). The algorithm starts off with each pixel in its own separate component. It proceeds to scan through the image, checking, for each pixel, whether it has the same color as its neighbor to the west and whether it has the same color as the neighbor to its south. Whenever either answer is "yes," it checks to see if its similarly colored neighbor has already been placed in its component (or vice versa). If not, it merges the component of its neighbor with the component to which it currently belongs. At the end of the scan, the components have all been properly determined.

This algorithm makes use of a special data structure called an up-tree that in turn efficiently implements the merging of components and the looking up to find out what component a particular pixel belongs to.

The following Python program represents an image as a list of lists. The function CC computes the 4-connected components of its argument. It produces an array of connected-component numbers using the function RENDER. The function INIT_UNION_FIND initializes a collection of up-trees (a forest of up-trees). Each up-tree is a linked hierarchy made out of nodes and links. Each element of the 2D array UPTREE_ARRAY holds one node. Each node is represented by a pair (ii, jj), which serves as a link to its parent. The values ii and jj are the coordinates of its parent in the array. If they are same as the node's coordinates, then this node is a root.

Each root serves as a representative for one connected component in the image. The link from a node allows the finding of its connected component. The FIND operation keeps following links until a root is found. Then it returns that root. The UNION operation takes as arguments two roots. It merges the two corresponding components by making one of the roots a child of the other.

```
1    '''ConnectedComponents.py
2    Computes a map of the 4-connected components of an image.'''
3
4    INPUT_IMAGE = [\
5    [0, 1, 0, 1],\
6    [0, 0, 0, 1],\
7    [1, 1, 1, 1],\
8    [0, 1, 0, 0]]
9
10   def CC(im):
11       result = clone(im)
12       INIT_UNION_FIND(result)
13       for i in range(len(im)):
14           for j in range(len(im[0])):
15               if j>0:
16                   v1 = im[i][j] # getPixel
17                   v2 = im[i][j-1]
18                   if v1==v2:
19                       c1 = FIND(i,j)
20                       c2 = FIND(i,j-1)
21                       if c1 != c2:
22                           UNION(c1, c2)
23               if i>0:
24                   v1 = im[i][j]
25                   v2 = im[i-1][j]
26                   if v1==v2:
27                       c1 = FIND(i,j)
28                       c2 = FIND(i-1,j)
29                       if c1 != c2:
30                           UNION(c1, c2)
31       return RENDER()
32
33   def clone(image):
34       # Returns a copy of the list of list: image.
35       return [row[:] for row in image]
36
37   UPTREE_ARRAY = None
```

```
38
39    def INIT_UNION_FIND(im):
40        global UPTREE_ARRAY
41        UPTREE_ARRAY = clone(im)
42        for i in range(len(im)):
43            for j in range(len(im[0])):
44                # Make each entry a root:
45                UPTREE_ARRAY[i][j] = (i, j)
46        #print_image(UPTREE_ARRAY, useSeparator=True)
47
48    def print_image(im, useSeparator=False):
49        if useSeparator: print "-----"
50        for row in im:
51            print str(row)
52
53    def FIND(i, j):
54        global UPTREE_ARRAY
55        (ii, jj) = UPTREE_ARRAY[i][j]
56        if ii==i and jj==j:  # At root?
57            return (ii, jj)  # We've found the root.
58        else: return FIND(ii, jj) # Recursive search from parent.
59
60    def UNION(c1, c2):
61        (i, j) = c2
62        global UPTREE_ARRAY
63        UPTREE_ARRAY[i][j] = c1
64
65    def RENDER():
66        global UPTREE_ARRAY
67        n = 0 # components found so far: 0
68        #print_image(UPTREE_ARRAY, useSeparator=True)
69        out = clone(UPTREE_ARRAY)
70        dic = {} # mapping from roots to cc numbers.
71        for i in range(len(out)):
72            for j in range(len(out[0])):
73                (ii, jj) = FIND(i, j)
74                if i==ii and j==jj:  # at a root?
75                    n += 1          # Yes, new component.
76                    dic[(i,j)]=n  # Register n with the coords.
77        # The dictionary is now complete.
78        # Use it to assign each pixel its cc number.
79        for i in range(len(out)):
80            for j in range(len(out[0])):
81                out[i][j] = dic[FIND(i, j)]
```

```
82        return out
83
84   print_image(CC(INPUT_IMAGE))
```

The following is the result printed by this program. From this we can see that there are five 4-connected components. Each has its own number.

```
[2, 1, 2, 4]
[2, 2, 2, 4]
[4, 4, 4, 4]
[3, 4, 5, 5]
```

   The concept of connected components is important not only in image processing but also in analysis of networks such as parts of the Internet. A connected-components algorithm provides a way to identify all the parts of a structure that are connected to each other. It can be used to determine, in an image of a printed circuit board, whether one terminal is electrically connected to another. It can also be used in an image of a maze to determine whether any solution path exists between the starting point and the goal.

17.6   Morphology

Now that we have considered ways of finding regions in an image, let's consider how the shapes of regions can be manipulated and measured. An important family of techniques falls under the popular name, mathematical morphology. The key image-processing operations in this family are erosion, dilation, opening, closing, and the hit-or-miss operation. We will assume, as is customary for these operations, that the region or regions of interest are represented as ones in a binary image.

17.6.1   Structuring Elements

When we perform morphological operations on binary images, we normally will combine one binary image (the original, which contains the regions of interest) with another, usually small, binary image called a structuring element. Figure 17.12a shows a 9-by-11 binary image that will serve as an example of an original binary image. The structuring element defines a shape of interest. As one example of a structuring element, consider figure 17.12b. Let's consider some ways in which the original binary image can be processed using the structuring element. It is normal to associate an origin with a structuring element. The origin of a structuring element is a point of reference. Typically, the origin is at the center of the structuring element, but it need not be. In figure 17.12b, the central pixel is highlighted with a thicker border to indicate that its center serves as its origin.

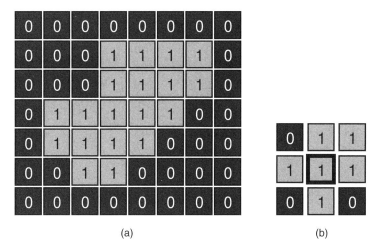

Figure 17.12
Two binary images: (a) one representing a shape to be processed and (b) a structuring element representing a diagonally oriented arrow shape.

17.6.2 Erosion and Dilation

For our first morphological operation we will take the *erosion* of the original by the structuring element. The erosion is an image of the same size as the original, where the erosion contains a 1 at a certain position (x, y) if and only if the structuring element, when positioned with its origin at (x, y) fits within the ones of the original. By "fits" we mean that for each 1 in the structuring element, the corresponding element of the original is also a 1. The erosion for the original and structuring element is shown in figure 17.13a. It is almost always the case that erosion causes some of the original's 1 pixels to become 0 pixels. These pixels are eroded away.

Erosion has several uses. One is to get rid of isolated 1 pixels that might represent noise. Another is to directly find occurrences of a shape (represented by the structuring element) in the original. One more use is as part of a more complex shape-detection operation, such as the hit-or-miss operator described later.

Another operation, *dilation*, is closely related to erosion. In dilation, the structuring element is placed repeatedly at all the positions where there are ones in the original. The ones of the structuring element serve as bristles of a paintbrush, and the output image has a 1 at a pixel if any of the structuring element's ones touch it in any of the placements. The dilation of our example original and structuring element is shown in figure 17.13b.

In some cases, dilation may have the effect of inverting an erosion. However, in the general case, neither erosion nor dilation are invertible operations. This is easy to see for erosion in the case of an original containing an isolated 1. Assuming the structuring element has a pair of adjacent ones in it, the isolated 1 will be wiped out, and it will not be restored

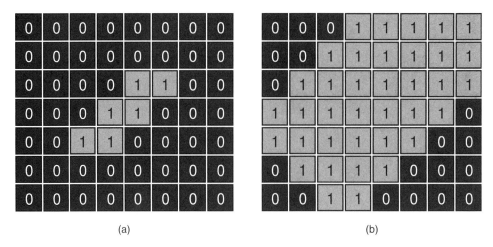

(a)   (b)

Figure 17.13
Results of (a) erosion and (b) dilation of the original with the structuring element of figure 17.12.

by dilation with that structuring element. Similarly for dilation, if the original contains an isolated 0, dilation with a structuring element in the form of a small disk or box of width 2 or more will cause the hole to be filled. Erosion with the same structuring element will not restore the hole.

17.6.3   Opening and Closing

Although erosion and dilation are not inverses, they tend to be partial inverses, and the changes caused by applying one and then the other can be desirable in some applications. If erosion is applied, and then dilation, with the same structuring element, the combination is known as *opening*. If dilation is performed first, and then erosion with the same structuring element, the combination is known as *closing*. The results of opening and closing for the example original and structuring element are shown in figure 17.14. Both opening and closing are typically used to eliminate small noise regions of either ones (opening) or zeros (closing). Although erosion alone typically eliminates small regions of ones, opening is often preferable because the remaining regions are more likely to have approximately the same areas and shapes as before the operation. The same can be said for closing and dilation.

17.6.4   Hit-or-Miss Transforms

In order to detect exact occurrences of a structuring element in an image, we can combine an erosion step with another step in which erosion is applied to the complement (negative) of the image using a complementary structuring element. This results in two images. If at a particular pixel position there is a one in both images, then the output also gets a one.

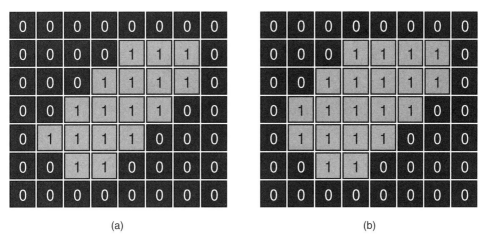

(a)   (b)

Figure 17.14
Results of (a) opening and (b) closing of the original with the structuring element of figure 17.12.

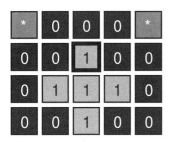

Figure 17.15
Combined structuring element and complementary structuring element for a hit-or-miss transform. The ones represent ones of the main structuring element; the zeros represent the complementary structuring element. The remaining pixels are marked with an asterish and represent "don't-care" entries.

Otherwise the output gets a zero. The structuring element and the complementary one can be combined as shown in figure 17.15.

We can summarize the effect of a hit-or-miss transform as follows:

```
HitOrMiss(Orig, StructElt) =
  intersect(Erode(Orig, StructElt), Erode(1-Orig, 1-StructElt))
```

The result of applying this hit-or-miss transform (having the structuring element shown) to the original shown in figure 17.16a is shown in figure 17.16b. As can be seen, the upward-pointing arrowhead shape of the structuring element occurs at three locations in the original, and there are three ones in the hit-or-miss result.

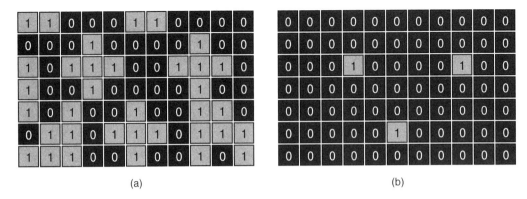

(a)   (b)

Figure 17.16
(a) A binary image and (a) the results of a hit-or-miss transform using the structuring element of figure 17.15.

17.7   Other Features

Morphological operations, such as the hit-or-miss transform, can be used to detect the presence of certain kinds of shapes that can be described with structuring elements. In order for pattern recognition to work on examples where many aspects of the image (the pose of the object, the scale, the contrast and color of lighting, for example) can change, other features are usually needed. Let's consider a few of them. Many of them are statistics of one kind or another, such as a mean, a variance, or a property of a histogram.

Although color is a property that is subject to changes in lighting, camera white balance, and factors such as weather in the case of outdoor scenes, it is sometimes just the thing for differentiating between, say apples and oranges. The average hue of the pixels in a region, can work well as a characteristic of the region provided it is computed only over pixels having some reasonable level of color saturation (such as 0.1). That's because at saturation zero, a color's hue is meaningless. Average saturation can also be a useful feature; one can imagine it being used to distinguish old, weathered cars from brand new ones (provided the new cars are not gray, white, or black). The set of dominant colors in an image can also serve as a descriptive summary of an image. Such a description can be constructed using a method similar to that used in GIF encoding: the colors of an image are clustered into groups, and each group is represented by an average or a central color of the group. Another way to get useful color features is to map from the given color representation (typically RGB or HSV) to another, such as the CMYK (a printing-oriented represention using cyan, magenta, yellow, and black), or CIEXYZ (a perception-oriented representation in which chromaticity and luminance are separated).

Texture usually refers to the characteristics of small areas of an image. These might be micropatterns of dots, stripes, or small shapes, or they might be fairly random patterns of color. However, we assume that they can be usefully described in terms of a few categories or measurements. "Thin vertical stripes" versus "wide diagonal stripes" can explain the difference in appearance between two regions of an image that in turn represent different surfaces in a scene. There are many easily computed measures that may be useful texture descriptors: proportion of pixels having vertical edges passing through them; standard deviation of hue within a small region; proportion of black pixels surrounded on four sides by white pixels, etc. More sophisticated measures of texture can be based on the statistics of regions after being filtered with a variety of high-pass filters.

In describing the shapes of regions, two families of methods can be distinguished: those that represent aspects of the boundary of the shape and those that are based on the interior. For example, perimeter is a boundary property, whereas area is an interior property. Counting corners gives a useful boundary property. Computing the 2D Fourier transform of a shape leads to various properties that can be mostly about the interior, provided that the boundary has been blurred or high-frequency components of the transform ignored. If the boundary of a shape is represented in a polar form (with the radius as a function of angle where the pole is at the centroid of the shape), then various function properties, including a one-dimensional Fourier transform, can be used to derive shape measures. How curvy is the boundary? How many peaks are there in the radius function? Another approach to shape analysis is the structural one: a typical complex shape (such as that of the human body) can be described as a collection of parts (head, torso, limbs, etc.) and their relationships. In the next chapter, we'll assume that features for images are available and that the issue is the organization and/or classification of images according to features.

17.8 Exercises

1. a. Modify the Python code for the Roberts cross operator so that it computes not only an edge-strength image but an edge-direction image in which each pixel value, in the range 0 to 255, represents an angle in the range 0 to 2π. For example, the value 33 would represent the angle $33 \cdot 2\pi/256$. In principle, the direction is based on the arc tangent of g_y/g_x, where g_x is the horizontal gradient and g_y is the vertical gradient. However, the Roberts operator estimates two diagonal gradients, and so the angles will be off by $\pi/4$. Also, there is a problem with the ratio g_y/g_x when g_x is zero. Even if g_x is nonzero but of very small magnitude, the ratio may not give an accurate value for the angle. Therefore, when $|g_x| < |g_y|$, one should compute the arctangent of the ratio g_x/g_y and then take the complement of the resulting angle.

b. Find a highly directionally textured image, such as a photograph of Vincent Van Gogh's painting, *Starry Night*. Then apply your directional operator to it. Present the angle results as a monochrome image in which black represents the zero angle and white represents $255/256 \cdot 2\pi$.

c. Using the results of (b), create a composite image in which the edge angle at a pixel is represented by the hue of your rendering's pixel and edge strength by the value (intensity) of that pixel. Hue values should range from 0 to 1.

2. Compare the results of the Roberts cross operator on paintings by Vincent Van Gogh and Auguste Renoir.

a. Taking one painting from each artist, compute edge images and capture them, presenting them in a document. Identify the paintings and where you found them.

b. Explain the different edge results in terms of the painting techniques used by each artist. (For example, look closely at the style of brush strokes in the paintings.)

c. Consider the average edge intensity over the pixels of the image. Come up with a rule to decide, on the basis of this average intensity, for an unknown painting, whether it is more likely by Van Gogh or by Renoir.

d. Take a second painting by Van Gogh and a second painting by Renoir and test your rule. What paintings are you using? Does your rule work? Why or why not?

3. The contour-following results shown in figure 17.6 were produced by a Python program called `ContourFollower.py`. It uses two thresholds: one to decide whether there is enough contrast between two adjacent pixels to start a new contour, and the other to decide whether there is enough contrast to continue the current contour. (If there is not enough to continue, it terminates the contour.) Modify this program to incorporate the following features:

a. Instead of dead-ending when the contrast is too low, your program will backtrack and try to extend the contour from the previous choice point along the direction having the next-best contrast value.

b. As it backtracks, it will keep track of the length of the longest path from a turnaround point (a "leaf" of a tree of explored paths) to the current point. At each choice point, it will maintain a record of which of the explored directions offers the longest contour. When it backtracks all the way to the beginning of the contour and cannot go in any more directions, it will go ahead and re-mark the longest contour as the final contour that starts at the current starting location.

c. At each decision point, after backtracking to it, a rating for the contour portion just explored will be computed that takes not only length, but also curvature, into consideration. A good contour should not have too many high-frequency wiggles, but should be relatively smooth, with only a relatively small number of hairpin turns. For example, a direction sequence NENENE approximates a diagonal line (in the northeast direction) without extra bends, but a sequence NESENE represents a wiggly horizontal line. In the end, the highest-rated contour from each starting point should be shown.

d. Make some additional improvement to your algorithm. This might be an ability to take color information into account or to filter out short contours.

4. Suppose that the contour shown in figure 17.7b is traversed clockwise instead of counterclockwise. What will be its new chain code (using the symbols 0, 1, 2, and 3)?

5. Chain codes are sometimes used as a form of image compression.

a. What information, besides the chain code of each contour, would need to be kept in a file that represents a color image (RGB with 8 bits of information per color component) so that the RGB image could be reconstructed with no loss of information?

b. What characteristics should an image have in order for the chain code representation to achieve good compression?

6. In some types of images, the chain-code representations of the contours tend to contain long, uniform subsequences. For example, a rectangular contour might have this representation: "11111222222223333300000000". The repeated ones form a run, as do the repeated twos, etc. When long runs are common, it may be more efficient to describe each contour as a list of runs rather than a sequence of elementary vectors. Each run can be described as a pair (length, direction). Some conventions are necessary to separate the pairs and the halves of each pair. For example, the rectangular contour above might be represented as "5*1,8*2,5*3,8*0". This is a form of run-length coding.

a. Give the run-length coding for the contour of figure 17.7b.

b. How does the length of this string compare with the length of the original chain code for this contour?

c. At what average run length does run-length coding become advantageous over standard chain coding, assuming we are using, as a measure of size, string length and the coding conventions presented?

7. One advantage of the polar line representation over the slope-intercept representation is the ability to handle vertical lines. What is the polar line representation for a vertical line passing through the point $(x, y) = (5, 0)$?

8. Give the (θ, ρ) parameters for the polar representations of the following lines:

a. the horizontal line having y-intercept 5

b. the 45-degree line given by $y = x$

c. the 45-degree line given by $y = x + 10$

d. the 45-degree line given by $y = x - 10$

9. Give the slope-intercept representation for each of the following lines:

a. $\theta = \pi/6, \rho = 10$

b. $\theta = \pi/8, \rho = 0$

c. $\theta = \pi, \rho = 13$

10. Develop a program to estimate the volume of a box using a photograph of it.

a. With a camera set up on a tripod, take pictures of five boxes of different sizes, so that for each box three faces are visible. To simplify the following steps, the views should be controlled as follows: (1) The background should be simple, ideally a flat, untextured wall and/or floor. (2) The distance from the camera to each box should be kept constant. (3) The boxes should not have markings on them. (4) The lighting should be arranged so that there are clear boundaries between each pair of visible faces for each box, and so that the faces contrast with the background. (5) The poses of the boxes should be similar. For example, the front faces of the posed boxes should be in the same plane, as should the visible side faces. The tops, naturally, will be in parallel planes.

b. Compute the Hough transform of each image and use it to determine the endpoints of segments representing edges along the width, depth, and height of the box.

c. Automate the previous step with Python code so that a single function can be called for each image to compute the Hough transform and return the endpoints of the segments.

d. For each box, compute the length of the segments representing the (foreshortened) width (d_w), length (d_l), and height (d_h). By measuring the true dimensions of one of the boxes, determine three constants, c_w, c_l, and c_h, that can be used to turn the line-segment lengths into good estimates of the real dimensions. What are the values of your constants?

e. Automate the previous step so that d_w, etc., are computed right after the segments are computed.

f. Using the constants and measurements from the previous steps, estimate the true dimensions of each box.

g. Automate the previous step and integrate it with the rest of your code. Finally, make your code output the estimated volume of each box, given the box's photograph as input.

11. What is the maximum number of 8-connected components that a 5-by-5 binary image can have?

12. Create a 3-by-5 binary image that has exactly six 4-connected components, with four of them using ones and the other two using zeros.

13. Create a single 5-by-5 binary image that has the following numbers of connected components: six 4-connected components of ones, four 4-connected components of zeros, two 8-connected components of ones, two 8-connected components of zeros.

14. Modify the connected-components program so that it takes its input from a PixelMath image and puts its output in another PixelMath image. Use a PixelMath image's red and green components to hold the (`ii`, `jj`) values of the `UPTREE_ARRAY`. In addition to the result containing an integer component number for each pixel, create an image in which each component is given a random, unique RGB color.

15. Consider a 3-by-1 structuring element consisting of all ones (a vertical bar of length 3). Determine the results of the following operations, using this structuring element and the

original binary image of figure 17.12a. Assume that the origin of the structuring element is in its center.

a. erosion

b. dilation

c. opening

d. closing

16. Design a structuring element for the hit-or-miss transform that will detect at least parts of the vertical strokes of printed text. Use the following image: Stamps-aligned-reduced.jpg available at this book's website. Convert it to a monochrome image and threshold it at 125. The structuring element should be in a 4-columns by 3-rows array. Start with the following 3-by-3 structuring element and adjust it so that it does as good a job as you can make it do.

*	1	*
0	1	0
*	1	*

Once it has reported on where it has found vertical strokes, dilate the results by 10 vertically and then 30 horizontally. Create an average of this image and the original stamps image to see how well the regions containing text have been identified. You may use and edit the Formula Page document `TextInStamps.pfp` to facilitate experimentation. (This document is also available at the book's website.)

18 Pattern Recognition

18.1 Overview

In chapter 17 we considered how features can be extracted from images.

Now let's consider how multiple features can be used to make such decisions as "What category of scenes (landscape, cityscape, flower picture) does the image represent?" or "How could this collection of images be automatically divided up into groups so that the images within each group have similar characteristics?"

18.1.1 Motivation

There are many existing and possible applications for automatic classification of images. A good example is medical chest X-ray analysis, where the question can be "Is there anything that looks like a lung tumor in this image?" By automatically screening images such as X-rays, it is possible to improve the accuracy of medical professionals and reduce the likelihood of misdiagnosis.

Another family of applications for pattern recognition techniques is information indexing and retrieval. Although a search engine can catalog web pages according to the keywords they contain, it is a more challenging matter to catalog images by the objects they depict. By automatically recognizing objects or scene types, search engine results can be improved.

Applications such as medical image analysis and search-engine image classification require a combination of image feature extraction and decision making. Chapter 17 focused mostly on feature extraction. This chapter focuses more on decision making. However, in order to illustrate the whole process, we'll have more to say about the feature extraction topic as well.

18.1.2 Training and Testing

There are two main kinds of pattern recognition activities: learning patterns and recognizing patterns. In the learning phase, a classification system acquires information about the different categories and the criteria for deciding which category a new example belongs to. In the recognition or classification phase, examples (which may or may not have been seen during the learning phase) are presented to the system and are classified; they are assigned to one of the categories learned in the first phase.

The learning happens in one of two ways: supervised or unsupervised. Supervised learning involves a process called training. Training requires a set of examples of inputs to the pattern recognition system, where the category for each example is known and provided. Such a set is called a *training set*. For example, a training set for learning to recognize chairs would normally consist of various images of chairs (positive training examples) and some images not containing chairs (negative training example). Sometimes training is performed by presenting a sequence of training examples to the classification system, having it try to classify each example as it is presented. When it makes a mistake, it is given the correct category as feedback. The use of feedback is the reason this kind of learning is called supervised.

In unsupervised learning, the pattern recognition system is not given any feedback about how to classify input examples. It typically makes up its own set of categories, using whatever features are available to it. This is typically done by taking a set of examples (with no category assignments) and "collecting" them into a set of groups called clusters. The system tries to keep the members of any one cluster similar to each other, usually in terms of a given distance metric.

In this chapter we'll start with a straightforward classification method (assuming learning, supervised or unsupervised) has already been done. The method is called K-nearest-neighbor classification. Then we will consider supervised learning and classification with a family of classifiers called perceptrons. We'll also look at some more powerful classifiers that are generalizations of perceptrons. Finally, we'll look at two methods for unsupervised learning: the K-means clustering method and hierarchical clustering.

18.2 K-Nearest-Neighbor Classification

Here we'll consider a simple and general way to classify a new example, provided that a set of preclassified examples is readily available. It's called the K-nearest-neighbor method, or KNN, for short. We call our objects to be classified examples. For an image classifier, each example would be an image.

In the KNN method (and many others), we assume that a distance function $d(E_1, E_2)$ is given that takes a pair of examples and returns a non-negative value that indicates how far apart the examples are (in some space, possibly a high-dimensional one). For example, suppose E_1 and E_2 are images, represented by their average RGB colors. Then the space is three-dimensional (with axes for R, G, and B) and the distance metric could be

$$d(E_1, E_2) = \sqrt{(R_1 - R_2)^2 + (G_1 - G_2)^2 + (B_1 - B_2)^2}.$$

The K in KNN indicates that the method needs a parameter K to tell it how many nearest neighbors to use during classification. For example, using $K = 5$ will tell it to use five nearest neighbors when classifying.

18.2.1 Method Description

Here is how a new example E' is classified by the KNN method. For each of the given preclassified examples, $E_0, \ldots, E_{N-1}$, compute its distance $d(E_i, E')$ to E'. The result is a list of distances $d_0, \ldots, d_{N-1}$. Find the K smallest of these and take note of the corresponding examples. These examples are the K nearest neighbors of E'. Next, the method goes through these K examples, counting up how many belong to the first category, second category, etc. The category with the most representatives is the category to which E' is assigned. If there is a tie, then it can be broken arbitrarily.

18.2.2 What Value of K for KNN?

If $K = 1$, the method is fast and simple to implement. The new example E' is assigned to the category of its nearest neighbor among the preclassified examples. One reason that this might not be the best way to classify comes down to the fact that there might be outliers in the original set of examples. An outlier is an anomalous case—an exception that might be present because of an error or a chance occurrence. When $K = 1$, if E' happens to have the outlier as its nearest neighbor, it falls victim to the outlier. Now consider what would happen with $K = 3$. Although the outlier is the nearest neighbor, there are probably two more neighbors, in another cluster, that outvote the outlier and save E' from being misclassified. This is illustrated in figure 18.1.

In general, raising K to higher values tends to reduce the influence of individual examples, so that a new example tends to be classified on the basis of multiple votes. On the other hand, if there are not many preclassified examples available, their power to correctly discriminate will go down as K goes up. For example, if, there are only K preclassified examples, then these will always be the same K nearest neighbors of a new example, and the new example will be classified the same way no matter where it lies in the space.

One of the nice features of the KNN method is that it's easy to implement. In fact, it doesn't need a training phase because it works directly from the training set of examples.

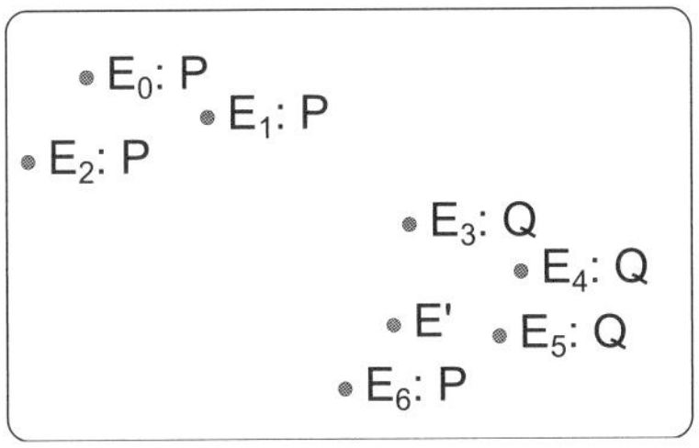

Figure 18.1
Two clusters (Ps and Qs) and a new example E'. Point E_6 is an outlier of cluster P. The KNN method with $K = 1$ classifies E' as a P because its closest neighbor is E_6. However, with $K = 3$, KNN classifies E' as a Q because two of its three nearest neighbors, E_3 and E_5, are in category Q.

18.2.3 Code in Python

The following program presents a simple implementation and demonstration of the K-nearest-neighbor method. These aspects of it may be instructive:

1. the representation of each example as a list, with example number, first feature (*x* coordinate value), second feature (*y* coordinate value), and category to which it belongs

2. the use of the Python functional programming capabilities (with map and lambda) for concise description of list processing

3. the use of a Python dictionary data structure (here it's votes) to keep counts for multiple categories

4. a way to make printouts more grammatical (handling singular and plural cases properly)

```
 1   '''KNN.py
 2   A simple demonstration of K-Nearest-Neighbor classification.
 3
 4   The data in the demo is consistent with the figure in the text.
 5   '''
 6
 7   EXAMPLES = [\
 8   [0, 184, 142, 'P'],
 9   [1, 290, 176, 'P'],
10   [2, 133, 213, 'P'],
11   [3, 467, 268, 'Q'],
12   [4, 564, 308, 'Q'],
13   [5, 545, 363, 'Q'],
14   [6, 410, 408, 'P']]
15
16   Eprime = ["'", 453, 353, '?']
17
18   def KNN(K, newExample, distFn):
19      global EXAMPLES
20      # Compute the distances from newExample to each of EXAMPLES
21      # and save a list of pairs (example, distance):
22      pairs = map(lambda e: (e, distFn(e, newExample)), EXAMPLES)
23      # Sort the pairs in order of increasing distance:
24      pairs.sort(key=lambda pair: pair[1])
25      # Take only the first K of them:
26      topK = pairs[:K]
27      # List only the examples and not the distances:
28      voters = map(lambda pair: pair[0], topK)
29      # Tally up the votes:
30      votes = {'P': 0, 'Q':0}
```

```
31      for voter in voters:
32          votes[voter[3]]+=1
33      # Report the votes:
34      Ps = votes['P']; Qs = votes['Q']
35      print "Out of "+str(K)+" nearest neighbor"+\
36          possiblePlural(K==1)+", "+\
37          str(Ps)+" say"+possiblePlural(Ps!=1)+" P, and "+str(Qs)+\
38          " say"+possiblePlural(Qs!=1)+" Q."
39      if Ps >= Qs: ans='P.'
40      else: ans='Q.'
41      print "Therefore, we classify the new example as a "+ans
42
43  def possiblePlural(cond):
44      # If plural, return blank; if singular, "s".
45      # Note usage varies for verbs and nouns.
46      if cond: return ""
47      else: return "s"
48
49  from math import sqrt
50  # Here is a pretty standard distance function:
51  def two_dim_euclidean(e1, e2):
52      x1=e1[1]; y1=e1[2]
53      x2=e2[1]; y2=e2[2]
54      return sqrt((x1-x2)**2+(y1-y2)**2)
55
56  KNN(1, Eprime, two_dim_euclidean)
57  KNN(3, Eprime, two_dim_euclidean)
```

After this program has been run, the following lines are printed.

```
Out of 1 nearest neighbor, 1 says P, and 0 say Q.
Therefore, we classify the new examples as a P.
Out of 3 nearest neighbors, 1 says P, and 2 say Q.
Therefore, we classify the new examples as a Q.
```

From an efficiency point of view, it might not be best to always sort the list of pairs, as done in line 24. If *K* is small compared with the number of examples, it may be more efficient to find the minimum-distance item, then the second minimum, etc. However, for the small number of examples in the current demonstration, the use of the sort method is not very costly and it keeps the program simple.

Notice that the sort method has been supplied an optional argument: a function that should be used by the sort method to obtain, from each pair on the list, the actual value that should be compared (with others) during the sorting. The values to be compared are the distances, which are the second components (with index 1) in each pair.

This discussion of sorting leads us to a point of criticism for the KNN method in general. If the number of preclassified examples is very large, then it will take a lot of time to classify each new example. In such a case, some additional work could be done to reduce the set of examples to a representative subset. Alternatively, we could use a different kind of method entirely, one that processes (and effectively summarizes) its training set, so that new examples can be handled expeditiously. A popular family of techniques that do this is known as the perceptrons.

18.3 Perceptrons

A perceptron is a type of classifier that can be first trained, using a supervised learning process, and then applied to new examples. The basic organization of a perceptron was inspired by what neurophysiologists learned about brain neurons in the 1940s. In fact, many people call perceptrons neural networks. (However, there are many different kinds of computational structures called neural networks, and perceptrons are just one kind.)

18.3.1 The Basic Perceptron

A basic perceptron is a simple mathematical device (actually a function) that takes as its input a vector (such as a list of feature values) and produces as its output a binary classification (e.g., yes-no, or zero-one, or true-false). The basic perceptron has within it a vector of weights (a list of real numbers, one for each component of the input vector). It also has within it a real number called its threshold, which it uses in the decision step.

The perceptron works to classify an input vector X as follows. For each component x_i of the input, a product $w_i x_i$ is formed with the corresonding weight. These products are added up, producing a value $g(X) = \sum_{i=0}^{n-1} w_i x_i$. This sum is compared with the threshold θ, and if it is greater than or equal to it, the perceptron outputs 1. Otherwise it outputs 0.

This perceptron model is shown in figure 18.2. The components x_i of the input vector X are shown at the left. The weights w_i are drawn next to each incoming branch (analogous to a dendrite of a biological neuron), and it is understood that each weight multiplies its corresponding input. The box containing Σ represents a summation function, adding all of its inputs. The next box contains the step-function icon, and it represents the thresholding function, which compares its input with the threshold θ. The output of the perceptron is labeled y. There are more sophisticated types of perceptrons that can have multiple-valued outputs, but we will not discuss them here.

18.3.2 Training a Perceptron

An attractive feature of perceptrons is that it is possible for them to be trained to classify patterns. Not all kinds of patterns can be handled, as we'll see. However, there are many situations where perceptrons are useful.

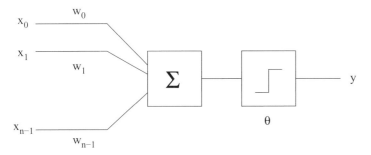

Figure 18.2
The basic perceptron model.

The idea of training is that the weights (and perhaps the threshold, too) of a perceptron need to be set to good values in order for a perceptron to correctly distinguish between the positive and the negative examples of the vectors to be classified. Instead of trying to engineer the weights, we can try a method to find them automatically, and that is to let the perceptron try to classify examples, and whenever it makes a mistake, it gets feedback that it can take into consideration in future decisions.

In more detail, here is how perceptron training typically works. We begin with a perceptron having the right number of inputs and some arbitrary set of weights (perhaps all zero, perhaps random, or perhaps based on a human designer's guess at reasonable values). We also start out with a training set of examples consisting of some positive examples and some negatives ones. Each example is represented as a vector of feature values. The set is finite. However, these examples will be presented to our perceptron in a sequence that might not have any bound on its length. That is, the presentation can repeat the examples as often as necessary. The order in which examples are presented is called the *training sequence*. It is important that all examples be adequately represented in the training sequence. In general, the sequence must repeat all the training examples (not just some of them) over and over, as long as necessary.

Each time an example is presented to the perceptron, the perceptron classifies it using its current weights. If the example (whether positive or negative) is classified correctly, then the next example in the training sequence is presented. If the example is misclassified, there are two cases: If it's a positive example classified as negative, the weights are too low; they are all raised by adding a small multiple (for example, 0.1) of the example vector to the weight vector. If it's a negative example classified as positive, the weights are too high, and the small multiple is subtracted instead of added.

Training ends when either a weight vector has been found that causes all training examples to be classified correctly, or a limit on the number of iterations of training has been reached. Such a limit can be either one set in advance or one determined during the iteration on the basis of progress being made or not. Having some limit is important because there are situations that could lead to training failing to complete.

Figure 18.3
Illustration of the linear separability of training sets: (a) a linearly separable case and (b) one that is not linearly separable.

The most obvious case of training never finishing (without a limit being used) occurs if the same training example occurs in both the positive and the negative groups. If it's correctly classified when considered as a positive, then it will be incorrectly classified when it is considered as belonging to the negatives.

This is a special case of the more general condition necessary for training to converge: the positive training examples must be linearly separable from the negative ones. In the case of two-dimensional vectors, where each example can be represented as a point on the plane, this means that it is possible to draw a straight line so that all the positive examples' points are on one side and all the negatives' are on the other. Figure 18.3 illustrates this idea. The training set shown in (a) is linearly separable, but that in (b) is not.

18.3.3 A Program for Perceptron Training

Part of the beauty of the perceptron model is just how simple its training algorithm is. Here is an excerpt of a sample implementation:

```
1    while i<max_iterations:
2      X = XVECTORS[K % NEXAMPLES] # next training example
3      # Try it with the current weights:
4      trial_result = perceptron_classify(X, W)
5      if (trial_result==1 and isPositive(example)) or \
6         (trial_result==0 and isNegative(example)):
7          # This example has been classified correctly.
8          continue
9      else:
10       # This example was misclassified.
11       if trial_result==1 and isNegative(example):
12         # It was a false positive, so lower the weights.
13         updateWeights(W, -C, X)
```

```
14              else:
15                  # It was a false negative, so raise the weights.
16                  updateWeights(W, C, X)
17
18      def updateWeights(W, f, X):
19          '''Apply the perceptron learning rule. The fraction f
20              is either c or -c, where c is the learning rate,'''
21          for i in range(len(W)):
22            W[i] += f*X[i]
```

This code consists of two sections: a main loop on lines 1–16 and a function `updateWeights` on lines 18–22. During each iteration of the main loop the program takes one of the training examples and classifies it using the current weights. If the example is misclassified as a positive example (a "false positive") or if it's misclassified as a negative examples (i.e., a false negative), then `updateWeights` is called to adjust the classification boundary (a point, line, plane or hyperplane), moving it in the direction of the point represented by the example.

Figure 18.4 illustrates a two-dimensional classification boundary (a straight line) after convergence of the training procedure. The line separates the points labeled P from those labeled Q.

18.4 The *K*-Means Clustering Method

Classification devices such as perceptrons require predefined categories, sometimes called *classes*. They can be trained using training data, where each training instance consists of an input vector and the class to which it belongs.

In many applications, the categories are not known in advance, and it is important to analyze the data to find natural groupings into subcollections called clusters. An example of an application where this is needed is in an interface for searching the web or searching a database for images. When the images are retrieved using a query, they may be ranked by relevance, but simply showing a list of the icons may not be as helpful as showing groups of similar images so that the user can better understand the nature of the results of the query.

In order to automatically perform this grouping, or clustering, there are many algorithms that have been devised. One of the most popular is called the *K-means* algorithm. With this method, each example (e.g., image) is first analyzed and represented by a vector of numeric feature values. For example, the percentage of red pixels in the image could be such a feature (with some suitable rule for deciding whether a pixel should be counted as red).

The *K*-means algorithm works as follows:

1. The N data vectors `D[i]` are input.
The desired number of clusters, K, is input.

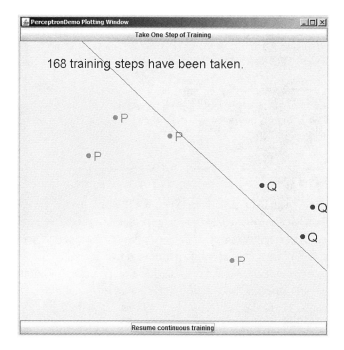

Figure 18.4
Screen shot of the perceptron training program described in the text after training is complete.

2. An initial set of K cluster centers is created as follows: For each cluster, one of the data elements is selected at random and designated as the center of the cluster. (No two clusters are given the same center.)

3. The following steps are repeated until either no updates take place or a given maximum number of iterations is reached.

a. Each data point is assigned to the cluster of the closest center.

b. The coordinates of each center are updated to be the centroid (mean point) of the points in the cluster.

The K-means algorithm tends to find clusters that are plausible, but often they are not optimal in terms of minimizing the average distances between cluster centers and their cluster members. The algorithm is greedy in the sense that it immediately assigns each data point to the cluster having the closest center, regardless of whether there should be a center in that vicinity at all. Also, because the algorithm starts with a random selection of cluster centers, the results can be somewhat unpredictable.

Figure 18.5 illustrates four of the numerous possible results of clustering eight data points (in a two-dimensional feature space) using the K-means algorithm. In each of the cases

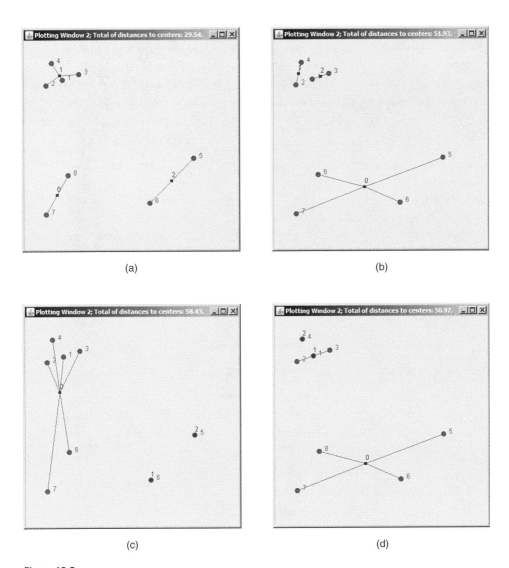

Figure 18.5
Results of clustering eight data points into three clusters with the K-means algorithm. Owing to the randomness of the initial selection of cluster centers, the clusters can turn out differently, although the optimal arrangement (a) is most frequent.

shown here, $K = 3$, and the algorithm ran for a maximum of three iterations. In each case, the algorithm converged, meaning that the cluster centers stabilized. Each plot shows, not only the original data and the cluster centers found, but also graph edges from each cluster center to each of the members of its cluster. The clusters of figure 18.5a are optimal in the sense that the total of the edge distances (29.54) is minimal.

18.5   References

Duda, R., Hart, P., and Stork, D. 2000. *Pattern Classification*, 2d ed. New York: Wiley-Interscience.

18.6   Exercises

1. Use K-nearest-neighbor classification on the following examples of apples and oranges. Each example is described by two numbers: x_0 is the average hue for the object and x_1 is the average color saturation.

Training examples of apples: [0.92, 0.37], [0.97, 0.48], [0.01, 0.29].

Training examples of oranges: [0.21, 0.52], [0.14, 0.36], [0.09, 0.61].

Test examples of apples: [0.02, 0.24], [0.90, 0.51], [0.04, 0.39].

Test examples of oranges: [0.17, 0.60], [0.14, 0.25], [0.12, 0.39].

a. Using $K = 1$, find the numbers of true positives, false positives, true negatives and false negatives, relative to correct classification of apples. (An apple classified as an apple is a true positive, whereas an apple classified as an orange is a false negative.)

b. Using the same classification results, describe them from the point of view of oranges. (An apple classified as an apple is now a true negative, etc.)

c. What are the numbers, with apples as positives, when $K = 3$?

d. What are the numbers, again with apples as positives, when $K = 5$?

2. Give a set of twenty-five weights for a perceptron that could recognize instances of the letter Q in a 5-by-5 binary format.

3. Download the KMeans.py program from the text's website and run the clustering program ten times with the simple-data.txt data set and $K = 2$. How many different configurations of clusters do you observe and how frequently did each occur?

4. A City-block distance is defined as follows:

$$d((x_0, y_0), (x_1, y_1)) = |x_0 - x_1| + |y_0 - y_1|$$

Modify the KMeans.py program to use the city-block distance instead of the Euclidean distance. Then run the program with the simple-data.txt data set ten times, noting the characteristics of the results. Compare the results with those obtained using the Euclidean distance:

$$d((x_0, y_0), (x_1, y_1)) = \sqrt{(x_0 - x_1)^2 + (y_0 - y_1)^2}$$

5. (project) Build a collection of images that naturally fall into three or four categories. Write a program to analyze each image and build a catalog of the images with at least two features per image that are relevant to the categorization. Then use the K-means algorithm to try to discover the natural clustering in your image collection. Describe any disparities between your original categories and the clusters found.

19 Computational Photography

19.1 Overview

The previous chapters have more or less taken for granted that a digital camera gives us an image, without questioning the assumptions about how the image depends on the scene. In this chapter we consider some of the ways in which computing power is changing the process of capturing a scene in an image.

We start with some basic photographic concepts: dynamic range (the range from light to dark), focus (optical sharpness), and spatial resolution (potential for detail). Then we consider the use of geometric distortion by mirrors to put more information into images, the use of structured illumination to obtain more information about the scene, and the use of computing in postprocessing to eliminate defects.

19.2 High-Dynamic-Range Photography

For approximately the first 100 years of photography, a challenge for all photographers when taking a picture was to set an appropriate shutter speed and/or aperture (f-stop setting for the iris within the lens optics). Amateurs often guessed at the settings and ended up with overexposed or underexposed shots. The use of a light meter became common in the 1950s and by the 1970s most cameras had these built in. Still, pictures could be under- or overexposed as a result of conditions such as backlighting, reflections, or shadows. A typical photographer's technique to protect against such issues is bracketing the exposure by taking a series of pictures in a range of exposures around the one predicted to be best. By the year 2000, typical consumer-level digital cameras had reasonably good automatic exposure mechanisms and manual overrides to adjust for backlighting and other conditions. Professionals still use bracketing for its extra assurance of good exposure and some additional flexibility in the postprocessing. However, most amateurs now don't worry about the issue.

Nevertheless, no matter how good the automatic exposure mechanisms are, they don't overcome a longstanding limitation of digital cameras: the range from dark to light that they capture has been fairly limited. A picture that contained both highly illuminated objects and objects in shadow could not show much detail in both. Camera technology is moving forward to overcome this limitation. By redesigning the sensor array, the image format, and the processing of the sensor data, it is possible to get not just 8, but 12 bits per pixel color component of valid intensity data in a dynamic range four to sixteen times greater than in the past.

There are two consequences of this new capability: (1) The need to bracket an exposure to increase the likelihood of effectively capturing the image scene features is reduced. (2) The camera compresses such a wide dynamic range into one image that it can carry more information about the scene than before. In this way, it better matches the ability of the human eye to perceive a wide dynamic range. It even improves on the human eye in that the human eye may need time to dark-adapt to a particular scene, whereas a camera does it almost instantly.

One technique for achieving higher dynamic range in a camera is to alter the sensor array so that the photosites within a neighborhood have different degrees of sensitivity to light. As with Bayer mosaicing for achieving separate sensitivities to different colors, this can be achieved by overlaying filtering material on different photosites within the array. When engineered carefully, an increase in dynamic range of a factor of 4 or 16 can be obtained with only a slight degradation in spatial resolution (approximately 15 percent; Kuthirummel et al., 2010; Yasuma et al., 2010).

19.2.1 A Simple HDR Method

Here we give a method for creating a high-dynamic-range image and then tone-mapping it to an output image suitable for viewing.   The Python program that created the example in figure 19.1 (plate 32) is shown here. We assume that the original images, at different exposures, are in the folder Reduced-Still-Life. Ordinary PixelMath image windows hold these images during the execution. For extra precision, the program uses complex color images for HDR array and the array of weights required by the method. The imaginary parts of the complex numbers are not used.

The formula used to map the pixels at various exposures into HDR values makes the assumption that raising the pixel value to the power 2.2 and then multiplying by an exposure time and a camera constant will give reasonable results. If one wishes to get a more accurate high-dynamic-range image, a more complicated camera calibration procedure will be required.

(a)   (b)

(c)   (d)

Figure 19.1 (plate 32)

Example of input images and output image for high-dynamic-range imaging. (a) exposure for 1/60 second, (b) exposure for 1 second, (c) exposure for 15 second, and (d) tone-mapped result.

```
1    FOLDER = "Reduced-Still-Life"
2    HDRWIN = None      # Window for the HDR array
3    TOTALWEIGHT = None # Window for the weights array
4    OUTPUTWIN = None   # Window for the tone-mapped output image
5    CONST = 200        # Used in the mappings to and from HDR values
6
7    # Map pixels from one input image into HDR values and weights:
8    def process(folder, filename, shutter_speed):
9      global HDRWIN, TOTALWEIGHT, FOLDER, CONST
10     print "Preparing to read in the image file: "+filename
11     srcwin = pmOpenImage(0, folder+"/"+filename)
12     width = pmGetImageWidth(srcwin)
13     height = pmGetImageHeight(srcwin)
14     if not HDRWIN:
15       HDRWIN = pmNewImage(0, "HDR", width, height, 0, 0, 0)
16       pmSetComplex(HDRWIN) # For extra pixel precision
17       TOTALWEIGHT = pmNewImage(0,"Total Weight",width,height,0,0,0)
18       pmSetComplex(TOTALWEIGHT) # Again, extra precision
19     pmSetSource1(srcwin)
20     pmSetDestination(TOTALWEIGHT)
21     f="complex(dest(x,y)+200*\
22         pow(2.718,-pow((S1(x,y)-127.5)/65,2)),0)"
23     pmSetFormula(f)
24     pmCompute()
25     pmSetSource2(TOTALWEIGHT)
26     pmSetDestination(HDRWIN)
27     exposureFac = 1.0/shutter_speed
28     f="complex(dest(x,y)+REAL2(x,y)*pow(S1(x,y), 2.2)*"+\
29         str(exposureFac)+" * "+str(CONST)+",0.0)"
30     pmSetFormula(f)
31     pmCompute()
32
33   # To get correct weighted average HDR values, we
34   # divide HDR values by corresponding total weights.
35   def normalize_by_weights():
36     global HDRWIN, TOTALWEIGHT
37     pmSetSource1(TOTALWEIGHT)
38     pmSetDestination(HDRWIN)
39     pmSetFormula("complex(dest(x,y)/real1(x,y), 0.0)")
40     pmCompute()
41
42   # The tone_map routine has the job of mapping back the values
43   # from the HDR image to a normal image.  The contrast and
44   # brightness can be adjusted by changing the arguments.
45
46   def tone_map(factor, power):
```

```
47      global HDRWIN, OUTPUTWIN
48      width = pmGetImageWidth(HDRWIN)
49      height = pmGetImageHeight(HDRWIN)
50      if not OUTPUTWIN:
51        OUTPUTWIN = pmNewImage(0,"Output",width,height,0,128,0)
52        # Initialize to green to show that the output is coming.
53      pmSetSource1(HDRWIN)
54      pmSetDestination(OUTPUTWIN)
55      f=str(factor)+"*pow(S1(x,y)/"+str(CONST)+", "+str(power)+")"
56      pmSetFormula(f)
57      pmCompute()
58
59    def main():
60      print "Starting to read in images"
61      process(FOLDER, "REDUCED-still-life-1-1-60th.JPG",
62              1.0/30) # actual shutter speed = 1/60
63      process(FOLDER, "REDUCED-still-life-6-1-half.JPG",
64              1.0/2)
65      process(FOLDER, "REDUCED-still-life-11-15-secs.JPG",
66              8.0) # actual shutter speed = 15 sec.
67      normalize_by_weights()
68      tone_map(5, 1.0/4)
69
70    main()
```

When working with a program such as this, the user typically needs to manually adjust the tone-mapping parameters to obtain the desired effect. The tone-mapping formula used here is a simple one. More complicated techniques, such as histogram equalization, might be helpful in trying to get an aesthetically pleasing mapping of the HDR image to a normal (8 bits per pixel color component) image. The tone-mapped result shown in figure 19.1d has had an additional step of enhancement (a color saturation boost by a factor of 2) to restore most of the color vitality lost in the averaging process used to construct the high-dynamic-range image.

19.3 Automatic Focus Methods

Most of the popular digital cameras on the market today offer some form of automatic focusing. There are a variety of techniques that can be used for this, but perhaps the most important one is measuring (by computing) and maximizing sharpness. By applying operators that are sensitive to edges and fine textures in an image, sharpness values can be computed for regions of images. Then, by taking images of representative parts of the visual field at different focus settings, the best focus setting can be determined by comparing sharpness values.

Let's now consider two representative sharpness measures. The Brenner sharpness is defined as follows:

$$\text{Brenner}(I) = \sum_x \sum_y (I(x+2, y) - I(x, y))^2$$

Of all the popular sharpness measures, this is the simplest to compute. It has a disadvantage, however, of not responding well if the differences in an image are vertically rather than horizontally oriented. This problem can be overcome by the Tenengrad sharpness, defined this way:

$$\text{Tenengrad}(I) = \sum_x \sum_y \begin{cases} E(I, x, y), & \text{if } E(I, x, y) > t \\ 0, & \text{otherwise.} \end{cases}$$

where

$$E(I, x, y) = G_x(I, x, y)^2 + G_y(I, x, y)^2$$

and $G_x(I, x, y)$ and $G_y(I, x, y)$ are approximations of the horizontal and vertical gradients of the image I at (x, y). The approximations are based on the Sobel edge detector (see chapter 17). The threshold t can serve to reduce the effects of slow changes in the image.

Figure 19.2 (plate 33) shows two kinds of sharpness as functions of focus setting. The lower curve gives the Brenner sharpness and the upper gives the Tenengrad sharpness. The data for the graph were produced from a sequence of thirty-three photos taken across the full range of focus settings of the standard lens on a Nikon D40X camera. Two images from

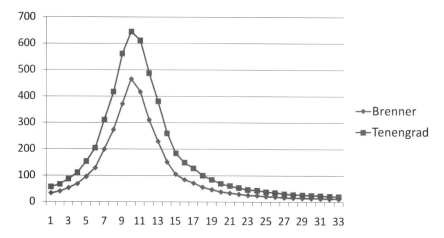

Figure 19.2 (plate 33)
Sharpness as a function of focus setting. The lower curve gives the Brenner sharpness and the upper curve gives the Tenengrad sharpness. The best focus is achieved in the tenth frame, where both types of sharpness are maximized.

(a)   (b)

Figure 19.3 (plate 34)
The first and tenth frames in the sequences of images used to demonstrate autofocus. Frame 10 achieves the best focus.

this sequence are presented in figure 19.3 (plate 34). On the left is the first in the sequence, which is very out of focus and which has low Brenner as well as low Tenengrad sharpness. On the right is the tenth frame of the sequence, at which both Brenner and Tenengrad sharpness measures are at a maximum.

Autofocus techniques, while using simple principles, may be quite sophisticated in order to deal with issues such as the following: (1) multiple objects of interest in the scene, occurring at different depths, (2) hypersensitivity of sharpness to focus setting, particularly in the case of microscopy, (3) ambiguity in what parts of the scene are "important." As a result, obtaining good focus is still a photographer's art. Optimal focus is best achieved by the photographer and the camera's autofocus system in a partnership. In fully automated imaging environments, extra care must be given to autofocus methods, such as extra tests to make sure focus values are reasonable, so that the imaging can be retried if they are not.

19.4 Multiple-Focus Photography

In typical industrial and medical applications, a sharply focused image is desired, with as much of the scene in focus as possible. Even when parts of the scene lie at different depths, and when a single exposure would have a limited depth of field, it is possible to capture a set of images of the same scene at different focus settings and combine them into one image that has everything sharp. The result is a very high-depth-of-field (HDF) photograph. The details of such techniques are beyond the scope of this text. However, one approach is to compute the gradient of each image, combine the gradient images (e.g., by addition), and then solve for an image that is consistent with the combined gradients.

In art photography, however, one often wants the main subject in focus, with the background and other objects intentionally out of focus. Rather than carefully focusing and shooting, it is possible to capture many images at different focus settings and work later, with the computer, to produce an image with just the right focus. Interpolation of focus (between focus settings) can take advantage of image deconvolution techniques. This means it is possible to simulate a focus setting that is not captured directly. Consequently, the options for artists to control focus effects are increasing.

19.5 Ultra-High-Resolution Photography

The trend of camera developers to provide more and more megapixels shows no signs of stopping. However, this brings some challenges to users. Typically, large images are reduced before being sent to online social-networking sites or as email attachments. Large images also place large demands on computer memory (in both hard disks and RAM) and processors. It can take more time to interactively view a large image, owing to slowdowns in zooming and panning.

Real technical challenges in achieving large image capabilities in cameras are (1) the trend toward physically smaller cameras, which makes it difficult to have a good enough lens to get good optical data, and consequently, (2) decreasing signal-to-noise ratios in the pixel data. To some extent, the additional noise in high-resolution images can be filtered out using image denoising algorithms, but higher spatial resolution clearly comes at a cost in terms of the quality of the new, smaller pixels.

Another approach to obtaining large images is by capturing multiple images and stitching them together. This can overcome the problem of low-quality pixels, though it has its own challenges in terms of the stitching. An impressive example image produced with this approach is the 222-megapixel Machu Picchu picture by Andre Gunther online at http://www.aguntherphotography.com/machupicchu_222mp.html.

An interesting line of development is wide field-of-view cameras. These include circular panorama imaging (e.g., 360-degree views around an "equator") and spherical panorama cameras. We consider these in the next section.

19.6 Catadioptric Imaging

Catadioptric imaging is photography using optical systems that combine lenses and mirrors. Catadioptric cameras typically produce an anamorphic image at the digital sensor. This image can be digitally mapped to a natural-looking panorama or other view. Some catadioptric cameras capture 360-degree panoramas seamlessly. Others capture multiple images (embedded in one digital image) that can be processed to obtain a three-dimensional model of the subject. Another application of catadioptric cameras is obtaining hyper-wide-angle views.

Figure 19.4 shows a 360-degree panorama produced from the anamorphic image shown in figure 19.5, which was captured by a catadioptric camera developed at Columbia University.

Figure 19.4
Panorama obtained from an anamorphic photograph taken with a catadioptric camera. Courtesy of Shree Nayar.

Figure 19.5
Anamorphic image corresponding to the football field panorama. Courtesy of Shree Nayar.

While the catadioptric camera itself could have been designed to use photographic film instead of a digital sensor, the computer plays a crucial role in mapping an anamorphic image into useful views. A key application is video capture of the participants around a conference table, so that the activity can be shared with remote participants or recorded.

19.7 Separating Direct and Global Illumination

Let's now consider another innovative use of photography supported by computation for capturing more information about the scene than is done in a traditional photo. In this case, rather than capture a panorama, the goal is to capture more information about each visible point in a scene. In order to understand what the new information consists of, we first discuss illumination in a scene.

Let's assume that there is a single light source (such as the sun or an electric lamp) illuminating a scene. A viewer with eye (or camera) at a viewpoint V looking at a particular point P on a surface in the scene receives light from P that depends on something called the radiance at P in the direction of V. The amount received also depends on the distance of P from V. The *radiance* at P in the direction towards V is a measure of light, per unit of solid angle, leaving P in the direction of V. (Solid angle itself can be thought of as a property of a cone that corresponds to the fraction of the area of a unit sphere that is cut out by the intersection of the cone with the sphere when the center of the cone is placed at the center of the sphere.) We may assume that radiance is colored light with red, green, and blue components, but we could also work with radiance in monochrome.

This radiance can be divided into two parts. One is the portion of light coming to P directly from the light source and reflected by the surface in the direction of V. This is known as the direct-illumination portion of the radiance, R_d. The other exists because there is, in general, more light arriving at P than only that directly from the source. Light from the source can reach P indirectly by first hitting another point P' on the surface, reflecting there, and then arriving at P. Light can also reach P after being scattered by dust particles in the air. Not only that, light might also reach P by entering the surface material (which may be translucent) at any point, reflecting and refracting internally to the material, and then exiting at P. The component of radiance at P due to light arriving along all of these indirect routes we call the global-illumination portion of the radiance, R_g.

When we take an ordinary photograph of the scene, we get a measure of the total radiance at each surface point P represented by a pixel position, in the direction towards V. This total radiance at P is the sum of the direct-illumination component and the global-illumination component:

$$R_t = R_d + R_g$$

By applying a technique due to Gurunandan Krishnan, Shree Nayar and their associates, it is possible to efficiently obtain quite accurate separate values of R_d and R_g. Then, with these separate values, it is possible to better infer surface properties such specularity (glossiness), opacity, and color. The information can be used for pattern recognition or for synthesizing new images with special effects.

The basic principle for separation assumes that the photographer or camera system has some control over the illumination of the scene, either by controlling the light source itself or by casting shadows on the scene. In the simplest case, suppose we wish to obtain separate R_d and R_g values for one point P in the scene. By casting a very small shadow on P, the direct-illumination component is completely suppressed, and the radiance value for P captured by the camera will be R_g. Moving the shadow to cover one point and then another will permit obtaining values of R_g at every pixel location. Of course, we also obtain R_t by measuring the radiance at P without any shadow there. Once we have R_g and R_t, it is easy to obtain the direct-illumination component by subtraction:

$$R_d = R_t - R_g$$

The main problem with this basic method is that it is slow. This is because it requires a separate shadowing and image capture step for each and every pixel position. Krishnan and Nayar showed how to compute the separate radiance components much more quickly by using shadows of meshes (or alternatively, illumination by checkerboard patterns). This permits putting up to half of the pixels in shadow simultaneously. Assuming that the global illumination varies gradually across the image, the use of high-spatial-frequency meshes or checkerboards has only an overall scaling effect on the global illumination. Their method proceeds as follows. A series of photographs are taken of the scene with different shadowing or checkerboarded illumination. Each scene position P should be completely in shadow in at least one of the photographs in the series. Also, P should be completely out of shadow in at least one photograph.

Among the radiance values measured for P, the minimal value then represents cR_g, and the maximal value represents R_t. Here, c is a scaling constant that corresponds to the fraction of each image that is in shadow. For example, if half of the pixel positions are in shadow, then $c = 1/2$, and half of the normal amount of light reaches the scene, which reduces the global illumination by $1/2$ everywhere. To obtain the correct R_g value from the minimum radiance value, we divide by c, which amounts to multiplying by 2 in the case $c = 1/2$. In theory the number of photographs in the series could be as small as two, if the shadows could be perfectly lined up with pixel positions. However, in practice more images are needed. Krishnan and Nayar typically used 20 or more images in a series for this purpose.

The results of applying this method are striking. As shown in figure 19.6 (plate 35), the global illumination image for a bowl of eggs clearly reveals the interreflections between the eggs, and the color differences between the direct (blue) and global components (green or burgundy) for grapes are surprising.

Figure 19.6 (plate 35)
(a) Normal photograph of eggs in a basket, (b) image representing only direct illumination, (c) image representing only global illumination, (d) normal photograph of grapes and cheese, (e) direct illumination only, and (f) global illumination only. Courtesy of Shree Nayar.

19.8   Image Inpainting

One of the most impressive developments during the decade starting in 2000 has been inpainting methods. When a photograph has scratches, damaged areas, or simply missing material, the missing ones can be automatically or interactively filled in using inpainting methods. Some of these methods can also be used to blend patches of one photo into another photo in such a way that it is difficult or impossible to see the seams.

An inpainting problem usually involves two input images: a damaged image or other image requiring inpainting, and a mask image that identifies which pixel positions are to be inpainted. In addition, one may have some kind of model for the image that can serve as a guide for the inpainting. Such a model might take the form of a smoothness constraint on the pixel values or it might be expressed in terms of statistical properties of the textures in the image.

The simplest methods work well in simple situations where only a few pixels are missing or where the area affected is uniform. More complex methods are needed when the areas to be filled in are large or where there are important geometric or textural features in the areas to be inpainted.

19.8.1   Finding the Average Color of a Set of Pixels
Our first experiment with inpainting is simply to find the average color among the pixels bordering the region to be inpainted and then to color in the missing pixels with that color. This method works particularly well when the section of the image containing the area to

be inpainted is of uniform or almost uniform color. It doesn't work so well when the area to be inpainted requires multiple colors. However, it serves as a starting point for more sophisticated techniques.

Here are the steps involved in this method. We assume A is a monochome image.

1. Read in image A, which needs inpainting.

2. Read in image B, a binary image whose 1-valued pixels indicate the inpainting region of A.

3. Compute a binary image C from B. There will be a 1 at (i, j) in C provided there is a 0 at (i, j) in B and a 1 in B at at least one of $(i - 1, j)$, $(i, j - 1)$, $(i + 1, j)$ and $(i, j + 1)$.

4. Add up the values of pixels in A that correspond to the ones of C, obtaining SUM.

5. Count the number of ones in C, obtaining PERIMETER.

6. Divide SUM by PERIMETER, getting AVERAGE.

7. Compute D, the inpainted image, by taking the pixel value to be AVERAGE if there is a 1 in image B at this position, and taking the value of A at the position otherwise.

To apply this method for color images, one can simply determine three average values for red, green, and blue, and thus get an average color. An example of inpainting with this averaging method is shown in figure 19.7b (plate 36).

If the inpainting problem requires multiple colors, owing to complexity in the image, then the method discussed here can be adapted somewhat. The overall inpainting region can be broken up, either manually or with the help of the computer, and inpainting peformed separately on each piece. That way, each piece is colored with a color that is an average of boundary pixel colors closer to that piece.

19.8.2 Inpainting by Diffusion

Our second experiment is to use a repeated, weighted averaging process that performs inpainting in a manner more like that used by professionals: working from the boundary of the region to be inpainted in toward the center. In this method, each pixel being inpainted sets its own color to a weighted average of the colors of its neighbors. This can be performed in a series of iterations so that in each iteration all pixels within the inpainting region have their values adjusted.

Using an equal weighting of each of the four (north, east, south, and west) neighbors, pixels to be inpainted are influenced by their neighbors. The colors they eventually take on depend on the colors of the closer boundary pixels. This automatically adapts the colors of inpainted pixels to colors around them rather than to colors in distant parts of the image.

The following Python script implements this diffusion process in PixelMath. It begins by loading two images from files. The variable `damaged` holds the window number of the image to be repaired, and `mask` is an image of the same size, whose pixels are either black or

white. White pixels mark locations to be inpainted in the damaged image. Then four more
image windows are opened with initially black images of the same size as the damaged and
mask images.

```
1    damaged = pmOpenImage(0, '../Inpainting/UW-Quad-damaged.png')
2
3    mask = pmOpenImage(0, '../Inpainting/Mask2.png')
4    w = pmGetImageWidth(mask)
5    h = pmGetImageHeight(mask)
6
7    current = pmNewImage(0, "Current version", w, h, 0, 0, 0)
8    updated = pmNewImage(0, "updated version", w, h, 0, 0, 0)
9    diff    = pmNewImage(0, "Difference of last two", w, h, 0, 0, 0)
10   accum   = pmNewImage(0, "Accumulator (temporary)", w, h, 0, 0, 0)
11
12   pmPositionWindow(updated, 700, 300, 2*w, 2*h)
13   pmZoom(updated, w/2, h/2)
14
15   pmSetSource1(damaged)
16   pmSetSource2(mask)
17   pmSetDestination(current)
18   pmSetFormula("S1(x,y)")
19   pmCompute()
20
21   def clearAccums():
22     pmSetRedAccumulator(0)
23     pmSetGreenAccumulator(0)
24     pmSetBlueAccumulator(0)
25
26   n = 300
27   for i in range(n):
28     # perform relaxation:
29     pmSetSource1(current)
30     pmSetDestination(updated)
31     pmSetFormula("if Red2(x,y)>0 then 0.25*"+\
32       "(S1(x-1,y)+S1(x,y-1)+S1(x+1,y)+S1(x,y+1)) else S1(x,y)")
33     pmCompute()
34
35     # compute difference:
36     pmSetSource2(updated)
37     pmSetDestination(diff)
38     pmSetFormula("abs(s1(x,y)-s2(x,y))")
39     pmCompute()
```

```
40
41      # find the total of the differences
42      clearAccums()
43      pmSetSource1(diff)
44      pmSetDestination(accum)
45      pmSetFormula('putinac(getac+S1(x,y))')
46      pmCompute()
47      # Here are the totals, possible quite large:
48
49      red = pmReadRedAccumulator()
50      green = pmReadGreenAccumulator()
51      blue = pmReadBlueAccumulator()
52      totalDifference = red+green+blue
53      print "Iteration "+str(i)+\
54        ", Total of differences: "+str(totalDifference)
55
56      if totalDifference < 5: break
57
58      # prepare for next iteration:
59      pmSetSource1(updated)
60      pmSetSource2(mask)
61      pmSetDestination(current)
62      pmSetFormula('S1(x,y)')
63      pmCompute()
```

The results of this process can be seen in figure 19.7c. For the example shown, the loop was allowed to run 137 times. At this point the total difference in pixel values from one iteration to the next had decreased to less than 4.

Although this method does a good job of adapting the colors of inpainted pixels to their surrounding colors, it still has a significant limitation: the inpainting it produces is always smooth, even in areas where the surrounding pixels have fine texture. Also, if there are image edges (e.g., the outline of an object like a tree branch or the border of the sidewalk in figure 19.7), these edges turn into blurs within the inpainted region.

19.8.3   Diffusion with Barriers

In an interactive context, the quality of inpainting using the diffusion method can be significantly improved if a user is allowed to create barriers where the diffusion will stop. The combination of barriers and diffusion represent a human–machine collaborative approach to solving an inpainting problem. A barrier is a 2-pixel-wide wall of specially marked pixel locations. During the diffusion, a barrier pixel is allowed to take a value from a nonbarrier pixel, but not from another barrier pixel. Thus it generally receives the color of pixels on

Figure 19.7 (plate 36)
Inpainting: (a) original damaged image, (b) inpainting with the average boundary color, (c) simple diffusion method, and (d) diffusion with barriers.

the side of the wall that it faces and not from the other side. The results of such a method are shown in figure 19.7d.   Some of the recent work on inpainting that overcomes these limitations is described in the next section.

19.8.4 Advanced Methods
Here we mention more advanced methods of inpainting to explain their main ideas without giving details or implementations.

Extending Contours into the Inpainting Region   A limitation of the diffusion method discussed here is that it doesn't explicitly handle contours of the image near the inpainting zone. Diffusion actually tends to avoid sharp edges within the inpainting zone, even if sharp edges abut the zone. Although barriers can overcome this, they require manual intervention and thus are sometimes impractical. Another approach is to automatically detect and extend isophotes. An *isophote* is a contour of constant pixel value, similar to an isobar (constant barometric pressure) in a weather map or a constant-elevation contour on a topographical map. Important isophotes of an image are analogous to ridges and valleys in topography. Significant isophotes (such as edges) may or may not exist at particular places, but if they do, they should be extended, in whatever direction they seem to be going, into the inpainting zone. Isophotes can be detected with local neighborhood processing that is analogous to edge detection, with the result that at each pixel an isophote's strength and direction are obtained. Suitably strong isophotes are identified and extended into the inpainting zone. Once the isophotes have been extended and painted, the remaining pixels within the inpainting zone can be given the color of their closest isophote or can be given colors via diffusion. This technique often produces better results than straight diffusion.

Textural Inpainting Using Dictionaries   Both diffusion and isophote extension have the problem that the inpainting region tends to acquire a smooth texture, even if the textures elsewhere in the image are not smooth. A way to overcome this is to use the rest of the image (and even related images, if they are available) to build a dictionary of textures that can be used to fill in the inpainting zones. A dictionary of textures is essentially a list of small patches of the image. To inpaint then is to work at the border of the inpainting zone, at each pixel (or neighborhood of pixels) going through the dictionary looking for patches having parts (for example, the left half, top half) that match up well with the nearby pixels. The patch is placed so that it lies partly on painted pixels and partly on unpainted pixels, and the unpainted ones are given the corresponding values from the patch. The matching can make use of image distances such as those used for choosing tiles in photomosaic algorithms. Good results have been reported in the literature using this general approach.

19.8.5 Applications of Inpainting

Although the most obvious application of image inpainting is repairing damage in old photographs that is due to scratches, dirt, and other degradation, the technique can be used for other purposes, too. Inpainting can be used as glue to fill in the seams between a patch and an artificially created hole in an image. For example, suppose a portrait snapshot of a person nicely captures a beautiful smile, but the person blinked. If another photo is available with the same pose and exposure, except that the eyes are open, then the open eyes can be copied and pasted into the image with the closed eyes. To hide the cut, the hole should be a little bigger than the patch, and then inpainting can be used to fill in the gap automatically.

Inpainting can also be combined with blending, so that a patch that is larger than the hole it goes into can be combined continuously with the larger image. The PatchMatch method of Barnes et al. (2009) can be used not only for inpainting but also for reshuffling an image—changing the number of windows on a building or the number of fenceposts in a fence, for example.

It is also possible to use inpainting within an interactive image editing application. Even simple diffusion methods can be very effective if a user is able to erect barriers that allow discontinuities within the inpainted regions.

Inpainting techniques remain an area of intensive research. Not only is there the challenge of doing a good job of inpainting when the regions to be inpainted increase in size and complexity, but there also is difficulty in managing the interplay between the modeling of the images to be inpainted and the algorithms that take advantage of the models. Some of the most visually striking results require complex algorithms and long computation times. Thus another challenge is creating fast algorithms for high-quality inpainting.

19.9   Other Developments

Kits for computational photography are being developed. A group at Stanford University is developing the Stanford Frankencamera whose subsystems are under the control of a built-in computer running the Linux operating system. An experimenter can write programs that access the camera's metering, focusing system, demosaicing, denoising, white balancing, and other mechanisms. For more information, see http://graphics.stanford.edu/courses/cs448a-10/.

19.10   References

Barnes, C., Shechtman, E., Finkelstein, A., and Goldman, D. B. 2009. PatchMatch: A randomized correspondence algorithm for structural image editing. *ACM Transactions on Graphics*, Vol. 28, No. 3 (*Proc. ACM SIGGRAPH 2009*).

Bertalmio, M., Sapiro, G., Ballester, C., and Caselles, V. 2000. Image inpainting. *Proc. SIGGRAPH 2000*, July, pp. 417–424.

Bitouk, D., Kumar, N., Dhillon, S., Belhumeur, P., and Nayar, S. 2008. Face swapping: Automatically replacing faces in photographs. *ACM Transactions on Graphics*, Vol. 27, No. 3 (*Proc. ACM SIGGRAPH 2008*).

Kopf, J., Uyttendaele, M., Deussen, O., and Cohen, M. F. 2007. Capturing and viewing gigapixel images. *ACM Transactions on Graphics*, Vol. 26, No. 3 (*Proc. SIGGRAPH 2007*).

Kuthirummal, S., Nagahara, H., Zhou, C., and Nayar, S. K. 2010. Flexible depth of field photography. *IEEE Transactions on Pattern Analysis and Machine Intelligence*, March, 2010. Available at http://doi.ieeecomputersociety.org/10.1109/TPAMI.2010.66.

Kutulakos, K., Piestun, R., and Raskar, R. (eds.) 2010. *Proceedings of the International Conference on Computational Photography* (ICCP 10). Los Alamitos, CA: IEEE Computer Society.

Krishnan, G., and Nayar, S. K. 2009. Towards a true spherical camera. *Proc. SPIE Human Vision and Electronic Imaging*. January 2009.

Moreno-Noguer, F., Belhumeur, P. N., and Nayar, S. K. 2007. Active refocusing of images and videos. *ACM Transactions on Graphics*, Vol. 26, No. 3 (*Proc. ACM SIGGRAPH 2007*).

Raskar, R. 2009. Computational photography: Epsilon to coded photography. In F. Nielsen (ed.) *Proc. Emerging Trends Visual Computing 2008*, LNCS 5416, Berlin: Springer, pp. 238–253. Also available at http://web.media.mit.edu/ raskar/ Talks/ETCVparis08/ raskarCompPhotoEpsilonCodedETVC08paper.pdf.

Sapiro, G. 2002. Image inpainting. *SIAM News*, Vol. 35, No. 4. Available at http://www.siam.org/pdf/news/427.pdf.

Yasuma, F., Mitsunaga, T., Iso, D., and Nayar, S. K. 2010. Generalized assorted pixel camera: Post-capture control of resolution, dynamic range and spectrum. *IEEE Transactions on Image Processing*, Vol. 19, No. 9, September, 2010, pp. 2241–2253.

Yeo, T. T. E., Ong, S. H., Jayasooriah, and Sinniah, R. 1993. Autofocusing for tissue microscopy. *Image and Vision Computing*, Vol. 11, No. 10, pp. 629–639.

19.11 Exercises

1. Suppose that three monochrome photographs of the same scene have been taken with different exposures in an attempt to bracket the best exposure setting. (Same camera settings, except for the shutter speeds, which were 1/200 second 1/100 second, and 1/50 second, and the scene is assumed to be motionless.) Assume the pixels of these images are represented with 8 bits each. We wish to combine these images into a single high-dynamic-range image in which we allocate 10 bits per pixel. Considering one particular pixel location, let's assume that the values for the pixel in the three input images are 75, 2, and 0. What would be a reasonable way to compute an appropriate pixel value in the output image? What value do you get for this example? Why does that value make sense?

2. Using the method and code described in this chapter, create a high-dynamic-range image using a digital camera that permits manual setting of aperture and shutter speed, taking three individual exposures with a fixed lens aperture (e.g., f/11): one at the exposure value (EV) chosen by your camera's automatic exposure system, one at one fourth that shutter speed, and one at four times that shutter speed.

3. Using the FocusSequence of images provided at http://www.cs.washington.edu/pixels (which are the images used to produce the data in figure 19.2), and slightly modifying the Python code (also at this website), produce a new graph that shows three Brenner sharpness curves: (a) the one shown in figure 19.2, (b) one in which the computation is limited to a rectangular region within the red flower, and (c) one in which the computation is limited to a region containing only lines on the wall in the background. According to the sharpness values, which frame has the best focus for the red flower? Which frame has the best focus for the wall in the background?

   Note: An easy way to plot the graph, if you have access to Microsoft Excel, is to first create a text file containing the sharpness data (copying from the PixelMath Python history pane and pasting into an editor such as Emacs, WordPad, Word, or TextEdit), and then load that file into Excel as a comma-delimited data file. Once the data are in Excel, select the cells containing the data, click on the Insert tab, and then choose a chart of the line-graph type.

4. Take a sequence of images of the same scene but with sixteen different focus settings, in a smooth progression from near to far. Compute both the Brenner sharpness and the Tenengrad sharpness of each image and plot the values in a graph. Select the focus setting(s) at which the sharpness values are maximized. How do the focus settings compare?

5. Capture two registered images of the same scene (using an ordinary digital camera), with one focused on an object close to the camera and the other focused on the distant background. Compute for each pixel of each image a sharpness value and combine them to give a map in which each pixel of the map tells which of the two images is in better focus. Finally, combine the two captured images using the map so that the resulting image is sharp almost everywhere.

6. In Krishnan and Nayar's method for obtaining separate images of a scene for direct illumination and global illumination, at a certain pixel brightness values B1 and B2 are captured using two different structured illumination patterns (complementary checkerboards). Suppose B1 = 50 and B2 = 35. Suppose B1 is obtained when the pixel is completely illuminated and B2 is obtained when the pixel is completely in shadow. If $c = 0.5$, then what are the corresponding values of R_d and R_g?

7. Find (or shoot) a pair of digital photos of the same person in the same pose where in the first image the person is smiling but has his or her eyes closed, and in the second image the person's eyes are open but the smile is missing. Using an image editing tool such as Microsoft Paint, remove the eyes that are closed from the first image, leaving a little extra space to be filled in later. Then copy the eyes from the second image and paste them into the first. There should be a gap of say, black pixels, around the pasted-in eyes that has yet to be filled. Then, in PixelMath explore the use of image inpainting with the diffusion method as a means to fill the gaps. How natural (or artificial) does the splice seem to be?

20 Selected Applications

20.1 Overview

This chapter presents three more advanced applications of Python to image manipulation than we have seen earlier. The first is a program for creating morphing sequences, in which one image changes gradually into another through a combination of warping and cross-fading. The second is a program for constructing photomosaics from many images. The third application is a game involving images and a transformed version of them. The first and third of these provide graphical user interfaces. All three require keeping track of multiple images within a program.

20.2 Morphing

In chapters 5 and 6 we saw various geometric distortions of images. We have also seen dissolves (cross-fades). In this section we consider a way of turning one image continuously into another using a combination of these techniques. However, we are not going to simply use a fixed formula to do the geometric distortions. Rather, we'll develop a way to describe organic-looking, situation-specific geometric distortions that we call warps. Then the geometric distortions will be closely related to the shapes and arrangements of features in the particular images we are working with.

We'll call our combination of warping and dissolving morphing. It is an important technique, with applications in movie special effects. The warping alone is also important, with applications in image alignments and comparing images.

We use concepts from geometry to design and implement the warping transformations. The key concept is that of the affine transformation. Other concepts are the Euclidean distance and the notion of weighted averages of displacements. There is a PixelMath and Python program available for experimentation with the morphing method we present, and it is described later in this section.

20.2.1 Affine Transformations

Now we introduce an important class of transformations, useful not only in warping, but in graphics systems more generally.

We define an *affine transformation* of a point in two-dimensional space to be any combination of coordinate translations, scale changes, rotations, and skews. Alternatively, an affine transformation is any transformation implemented using a pair of linear equations of the following form:

$$x' = a_1 x + b_1 y + c_1$$

$$y' = a_2 x + b_2 y + c_2$$

Here the point (x, y) is mapped by the affine transformation to the point (x', y'). The values a_1, b_1, c_1, a_2, b_2, and c_2 are constants that specify the particular affine transformation.

As an example of an affine transformation, consider the following equations:

$$x' = 0.4268x - 0.3659y + 110.3659$$

$$y' = 0.1220x + 0.6098y + 49.3902$$

To implement this in PixelMath, we must first invert the transformation so that for each destination pixel we have the coordinates of the source pixel that corresponds to it. The result of solving for x and y is the pair of equations

$$x = 2.0x' + 1.2y' - 280$$

$$y = -0.4x' + 1.4y' - 25$$

The transformation is implemented in PixelMath by the formula

```
S1(2.0*x + 1.2*y - 280, -0.4*x + 1.4*y - 25)
```

An original and the result of applying this formula are shown in figure 20.1.

An affine transformation is limited in the kind of distortion it can cause to an image. For example, parallel lines in the source image will remain parallel in the destination. Also, the ratio of areas of two regions in the source image will be equal to the ratio of areas of the corresponding regions in the destination. Another property of affine transformation is that any collinear points in the source map to collinear points in the destination. Also, the ratios of distances of these points from one another are preserved by the transformation. For example, if M_1 is the midpoint of the segment from P_1 to Q_1 in the source, and the corresponding points are M_2, P_2, and Q_2 in the destination, then M_2 is the midpoint between P_2 and Q_2.

Figure 20.1
An example of an affine transformation. Some degree of scaling, rotation, skew, and translation can all be seen here.

Although a single affine transformation is limited in the kind of change it can cause to an image, we'll be able to get more organic transformations by blending two or more affine transformations together. Thus affine transformations can serve as building blocks for more complex transformations.

20.2.2 Transformations from Line Segment Pairs

Let's consider the idea of mapping one line segment to another via an affine transformation. If we have a line segment $L_1 = (P_1, Q_1)$, and we wish to map it to another line segment $L_2 = (P_2, Q_2)$, we can accomplish this as follows: First translate L_1 [getting $L'_1 = (P'_1, Q'_1)$] so that P'_1 is on top of P_2. Then scale L'_1 without moving P'_1 so that it is the same length as L_2, getting $L''_1 = (P''_1, Q''_1)$. Finally rotate L''_1 to get L_2. The overall transformation is affine because it consists of a translation, scaling, and rotation.

Note that there are some affine transformations that cannot be specified in this manner. For example, scaling in both x and y at the same time is an affine transformation, but it cannot be expressed in our two-line segment method.

Now that we have seen how a pair of line segments specifies an affine transformation, let's consider how an arbitrary point [not necessarily on the line segment(s)] is mapped by the transformation. Consider the point R_d in figure 20.2. We wish to determine the point R_s in the source that corresponds to it. To accomplish this, we compute two quantities, u and v, that relate R_d to P_d and Q_d. We can then use u and v, together with P_s and Q_s,

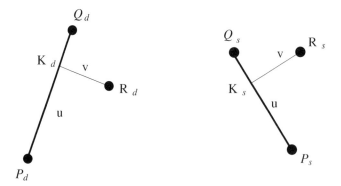

Figure 20.2
A pair of line segments that specify an affine transformation.

to determine the coordinates of R_s. To understand what u and v represent, draw a line segment starting at R_d, perpendicular to and approaching the line passing through P_d and Q_d. The length of the segment from R_d to the line is v. The diagram shows the perpendicular segment intersecting the line somewhere between P_d and Q_d. This need not be the case. The intersection could be on the other side of Q_d or the other side of P_d. Wherever the intersection lies (let's call the point of intersection K_d), we can define a distance $\delta(P_d, K_d)$ from P_d to K_d. If K_d lies on the other side of P_d, the distance is negative. We define u to be the ratio $\delta(P_d, K_d)/\delta(P_d, Q_d)$. Thus u represents the fraction of the way from P_d to Q_d that the projection of R_d onto the line lies.

   To determine the point R_s, we use u and v as follows. Starting at P_s we move fraction u of the way to Q_s. (If u is negative, we move in the opposite direction.) That takes us to a point K_s on the line. If u is greater than 1, then the point K_s lies somewhere beyond Q_s. Next, we move in a direction perpendicular to the line through P_s and Q_s. (Whether we go right or left depends on whether v is positive or negative.) We move in this direction for a distance of $|v|$ and that brings us to R_s.

   In the sample morphing application, the parameters u and v are computed by the function `pointLineDist` in the file `pointLineDist.py`. It works by first translating R_d by $-P_d$, then applying a rotation that has the effect of making the line through P_d and Q_d vertical (and the line through K_d and R_d horizontal). Then u is ratio of the y coordinates of the transformed R_d and Q_d, and v is the x coordinate of the transformed R_d. (See the code for further details.)

20.2.3   Blending Segment-Pair Transformations

If we have many segment pairs, they all pull the image in different directions. What we'd like is for them to work together in such a way that each one most strongly affects the pixels near it, and pixels distant from several lines are affected by all the lines in their vicinity.

Here is the idea behind our blending method. Each affine transformation induces a displacement on each point. The displacement is the amount of translation the point undergoes. We can describe the displacement for each point (x, y) as (dx, dy).

Each affine transformation wants to pull the point in a different direction and give it a different displacement. To blend the effect of the various affine transforms, we take a weighted average of these displacements. Weighting for each displacement is dependent on the closeness of the point (x, y) to the line segment that controls that displacement. This is specified more clearly in the code for the morphing program.

20.2.4 Full Morphing with the Beier-Neely Method

A full morphing transition is a sequence of frames that represents a smooth series of steps from a starting image to a target image. Let us assume that there are $n + 1$ frames in this sequence: $F_0, F_1, \ldots, F_i, \ldots, F_{n-1}, F_n$. The starting image is the same as F_0 and the target image is F_n. The frames $F_1, \ldots, F_{n-1}$ are in-between images, also known as interpolated images.

Each in-between image is a weighted sum of two warped images W_{is} and W_{it}. The first is a warped version of the starting image and the second is a warped version of the target. These two images are warped in such a way that (1) corresponding features, such as eyes, line up with each other; (2) the warped starting image W_{is} goes i/n of the way toward a warp from the start all the way to line up with the target; and (3) the warped target image W_{it} is $(n - i)/n$ of the way from the target image to a warped version of it that lines up with the start.

In order to produce the image W_{is}, we need a set of line segment pairs whose source segments line up with features in the starting image and whose destination segments bring the features a fraction of the way toward lining up with the target. Assuming that the morph designer has provided a set of line segment pairs K_{st} that align the starting image's features with the target image's features, we can compute a new set of line segment pairs K_{is} by interpolation for computing W_{is}. Similarly, to compute W_{it}, we need a set of line segment pairs K_{it} that will let the target image warp back to align with W_{is}. To obtain an appropriate set of line segment pairs K_{it} for this, we simply take the destination lines of K_{is} as the source lines of K_{it} and the destination lines of the overall alignment K_{st} as the destination lines of K_{it}.

We consider two different methods of interpolating the line segment pairs. Given a line segment pair (L_s, L_t), we need a new line segment pair (L_s, L_i) where L_i is i/n of the way between L_s and L_t. The first method is to use a weighted average of the coordinates. This means that each endpoint of L_i is i/n of the way between the corresponding endpoints of L_s and L_t. This method has some aesthetic drawbacks when the warps involve rotation of the line segments. For example, if a line segment is rotated 180 degrees around its center, then half-way through the interpolation sequence, the segment's endpoints will coincide and it will have length zero. The warped image will have a singularity at this step and will lose all its shape information.

Our second method for interpolating line segments is to determine the midpoint, length, and angle of the starting and target segments and then interpolate these (linearly) and generate a new line segment that has the interpolated parameters. The second method of interpolation usually avoids these singularities, though at a slight cost in complexity and the possibility of some occasional strange behavior. The strange behavior can happen when a rotation of the line by approximately 180 degrees is required. The rotation can go either clockwise or counterclockwise. Presumably its goes in the way that minimizes the change in angle. If two nearby line segment pairs have to do this, but one goes clockwise while the other goes counterclockwise (owing to slight angular differences), then the interpolated lines might cross and cause a warping singularity. With either interpolation scheme, singularities can be avoided or fixed by the morph designer.

20.2.5 How to Use the PixelMath Morphing App

A PixelMath application program called MorphingGUI is available that not only implements the Beier-Neely method of morphing but provides a user interface for editing the sets of line segment pairs that control a morphing sequence. Figure 20.3 (plate 37) shows a screen shot of the program after a morphing sequence has been computed. The original source and target images are shown at the top, with a set of line segment pairs drawn on them. The source image is the Mona Lisa and the target image shows a tiger. Our set of line segment pairs has two pairs in it. They have been drawn and edited using the drawing tool included in the program.

A seven-frame sequence was desired, meaning that five in-between frames were to be created. The five in-between images of the morphing sequence (the sequence minus the source and target images) are shown in the second row of figure 20.3. The third row shows the warped versions of the source image and the fourth row shows the warped versions of the target image. From the original set of line segment pairs, five new ones were interpolated for use in generating the warped starting images. From each of these new sets (which are for warping the source image), another set was formed for warping the target image back to match the warped source. The interpolated lines can be seen in the second row of images (on top of the in-between images).

To run the program, make sure that the following files are in the default directory: MorphingGUI.py, SetOfSegmentPairs.py, BlendedWarps.py, makeMapperFunction.py, pointLineDist.py, and oneLinePair.py. Next, load the file MorphingGUI.py into a Pixel-Math Python buffer and evaluate the buffer. The program can be run in either of two modes, which can be chosen from the menu. "Select either Use PixelMath Image Frames" or not. If using PixelMath image frames, the images loaded for computing the morphing sequence will be shown in separate zoomable windows. Otherwise, all images will be shown on the

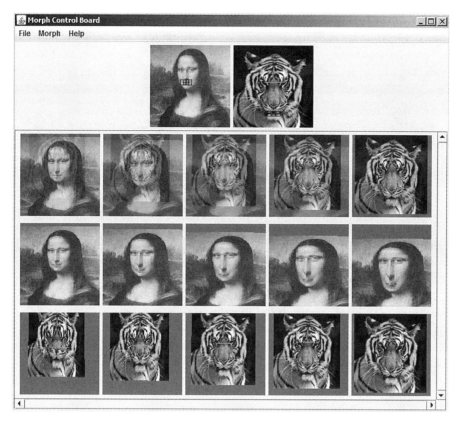

Figure 20.3 (plate 37)
Screen shot of the MorphingGUI program.

main graphical interface window. (The starting image and target image for the morph are specified in the code. This can be changed by editing the code.) The starting and target images are always shown on the interface, and a drawing facility is turned on so that a set of line segment pairs can be created or edited. The File menu of the application is for accessing files that represent sets of line segment pairs. To create a new set of line segment pairs, either start up the program and start drawing, or, if some other set is currently being edited, save it and then select "New" from the File menu. To draw a line segment, click on either the starting or target image and drag. One line segment will be created in each side: one in the start and one in the target. This initial clicking and dragging will affect both copies. However, subsequent editing operations on the line segment affect only one copy, thus allowing them to be different from start to target.

The following drawing affordances are available: creating new segments (described here), selecting (click on the line), moving by midpoint (translating the segment), moving by endpoint (leaving the other endpoint fixed), deleting, and sending a segment to the back of the priority list (the list used by the system during selecting). When a line segment is selected, handles appear on its midpoint and endpoints. Clicking and dragging a handle will either translate the segment or adjust the position of one of its endpoints. To delete or adjust the selection priority of a segment, right-click on the segment and choose the desired operation from a popup menu that appears.

20.2.6 Structure of the Morphing App

The morphing application is implemented in six separate Python source files. The main program is in MorphingGUI.py. This file defines a new class MorphControlBoard that subclasses javax.swing.JFrame and thus represents a customized window on the screen. It also defines a class ImagePanel whose instances are used to contain images within the overall Morph-ControlBoard window. This class implements the methods that support drawing and editing line segment pairs. At the end of MorphingGUI.py are global assignments that specify which image files to use for the source and target of the morphing, and how many in-between frames to create.

The file SetOfSegmentPairs.py defines a class SetOfLineSegmentPairs with methods that support creating and removing pairs, finding "hits" given mouse coordinates, and converting to and from strings. Also in this file are definitions for the classes Segment (a line segment) and Pair (a pair of line segments).

The file PointLineDist.py defines a function pointLineDist that computes the parameters u and v defined earlier. (The value of v is the perpendicular distance from the given point to the given line.)

The functionality to compute the affine transformation specified by one pair of line segments is provided in the file oneLinePair.py. The function findSourceCoords obtains the (x, y) coordinates of the source point R_s corresponding to destination point R_d (see figure 20.2).

MorphMapper.py defines a class of callable objects, each of which can compute one affine transform. When an instance is created, the parameters of the affine transform are encapsulated. Whenever the instance is called with a particular destination point (x_d, y_d), the corresponding source point (x_s, y_s) is computed. Also returned is the distance of the destination point from the destination segment (which is not always the same as the point's distance v from the full line) and a weight based on this distance that is later used in blending the effects of multiple affine transforms on the point.

Finally, the file BlendedWarps.py implements the blending of multiple affine transforms using the method of Beier and Neely. It applies each of a set of affine transforms to each point, producing a set of displacements. It computes a weighted average of the displacements, based on the weights returned by the MorphMapper instances, and applies these average displacements to determine the source point for each destination point.

20.2.7 Discussion

There are many things to consider when producing an aesthetically pleasing morphing sequence. The source and target images should be roughly compatible. If they have very different sizes, then the scale difference may be too obtrusive. Another issue is dealing with the boundaries of the images, which may look unattractive as they become visible within interpolated frames. One approach to overcoming this is to use larger, perhaps padded, images when creating the morphing sequence and then to crop the results. This has a disadvantage in terms of extra computation time, however. Another approach is to prepare the source and target images so that their boundaries blend gradually into the background (gray in the given morphing application). Then the boundaries will be less obtrusive, although the gray surrounds might still be undesired.

The placement of line segments for the in-between frames does not have to follow a strict formula. The positions of line segments for in-between frames can, in theory, be edited manually for tighter artist control of the morphing sequence.

The applications for morphing are not limited to creating direct blends from one image to another. A less direct example involves creating a time-varying stereogram in which the depth image morphs from a source to a target. The carrier image could be constant, or it could evolve during the sequence.

The warping method presented here can be used not only for morphing but also to align a pair of images so that they can be compared or combined. For example, averaging multiple images of the same object is a way to reduce imaging noise. However, if the images are not aligned, the average might be unduly blurry. By aligning them first using warping, the results will be sharper.

Morphing itself is a good example of a technique that combines image processing and art. Without the computer, the warping and averaging would be impractical. Without the hand of an artist, the organic and aesthetic aspects of morphing would be missing.

20.3 Photomosaics with Many Images

In chapter 9 we considered the topic of photomosaics and described a method for replicating and adjusting a single tile image to render a subject image. The entire construction required essentially only one PixelMath formula:

```
S1(x/w2, y/h2) * (s2(x mod w2, y mod h2)-32)/96
```

In this formula, S1 represents the subject image and S2 is the tile. Taking the product causes each pixel in the copy of the tile representing a particular subject pixel to be adjusted in color so that the tile copy as a whole effectively represents the subject pixel.

The chief limitation of the single-tile method is that it doesn't use multiple images for the tiles. Now we present a way, using Python, to overcome that. Furthermore, the Python program sets the stage for much more control over the process of constructing photomosaics, including the criteria used to select the best tile for a particular part of the photomosaic.

The method we describe here consists of two parts. The first part is preparing the collection of tile images to facilitate the second part, in which the photomosaic is constructed. Although construction of photomosaics is essentially an art form in its own right, the principles that underlie the construction process are essential in other applications, especially image information retrieval using the "query by contents" approach.

20.3.1 Preparing a Database of Images

Before we can construct a multiimage photomosaic, we need a collection of images to use as tiles. In addition, the collection needs a little bit of organization. Obtaining a set of images can be a matter of going out and shooting photos, downloading images from the Internet, or selecting a set of images from one's own preexisting collection. Let's assume the images have been collected and put into a folder, SelectedImages.

The next step is to prepare resized versions of the selected images. At this book's website is a program, `MakeTiles.py`, that can be helpful in doing that. It traverses a folder tree (in the manner of `MakeReductions.py`, presented in chapter 15) looking for image files, and it creates a 128-by-128 tile from each image found.

After creating the tile images, the final step in preparation is a packing step in which the tiles are packed into one (or a few) large images. Prior to packing, the user must create a list of the image files to be used as tiles and put this list into a text file named `image-list.txt`. The easiest way to do this in the Windows operating system is to open up a Command Prompt window in the folder containing the tile images (assuming they are now all in one folder) and type

```
ls *.jpg > image-list.txt
```

However, the file could also be created by typing the names of the image files directly into it with an editing program.

Once the file `image-list.txt` is ready, the large database images full of tiles can be prepared by running the Python program

```
MakePhotomosaicDBImage.py
```

This works by opening a particular folder and looking for the file `image-list.txt`, which should be a list of all the image files in that folder that are to be used. Some of the parameters of this program can be easily changed by editing the file before running it in PixelMath. For example, the size of the database image can be controlled. It is set up here to create a

2048-by-1024 image, which is sufficient for a 16-by-8 array of tiles (128 tiles). The program does not require exactly 128 tile images, but if you have a lot fewer than that, then you might as well reduce the size of the large image to 1024 by 1024 or less. If you wish to have only four rows of tiles rather than eight, reduce the height of the large image to 512 and change the second to last line of the program from if row==8: row=0; col=0 to if row==4: row=0; col=0.

Once the database image has been constructed, it can be used to create many photomosaics using different subject images or using the same subject image but with different construction parameters.

```
'''MakePhotomosaicDBImage.py
This is a program to create a big tiled image of macropixels for
use in creating Photomosaics.
'''
def makeInitialDBImage():
  # The prefix specifies the folder of tile images.
  prefix = 'Flower-tiles-128/'
  image_list_file = open(prefix + 'image-list.txt', 'r')

  all_image_filenames = image_list_file.read()

  filenames = all_image_filenames.split('\n')
  storageWindow = pmNewImage(0, 'Macro-pixel Storage Image',\
                       2048, 1024, 0,0,0)
  miniImageWindow = pmNewImage(0, 'Tile Image', 128, 128, 0,0,0)
  pmSetSource1(storageWindow)
  pmSetSource2(miniImageWindow)
  pmSetDestination(storageWindow)
  row = 0; col = 0
  for fn in filenames:
    if fn=='': continue
    print 'This filename is ' + fn
    pmOpenImage(miniImageWindow, prefix + fn)
    formula = 'S1(x,y)+if {floor(x/128)='+str(col)+\
              ' and floor(y/128)='+str(row)+\
              '} then S2(x mod 128, y mod 128) else 0'
    print formula
    pmSetFormula(formula)
    pmCompute()
    row += 1
    if row==8:  row=0; col+=1

makeInitialDBImage()
```

Figure 20.4 (plate 38)
Large database image that holds many tiles, prepared by `MakePhotomosaicDBImage.py`, ready for use in a
photomosaic construction.

The result of running `MakePhotomosaicDBImage.py` is an image such as that shown in figure 20.4
(plate 38). Notice that this image is not completely full. This allows some flexibility in
creating tile databases.

20.3.2 Photomosaic Construction

The program for constructing photomosaics first reads in one or more of the large database
images prepared by `MakePhotomosaicDBImage.py`, and it analyzes the tiles within them, creating internal data structures that it will use during the construction process. It also reads in
the subject image. Then it scans through the subject image, considering a small zone at a
time. For each zone, it selects a tile that fits the criteria for representing that zone and then
it puts a copy of that tile, with some adjustment, into the output image array.

Here is how the tiles are processed before constructing a photomosaic. The program reads
in a set of images that represent a database of tile images. Each tile is assumed to be 128 by
128, and each input image here can contain any number of tiles. If a database image is 128
by 128, then it is assumed to contain a single tile. In any case it should be of dimensions ($m \times$
128) by ($n \times 128$) where m and n are integers. Although these images may all have different
sizes, the tiles are left in these images since they provide a convenient storage format.

However, some basic information about each tile is computed and stored in some lists.
Here is what we register for each tile:

1. the number of the window it occurs in

2. its tile column index (0, or 1, or etc.)

3. its tile row index

4. its average color—one RGB triple

5. a 4 by 4 reduced version of it represented as a list of sixteen RGB triples

These lists are used during the construction, with item 5 used for matching, item 4 used for adjustment, and items 1, 2, and 3 used to obtain the tile when the decision to use it has been reached.

Here is how the zones of the subject image are processed. The photomosaic is constructed by repeatedly considering a small area of the image to be rendered, creating a 4-by-4 reduction of it, and comparing this reduction with a similar reduction of each tile. The tile with the closest match on the basis of the reductions is selected for use in that area of the image. The tile's colors are adjusted before it is drawn, using the average color of the tile as a reference, so that the colors more accurately reflect the color needed by the large image in that area.

```
1    '''PhotomosaicsWithPython.py
2    This program reads in one or mo.; tile-database images and one
3    subject image. Then it constructs a photomosaic version of the
4    subject image using the tile images.
5    '''
6
7    TILE_WIDTH = 128
8    TILE_HEIGHT = 128
9
10   # The following list of filenames can be arbitrarily long.
11   # Each file should name an image that holds one or more
12                           # 128x128 tile images.
13   DBImage_filenames = ['FlowerDBImage.JPG']
14   prefix = ''              # Change if your database images
15                            # are not in current folder.
16   TILES_PACKAGED_IN = []   # Window num of database image
17                            # containing the tile.
18   TILES_COLUMN_INDEX = []  # Horiz. pos. of tile in its
19                            # database image (0, 1, 2, 3)
20   TILES_ROW_INDEX = []     # Vert. pos. of tile in its
21                            # database image.
22   TILES_AVG_COLOR = []     # RGB value representing the average
23                            # color of the tile.
24   TILES_4X4_REDUCTION = []# A list of 16 RGB triples,
25                            # used in matching.
26
27   # NTILES tells how many of the tiles read in should be used.
```

```
28   NTILES=92 # Any additional tiles will be ignored.
29
30   def load_image_database():
31     for dbimage in DBImage_filenames:
32       wn = pmOpenImage(0, prefix + dbimage)
33       w = pmGetImageWidth(wn)
34       h = pmGetImageHeight(wn)
35       ncols = w / TILE_WIDTH
36       nrows = h / TILE_HEIGHT
37
38       count = 0
39       print 'Image '+dbimage+ ' has width '+str(w)+\
40             ' and height '+str(h)+' and seems to have '+\
41             str(ncols*nrows)+' tiles.'
42       for j in range(ncols):
43         for i in range(nrows):
44           # Processing a tile:
45           TILES_PACKAGED_IN.append(wn)
46           TILES_COLUMN_INDEX.append(j)
47           TILES_ROW_INDEX.append(i)
48           four_by_four = reduce_tile(wn,i,j)
49           TILES_4X4_REDUCTION.append(four_by_four)
50           avg = get_RGB_avg(four_by_four)
51           TILES_AVG_COLOR.append(avg)
52           count += 1
53           if count==NTILES: return
54
55   def reduce_tile(wn,i,j):
56     reduction = []
57     horiz_factor = TILE_WIDTH / 4
58     vert_factor = TILE_HEIGHT / 4
59     xstart = j*TILE_WIDTH
60     ystart = i*TILE_HEIGHT
61     averaging_factor = horiz_factor*vert_factor
62     for mx in range(4):
63       for my in range(4):
64         r=0; g=0; b=0
65         for x in range(horiz_factor):
66           for y in range(vert_factor):
67             rgb = pmGetPixel(wn,xstart + mx*horiz_factor + x,
68                                 ystart + my*vert_factor  + y)
69             r+=rgb[0]; g+=rgb[1]; b+=rgb[2]
70         avg_r = r/averaging_factor
71         avg_g = g/averaging_factor
72         avg_b = b/averaging_factor
73         reduction.append((avg_r, avg_g, avg_b))
```

```
74      return reduction
75
76   def get_RGB_avg(rgb_list):
77     r = 0; g = 0; b = 0
78     the_len = len(rgb_list)
79     for (dr, dg, db) in rgb_list:
80       r+=dr; g+=dg; b+=db
81     print 'Average RGB for this tile or patch: '+\
82           str((r/the_len, g/the_len, b/the_len))
83     return (r/the_len, g/the_len, b/the_len)
84
85   def print_database_info():
86     print 'TILES_PACKAGED_IN = ' + str(TILES_PACKAGED_IN)
87     print 'TILES_AVG_COLOR   = ' + str(TILES_AVG_COLOR)
88
89   load_image_database()
90   print_database_info()
91
92   ''' We assume that the database of tile images is now loaded.
93   Now we load in the original image and compute a slightly reduced
94   version that we call the 'subject' image. This is the main image
95   to be rendered using the tiles.
96   '''
97   path = 'AnnaAtConservatory2.jpg'
98   ORIG = pmOpenImage(0, path)
99   SUBJ_WIDTH  = 256
100  SUBJ_HEIGHT = 256
101  subj = pmNewImage(0, 'Subject image to be rendered',\
102                    SUBJ_WIDTH, SUBJ_HEIGHT, 0,0,0)
103  pmSetFormula('S1(x*w1/w,y*h1/h)')
104  pmSetSource1(ORIG); pmSetDestination(subj); pmCompute()
105
106  ''' And now we create a blank image to hold the photomosaic.
107  '''
108  TILE_H_COVERAGE = 8 # Horiz. size of a subject image zone.
109  TILE_V_COVERAGE = 8 # Vert.   "
110  EFFECTIVE_TILE_WIDTH = 32 # Not more than width of tiles in DB
111  EFFECTIVE_TILE_HEIGHT= 32
112  PHOTOM_WIDTH  = SUBJ_WIDTH * EFFECTIVE_TILE_WIDTH /TILE_H_COVERAGE
113  PHOTOM_HEIGHT = SUBJ_HEIGHT* EFFECTIVE_TILE_HEIGHT/TILE_V_COVERAGE
114
115  NROWS_OF_TILES = PHOTOM_HEIGHT / EFFECTIVE_TILE_HEIGHT
116  NCOLS_OF_TILES = PHOTOM_WIDTH / EFFECTIVE_TILE_WIDTH
117  print 'There will be ' + str(NROWS_OF_TILES)+' rows of tiles'
118  print 'There will be ' + str(NCOLS_OF_TILES)+' columns of tiles'
```

```
119
120    PHOTOM = pmNewImage(0, 'Photomosaic', PHOTOM_WIDTH,
121                        PHOTOM_HEIGHT, 0,0,0)
122
123    # Returns the sum of the squares of the differences of
124    # two sets of RGB values:
125    def colorDistance(c1, c2):
126     dr = c1[0]-c2[0]
127     dg = c1[1]-c2[1]
128     db = c1[2]-c2[2]
129     return dr*dr + dg*dg + db*db
130
131    def reduced_patch_distance(p1, p2):
132      color_distances = map(colorDistance, p1, p2)
133      return reduce(lambda x,y: x+y, color_distances)
134
135    def computePhotomosaic():
136      # Loop through all the "effective tile" locations
137      for i in range(NROWS_OF_TILES):
138        for j in range(NCOLS_OF_TILES):
139          # Compute a reduced (4 by 4) version of the corresponding
140          # patch of the subject image:
141          #print 'Preparing to render patch ('+str(i)+','+str(j)+')'
142          patch_reduction = reduce_patch(i, j)
143          avg = get_RGB_avg(patch_reduction)
144          index_of_best_tile = choose_best_tile(patch_reduction, avg)
145          render_patch(i,j,index_of_best_tile, avg)
146
147    def choose_best_tile(patch_reduction, avgRGB):
148      '''This computes the sum of the pixel distances between the
149      adjusted representative values from each tile and the reduced
150      patch pixels passed in. Selects tile with minimum distance.
151      '''
152      best = -1
153      best_dist = 100000
154      for i in range(NTILES):
155        this_dist = reduced_patch_distance(patch_reduction,\
156                                          TILES_4X4_REDUCTION[i])
157        if this_dist < best_dist:
158          best = i; best_dist = this_dist
159      #print "best_dist = "+str(best_dist)+\
160      # "; best tile index = "+str(best)
161      return best
162
163    def compute_RGB_scale_factors(color1, color2):
```

```
165    scale_red = (color2[0]+0.0)/(color1[0]+1.0)
166    scale_green = (color2[1]+0.0)/(color1[1]+1.0)
167    scale_blue = (color2[2]+0.0)/(color1[2]+1.0)
168    return (scale_red, scale_green, scale_blue)
169
170  def render_patch(i,j,tile_idx,patch_avg):
171    tile_win = TILES_PACKAGED_IN[tile_idx]
172    tile_row = TILES_ROW_INDEX[tile_idx]
173    tile_col = TILES_COLUMN_INDEX[tile_idx]
174    tile_rgb = TILES_AVG_COLOR[tile_idx]
175    (scale_red, scale_green, scale_blue) =\
176      compute_RGB_scale_factors(tile_rgb, patch_avg)
177    #print "Scale factors for R,G, and B are: "+\
178    #  str(scale_red)+','+str(scale_green)+','+str(scale_blue)
179    x_mos_start = j*EFFECTIVE_TILE_WIDTH
180    y_mos_start = i*EFFECTIVE_TILE_HEIGHT
181    x_tile_start = tile_col*TILE_WIDTH
182    y_tile_start = tile_row*TILE_HEIGHT
183    x_tile = x_tile_start
184    x_mos = x_mos_start
185    for dx_mos in range(EFFECTIVE_TILE_WIDTH):
186      y_tile = y_tile_start
187      y_mos = y_mos_start
188      for dy_mos in range(EFFECTIVE_TILE_HEIGHT):
189        tile_pixel = pmGetPixel(tile_win, int(x_tile), int(y_tile))
190        new_r = scale_red * tile_pixel[0]
191        new_g = scale_green*tile_pixel[1]
192        new_b = scale_blue* tile_pixel[2]
193        pmSetPixel(PHOTOM, int(x_mos), int(y_mos),\
194                   int(new_r), int(new_g), int(new_b))
195        y_mos += 1
196        y_tile += (TILE_HEIGHT + 0.0) / EFFECTIVE_TILE_HEIGHT
197      x_mos += 1
198      x_tile += (TILE_WIDTH + 0.0) / EFFECTIVE_TILE_WIDTH
199
200  def reduce_patch(i,j):
201    reduction = []
202    horiz_factor = (SUBJ_WIDTH/NCOLS_OF_TILES)  / 4
203    vert_factor  = (SUBJ_HEIGHT/NROWS_OF_TILES) / 4
204    xstart = j*(SUBJ_WIDTH/NCOLS_OF_TILES)
205    ystart = i*(SUBJ_HEIGHT/NROWS_OF_TILES)
206    averaging_factor = horiz_factor*vert_factor
207    for mx in range(4):
208      for my in range(4):
209        r=0; g=0; b=0
```

```
210          for x in range(horiz_factor):
211             for y in range(vert_factor):
212                 rgb = pmGetPixel(subj,xstart + mx*horiz_factor + x,
213                                  ystart + my*vert_factor + y)
214              r+=rgb[0]; g+=rgb[1]; b+=rgb[2]
215          avg_r = r/averaging_factor
216          avg_g = g/averaging_factor
217          avg_b = b/averaging_factor
218          reduction.append((avg_r, avg_g, avg_b))
219      return reduction
220
221  computePhotomosaic()
```

The program selects the best tile for each patch, but it does not consider that it might have just used the tile for a neighboring position in the course of this decision. (Adding a consideration for avoiding adjacent occurrences of the same tile is left as an exercise.) It may take a minute or more to compute the photomosaic, depending on the speed of one's computer, the number of tiles in the database, and the size of the photomosaic being constructed.

20.3.3   Results and Discussion

A photomosaic made with this program is shown in figure 1.2 in chapter 1. When making the photomosaic, one can not only control the size of the final result and the effective tile size, but one can also adjust NTILES so that only some of the tiles are allowed in the photomosaic. One strategy for creating a photomosaic is to prepare the database of tiles (in part by editing the file image-list.txt) so that the best tiles are located early in the list. Sometimes there are tile images that depict scenes that are less relevant to the theme of a photomosaic, yet the tiles have an important overall color to contribute to the collection. Then there may be tiles that are questionable on grounds of both content and color. Those can be put at the end of the list. Then during the construction NTILES can be set to omit them, and if the result is unsatisfactory for lack of enough tiles, to include them.

The ultimate quality of a photomosaic depends on many factors, including the quality of the subject image and the tile images. It's also important to have an adequate set of tile images so that the photomosaic is not only well rendered from an optical point of view but also contains the variety and interest that is possible with the medium. Technically, the quality of the image matching method can also make a difference between having a good photomosaic and an excellent one. The more relevant the criteria used in the matching, the more likely that best decisions can be made by the software. The method here uses limited subtile (and subzone) color information (the 4-by-4 summaries). Other criteria that can be used include location, orientation, and strength of edges. The use of semantic criteria leads to endless possibilities (using images of eyes to render eyes, images of lips to render lips, for example). Finkelstein and Farrier's (1994) photomosaic of John F. Kennedy made out of images of Marilyn Monroe suggest the semantic connections that can be used between tiles and subject.

Photomosaics can be taken to advanced levels of expressiveness and technical feats. They can be wrapped as textures onto 3D shapes, made into animations, and embedded within other images. Robert Silvers has made photomosaic creation a profession and holds a patent on the basic process (Silvers, 2010).

The matching of tiles to zones of the subject image is at the heart of creating a photomosaic. Image matching is an important topic in its own right. As mentioned previously, it is a key technical issue for the retrieval of images from image databases or from the World Wide Web. A research system called *QBIC* (Query By Image Contents) was developed at IBM and was influential in helping launch a train of research related to tools for querying image databases on the basis of appearance, not semantic tags. QBIC itself is used in the image query facility of the Russian Hermitage Museum's website, which won the "Best Internet Site in Russia" award from the Russian Internet Academy. A different kind of image matching is the subject of the next section. It's about having humans do the image matching in a game format.

20.4 An Image-Matching Game

20.4.1 Overview

This section presents a pair of programs. The first transforms a collection of images to produce virtual cards for a game. The second administers the game. The main purpose of this section is to illustrate the structure of such programs and to describe how they are developed.

The game is called Transcentration. It is based on a memory game played with cards that is sometimes called Concentration. In Concentration, which uses a standard deck of fifty-two playing cards, the cards are shuffled and laid out face down in a 4-by-13 array (or any other convenient arrangement). Two or more players take turns trying to find matching pairs of cards. For example, player 1 might choose to turn over a card that turns out to be the 7 of hearts. Then that player chooses another card. If it is also a red seven (the 7 of diamonds), then the player wins that pair and removes it from the array, putting it in his or her pile of captured cards. Each time a player matches in this way, he or she gets to take another turn immediately. If a player does not make a match, the cards must be returned to their places facedown in the array. The game ends when all the cards have been captured, and the player with the most pairs wins.

In Transcentration, the cards are different. Instead of ranks and suits, they have images. The images come in pairs: original and transform. In order to match a pair, a player must choose the original and its transform. There are two modes of play, to make the game more

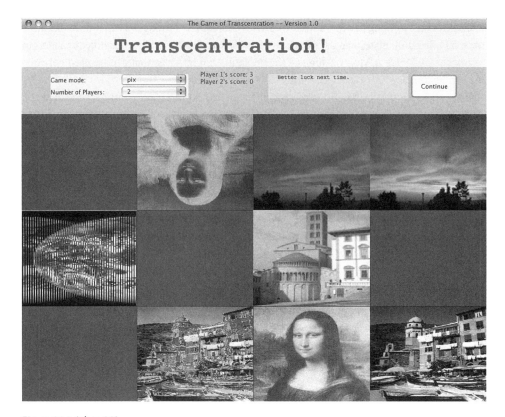

Figure 20.5 (plate 39)
Transcentration game screen shot. At this point in the game, four of twelve cards remain unmatched and face down (purple). Each of the others has been matched with its transform or inverse transform and is shown face up.

fun and challenging: pix mode (as just described) and formulas mode. In formulas mode, the original images do not appear on their cards. Instead, the formulas used to transform the originals are shown. To play well, a player should inspect the formulas when they are turned over, examine the transformed images, and understand the relationship. Figure 20.5 (plate 39) is a screen shot from a Transcentration game.

20.4.2 The Program TranscentrationMakeDistortions

The game can be played with almost any images and PixelMath calculator formulas. This first program, TranscentrationMakeDistortions.py, takes a list of images and a list of formulas and applies the formulas to the images in corresponding order. Someone who wants to set up the game with a special set of images and transformations has only to put all the image files in a folder called ORIGINALS, make a list of the images and put it in a file called active-images-list.txt, and make a list of transformation formulas and put it in a file called active-formulas-list.txt. The program will take it from there. It will read in the two lists and for each corresponding pair it will create a filename. It will check to see if a file with that name already exists, and if so, it will not create a new one but will skip that transformation. If no file exists with the name, it will read in the specified original image, apply the transformation and then save the transformed image in the folder TRANSFORMED under the file name that was created.

In order to apply the formulas to the original images, the program makes use of Pixel-Math's image windows and calculator. Here is the Python source code for it:

```
'''TranscentrationMakeDistortions.py

This program performs some setup prior to running a game of
"Transcentration".

It reads in a file containing a list of image file names,
and then it reads in a list of transformation formulas.  In
the current version, these are assumed to be in a one-to-one
correspondence, though actually there is no problem if there
are more formulas than images.

For each image on the list of images, the corresponding
formula is taken from the list of formulas and a file name
is constructed using the image file name and the first part
(the 'name') of the formula.  Next we check to see if a file
with this constructed file name exists in the folder
TRANSFORMED.  If so, we skip this image and this formula and
go on to the next one.  If the file does NOT exist, we
transform the image with its formula and create a new image
file with the constructed name and put it in the TRANSFORMED
folder.

In this way, it will not be necessary to create any new
image files when the game is actually played, since this
program will have constructed them.

(However, this could be called on-demand by the game program
to set up a custom arrangement.)

'''
PATH = '../Transcentration/'

# Read in a file containing a list of image files to use.
image_list_file =\
```

```
35      open(PATH+'ORIGINALS/active-images-list.txt', 'r')
36    image_files = image_list_file.readlines()
37
38    formula_list_file =\
39      open(PATH+'TRANSFORMED/active-formulas-list.txt', 'r')
40    formulas = formula_list_file.readlines()
41
42    i = 0
43    for line in image_files:
44      line = line[:-1]
45      print line
46      formula_line = formulas[i][:-1]
47      i += 1
48      comment = True
49      if formula_line[0]!='#': comment = False
50      while comment:
51        formula_line = formulas[i][:-1]
52        i += 1
53        comment = True
54        if formula_line[0]!='#': comment = False
55
56      print formula_line
57      pos = formula_line.find(':')
58      formula_name = formula_line[:pos]
59      formula = formula_line[pos+1:]
60      transname = formula_name
61      new_name = line[:-4]+'-'+transname+'.png'
62      # Check to see if the transformed image file already exists.
63      try:
64        file = open(PATH+'TRANSFORMED/'+new_name, 'r');
65        exists = True
66      except: exists = False
67      # If not, then create it:
68      if not exists:
69        win1 = pmOpenTwo(PATH+'ORIGINALS/'+line)
70        win2= win1+1 # pmCloneImage(win1)
71        pmSetSource1(win1)
72        pmSetDestination(win2)
73        pmSetFormula(formula)
74        pmCompute()
75        pmSaveImageAs(win2, PATH+'TRANSFORMED/'+new_name);
76        print 'Wrote image file: '+PATH+'TRANSFORMED/'+new_name
77      else:
78        print 'The file: '+PATH+'TRANSFORMED/'+new_name+\
79              ' already exists.'
```

There are two features of this program that should be noted, having to do with how formulas are represented. The file `active-formulas-list.txt` generally has one line per formula, except that it may contain comment lines whose first character is #. This allows the person who is writing these formulas to keep notes in the file without affecting how the formulas will work or look in the game. The other aspect of formula representation in the file is that each formula must have a name. The purpose of the name is to support automatic creation of a unique filename for each transformed image. The filename for a transformed image consists of two parts: one for the original image and one for the formula. The part for the original image is the original filename minus its extension (e.g., "mountain" for "mountain.jpg"). However, since PixelMath formulas can contain many characters that are not good in filenames, it is necessary to have a separate name to represent the formula. An example of a legal line in the file `active-formulas-list.txt` is this:

```
photonegative: 255-Source1(x,y)
```

Here a colon and space are used to separate the formula name from the formula itself.

This program only has to be run when a new set of images and/or transforms is wanted for the Transcentration game. Once created, the same images can be used over and over for any number of sessions playing the game. The next section describes the program that runs the game.

20.4.3 The Program `TranscentrationRunGame`
The program about to be presented is a good example of a Jython program that takes advantage of what's special about Jython: its ready access to the Java runtime libraries. It uses the graphical user interface facilities of the Java environment extensively, with two important consequences. The resulting program is platform-independent, and so it can run on Windows, Linux, and Mac OS/X computers. It also is considerably simpler to express the interface in Python than it would be in Java, owing to Java's heavier syntax.

In order to explain the organization of this program and how it was developed, two versions of the program are given here: a skeleton version and the full version. The skeleton version exhibits most of the tricks required to build the interface and work with Java images in Jython. (Note that this program can run in PixelMath's Python environment, but unlike TranscentrationMakeDistortions, does not actually call PixelMath functions. It only needs Jython.) A good way to understand this program is to first download and run it, playing the game; then read over the skeleton version of the code (especially the comments embedded in the program), and then read the full program.

20.4.4 Skeleton Version
Here is the skeleton version of the program. It's compilable and runnable, but it doesn't do much other than show the framework into which the game will be put.

```python
'''  TranscentrationRunGameV01.py
  GUI skeleton for the program that will
  run a game of Transcentration.

Version 01: Simply reads in all the images and displays them
in a reasonable array.  Thus it illustrates the basics of
the GUI and how to deal with images in a Jython application.

It also detects mouse clicks, using a class called
TranscentrationMouseAdapter, but it doesn't do anything more
than report the clicks in the console.

This version DOES NOT organize the images according to the
game specification.  It DOES NOT handle the playing.
'''

import javax.swing as swing
import javax.imageio as imageio
from java.awt.event import MouseAdapter
import math

# The PATH should lead from the default PixelMath user directory
# to the folder where the Transcentration files and folders are.
PATH = '../Transcentration/'

# The following class specializes a Swing JPanel to represent
# the game board.
class Board(swing.JPanel):

  # Constructor for the class.
  def __init__(self, title):
    self.originalImages = []
    self.transformedImages = []
    # The following 3 members get created by other methods:
    #self.nr = 0
    #self.nc = 0
    #self.num_originals = 0
    # The next call determines how big to paint the images.
    self.setCardSize(200,170)
    # Next, associate a mouse handler with the board.
    self.addMouseListener(Board.BoardMouseAdapter())

  # Set the width and height for the "cards" of the game.
  def setCardSize(self, w, h):
    self.w = w
    self.h = h
```

```
47
48      # Determine the board's overall width and height.
49      def getDimensions(self):
50        return (int(self.w*self.nc), int(self.h*self.nr))
51
52      # Here we override the JPanel paintComponent method so that
53      # we control how the board is rendered.
54      def paintComponent(self, g):
55        i = 0; j = 0
56        k = 0
57        for image in self.originalImages + self.transformedImages:
58          g.drawImage(image, j*self.w, i*self.h, self.w, self.h, self)
59          k += 1
60          j += 1
61          if j == self.nc:
62            i += 1; j = 0
63
64      # To load one image from a file, we use the Java ImageIO class.
65      def loadImage(self, filename, whichList):
66        try:
67          f = open(filename,'r')
68          image = imageio.ImageIO.read(f)
69          whichList.append(image)
70          #w = image.getWidth(b)
71          #h = image.getHeight(b)
72          # Note: we don't currently make use of the actual width
73          # and height of each image. Instead we force all the
74          # widths to be the same when we paint the images. A more
75          # sophisticated way to show the images could use scaling
76          # and padding to maintain the original aspect ratios.
77        except:
78          print "Could not read an image named: "+filename
79          print " There could be a path problem, "+\
80                "or the image may need to be created."
81
82      # Read in all the images needed for a game of Transcentration.
83      def loadAllImages(self):
84        # Read in two files, and figure out the names of
85        # all the images needed.
86
87        # First read in a file containing a list of image originals.
88        global PATH
89        image_list_file =\
90          open(PATH+'ORIGINALS/active-images-list.txt', 'r')
91        image_files = image_list_file.readlines()
```

```
 92
 93        formula_list_file =\
 94          open(PATH+'TRANSFORMED/active-formulas-list.txt', 'r')
 95        formulas = formula_list_file.readlines()
 96
 97        i = 0 # index of current line in the formulas file.
 98        k = 0 # count of the number of originals
 99        for image_line in image_files:
100          image_fn = image_line[:-1] # remove trailing newline.
101          formula_line = formulas[i][:-1] # get a line, remove newline
102          i += 1
103          # If this formula_line starts with '#' then
104          # it is a comment and should be skipped.
105          comment = True
106          if formula_line[0]!='#': comment = False
107          while comment:
108            formula_line = formulas[i][:-1]
109            i += 1
110            comment = True
111            if formula_line[0]!='#': comment = False
112
113          print 'Processing formula line: '+formula_line
114          pos = formula_line.find(':')      # Find end of formula name
115          formula_name = formula_line[:pos] # Get formula name.
116          formula = formula_line[pos+1:]    # Get formula itself.
117          new_name = image_fn[:-4]+'-'+formula_name+'.png' # file name
118
119          # Read both the original and the transformed version.
120          self.loadImage(PATH+'ORIGINALS/'+image_fn,\
121                         self.originalImages)
122          k += 1
123          self.loadImage(PATH+'TRANSFORMED/'+new_name,\
124                         self.transformedImages)
125
126        self.num_originals = k      # Save number of originals
127        total = 2*k                 # total number of images read in.
128        if total > 16: self.nc = 6  # Set number of columns for board.
129        else: self.nc = 4
130        self.nr = math.ceil((0.0+total)/self.nc) # Set number of rows.
131
132      # A convenience method combining the functionality of
133      # getDimensions, the Swing method setSize, and which
134      # returns the dimenions to the caller.
135      def setAndReturnDimensions(self):
136        dims = self.getDimensions()
137        self.setSize(dims[0], dims[1])
```

```
138        return dims
139
140     # Here's a skeleton of a handler for mouse clicks.
141     # It is an inner class of Board, with access to its members.
142     class BoardMouseAdapter(MouseAdapter):
143       def mouseClicked(self, event):
144         print 'The mouse was clicked...' + str(event)
145
146   # Here's most of the top-level executable code for this program:
147   windowTitle = "The Game of Transcentration -- Version 0.1"
148   j = swing.JFrame(windowTitle) # Create a window.
149   b = Board(False)              # Create the board.
150   b.loadAllImages()             # Load all the images.
151   # Set the board size so all images show.
152   boardDimensions = b.setAndReturnDimensions()
153   j.getContentPane().add(b)     # Add the board to the window.
154   # Set the window size so the whole board shows.
155   j.setSize(boardDimensions[0],boardDimensions[1]+20)
156   j.show() # Show the window.
```

This skeleton version is a relatively short 2.5 pages of code. Most of it defined the class called Board. It serves as a compilable and runnable shell for the game. In the full version, which follows, this shell is filled in.

20.4.5 Full Version of TranscentrationRunGame
Here is the full version of the program. It uses a software architecture known as the model-view-controller structure. There are three principal object-oriented classes in the program: class Game, which can be thought of as the logical model for Transcentration; class Board, which we can think of as the view; and class ControlPanel, which handles much of the control functionality of the program.

This version adds the following classes to what is in the skeleton version:

1. A class called Game, which has methods to arrange the cards at the beginning of the game and to enforce game rules and respond to user actions. The game has access to the board, and the board has access to the game. Most of the game operation is handled within the Game class.

2. A class called ControlPanel, which contains some subpanels and Swing widgets for controlling and showing the status of the game.

3. A class called TitlePanel, which simply displays the title of the game.

The code that is new is mostly at the end in the class Game, but there are a few lines elsewhere, with the changes indicated as "# V02." if on the same line or "# V02:" if on the next line.

The Game class maintains a list called cardArray which has one element for each place on the board. Some of the places might not be used, in which case a blank board item is placed there. In general, each place in the cardArray (which is really a one-dimensional list, but serves to hold the content of a conceptually two-dimensional array) holds an instance of the BoardItem structure. This structure is defined by the inner class (within the Game class) called BoardItem. The BoardItem object tells, for a given place on the board, whether it contains anything, whether what it contains is an original image or a transform image, the index of the image within its particular list (either originals of transforms), its own index in the cardArray list, and the index of its mate within the cardArray list. When the game is set up, a bunch of these BoardItem instances are made up so that the arrangement of cards on the board is random. The information is organized so that the program can determine, when the game is played, whether or not two cards selected by the user actually match each other.

As mentioned, the game can be played in two modes. The pix mode is the default. In this mode, each corresponding pair of cards is displayed using images: one is the original and the other is a transformation of it. In the formulas mode, only the transformed image is shown as an image. The original is not shown, but the formula used to transform it is shown instead.

```
1    ''' TranscentrationRunGameV03.py
2      The program that runs a game of Transcentration.
3    '''
4    import javax.swing as swing
5    import javax.imageio as imageio
6    import java.util.Random as Random   # V02.
7    from java.awt import Color, BorderLayout, FlowLayout,\
8      GridLayout, Dimension, Font
9    from java.awt.event import MouseAdapter
10   import math
11
12   # The PATH should lead from the default PixelMath user
13   # directory to the folder where the Transcentration files
14   # and folders are.
15   PATH = '../Transcentration/'
16
17   # The following class specializes a Swing JPanel to
18   # represent the game board.
19   class Board(swing.JPanel):
20
21     # Constructor for the class.
22     def __init__(self, game): # V02. (adds Game param).
```

```
23        self.game = game # VO2.
24        self.originalImages = []
25        self.transformedImages = []
26        self.formulas = []
27        # The following 3 members get created by other methods:
28        #self.nr = 0
29        #self.nc = 0
30        #self.num_originals = 0
31        # The next call determines how big to paint the images.
32        #self.setCardSize(200,170)
33        self.setCardSize(250,200)
34        # Next, associate a mouse handler with the board.
35        self.addMouseListener(Board.BoardMouseAdapter())
36
37    # Set the width and height for the "cards" of the game.
38    def setCardSize(self, w, h):
39      self.w = w
40      self.h = h
41
42    # Determine with board's overall width and height.
43    def getDimensions(self):
44      return (int(self.w*self.nc), int(self.h*self.nr))
45
46    # Here we override the JPanel paintComponent method so
47    # that we control how the board is rendered.
48    def paintComponent(self, g):
49      i = 0; j = 0
50      k = 0
51      # VO2: (Contents of the loop have been changed, too)
52      backSideColor = Color(128, 0, 192)
53      borderColor = Color(0, 0, 128)
54      cards = self.game.cardArray
55      if cards==None: return
56      for item in cards:
57        if not item.isEmpty:
58          if item.isVisible:
59            if item.isXform:
60              image = self.transformedImages[item.imageIDX]
61              g.drawImage(image, j*self.w, i*self.h,\
62                          self.w, self.h, self)
63            else:
64              if self.game.getMode()=='formulas':
65                g.setColor(borderColor)
66                g.drawString(self.game.getFormula(item.transIDX),\
67                             j*self.w, int((i+0.5)*self.h))
68              else:
```

```
69                         image = self.originalImages[item.imageIDX]
70                         g.drawImage(image, j*self.w, i*self.h,\
71                               self.w, self.h, self)
72                    else:
73                       # Show a colored rectangle, when the card is hidden.
74                       g.setColor(backSideColor)
75                       g.fillRect(j*self.w, i*self.h, self.w, self.h)
76                       g.setColor(borderColor)
77                       g.drawRect(j*self.w, i*self.h, self.w, self.h)
78                 k += 1
79                 j += 1
80                 if j == self.nc:
81                   i += 1; j = 0
82
83        # To load one image from a file, we use the Java ImageIO class.
84        def loadImage(self, filename, whichList):
85          try:
86            f = open(filename,'r')
87            image = imageio.ImageIO.read(f)
88            whichList.append(image)
89            #w = image.getWidth(b)
90            #h = image.getHeight(b)
91            # Note: we don't currently make use of the actual
92            # width and height of each image. Instead we force
93            # all the widths to be the same when we paint the images.
94            # A more sophisticated way to show the images might involve
95            # scaling and padding to maintain the original aspect ratios
96          except:
97            print "Could not read an image named: "+filename
98            print " There could be a path problem, "+\
99                "or the image may need to be created."
100
101       # Read in all the images we need for a game of Transcentration.
102       def loadAllImages(self):
103         # Read in two files, and figure out the names of
104         # all the images needed.
105
106         # First read in a file containing a list of image originals.
107         global PATH
108         image_list_file =\
109           open(PATH+'ORIGINALS/active-images-list.txt', 'r')
110         image_files = image_list_file.readlines()
111
112         formula_list_file =\
113           open(PATH+'TRANSFORMED/active-formulas-list.txt', 'r')
114         formulas = formula_list_file.readlines()
```

```
115
116    i = 0 # index of current line in the formulas file.
117    k = 0 # count of the number of originals
118    for image_line in image_files:
119      image_fn = image_line[:-1] # remove trailing newline char.
120      formula_line = formulas[i][:-1] # get a line, remove newline
121      i += 1
122      # If this formula_line starts with '#' then
123      # it is a comment and should be skipped.
124      comment = True
125      if formula_line[0]!='#': comment = False
126      while comment:
127        formula_line = formulas[i][:-1]
128        i += 1
129        comment = True
130        if formula_line[0]!='#': comment = False
131
132      #print 'Processing formula line: '+formula_line
133      pos = formula_line.find(':')      # Find end of formula name
134      formula_name = formula_line[:pos] # Get formula name.
135      formula = formula_line[pos+1:]    # Get formula itself.
136      new_name = image_fn[:-4]+'-'+formula_name+'.png' # file name
137
138      # Read both the original and the transformed version.
139      self.loadImage(PATH+'ORIGINALS/'+image_fn,\
140                     self.originalImages)
141      k += 1
142      self.loadImage(PATH+'TRANSFORMED/'+new_name, \
143        self.transformedImages)
144      self.formulas.append(formula) # Used only in "formulas" mode
145
146    self.num_originals = k      # Save number of originals
147    total = 2*k                 # total number of images read in.
148    if total > 16: self.nc = 6  # Set number of columns for board.
149    else: self.nc = 4
150    self.nr = math.ceil((0.0+total)/self.nc) # Set number of rows.
151
152  # A convenience method that combines the functionality of
153  # getDimensions, the Swing method setSize, and which returns
154  # the dimenions to the caller.
155  def setAndReturnDimensions(self):
156    dims = self.getDimensions()
157    self.setPreferredSize(Dimension(dims[0],dims[1]))
158    return dims
159
160  # Here's a skeleton of a handler for mouse clicks.
```

```
161    # It is an inner class of Board, with access to its members.
162    class BoardMouseAdapter(MouseAdapter):
163      def mouseClicked(self, event):
164        board = event.getSource()
165        board.game.handleMouseClick(event)
```

At this point, the definition of class Board is complete. Its last component, defined here, is the inner class BoardMouseAdapter, which specifies that any mouse click on the board will be handled by a method in the class Game called handleMouseClick.

The logic of the game is represented by the class Game, which is defined next. Its methods include an initialization method, a method dealTheCards, and additional methods: startGame, quitGame, proceedToNextTurn, getMode, handleMouseClick, chooseAndRemove, flipCard, and getFormula. An inner class, BoardItem, of class Game is also defined here. These are described further in the comments.

```
166    class Game:
167
168      def __init__(self, c):
169        self.controlPanel = c
170        self.board = Board(self)      # Create the board.
171        self.cardArray = None
172
173        self.board.loadAllImages()   # Load all the images.
174        # Set the board size so all images show.
175        self.boardDimensions = self.board.setAndReturnDimensions()
176
177        self.scores=[0,0,0,0]
178        self.playing = False
179
180      def dealTheCards(self):
181        # Create the array of board items:
182        blankItem = Game.BoardItem(False,0,0,0,False,True)
183        self.blankItem = blankItem
184        nOriginals = self.board.num_originals
185        # nSlots tells how many of the board positions we'll use.
186        # There may be unused ones, if rows don't come out even.
187        nSlots = 2*nOriginals
188        self.cardArray = int(self.board.nc*self.board.nr)*[blankItem]
189
190        # Fill it with a randomized ordering of the cards:
```

```
191       self.rg = Random() # Initialize a random num. generator.
192       # iOA lists the indexes of originals available.
193       # iTA lists the indexes of transformed images available.
194       iOA = range(nOriginals)
195       iTA = range(nOriginals)
196       # slotsLeft lists the slots still available for cards.
197       slotsLeft = range(nSlots)
198       for i in range(nOriginals):
199         # Choose a random place on the board for one card:
200         slot1 = self.chooseAndRemove(slotsLeft)
201         # Find a spot for its mate:
202         slot2 = self.chooseAndRemove(slotsLeft)
203         # Put in an item for the original in this slot.
204         origItem = Game.BoardItem(False, i, slot1, slot2,\
205                                   False, False)
206         self.cardArray[slot1] = origItem
207         # Put in an item for the transform in the other slot.
208         transItem = Game.BoardItem(True, i, slot1, slot2,\
209                                    False, False)
210         self.cardArray[slot2] = transItem
211         #print "slot1 = "+str(slot1)+"; sot2 = "+str(slot2)
212         #print "slotsLeft: " + str(slotsLeft)
213       self.cardsLeft = 2*nOriginals
214
215   def startGame(self):
216     g=self
217     c=g.controlPanel
218     g.scores = [0,0,0,0]      # Initialize scores
219     c.updateScoreDisplay(None)
220     g.whoseTurn = 1
221     g.turnPhase = 0
222     g.playing = True
223     g.dealTheCards()
224     c.msg(['Game started.',
225           'Player 1 click on a card.'])
226     self.board.repaint()
227
228   def quitGame(self):
229     self.playing = False
230     self.controlPanel.msg(['You have Quit the game.',
231                            'To play a new game, press Start.'])
232     self.controlPanel.changeButtonLabel("Start")
233
234   def proceedToNextTurn(self):
235     g=self
236     c=g.controlPanel
```

```
237        c.changeButtonLabel("Quit") # Assume game continues.
238        g.turnPhase = 0
239        if g.playerJustMatched:
240          g.cardArray[g.firstCard] =g.blankItem
241          g.cardArray[g.secondCard]=g.blankItem
242          if g.cardsLeft == 0:
243            g.playing = False
244            highestScore = max(g.scores)
245            winners =\
246              map(lambda w:w+1, indexes(g.scores, highestScore))
247            if len(winners)==1:
248              c.msg(['Game Over',\
249                      'Congrats to Player '+str(winners[0])+'!'])
250            else:
251              winnerSequence =\
252                reduce(lambda w1,w2:str(w1)+', '+str(w2), winners)
253              c.msg(['Game Over',\
254                      'Congrats to Players '+winnerSequence+'!'])
255
256            c.changeButtonLabel("Start")
257            return
258          else:
259            g.board.repaint()
260            c.msg(['Take another turn!'])
261            return
262        else:
263          # put back the cards turned over; advance to next turn.
264          g.flipCard(g.firstCard)
265          g.flipCard(g.secondCard)
266          g.whoseTurn = (g.whoseTurn % c.getNPlayers()) + 1
267          g.board.repaint()
268          c.msg(['Player '+str(g.whoseTurn),\
269                  'Choose your first card.'])
270
271    def getMode(self):
272      return self.controlPanel.modeChoice.getSelectedItem()
273
274    def handleMouseClick(self, event):
275      board = event.getSource()
276      g = self
277      c = g.controlPanel
278      if not g.playing:
279        c.msg(['You are not currently playing a game.',
280                'To start a game, press "Start".'])
281        return
```

```
282      if g.turnPhase==2:
283        c.msg(['You must click Continue.'])
284        return
285      x = event.getX()
286      y = event.getY()
287      col = x/board.w
288      row = y/board.h
289      idx = row*board.nc + col
290      if idx >= 2*board.num_originals: return
291      item = g.cardArray[idx]
292      if item.isEmpty:
293        c.msg(['There is no card there.',
294                'Try again.'])
295        return
296      if g.turnPhase==0:
297        g.flipCard(idx)
298        g.firstCard = idx
299        if item.isXform:
300          g.mateNeeded = item.origIDX
301        else:
302          g.mateNeeded = item.transIDX
303        g.turnPhase=1
304        c.msg(['Now choose the card that',
305                'you think matches.'])
306        board.repaint()
307        return
308      if g.turnPhase==1:
309        g.secondCard = idx
310        g.flipCard(idx)
311        if idx==g.mateNeeded:
312          g.playerJustMatched = True
313          c.msg(['Good Job!'])
314          g.scores[g.whoseTurn-1] += 1
315          c.updateScoreDisplay(None)
316          board.repaint()
317          g.cardsLeft -= 2
318        else:
319          g.playerJustMatched = False
320          c.msg(['Better luck next time.'])
321        g.turnPhase=2 # The phase where we wait
322        # for the user to click on the Continue button.
323        c.changeButtonLabel('Continue')
324        board.repaint()
325
326
327   class BoardItem:
```

```
328        def __init__(self, isXform, imageIDX, origIDX, transIDX,\
329            isVisible, isEmpty):
330          self.isXform = isXform
331          self.imageIDX = imageIDX
332          self.origIDX = origIDX
333          self.transIDX = transIDX
334          self.isVisible = isVisible
335          self.isEmpty = isEmpty
336
337      # Randomly select an item from a list.
338      # Remove it from the list and return the item.
339      def chooseAndRemove(self, aList):
340        # Choose a random index within the range:
341        index = self.rg.nextInt() % len(aList)
342        elt = aList[index]
343        aList.__delitem__(index)  # The method __delitem__ is a
344                                  # built-in method for lists.
345        return elt
346
347      # FlipCard:
348      def flipCard(self, idx):
349        bi = self.cardArray[idx]
350        bi.isVisible = not bi.isVisible
351
352      # Retrieve the formula used to produce the
353      # transformed image currently placed at itemIDX.
354      # This is needed when playing in "formulas" mode.
355      def getFormula(self, itemIDX):
356        transItem = self.cardArray[itemIDX] # info about that card
357        formulaIDX = transItem.imageIDX # index of its original
358            # in the list of originals.
359            # This is the same as the index of its formulas in
360            # the list of formulas. Now get the formula:
361        formula = self.board.formulas[formulaIDX]
362        return formula
```

Now that the game logic has been specified, we define a panel to hold the title and a control panel to hold the choice boxes, status displays, and the button used by the player(s) to advance in the game. The control panel contains a number of methods and two inner classes: ScorePanel and DialogPanel.

```
363   class TitlePanel(swing.JPanel):
364     def __init__(self):
365       self.setPreferredSize(Dimension(500,80))
366       self.font = Font('Courier', Font.BOLD, 48)
367
368     def paintComponent(self, g):
369       g.setColor(Color(64, 64, 255))
370       g.setFont(self.font)
371       g.drawString("Transcentration!", 200, 50)
372
373   # We define ControlPanel in order to organize the controls.
374   class ControlPanel(swing.JPanel):
375
376     def __init__(self):
377       self.setLayout(FlowLayout())
378       self.setPreferredSize(Dimension(500, 60))
379       self.setBackground(Color(192,192,212))
380
381       # Set up a small 2x2 subpanel on the left.
382       self.leftPanel=swing.JPanel()
383       self.leftPanel.setLayout(GridLayout(2,2))
384       self.leftPanel.setPreferredSize(Dimension(300,50))
385
386       label = swing.JLabel("Number of Players:")
387       label.setPreferredSize(Dimension(100,20))
388       self.leftPanel.add(label,0,0)
389       # Define the scorePanel now, because it is accessed
390       # by the updateScoreDisplay callback needed next.
391       self.scorePanel = ControlPanel.ScorePanel(self)
392       choice = swing.JComboBox([1,2,3,4],\
393         itemStateChanged=self.updateScoreDisplay)
394       choice.setPreferredSize(Dimension(65, 50))
395       self.leftPanel.add(choice,0,1)
396       self.nplayersChoice = choice
397       modeLabel = swing.JLabel("Game mode:")
398       self.leftPanel.add(modeLabel,1,0)
399       modeChoice = swing.JComboBox(['pix','formulas'])
400       self.modeChoice=modeChoice
401       self.leftPanel.add(modeChoice,1,1)
402       self.add(self.leftPanel)
403
404       # Now add the scorePanel to the control panel.
405       self.add(self.scorePanel)
406
407       # Set up a "dialog" panel where messages will be printed.
408       dialog=\
```

```
409        ControlPanel.DialogPanel(['Welcome to Transcentration!'])
410      dialog.setPreferredSize(Dimension(300,50))
411      self.dialog = dialog
412      self.add(dialog)
413
414      # Finally, set up a multipurpose button.
415      theButton =\
416        swing.JButton("Start", actionPerformed=self.handleButton)
417      theButton.setPreferredSize(Dimension(100, 50))
418      self.theButton = theButton
419      self.add(theButton)
420
421    # We need the following because the control panel is
422    # constructed before the game object. The linkage the other
423    # way is established after both are created.
424    def setGame(self, game):
425      self.game = game
426
427    def getNPlayers(self):
428      return self.nplayersChoice.getSelectedItem()
429
430    def msg(self, text):
431      self.dialog.setText(text)
432
433    def updateScoreDisplay(self,dummy):
434      self.scorePanel.repaint()
435
436    def handleButton(self, event):
437      buttonLabel = event.getActionCommand()
438      if buttonLabel=='Start':
439        self.changeButtonLabel('Quit')
440        self.game.startGame()
441      if buttonLabel=='Quit':
442        self.changeButtonLabel('Start')
443        self.game.quitGame()
444      if buttonLabel=='Continue':
445        self.changeButtonLabel('Quit')
446        self.game.proceedToNextTurn()
447
448    def changeButtonLabel(self, newLabel):
449      self.theButton.setLabel(newLabel)
450
451    class ScorePanel(swing.JPanel):
452      def __init__(self, cp):
453        self.cp = cp
454        self.setPreferredSize(Dimension(160,70))
```

```
455            self.backColor = Color(192,192,255)
456            self.setBackground(self.backColor)
457            self.setOpaque(True)
458
459        def paintComponent(self, g):
460            scoreColor = Color(128,0,0)
461            g.setColor(self.backColor)
462            g.fillRect(0,0,150,120)
463            g.setColor(scoreColor)
464            np = self.cp.nplayersChoice.getSelectedItem()
465            scores = self.cp.game.scores
466            for p in range(np):
467                p1 = p + 1
468                g.drawString("Player "+str(p1)+"'s score: "+\
469                                str(scores[p]),\
470                                20, 15*p1)
471
472      class DialogPanel(swing.JPanel):
473          def __init__(self, textLinesList):
474              self.text = textLinesList
475              self.bgColor=Color(212,212,230)
476              self.setBackground(self.bgColor)
477              self.textColor=Color(0,0,128)
478              self.dialogFont = Font('Courier', Font.PLAIN, 12)
479
480          def paintComponent(self, g):
481              g.setColor(self.bgColor)
482              g.fillRect(0,0,300,100);
483              g.setColor(self.textColor)
484              g.setFont(self.dialogFont)
485              for i in range(len(self.text)):
486                  g.drawString(self.text[i], 20, 10+(20*i))
487
488          def setText(self, text):
489              self.text = text
490              self.repaint()
491
492  # Helper function for finding the winner(s) of a game:
493  def indexes(lst, elt):
494      result=[]
495      for i in range(len(lst)):
496          if lst[i]==elt: result.append(i)
497      return result
498
499
500  # Here's most of this program's top-level executable code:
```

```
501   windowTitle = "The Game of Transcentration -- Version 0.1"
502   j = swing.JFrame(windowTitle) # Create a window.
503   # VO2: (4 lines moved to Game.__init__)
504   #b = Board(False)                # Create the board.
505   #b.loadAllImages()               # Load all the images.
506   # Set the board size so all images show.
507   # boardDimensions = b.setAndReturnDimensions()
508
509   # VO2: (create the title panel, control panel and game)
510   t = TitlePanel()
511   c = ControlPanel()
512   g = Game(c)
513   c.setGame(g)
514   j.setLayout(BorderLayout())
515   j.getContentPane().add(t, BorderLayout.NORTH)
516   j.getContentPane().add(c, BorderLayout.CENTER)
517
518   # VO2: (access board via the game in the next 2-3 lines)
519   # Add board to window:
520   j.getContentPane().add(g.board, BorderLayout.SOUTH)
521   # Set the window size so the whole board shows.
522   j.setSize(g.boardDimensions[0],g.boardDimensions[1]+200)
523   j.show() # Show the window.
```

The program ends with most of the top-level executable code. This code first establishes the window title. Then it creates an instance of a Swing JFrame (a window on the screen) and it gives the window the title. Then it creates instances of the main components of the game: TitlePanel, ControlPanel, and Game (which in turn creates an instance of Board in its initialization method). It then arranges the panels and the board within the window using a layout called BorderLayout. The final step is to show the window on the screen. The user can then play the game, and the program reacts to the actions of the user.

20.4.6 Discussion

The program TranscentrationRunGame shows a complete, nontrivial Python program that involves a graphical user interface. By looking at a skeleton version first and then a full version, it's somewhat easier to grasp what the development process is like for this kind of program. In order to avoid having a complex tangle of bugs, it's important to develop a complex program a little bit at a time, striving to keep the finished part bug-free, runnable, and understandable along the way.

This program has been created in one relatively large source-code file. Complex programs are typically created using multiple files. If additional features are added to this game, such as sound effects, or on-the-fly computation of image transforms, then it might be a good idea to separate the main classes of the program into different files.

20.5 References

Beier, T., and Neely, T. 1992. Feature-based metamorphosis. *Proc. ACM SIGGRAPH 1992*, pp. 35–42.

Bill, Robert W. 2002. *Jython for Java programmers*. Indianapolis, In Sans Technical Publishing.

Finkelstein, A., and Farrier, S. 1994. JFK-MM. www.cs.princeton.edu/ af/cool/jfk-mm.html.

Flickner, M., Sawhney, H., Niblack, W., Ashley, J., Huang, Q., Dom, B., Gorkani, M., Hafner, H., Lee, D., Petkovic, D., Steele, D., and Yanker, P. 1995. Query by Image and Video Content: The QBIC system. *IEEE Computer*, Vol. 28, No. 9, pp. 23–32.

Gustafsson, A. 1993. Interactive Image Warping. Ph.D. Dissertation, Dept. of Computer Science, Helsinki Univ. of Technology. Available online at http://www.gson.org/thesis/warping-thesis.pdf

Hermitage Museum Staff. 2010. QBIC Color and Layout Searches. Digital Collections web area. www.hermitagemuseum.org/fcgi-bin/db2www/qbicSearch.mac/-qbic?selLang=English.

Silvers, R. 2010. www.photomosaic.com.

Wolberg, G. 1990. *Digital Image Warping*. Los Alamitos, CA: IEEE Computer Society Press.

20.6 Exercises

1. With the image warping method of Beier and Neely, what happens to an image that is transformed using the following warp? The warp is controlled by two line segment pairs. In the source image the segments are parallel, but in the destination they form a cross.

2. Consider the two line segments and the point R specified below. Find the coordinates in the destination space of the point R', which is the image of R under the affine mapping specified by the two line segments, using the Beier-Neely method.

$$L = (P, Q) = ((0, 0), (0, 1))$$

$$L' = (P', Q') = ((3, 0), (5, 3))$$

$$R = (10, 10)$$

3. Using L and L' of the previous example, find an interpolated segment that is one-quarter of the way between L and L'.

4. Explain how one could use Beier-Neely transformations (maybe more than one) to blow up an image by a factor of 2 in each dimension.

5. Create a warp sequence that turns an image upside down. What happens in the middle of the sequence?

6. Create a warp sequence that causes an image to break up into disconnected regions. How did you do it?

7. Create a warp sequence that turns a human face inside out. How did you do it?

8. Create a morphing sequence that gradually turns a house into a castle.

9. Create a morphing sequence that gradually turns a goldfish into a shark.

10. Create a morphing sequence that gradually turns a salamander into a dragon.

11. Create a morphing sequence that turns an old jalopy into a new Porsche.

12. Consider an image warp specified by four line segment pairs as follows: For the source image, the segments form a square of side length s. The square is centered on the image. For the destination, the segments still form a square centered on the image, but it is reduced in size, with a side length $s/2$. Does this transform correctly shrink the image by a factor of 2 in each direction?

13. Using code from the morphing program, create a morphing slide-show program that can run a connected sequence of morphing transitions. There are two distinct ways to do this. The first uses a separate set of line segment pairs for each transition so that each transition can be defined independently of the previous one. The second method requires that the same number of line segments be used at each transition, and that the placement of the lines on a given image serves in both transitions involving that image (both when it is a destination and when it is a source). Although the second method may seem simpler, the first method has two advantages. It not only provides more flexibility in the transitions, the existing morphing program can still be used by the show's designer to create the sets of line segment pairs that are needed.

14. Consider the multiple-tile-image method of making a photomosaic. Suppose we are considering a 32-by-32 region of the subject image and we wish to find a tile that best represents it. This region has a sharp boundary separating a left-side area of bright red from a right-side area of bright blue. The tile images consist of various photos of party balloons. What do you expect might happen as the method selects a tile for this region?

15. Assemble a collection of images for use in making photomosaics. Give a qualitative evaluation of this collection in terms of (a) its coverage of the color spectrum, (b) coherence to a theme, (c) visual consistency.

16. Convert the collection of the previous exercise into (a) a set of 128-by-128 tile images and (b) one or more database images, as described in the text.

17. Create a photomosaic using the database of tile images that you constructed in the previous exercise.

18. Modify the photomosaic construction program so that it can avoid using the same tile (a) twice in succession and (b) in neigboring positions either horizontally or vertically.

19. Further modify the program so that it may or may not avoid the repeated tile problem of the previous exercise, depending on an estimated aesthetic cost. The cost should depend on two factors: (a) how much worse the visual match quality (between the zone of the subject image to be rendered and the tile to render it) would be if a different tile from

the optimal one were used and (b) an arbitrary cost amount that you decide is the penalty for immediately repeating a tile. There may be two parts to the latter cost: the cost of a horizontal repetition and the cost of a vertical repetition. There could even be a (lesser) cost for a diagonal repetition. Demonstrate your new program by creating a photomosaic in which you can point to places where it decided one way and elsewhere decided the other, according to your cost criterion. You might need to add some tests and print statements to detect and provide clear evidence of such decisions.

20. (project) Build a graphical user interface for the photomosaic construction program. The interface should allow the user to manually select, from the top k tile choices (computed by the program), what tile should be used at each zone. Each time the user makes a selection, the tile should be plotted into the output array, and the program should go on to the next zone until the entire process is done. As an additional option, include a "back" button that allows retraction of the last choice, and if the user desires, the choice before that, etc. It should be possible to set the parameter k either at runtime or by changing the value of a global variable in the code before starting.

21. (project) A project similar to the previous one is to build an image query-by-contents search interface. Assuming that a database of images is set up in the same way as in the photomosaic construction program, create a user interface to query the database by either (a) loading an image to serve as the query or (b) drawing an image, as with the QBIC system described in the article by Flickner et al. (1995).

22. Modify the Transcentration game program so that all source images are the same. (Use a new image of your own.) The game can then be played in the formulas mode, so that a player matches the formula with the corresponding transformed version of that one image.

23. Modify the Trancentration game so that instead of pairs, triples are used. In each turn, a player reveals three cards and tries to match an original image, a formula, and the transformed version of that original using that formula. The number of cards placed on the board should now be a multiple of three. (This is a more challenging exercise because some of the program's data structures have to be reworked.)

24. Using some of the user-interface ideas of the Transcentration game, design and create a color-matching game that requires the players to match given colors by entering their RGB values (or in HSV mode, their HSV values).

APPENDIXES

A   Calculator Formulas

The PixelMath calculator accepts formulas in a standard syntax in which infix ordering is used for arithmetic operators such as +, −, *, /, and MOD, and prefix ordering is used for function calls, such as Sin(x), Source1(x,y), etc. The Formula Page interface also accepts these formulas.

A syntactically valid formula must be an arithmetic expression. In other words, the expression should provide a way to compute numbers. These numbers will be used as pixel values. If the numbers that result are less than 0, they are set to 0. If they are greater than 255, they are set to 255. Any fractional number like 93.8 will be truncated to an integer. So 93.8 would be converted to 93 before being stored in a pixel component. If the formula put in the calculator is not syntactically valid, then the PixelMath software will show an error message when the Compute button is clicked. Arithmetic expressions can involve subexpressions. Parentheses can be used to force groupings of the subexpressions.

Some expressions in a formula may be Boolean expressions. As indicated earlier, a Boolean expression is one whose result is the value True or the value False. For example, the expression "x > 7" is a Boolean expression. Boolean expressions are used as conditions in IF THEN ELSE constructs. They can be combined with logical operators such as AND, OR, and NOT. Boolean expressions involving subexpressions can use curly braces for grouping. When curly braces are used, they must enclose a valid boolean expression. The following is valid:

```
if {x<10 and y<10} or {x>20 and y>20} then 255 else 0
```

When mixing Boolean expressions and arithmetic expressions without parentheses or curly braces, the parser will use standard rules of precedence to interpret the formula. These groupings can be overridden by including parentheses or curly braces, depending on whether the immediate subexpression being grouped is arithmetic or Boolean. Note that putting parentheses around a Boolean expression or curly braces around an arithmetic expression will cause a syntax error. For example (x<y) is not allowed. Neither is {x+y}. Instead, one must use {x<y} and (x+y). This restriction helps prevent semantic errors in a formula by encouraging the user to be aware of the types of any grouped subexpressions in the formula.

Although each image is normally represented using 8 bits of red, 8 bits of green, and 8 bits of blue, PixelMath also supports a complex color image representation in which each pixel is represented by six floating-point values: red is represented by a complex number of the form $a_r + b_r i$, green by $a_g + b_g i$, and blue by $a_b + b_b i$. Here i represents $\sqrt{-1}$ and so each color is represented by a *complex number*. Formulas may refer to these components by making use of the COMPLEXCC function described in the next section. This representation is not used much in this book except in connection with the Fourier transform and filtering, where it is very important.

Functions

The following functions are recognized in the calculator:

LOG(x)   Logarithm, to the base 10, of x.

LN(x)   Natural logarithm (to the base e) of x.

SQR(x)   Square of x, i.e., x^2.

POW(x,y) x raised to the power y, that is, x^y.

SQRT(x)   The square root of x, that is, $\sqrt{x}$.

SIN(x)   The sine of x.

COS(x)   The cosine of x.

TAN(x)   The tangent of x.

ASIN(x)   The arc sine of x, in radians.

ACOS(x)   The arc cosine of x, in radians.

ATAN(x)   The arc tangent of x, in radians.

MIN(x,y)   The minimum of x and y.

MAX(x,y)   The maximum of x and y.

ABS(x)   The absolute value of x.

CEIL(x)   The ceiling of x. This is the smallest integer that is greater than or equal to x. It's sometimes written as $\lceil x \rceil$.

FLOOR(x)   The floor of x. This is the largest integer that is less than or equal to x. It's sometimes written as $\lfloor x \rfloor$.

ANGLE(x,y)   The angle of the vector (x, y), in radians. This is similar to the value of the arc tangent of y/x; however, it is defined even if x is zero. Results are in the range $[0, 2\pi]$.

SOURCE1(x,y) The value(s) of the pixel in the Source1 image at location (x, y). "Source1" is sort of an abbreviation of any or all of "Red," "Green," and "Blue." When the computation is being done for the destination's red component, "Source1" means "Red1," and similarly for Green and Blue. If the color toggles are set so that only green is being updated, then the expression "Source1(x,y)" will not actually reference the red and blue components. If x or y are noninteger values, then a weighted linear interpolation of the values of nearby pixels will be used to compute the returned value. (Interpolation can be disabled via the Python function `pmSetInterpolateSourcePixels` or made moot by applying the `FLOOR` function to x and y in the formula.)
"S1" can be used as an abbreviation for Source1.

SOURCE2(x,y) The value(s) of the pixel in the Source2 image at location (x, y). As for Source1, any or all of the red, green, and blue components may be accessed. "S2" can be used as an abbreviation for Source2.

RED1(x,y) The value of the red component of the Source1 image's pixel at location (x, y). The red value is used regardless of what destination components (R, G, or B) are enabled or disabled.

RED2(x,y) Like Red1, except for the Source2 image.

GREEN1(x,y) Like Red1, except that the green component is accessed.

GREEN2(x,y) Like Green1, except it uses the Source2 image.

BLUE1(x,y) Like Red1, except that the blue component is accessed.

BLUE2(x,y) Like Blue1, except that the Source2 image is used.

DESTINATION(x,y) Like Source1 or Source2, except that the current value of the pixel at (x, y) in the destination image is used. This is like having an additional source image. However, it is important to keep in mind that when using the destination image in this way, the order in which pixels are updated might affect the outcome.

CC(exp1,x,y) The first argument, exp1, should evaluate to either 0, 1, or 2. This controls whether the function will return the Red, Green, or Blue component of the Source1 image. The purpose of this function is to permit the selection of a color component on the basis of a computed expression.

COMPLEXCC(exp1,x,y,realorimaginary) This function is similar to `cc`, described earlier. However, it takes one more argument, `realorimaginary`, which should have a value 0 or 1. If the Source1 image does not have a complex-number representation, then COMPLEXCC acts like CC, ignoring the extra argument. However, if the Source1 image does have a complex-number representation, then either the real part or the imaginary part of the designated pixel's designated color component is returned, depending upon whether the value of `realorimaginary` is 0 or 1, respectively.

HUE1(x,y) The pixel in Source1 position (x, y) is accessed, and its RGB values are converted to an HSV triple. The hue value is returned. (The three HSV values are briefly cached in case any of them are needed in the evaluation of other parts of the formula for the current output pixel.)

SAT1(x,y)   The pixel in Source1 position (x, y) is accessed and its RGB values are converted to an HSV triple. The saturation value is returned. (The three HSV values are briefly cached in case any of them are needed in the evaluation of other parts of the formula for the current output pixel.)

VAL1(x,y)   The pixel in Source1 position (x, y) is accessed and its RGB values are converted to an HSV triple. The value is returned. (The three HSV values are briefly cached in case any of them are needed in the evaluation of other parts of the formula for the current output pixel.)

HUE2(x,y)   Like HUE1, except that the Source2 image is accessed.

SAT2(x,y)   Like SAT1, except that the Source2 image is accessed.

VAL2(x,y)   Like VAL1, except that the Source2 image is accessed.

RGB(exp1,exp2,exp3)   When PixelMath is computing the red component of the destination pixel, RGB returns the value of exp1. Similarly, the values of exp2 and exp3 are returned when computing green and blue components, respectively.

HSV(exp1,exp2,exp3)   Like RGB except that each expression is used to compute the destination pixel's hue, saturation, or value. For each destination pixel, the color that results from evaluating these expressions and interpreting them as hue, saturation, and value is converted back to RGB and stored in the destination pixel. If used as a subexpression, the values returned represent the R, G, and B values for the color defined by the subexpression. For example, whereas HSV(0.78, 1.0, 0.75) represents violet, the expression 0.5 * HSV(0.78, 1.0, 0.75) reduces each of this color's R, G, and B values by half, resulting in a darker color. (A similar effect could be obtained by reducing the V component of the HSV triple from 0.75 to 0.37.)

COMPLEX(exp1,exp2)   If the destination image has a complex-number representation, then exp1 expresses the value assigned to the real part of each destination pixel whereas exp2 gives the value for the imaginary part. For example, COMPLEX(x, y)-128 will assign each pixel a real-part value equal to its x coordinate value minus 128, and its imaginary part a value equal to its y coordinate minus 128. The real and imaginary parts of complex numbers are not limited to the range 0 to 255 in PixelMath, but can be arbitrary floating-point values with fractional parts and minus signs, and can be very small or very large.

The abbreviations S1(x,y) and S2(x,y) are available for SOURCE1(x,y), and SOURCE2(x,y), respectively. The abbreviations DEST(x,y) and D(x,y) are both equivalent to DESTINATION(x,y).

Binary Operators

The following Infix binary operators are recognized in the calculator:

MOD The expression a MOD b refers to the remainder after dividing a by b. The operator is only valid when a and b are non-negative integers and b is not zero.

DIV The expression a DIV b refers to the integer quotient after dividing a by b. The operator is only valid when a and b are non-negative integers and b is not zero. The DIV operator is known as integer division.

= The expression $a = b$ has the value True if a and b are equal in value, and false otherwise. The result is a Boolean value, and such an expression can be used as the condition in an IF THEN ELSE construct.

AND The expression a AND b makes sense provided that a and b are Boolean expressions. The result is True only if both a and b are true. It's false otherwise.

OR The expression a OR b makes sense provided that a and b are Boolean expressions. The result is True if either a, b, or both are true. It's false in the case that neither a nor b is true.

XOR The expression a XOR b makes sense provided that a and b are Boolean expressions. The result is True if either a or b is true, but not if both are true. It's false if neither a nor b is true, and it's false if both of them are true. This is called the exclusive-OR operation.

< The expression $a < b$ makes sense provided that a and b are both arithmetic expressions. It's true if the value of a is less than the value of b.

> The expression $a > b$ makes sense provided that a and b are both arithmetic expressions. It's true if the value of a is greater than the value of b.

≤ The expression $a \leq b$ makes sense provided that a and b are both arithmetic expressions. It's true if the value of a is less than or equal to the value of b.

≥ The expression $a \geq b$ makes sense provided that a and b are both arithmetic expressions. It's true if the value of a is greater than or equal to the value of b.

BAND This is the bitwise-AND operator. The expression a BAND b makes sense provided that a and b are arithmetic expressions that represent integers. The bits of the resulting integer are obtained by performing pairwise logical AND operations on corresponding bits of the values of a and b.

BOR This is the bitwise-OR operator. The expression a BOR b makes sense provided that a and b are arithmetic expressions that represent integers. The bits of the resulting integer are obtained by performing pairwise logical OR operations on corresponding bits of the values of a and b.

BXOR   This is the bitwise-exclusive-OR operator. The expression *a* BXOR *b* makes sense provided that *a* and *b* are arithmetic expressions that represent integers. The bits of the resulting integer are obtained by performing pairwise logical exclusive-OR operations on corresponding bits of the values of *a* and *b*.

Unary Operators

The following unary operators are recognized:

— Unary minus. In the expression −*a*, it takes the negative of *a*.

NOT   Logical negation. Assuming *a* is a Boolean expression, the expression NOT *a* returns false if *a* is true and true if *a* is false.

Symbols

The following symbols are recognized:

X   The *x* coordinate of the pixel currently being computed in the destination image.

Y   The *y* coordinate of the pixel currently being computed in the destination image.

RHO   The first coordinate of the pixel currently being computed in the destination image using polar coordinates. Equivalent to the distance (in pixel widths) from the current pixel to the center of the image. (Undefined if using Cartesian rather than polar mode.)

THETA   The second coordinate of the pixel currently being computed in the destination image using polar coordinates. Equivalent to the angle, in radians, between the ray going from the middle of the image to the right and the ray going from the middle of the image to the current pixel. (Undefined if using Cartesian rather than polar mode.)

XMAX   The largest *x*-coordinate value of any pixel in the currently selected destination image.

YMAX   The largest *y*-coordinate value of any pixel in the currently selected destination image.

XMAX1   The largest *x*-coordinate value of any pixel in the currently selected Source1 image.

YMAX1   The largest *y*-coordinate value of any pixel in the currently selected Source1 image.

XMAX2   The largest *x*-coordinate value of any pixel in the currently selected Source2 image.

YMAX2   The largest *y*-coordinate value of any pixel in the currently selected Source2 image.

W   The width, in pixels, of the currently selected destination image.

H   The height, in pixels, of the currently selected destination image.

*W*1   The width, in pixels, of the currently selected Source1 image.

*H*1   The height, in pixels, of the currently selected Source1 image.

*W*2   The width, in pixels, of the currently selected Source2 image.

*H*2   The height, in pixels, of the currently selected Source2 image.

PI   The value of π, or about 3.141592653589.

SQRTTWO   The value of $\sqrt{2}$ or about 1.414213562373.

E   The value of *e*, or about 2.718281828459.

Note that unnumbered symbols such as XMAX and W refer to characteristics of the destination image, whereas numbered symbols such as XMAX1 and W1 refer to characteristics of source images.

Ternary Operator

The following Infix ternary operator is recognized:

IF c THEN e_1 ELSE e_2   The expression represented here by *c* should be a Boolean expression. That is, it should have a value that is true or false. The expressions e_1 and e_2 should be arithmetic expressions. All three of these expressions are evaluated, and depending on whether the first expression is true or false, the value of the second or the third expression is returned, respectively. Here is an example of this construct: *If {x < 128} then Source1(x,y) else Source1(x-128, y)*

Accumulator Operators

Certain advanced image transformations make use of accumulators in the image-processing engine. This allows such things as efficiently counting certain pixels in each row of an image or finding the location of the largest red value in the image. There are three accumulators: one for each of R, G, and B. However, the user pretends there is only one accumulator. The system automatically uses the R accumulator when computing the red component, etc. Normal pixel computations do not access any of these accumulators. However, by storing and reading with the accumulators, it is possible to take advantage of the fact that the image-processing engine scans through the destination image processing the pixels in a particular order (bottom row first, left-to-right, working up to the top row). The accumulators are automatically set to zero before any formula is evaluated, but they are not reset to zero during the scan unless the formula causes them to be reset using the PUTINAC operator. There are two operators for manipulating the accumulators. One puts a value into the current accumulator and the other retrieves the value.

PUTINAC(e)   The value of the expression represented here by *e* is put in the accumulator. (It's the accumulator for whatever color component is currently being processed.) Here is an example of this construct: *PUTINAC(If x = 0 then 0 else (GETAC + 1))*. This causes a value to be stored in the accumulator every time a pixel color component is computed. At the start of each row of the image, the value 0 is put in the accumulator for each enabled color component. At subsequent row positions, the value of the accumulator is accessed and 1 is added to it. Then that new value is stored back in the accumulator. PUTINAC acts as a function in that it returns a value—the same value that it puts in the accumulator. So this example formula will store in each pixel the same value (up to a maximum value of 255) that it's putting in the accumulator at that point. The result is an image that's black at the left and that becomes gradually brighter to the right. In this case, it's the same image you would get using the formula x.

It is important to note when using PUTINAC that this is a special operation. If it is used inside of one of the two numeric expressions in an IF-THEN-ELSE operation, it will be performed whether the condition is true or false. This is because both parts of an IF expression are always evaluated. It's just that only one of the two resulting values is selected. Therefore, to store a value in the accumulator that depends on some condition, put the IF-THEN-ELSE part of the expression inside the PUTINAC's parentheses, just as shown in the example.

GETAC   The value of the accumulator (for the current color component) is returned, and so it can be used in the formula like any other numeric value. If nothing has been stored in the accumulator using a PUTINAC operation, then GETAC returns 0.

Additional Information

Precedence follows the conventional rules for mathematics, with multiplication and division taking precedence over addition and subtraction.

Using the expression DESTINATION(x,y) in a formula allows the current destination image to be used as an additional source. This function causes the current value of the pixel at (x, y) to be used in the calculation. It does not have anything to do with writing data into the destination; that is done automatically by the transformation engine whenever any formula is computed.

B Quick Reference—PixelMath Formulas

Identity transformations:
Source1(x,y)
S1(x,y)
RGB(Red1(x,y),Green1(x,y),Blue1(x,y))
HSV(Hue1(x,y),Sat1(x,y),Val1(x,y))
Source1(rho,theta) in polar mode

Additive brightening:
S1(x,y) + 50
Brightening and/or contrast enhancement:
2*S1(x,y) - 100
Thresholding:
If S1(x,y) < 128 then 0 else 255

Double exposure:
S1(x,y)+S2(x,y)
Monochrome conversion:
(Red1(x,y)+Green1(x,y)+Blue1(x,y))/3
Red1(x,y)

Color component permutation:
RGB(Green1(x,y),Blue1(x,y),Red1(x,y))

*Individual color component rotation -
color components get a little brighter,
except bright ones "wrap around" to dark:*
(S1(x,y)+32) mod 256
256 x 256 Palettes:
RGB(x,y,16*(x mod 16)+(y mod 16))
HSV(x/w, y/h, 0.75)

*Monochrome horizontal gradient in
256-pixel-wide image:*
x
Color circle in polar mode:
If rho<128 then
HSV(theta/(2*pi),rho/128,1) else 0

Flip upside-down:
S1(x,ymax-y)
S1(rho, -theta) in polar mode
Mirror image:
S1(xmax-x, y)

Horizontal stretch:
S1(x/2, y)
S1(0.5*x, y)
Vertical stretch:
S1(x, y/2)
S1(x, 0.5*y)
Reduce or enlarge to fit destination:
S1(x*w1/w, y*h1/w)

Repeated miniatures:
S1((x*3) mod w1, (y*4) mod h1)

Translate (shift) right 80 and up 50:
S1(x-80, y-50)
Translate with wraparound:
S1((x-80) mod w, (y-50) mod h)

Rotate 1 radian in polar mode:
S1(rho, theta-1)
Fisheye in polar mode:
S1(sqr(rho)/rhomax, theta)

Blue-screen compositing (needs two sources):
If hue1(x,y)>0.6 and hue1(x,y)<0.7
then S2(x,y) else S1(x,y)

Color saturation boost:
HSV(hue1(x,y),(1+sat1(x,y))/2,val1(x,y))
Double red only:
S1(x,y)*RGB(2,1,1)
Misalign color components:
S1(x-RGB(-5, 0, 5), y)

Note: For these transformations to work, all color toggles should be turned on (glowing), and transformations preceded by an asterisk need separate Source1 and destination windows.

C   Python Glossary

This glossary gives a summary for each of the functions in PixelMath Python and many standard Python functions. The arguments are indicated in a slanted typeface, with names intended to be suggestive of the data types required or normally used. Thus *e* indicates something that represents arbitrary data, *n* a number, *s* a string, etc. Sometimes the names are more descriptive, such as *windownum*.

Each entry is either labeled as a standard function, a function of PixelMath Python only, a reserved word (such as if), a module, a class, or a constant. An example use of the element is also given.

Any function with a name that begins with pm is a PixelMath Python function, usually providing access to PixelMath capabilities, and is not something found in standard Python. (All the other functions are compatible with standard Python.)

abs(*n*)   Returns the absolute value of the value of *n*. **function.**
```
abs(-5)    ## 5
```

and   This computes the logical *and* of its operands. Consider the expression
e_1 *and* e_2 *and* $\cdots$ *and* e_k
This evaluates the e_i in sequence until one of them evaluates to something false, at which point that last value is returned. Otherwise the value of the last expression is returned. **reserved word.**
```
3 < 4 and 3.5          ##  3.5, which is considered true.
3 < 4 and 0 and 4 < 5  ##  0, which is considered false.
```

append(e)   This inserts the element *e* onto the end of the list on which it is invoked. Nothing is returned but the list is modified. **method.**
```
a = [1, 2, 3]
a.append(10)
a   ##  [1, 2, 3, 10]
```

apply(*function, arglist*)   Applies the value of *function* to the given list of arguments. If the function normally takes *n* arguments, then *arglist* should have *n* elements. **function.**
```
apply(round, [1.2345, 1])   ##  1.2
```

atan(*n*)   Returns the arc tangent (in radians) of the value of *n*. **function in module** math.
```
math.atan(1.0)    ##   0.7853982
```

ceil(*n*)   Returns the smallest integer that is not smaller than the value of *n*. **function in module** math.
```
math.ceil(3.14)   ##   4
```

chr(*n*)   Returns the ASCII character whose code is the integer *n*. **function.**
```
chr(65)   ##   'A'
```

cos(*n*)   Returns the cosine of the value of *n*, which must be in radians. **function in module** math.
```
math.cos(math.pi / 4)   ##   0.7071
```

def *variable(args)   statements* establishes a variable naming a function. The arguments *args* are zero or more variables (e.g., *x*) or argument-specifying expressions such as *x = 5*, separated by commas. The body of the function is defined by the *statements*. **reserved word.**
```
def vlength(x, y):
  s = x*x + y*y
  return math.sqrt(s)
vlength(3, 4)   ##   5.0
```

class *variable(parent)   statements* establishes a variable naming a class. The parent is optional and if not used, no parentheses are used either. The statements of the class definition should specify the methods of the class. **reserved word.**

eval(*e*)   First computes the value of *e* and then computes the value of that expression. **function.**
```
myexp = "7 + 9"
eval(myexp)   ##   16
```

exp(*n*)   Returns e^n, where *e* is the base of natural logarithms, approximately 2.71828. **function in module** math.
```
math.exp(2)   ##   7.389056
```

float(*n*)   Converts *n* to a floating-point number, if it was not already a float. **function.**
```
float(3)   ##   3.0
```

floor(*n*)   Returns the largest integer less than or equal to *n*. **function in module** math.
```
math.float(3.9)   ##   3.0
```

if *condition   exp1*
else: exp2
Evaluates the *condition* expression and if nonzero, evaluates *exp1* and returns that; otherwise, evaluates *exp2* and returns that. **reserved word.**
```
if 2<3: "OK"
else: "BAD"
##   "OK"
```

int(*data*) Converts *data* to an int if possible. **function.**
```
int(math.pi)    ##  3
int("3")    ##  3
int(3)    ##  3
```

lambda *var*$_1$, ..., *var*$_n$: *exp* returns an unnamed function whose arguments are *var*$_1$, ..., *var*$_n$ and whose body is *exp*.
```
apply(lambda x: x+1, [5])    ##  6
```

list(*sequence*) Creates a list from the elements of *sequence* and returns the list. The *sequence* can be a tuple, a string, or another list, but if it's a list, then that list is returned without any copying. **function.**
```
list((1, 2, 3))    ##  [1, 2, 3]
```

log(*n*) Returns the logarithm of the value of *n* to the base *e*. **function in module** math.
```
math.log(8)    ##  2.0794415
math.log(8)/math.log(2)    ##  3.0
```

lower() Returns a copy of the string on which it is invoked, such that in the copy, any and all uppercase characters are converted to lowercase. **method** of the str class.
```
s = "AbCdE"
s.lower()          ##  'abcde'
```

map(*f*, *arglist*$_1$, *arglist*$_2$, ..., *arglist*$_n$) Here *f* must be a function that takes *n* arguments. The function *map* successively applies *f* to new argument lists formed from the first elements of each *arglist*$_i$, then the second elements, etc. The list of results is returned. **function.**
```
def f(x): return x*2
map(f, [0,1,2,3])    ##  [0,2,4,6]
def g(x,y): return x*x+y
map(g, [0,1,2,3], [100,200,300,400])    ##  [100, 201, 304, 409]
```

max(*a*, *b*) Returns either *a* or *b*, whichever is larger. **function.**
```
max(3,4)    ##  4
```

min(*a*, *b*) Returns either *a* or *b*, whichever is smaller. **function.**
```
min(3,4)    ##  3
```

not(*e*) Returns either False or True. If *e* evalutes to anything, meaning false, then *not* returns True. Otherwise, it returns False. **reserved word**.
```
not 4 > 3    ##  1
```

open(*filename*, *mode*) Attempts to open a file with the given name and mode. Both arguments must be strings. When successful, a file handle is returned. The mode should be 'r' for reading, 'w' for writing, or 'a' for appending. When the file has been completely read or written, a call to the *close* method should be made by the program. **function.**

```
try:
  f = open("MyData.txt", "r")
  data = f.read()
except IOError: print 'Could not read file'
```

or   This computes the logical *or* of its operands. Consider the expression
e_1 *or* e_2 *or* $\cdots$ *or* e_k.
This evaluates the e_i in sequence until one evaluates to a value considered true, at which
point it returns that value. Otherwise it returns the last value. **reserved word**.

```
3 < 4 or 3 > 4    ##  True
3 > 4 or 0        ##  0
```

pi   A constant in the `math` module whose value is a floating-point approximation to π.
constant in module math.

```
math.pi    ##  3.14159265
```

pmAlert(*str*)   Displays a modal dialog box with the string message *str*. The user can dis-
miss the box by clicking on "OK". See also *pmMessage*, which has additional options for
positioning on the screen, setting a title, and resizing. **function.**

pmCalculatorSetVisible(*tf*)   Shows or hides the calculator, depending on whether *tf* is `True`
or `False`. **function.**

pmCapturePixelMathState(*includePython*)   Returns a string that represents a Python script
that when executed will recreate much of the state of the current PixelMath session, including positions of the control windows and the contents of the Formula Page. If *includePython*
is True, the contents of the Python buffers (but not the history pane or input field) will also
be represented in the string. Since this string may itself include embedded Python scripts,
any occurrences of the triple single-quote delimiter (' ' ') are encoded in such as way as to
avoid being interpreted as the end of the script itself. (They are replaced by ! ' ! ' ! ' in this
context.) These are automatically converted back to triple single quotes when the script is
executed to restore the Python buffers. This function is useful in preparing demonstrations,
tutorials, laboratory activities, and customized environments. **function.**

pmCloneImage(*wn*)   Creates a copy of the image that exists in window *wn*, putting it into
a new window. It returns the number of the new window. **function.**

```
pmCloneImage(1)   ##  copies window 1 and returns new number
```

pmClose(*wn*)   Closes the window having window number *wn*. If *wn* $= -1$, then all of the
open image windows are closed. **function.**

```
pmClose(1)   ##  closes window number 1
```

pmColumnSums(*wn, whichcolor*)   Computes, for each column of the image, the total of all
the pixel values of the given color (specify either 0 for red, 1 for blue, or 2 for green.) The
result is returned as a one-dimensional array (list) of integer values, one for each column.
(See also `pmRowSums`.) **function.**

pmCompute() Simulates clicking on the Compute button on the PixelMath calculator. **function.**

pmDelete(*wn*) Deletes the image window numbered *wn* and frees up the memory it was using. Unlike with `pmSetVisible(False)`, the window cannot be restored with `pmSetVisible(True)`. **function.**

pmDeleteAllImages() Deletes all image windows and frees up the memory they were using. **function.**

pmEnableColors(*r, g, b*) Enables or disables each color component for updates. **function.**
`pmEnableColors(1, 0, 1)    ## Enables red and blue; disables green.`

pmExitAll() Closes all windows and exits from PixelMath. Note that no prompting is done for saving anything. This is a way to close up the program at the end of a scripted job in batch-mode style of use. **function.**

pmFFT(*wn1, wn2, inverse*) Performs a two-dimensional Fourier transform. The integers *wn1* and *wn2* must be the window numbers of two distinct existing image windows. Also, both of the images must have complex-number representations (see `pmSetComplex`). The widths of the two images must match, and the heights must also match. Furthermore, the widths and heights must be powers of 2. If *inverse* is false, then a forward transform is computed; otherwise, an inverse transform is computed. In either case, *wn1* specifies the source image and *wn2* designates the destination image. **function.**
`pmFFT(1, 2, false)    ## transforms 1 to 2.`

pmFormulaPageAddFormulaBar(*desc*) Creates a new formula bar using the *desc* string and adds it to the Formula Page after the last existing formula bar. The *desc* string must be in the format used in files created by saving the contents of the Formula Page. **function.**

pmFormulaPageClear() Removes all formula bars from the Formula Page. **function.**

pmFormulaPageCompute() Computes all formula bars on the Formula Page. If the page is not open, nothing is computed. **function.**

pmFormulaPageLoadFile(*fn*) **function.** Causes the file with name *fn* to be loaded into the Formula Page. If the file has an improper format, an error will result. If the file name starts with "server:" and PixelMath is being run from INFACT, then PixelMath will attempt to access the file (whose name is the rest of the string, without the "server:" prefix) from the server. Otherwise, it will attempt to load the file from the default Formula Page directory.

pmFormulaPageSetInfoText(*text*) The Formula Page information text is set to the string *text*. If the page is not open, nothing is done. **function.**

pmFormulaPageSetTitle(*text*) The Formula Page's title is set to the string *text*. If the page is not open, nothing is done. **function.**

pmGetAllWindowNumbers()   Returns a list of the window numbers of the images currently open in PixelMath. They are listed in the order in which the windows were created. **function.**

pmGetComplexPixel(*wn, x, y*)   Retrieves a pixel from the specified window, performing array bounds checking. The result is a Python tuple of six values. The form is (rr, ri, gr, gi, br, bi). The six floating-point values represent three complex numbers: the real and imaginary parts of the red component, green component, and blue component. If *x* and *y* refer to a point outside the image, then the tuple (127.0, 0.0, 127.0, 0.0, 127.0, 0.0) is returned (gray). If the image in the window with number *wn* does not have a complex-number representation, an error is reported. **function.**

pmGetFloat(*str*)   Displays a modal dialog box with the string message *str*. There is a textfield where the user can enter a floating-point number and there are two buttons, "OK" and "Cancel." If the user clicks on "OK" then whatever floating-point number the user has typed in the field is returned. If the user clicks "Cancel" then 0.0 is returned. If the user types something that is not a floating-point number and clicks "OK" then a message is printed on the Python listener history pane, and the user is prompted again for a floating-point number. Also see pmAlert. **function.**

```
tryPi = pmGetFloat('Estimate the value of pi.')
```

pmGetFormula()   Returns, as a string, a copy of the formula currently in the calculator's formula field. It's useful in programs that need to capture the formula last entered by the user. **function.**

pmGetImageHeight(*wn*)   Returns an integer giving the height of the image in the selected window, measured in pixels. For example, for an image 128 colums by 64 rows, the returned height would be 64. **function.**

pmGetImageWidth(*wn*)   Returns an integer giving the width of the image in the selected window, measured in pixels. For example, for an image 128 colums by 64 rows, the returned width would be 128. **function.**

pmGetInt(*str*)   Displays a modal dialog box with the string message *str*. There is a textfield where the user can enter an integer, and there are two buttons, "OK" and "Cancel." If the user clicks on "OK" then whatever integer the user has typed in the field is returned. If the user clicks "Cancel" then 0 is returned. If the user types something that is not an integer and clicks "OK" then a message is printed on the Python listener history pane, and the user is prompted again for an integer. Also see pmAlert. **function.**

```
age = pmGetInt('Enter your age')
```

pmGetInterpolateSourcePixels()   Returns True if interpolation is currently in use. The image-processing engine normally obtains pixel values from the source image(s) by performing a linear interpolation of the values of the four pixels closest to the requested point. The interpolation can be turned off, either to speed up access slightly or to ensure that actual pixel values are returned instead of synthesized ones; to do this, pmSetInterpolateSourcePixels is called with the argument False. **function.**

pmGetPixelQuickly(*wn, x, y*)   Returns an integer giving the combined R,G, and B values of the pixel at (x, y) in the image in window number *wn*. encoded as $R \cdot 256^2 + G \cdot 256 + B$. No bounds checking is done on x or y, so if either is out of range, the answer is unpredictable. **function.**

pmGetPixel(*wn, x, y*)   Returns pixel information. The RGB values of the pixel at (x, y) in the image in window number *wn* are returned as a tuple of three integers. The values of x and y are tested to make sure they refer to a valid pixel, and an error is reported if they do not. **function.**

pmGetRectangle(*wn*)   Returns the selection rectangle of the specified window as a 4-tuple `(x, y, width, height)`. **function.**

pmGetScreenSize()   Returns a tuple (of length 2) containing the width and height of the screen in pixels. For example, for a 1280-by-1024 screen, the returned tuple would be (1280, 1024). **function.**

pmGetString(*str*)   Displays a modal dialog box with the string message *str*. There is a textfield where the user can enter a string, and there are two buttons, "OK" and "Cancel." If the user clicks on "OK" then whatever string the user has typed in the field is returned. If the user clicks "Cancel" then the empty string is returned. Also see `pmAlert`. **function.**

```
name = pmGetString('Enter your name')
```

pmGetValidWindowNumbers()   Returns a list of integers representing the currently available image windows. **function.**

pmGetWindowSize(*wn*)   Returns a tuple containing the width and height of the selected window in pixels. The parameter *wn* should be an integer that indicates the selected window. If *wn* = 0, then the size of the calculator window is returned. Note the difference from `pmGetImageSize`. **function.**

pmHideProgress()   Suppresses the display of the progress bar during computations. This can be helpful if a computation is part of a transition effect during a presentation. (Also see `pmShowProgress`.) **function.**

pmHideSelections(*wn*)   Disables the displaying of the selection rectangle in the given window. This may be desirable during animations that use the rectangle to restrict computation in order to speed up the computation. (Also see `pmShowSelections`.) **function.**

pmHistogramBlue(*wn*)   Creates and returns a 256-element list containing counts of the number of occurrences of blue-value 0, blue-value 1, etc., up through blue-value 255 in the image in window *wn*. **function.**

pmHistogramGreen(*wn*)   Creates and returns a 256-element list containing counts of the number of occurrences of green-value 0, green-value 1, etc., up through green-value 255 in the image in window *wn*. **function.**

pmHistogramRed(*wn*)   Creates and returns a 256-element list containing counts of the number of occurrences of red-value 0, red-value 1, etc., up through red-value 255 in the image in window *wn*. **function.**

pmHSVtoRGB(*triple*)   Returns a new tuple of length 3 representing the RGB color values of the HSV value represented by *triple*. **function.**

```
pmHSVtoRGB((0.7778, 1.0, 0.7529))   ## (128, 0, 192)
```

pmMaximizeWindow(*wn*)   Makes image window number *wn* take up the whole screen. Note that the image itself may have to be zoomed one or more times to take advantage of the large window. **function.**

pmMessage(*msg, title, x, y, width, height*)   Pops up a dialog box having an "OK" button. The string *msg* is displayed in the box. The title bar of the dialog box has the string *title* shown in it. The location of the box on the screen and the width and height of the box are controlled by the remaining parameters. **function.**

```
pmMessage("Notice the change in color.", "Click OK to proceed", 100, 600, 400, 200)
```

pmNewComputedImage(*title, width, height, formula*)   Creates a new image and applies the given *formula* to set its contents. This function combines the effects of `pmNewImage`, `pmSetFormula`, and `pmCompute` for convenient handling of the common case where one wants to quickly set up an image with a formula. It bypasses the calculator's Destination and formula settings (temporarily setting them and then restoring them afterward), but it uses the calculator's other settings, such as RGB enablings, and coordinates mode and Source1 and Source2 settings. It returns the window number of the new image.

```
pmNewComputedImage("Ringing Paraboloid", 256,256, "(sqr(x)+sqr(y)) mod 256")
```
function.

pmNewImage(*wn, title, width, height, r, g, b*)   Creates a new image. If *wn* is 0, this creates a new window and a new image having the specified width, height, and color. If *windownum* is the number of an image window already on the screen, then the new image is put in that window, replacing whatever image is already there. If *wn* is an unused window number other than 0, a new window is created with that number. Example: `(pmNewImage(0, "My image", 400, 300, 0, 0, 128)` creates a new window with a 400-by-300 array of pixels, each of which is initialized to dark blue (0 red, 0 green, and 128 units of blue). This function returns an integer that is the window number for the newly created image window or for the existing image window. **function.**

pmOpenImage(*wn, filename*)   Opens an image from a file, either locally or on a web server, depending on whether PixelMath is being run as an application or a web-based applet. If *wn* is 0, this creates a new window with a unique window number and loads the specified image from a file or downloads the specified image from the server (depending upon whether the program is being run as an application or from a server). Then it returns an integer representing the number for the new window. If *wn* is the number of an image window already on the screen, the new image is put into that window rather than a new one. If *wn* is an unused window number other than 0, a new window is created with that number. Also, see the alternative calling form that takes an additional argument. **function.**

pmOpenImage(*wn, filename, sizeExpr*) Functions like the two-argument version, except that the image is resized to match the size specified by the string *sizeExpr*. The form of the string is the same as that used for size expressions in the Formula Page interface. It is either a comma-separated pair giving the width and height, such as "`256,128`", or it is a reference to another image, such as "`sizeOf(5)`". Note that the aspect ratio may be changed by the resizing.

pmOpenTwo(*filename*) Opens two copies of an image from a file, either locally or on a web server. This function always creates two new windows and downloads the specified image from the server or loads it from a file (depending upon whether the program is being run from a server or as an application). It rearranges the windows on the screen and makes the first copy of the image be the Source1 and Source2 choices while the second copy is made the destination choice. Then it returns an integer representing the window number for the first of the two new windows. The number for the second new window can be obtained by adding 1 to the returned value. This function offers programs a way to take advantage of the calculator File menu's "Open Two..." option. **function.**

pmPositionCalculator(*x, y*) Repositions and resizes the calculator. The *x* and *y* values specify where to put the upper-left corner of the window in terms of the screen's coordinates. The screen coordinates point (0,0) is assumed to be at the upper-left corner of the screen. **function.**

pmPositionFormulaPage(*x, y, width, height*) Repositions and resizes the Formula Page window. If it is not open, it is opened. If either *width* or *height* is zero, then only repositioning is done (no resizing). **function.**

pmPositionLaunchPad(*x, y, width, height*) If PixelMath is running as an application, repositions and resizes the launch pad window. **function.**

pmPositionPythonWindow(*x, y, width, height, bufheight*) Repositions and resizes the Python window. If the window is not open, it is opened. If either the *width* or *height* value is 0, then only repositioning is performed. The *x* and *y* values specify where to put the upper-left corner of the window in terms of the screen's coordinates. The screen-coordinates point (0,0) is assumed to be at the upper-left corner of the screen. (Note that the screen coordinates use a computer-graphics convention, whereas the image coordinates use a mathematics convention.) The *bufheight* value is used to set the height of the Python buffer pane in the window. The remaining height in the window is shared between the history pane and the input pane. **function.**

pmPositionWindow(*wn, x, y, width, height*) Repositions and resizes the specified image frame window. If either the *width* or *height* value is 0, then only repositioning is performed.

The *x* and *y* values specify where to put the upper-left corner of the window in terms of the screen's coordinates. The screen-coordinates point (0,0) is assumed to be at the upper-left corner of the screen. (Note that the screen coordinates use a computer-graphics convention, whereas the image coordinates use a mathematics convention.) **function.**

pmPythonWindowCloseCurrentBuffer()   Closes the currently open Python buffer. If there are unsaved changes in the buffer, the user is prompted to save. If the Python window is not open, nothing happens. **function.**

pmPythonWindowEvalCurrentBuffer()   If the Python window is not open, nothing happens. Also, if it is open, but there are no buffers, nothing happens. Otherwise, the currently open Python buffer is executed. **function.**

pmPythonWindowLoadFile(*filename*)   If the Python window is not open, it is opened. A new Python buffer is created into which the contents of the file given by *filename* are placed. **function**.

pmReadBlueAccumulator()   Returns the value from image engine's blue accumulator. **function.**

pmReadGreenAccumulator()   Returns the value from image engine's green accumulator. **function.**

pmReadRedAccumulator()   Returns the value from image engine's red accumulator. **function.**

pmRGBtoHSV(*triple*)   Returns a new tuple of length 3 representing the hue, saturation, and value of the RGB color value represented by *triple*. **function.**
```
pmRGBtoHSV((128, 0, 192))   ##  (0.7778, 1.0, 0.7529)
```

pmRowSums(*wn, whichcolor*)   Computes, for each row of the image, the total of all the pixel values of the given color (specify either 0 for red, 1 for blue, or 2 for green.) The result is returned as a one-dimensional array (list) of integer values, one for each row. The first row is the one at the top of the image (maximum *y* value) and the last is the one at the bottom, where $y = 0$. (See also `pmColumnSums`.) **function.**

pmSaveImageAs(*wn, filename*)   Saves the image in the specified window using the filename (which can include the full path) on the local hard disk. Requires appropriate security privileges. The filename should end in `.gif`, `.jpg`, or `.png`. The quality parameter for JPEG files can be adjusted using `pmSetJPEGQuality`. **function.**

pmSetBlueAccumulator(*val*)   Uses *val* to set the initial value for the image engine's blue accumulator. **function.**

pmSetCartesian() Sets the calculator's coordinate system to be a Cartesian one with origin at the lower-left corner of the image. Values of x range from 0 to xmax, and values of y range from 0 to ymax. **function.**

pmSetCartesianOrPolar(*polar*) If *polar* is True, sets the calculator's coordinate system to be a polar one (with the same effect as `pmSetPolar`. Otherwise, sets the coordinate system to be Cartesian (with the same effect as `pmSetCartesian`). **function.**

pmSetComplex(*wn*) There must already be a window with number *wn*. This function causes that window's image to become represented with complex numbers. This is required if the window is to be the source or destination for a Fourier transform or inverse transform. **function.**

pmSetComplexPixel(*wn, x, y, rr, ri, gr, gi, br, bi*) Stores a pixel in the specified window, performing array bounds checking. The pixel consists of six floating-point values that represent three complex numbers. *rr* and *ri* are the real and imaginary parts of the red component, etc. It is necessary to call `pmUpdateDisplay` after calling `pmSetComplexPixel` in order to see the changes in the displayed image. If the image in the window with the number *wn* does not have a complex-number representation, an error is reported. **function.**

pmSetDestination(*wn*) Sets the choice box for the destination to the chosen window. Assumes that no windows have been deleted; otherwise the count will be off. **function.**

pmSetFormula(*formula*) Puts a string into the formula box on the PixelMath calculator. This string should be in a form that is ready for the calculator, just like those that get entered by hand. Example: to negate the source image, use `pmSetFormula("255 - Source1(x,y)")` **function.**

pmSetGreenAccumulator(*val*) Uses *val* to set the initial value for the image engine's green accumulator. **function.**

pmSetInterpolateSourcePixels(*tf*) The image-processing engine normally obtains pixel values from the source image(s) by performing a linear interpolation of the values of the four pixels closest to the requested point. The interpolation can be turned off, either to speed up access slightly or to ensure that actual pixel values are returned instead of synthesized ones. Affected access functions include `Source1`, `S1`, `Source2`, `S2`, `Dest`, `Red1`, `Green1`, `Blue1`, `Red2`, `Green2`, `Blue2`, `DestRed`, `DestGreen`, `DestBlue`, `Real1`, `Imag1`, `Real2`, `Imag2`, `CC`, and `ComplexCC`, `Hue1`, `Sat1`, `Val1`, `Hue2`, `Sat2`, `Val2`. Note that hue, saturation, and value are computed from the interpolated RGB values and are not interpolated themselves, owing to the nonlinearity of combinations of hues or saturations. `pmSetInterpolateSourcePixels(False)` **function.**

pmSetJPEGQuality(*q*) Sets the quality parameter for saving images in JPEG format. Here *q* should be an integer in the range 0 to 100. If not set by the user, the default value of

90 is assumed. For greater compression but lower fidelity, use smaller values. (Also see `pmSaveImageAs`.) **function.**

pmSetPixelQuickly(*wn, x, y, c*)   Stores a pixel in the specified window without performing array bounds checking. The color is represented by an integer *c* in the format returned by `pmGetPixelQuickly`. Note: In order to see the change, the function `pmUpdateDisplay(wn)` should be called after the call(s) to `pmSetPixelQuickly`. **function.**

pmSetPixel(*wn, x, y, r, g, b*)   Stores a pixel in the specified window, performing array bounds checking. Note: It is not necessary to call `pmUpdateDisplay` after calling `pmSetPixel`; it's done automatically. **function.**

pmSetPolar(*s*)   Sets the calculator's coordinate system to be a polar one with its origin in the center of the image. Values of rho range from 0 to half the length of a diagonal of the image. Values of theta range from $-\pi$ to $+\pi$, with 0 radians being the angle along the ray from the center of the image to the right. **function.**

pmSetRectangle(*wn, x, y, width, height*)   Places the selection rectangle of the specified window so that one corner is at (x, y) and so that it will have the given *width* and *height*. **function.**

pmSetRedAccumulator(*val*)   Uses *val* to set the initial value for the image engine's red accumulator. **function.**

pmSetScanningOrder(*order*)   Sets the order in which pixels are computed during transformations with the calculator. The argument *order* should be an integer in the range 0 through 7. The value controls the order as follows:

```
0 row-major,  left-to-right, bottom-to-top (default)
1      "      right-to-left        "
2      "      left-to-right  top-to-bottom
3      "      right-to-left        "
4 column-maj, left-to-right, bottom-to-top
5      "      right-to-left        "
6      "      left-to-right  top-to-bottom
7      "      right-to-left        "
```

For most computations, the order does not matter. However, it can matter if the source and destination are the same and the formula accesses any pixels at a coordinate location different from (x, y), such as at $(x + 1, y)$. It can also make a difference if the accumulator-access operators PUTINAC or GETAC are used. The new scanning order remains in effect until the end of the session or until changed again. **function.**

pmSetSource1(*wn*)   Sets the choice box for Source1 to the chosen window. Assumes that no windows have been deleted; otherwise the count will be off. **function.**

pmSetSource2(*wn*)   Sets the choice box for Source2 to the chosen window. Assumes that no windows have been deleted; otherwise the count will be off. **function.**

pmSetVisible(*wn, tf*)   Shows or hides window number *wn*, depending on whether *tf* is `True` or `False`. **function.**

pmSetTitle(*wn, title*)   Takes a title represented as a string and makes the specified window have that title. **function.**

pmShowProgress()   Restores the display of the progress bar during computations. (Also see `pmHideProgress`.) **function.**

pmShowSelections(*wn*)   Enables the displaying of the selection rectangle in the given window. This undoes the effect of `pmHideSelections`. (Also see `pmHideSelections`.) **function.**

pmSleep(*millisec*)   Pauses execution for the given number of milliseconds. This can be useful when playing through a timed presentation of images and their transformations. **function.**

pmTotalBlue(*wn*)   Adds up all the blue values in the specified image and returns the total as an integer. **function.**

pmTotalGreen(*wn*)   Adds up all the green values in the specified image and returns the total as an integer. **function.**

pmTotalRed(*wn*)   Adds up all the red values in the specified image and returns the total as an integer. **function.**

pmZoom(*wn, x, y*)   Zooms the specified image window, using the point (*x,y*) as the focus of expansion. **function.**

pmUnzoom(*wn, x, y*)   Zooms out rather than in, using the specified window and focal point. **function.**

pmUpdateDisplay(*wn*)   Updates the display. This should be called after one or more calls to `pmSetPixelQuickly` so that the new pixel value and color can actually be seen. It takes enough time to execute this that it is not done automatically for `pmSetPixelQuickly`. However, it is automatically performed after each call to `pmSetPixel`. **function.**

pow(*x, y*)   Computes *x* to the *y* power. **function in module** math.

```
math.pow(2, 3)    ##  8
math.pow(math.e, 0)    ##  1.0
```

print(*e*)   Prints the value of *e*. **reserved word.**

raw_input(*s*)   Prints the value of *s*, which must be a string, as a prompt, and then waits for the user to enter an input string. The input string is returned. **function.**

read(*n*)   Attempts to read *n* bytes of data, or, if *n* is not given, all the data remaining in the file. The file must already be open (see open). **method** of the `file` class.

```
text = f.read()
```

reduce(*fun, lst*)   Applies the function, which should be defined for two arguments, as many times as needed, to the elements of *lst*, until a single value is obtained. That value is returned. **function.**

```
reduce(lambda a,b:a*b, [3, 4, 5])    ## 60
reduce(math.pow, [2, 3, 4])    ## 4096.0
```

reverse()   Changes the order of elements within a list. Note that the list is modified and nothing is returned. **method** of the class `list`.

```
a = [0, 1, 2]
a.reverse()
a    ## [2, 1, 0]
```

sin(*x*)   Returns $\sin x$ where x is in radians. **function in module** math.

```
math.sin(math.pi / 6)    ## 0.5
```

sort()   Sorts the elements within a list. Note that the list is modified and nothing is returned. **method** of the class `list`.

```
a = [7, 1, 2]
a.sort()
a          ## [1, 2, 7]
```

sqrt(*x*)   Returns the square root of the value of *x*. **function in module** math.

```
math.sqrt(3)    ## 1.7320508
```

str(*e*)   Returns a string version of the value of *e*. **function.**

```
str(range(3))    ## '[0, 1, 2]'
'From ' + str(10) + ' to ' + str(20)    ## 'From 10 to 20'
str(str)    ## "<type 'str'>"
```

upper()   Returns a copy of the string on which it is invoked, such that in the copy, any and all lowercase characters are converted to uppercase. **method** of the `str` class.

```
s = "AbCdE"
s.upper()    ## 'ABCDE'
```

write(*data*)   Attempts to write the data (which should be a string) to a file. The file must already be open for writing (see `open`). **method** of the `file` class.

```
f.write ("Some text.")
```

D Troubleshooting

This appendix provides an assortment of tips and ideas for resolving PixelMath problems.

1. "I have entered a formula into the PixelMath calculator and clicked on Compute, but nothing happens."

a. Make sure the Destination choice you have selected corresponds to the image window where you want to see the results.

b. Make sure that the Selection rectangle *in the destination image window* includes all the pixels that you wish to change. (Normally you will want to change all the pixels, so if you've accidentally left the selection set to a few pixels, you should redraw it around all the pixels.

c. Make sure the Source1 image choice corresponds to the image window that the calculator should use to get pixel values (if you are using Source1 in your formula).

d. Make sure that the Red, Green, or Blue color-component checkboxes are set so that something is actually going to be updated. For example, if these are all turned off, no changes can be made to the destination image at all.

e. Perhaps you have already applied the formula you are currently trying, and since it has already made the changes, you might not see anything new (particularly if your source and destination image windows are different).

f. The destination window may not be visible, if it has been minimized, or if it is hidden behind other windows. Bring it to the front by either unminimizing it or selecting it (e.g., in MS Windows NT, Vista, or Windows 7, by clicking on its button on the Task bar).

g. The relevant pixels in the destination window might not be visible if they are scrolled off the window or if they are too small to be seen, owing to zooming out. Make sure the pixels in which you expect to see changes are actually visible on the screen.

h. The transformation expression you have put in the calculator and applied to the image may be an identity transformation—one that has no visible effect on the image. You can test to see if this might be the case by temporarily replacing it with a different transformation [such as one that sets every pixel in the destination buffer to black (0,0,0)], and if that works, undo it and suspect a little more strongly that your formula may be an identity operation or one that is approximately an identity operation and so has little or no visible effect on the image.

2. "I don't see any of my images in the files list when I try to open an image."

a. If you are using the application rather than the web site, and you stored your images on your hard disk, they will only be visible to you again if you make sure that you are viewing the contents of the particular folder where you stored your image(s). Note also that PixelMath's file browser normally only shows JPG, GIF, and PNG files when loading or saving images.

b. If you are using PixelMath online with INFACT, and if you are using an account other than the one under which you uploaded your images(s), then you will not be able to see them unless they have been shared from the other account.

3. "When I open an image, downloading it from the server takes a long time."

This may be a result of your having a slow Internet connection. You can either try to get a faster connection, or you can select one of the smaller images on the web site.

4. "For some reason, the applet hangs in my browser and I cannot proceed."

The PixelMath applet runs in a Java-enabled browser such as Mozilla Firefox, Google Chrome, Apple Safari, or Microsoft Internet Explorer. These browsers call upon a Java Virtual Machine (or JVM) to execute the applet code. Sometimes these JVMs will hang up when particular situations arise. You will need to restart the applet. Before doing so, you might attempt to save any work you have done by (a) doing a screen capture, (b) cutting and pasting from the calculator's formula window into some text file, or (c) writing down some notes on a piece of paper about what you did to get to your current state. To restart the applet in Mozilla Firefox, hold down the Shift key and click on Reload Page. Then start up the calculator again as usual.

5. "The applet is still working, but I want to restart it."

You can reinitialize the applet using the Restart option on the calculator's File menu. Any image windows you have opened in the applet will be closed. However, any Python buffer you have open will stay open.

6. "My Python program seems to loop infinitely."

If you have written a Python program with an infinite or very long loop, you may have to completely shut down PixelMath to stop it. The Windows Task Manager is one way to stop PixelMath if it becomes unresponsive. On the Macintosh, the Force Quit option is similar.

7. "PixelMath says that there is not enough memory to load or process my image."

When PixelMath finds that there is not enough memory to handle an image normally, it can sometimes proceed, disabling the possibility of undoing an image transformation. However, it is recommended that you work with images small enough that this does not occur on your computer.

E Graphical User Interfaces

Programs intended to be run by a human operator often benefit from a graphical user interface. Such an interface allows a user to operate the program by clicking on buttons and selecting menu items, rather than typing lines of text at a prompt. This appendix gives a short introduction to exploiting the Jython software environment used in PixelMath to build such graphical interfaces.

Overview

PixelMath's Python implementation consists of three parts: a Python language interpreter called Jython, a Python window with panes and buffers for editing and runing programs, and a set of PixelMath functions such as pmOpenImage that allow Python programs to access PixelMath functionality.

Because Jython runs in a Java Runtime Environment, it has access to the standard Java code libraries, such as the Swing user-interface packages. Jython was designed to make it possible, and easy, to take advantage of that. The Swing components are written as Java classes. These include classes such as JFrame (for creating windows on the screen), JButton (for making pushbuttons in the interface), and JPanel (for organizing other components and for supporting graphical drawing). Python therefore uses its object-oriented class and instance features to access them. They can be subclassed, instantiated, their methods invoked, etc., all using Python syntax. Let's consider two examples. The first is minimal and it simply shows how to create and display a window containing a message.

A Tiny Example

The following example creates a window (called a JFrame in Java). It starts by importing two classes that it needs from the Swing libraries. Then it defines MyWindow to be a subclass of JFrame. The class definition contains one method definition, that for __init__, which specifies what happens right after construction of an instance of the class.

What happens is that a `JLabel` instance is created containing the text "Just a window" and this is saved as part of the object as the value of the member variable `label`. Doing this isn't enough to make the label show up as a graphical component of the window. That requires that the window's `add` method be called.

```
1    from javax.swing import JFrame, JLabel
2
3    class MyWindow(JFrame):
4      def __init__(self):
5        self.label = JLabel("Just a window")
6        self.add(self.label)
7
8    win = MyWindow()
9    win.setSize(200, 50)
10   win.setVisible(True)
```

The actual creation of an instance of `MyWindow` is done when line 8 is executed. The next line sets its width and height, and finally, line 10 causes it to be displayed.

Creating a program such as this is easy if the programmer knows what classes are available in Swing and what their methods are and do. There is less typing to do in Jython than in Java for an equivalent program because Python (and Jython) do not require type declarations. In order to learn about Swing classes, one may consult online documentation at Oracle.com. However, the documentation is written for Java rather than Jython programmers. An alternative is to examine the series of examples of Swing programming in Jython presented at the Python.org website: http://wiki.python.org/jython/SwingExamples.

An Example with Menus

The next example adds another feature to a window: a menu bar, a menu, and two menu items. A callback method `respond` is provided to handle the menu selections.

```
1    '''MenuGUI.py
2    A small example of using Swing to create a menu bar
3    and menu on a window. '''
4
5    from javax.swing import JFrame, JMenuBar, JMenu, JMenuItem
6
7    class MenuWindow(JFrame):
```

```
8     def __init__(self):
9       menuBar = JMenuBar()
10      appetizerMenu = JMenu("Seafood")
11      appetizerMenu.add(JMenuItem("Jackson Pollock",\
12                                  actionPerformed=self.respond))
13      appetizerMenu.add(JMenuItem("Cubism of Cuttlefish",\
14                                  actionPerformed=self.respond))
15      menuBar.add(appetizerMenu)
16      self.setJMenuBar(menuBar)
17
18    def respond(self, event):
19      item = event.getSource().text
20      if item[0]=="J":
21        response = "Do you want your Pollock on canvas?"
22      elif item[0]=="C":
23        response = "Squid Squares for you!"
24      else: response = "We don't have it."
25      print response
26
27  mwin = MenuWindow()
28  mwin.size=(300,100)
29  mwin.visible=True
```

The last two lines show how a direct Jython style makes it easier to set properties of Swing objects than Java does with its "getter" and "setter" methods.

Swing and PixelMath

The next example illustrates several possibilities for using Swing with PixelMath. One of these is allowing new PixelMath image windows to be created by the click of a button. Another is to allow image operations to be performed in the background by a separate thread of processing. A thorough understanding of this means learning about Java threads. However, the example may provide a starting point for readers who wish to explore the possibilities further.

```
1   ''' ComputeImagesFromGUI.py
2   This program combines Jython and Swing
3   to control PixelMath from a separate window.
4   '''
5   from java.lang import Runnable
```

```python
6    from java.util import Random
7    from java.util.concurrent import ExecutionException
8    from javax.swing import JButton, JFrame, JLabel, JPanel
9    from javax.swing import SwingWorker, SwingUtilities
10   from java.awt import GridLayout as awtGridLayout
11
12   # The following Python class is defined as a subclass of the
13   # Java Swing JFrame class, which represents a window
14   class ControlPanel(JFrame):
15     def __init__(self):
16       JFrame.__init__(self,
17                         "A Control Window for PixelMath Operations",
18                         defaultCloseOperation=JFrame.HIDE_ON_CLOSE)
19       # Set the layout scheme to "grid layout".
20       self.contentPane.setLayout(awtGridLayout(1, 2))
21       # create a panel to hold four buttons.
22       panel = JPanel(awtGridLayout(0, 1))
23       computeButton1 = JButton("Compute a ringing paraboloid")
24       computeButton2 = JButton("Compute a pattern of colors")
25       self.BeginRandomButton =
26           JButton("Start a stream of random colors")
27       self.EndRandomButton =
28           JButton("Stop the stream of random colors")
29       computeButton1.actionPerformed = lambda e: self.doCompute1()
30       computeButton2.actionPerformed = lambda e: self.doCompute2()
31       self.BeginRandomButton.actionPerformed =
32           lambda e: self.startRandom()
33       self.BeginRandomButton.enabled = True
34       self.EndRandomButton.actionPerformed =
35           lambda e: self.stopRandom()
36       self.EndRandomButton.enabled = False
37       panel.add(computeButton1)
38       panel.add(computeButton2)
39       panel.add(self.BeginRandomButton)
40       panel.add(self.EndRandomButton)
41       self.contentPane.add(panel)
42       label = JLabel('This is the control panel', JLabel.CENTER)
43       self.contentPane.add(label)
44       self.formulaLabel = JLabel('formula normally is shown here')
45       self.contentPane.add(self.formulaLabel)
46       self.pack()
47       self.setVisible(1) # Makes the window appear
48
49     def doCompute(self, formula):
50       self.formulaLabel.setText(formula)
51       # create worker thread to create one PixelMath image.
```

```
52        pi = ProcessImage(formula)
53        pi.execute() # start up this thread
54
55      def doCompute1(self):
56        print "You pressed Button 1"
57        self.doCompute("(sqr(x)+sqr(y))mod 256")
58
59      def doCompute2(self):
60        self.doCompute("RGB(x,y,0)")
61
62      def startRandom(self):
63        self.BeginRandomButton.enabled = False
64        self.EndRandomButton.enabled = True
65        # create worker thread to run an unlimited sequence of
66        # PixelMath operations.
67        self.randomColorProcess = ColorStream()
68        self.randomColorProcess.execute() # start up this thread
69
70      def stopRandom(self):
71        # respond to the stop button by cancelling the worker process.
72        self.BeginRandomButton.enabled = True
73        self.EndRandomButton.enabled = False
74        self.randomColorProcess.cancel(True)
75        self.randomColorProcess = None
76
77   class ProcessImage(SwingWorker):
78      def __init__(self, formula):
79        self.formula = formula
80        print "Creating the ProcessImage instance"
81        SwingWorker.__init__(self)
82      def doInBackground(self):
83        print "Beginning ProcessImage.doInBackground"
84        pmNewComputedImage("Nice picture", 256, 256, self.formula)
85      def done(self):
86        try:
87          self.get()  #close frame if abnormal completion
88        except ExecutionException, e:
89          hide(0)
90          print e.getCause()
91
92   class ColorStream(SwingWorker):
93      def __init__(self):
94        print "Creating the ColorStream instance"
95        SwingWorker.__init__(self)
96      def doInBackground(self):
```

```
97          print "Beginning ColorStream.doInBackground"
98          wn = pmNewComputedImage("Nice picture",
99                                      256, 256, "RGB(255,0,0)")
100         pmSetDestination(wn)
101         random_gen = Random()
102         while not self.isCancelled():
103            red = random_gen.nextInt() % 256
104            green = random_gen.nextInt() % 256
105            blue = random_gen.nextInt() % 256
106            pmSetFormula("RGB("+str(red)+",
107                         "+str(green)+",
108                         "+str(blue)+")")
109            pmCompute()
110
111      def done(self):
112         try:
113            self.get()  #close frame if abnormal completion
114         except ExecutionException, e:
115            hide(0)
116            print e.getCause()
117
118   class Runnable(Runnable):
119      def __init__(self, runMethod):
120         self._runMethod = runMethod
121
122      def run(self):
123         self._runMethod()
124
125   SwingUtilities.invokeLater(Runnable(ControlPanel))
```

This example is best studied by first running it and then examining the code that provides its features. The layout, as well as the image windows it creates, can be seen in figure E.1 (plate 40). One thing to be careful of is that the ColorStream process here, if modified, might take over the computer's processor and make PixelMath unresponsive. That might require using the Windows Task Manager or Macintosh's Force Quit tools to stop the program. On the other hand, a nice interface, and image processing taking place in a background process can be attractive features of an advanced image-processing project.

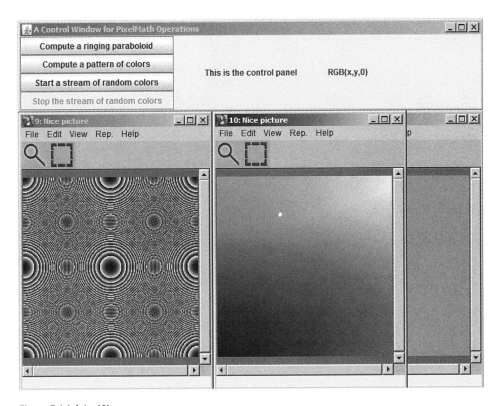

Figure E.1 (plate 40)
Screen shot of a program that computes PixelMath images from a graphical user interface. The interface uses buttons and labels.

Index